SAVING THE MEDITERRANEAN

New Directions in World Politics
Helen Milner and John Gerard Ruggie, General Editors

NEW DIRECTIONS IN WORLD POLITICS

Helen Milner and John Gerard Ruggie, General Editors

SAVING THE MEDITERRANEAN

The Politics of
International Environmental Cooperation

PETER M. HAAS

COLUMBIA UNIVERSITY PRESS   *New York*

Columbia University Press
New York   Chichester, West Sussex
Copyright © 1990 Columbia University Press
All rights reserved

Library of Congress Cataloging-in-Publication Data

Haas, Peter M.
Saving the Mediterranean : the politics of international
environmental cooperation / Peter M. Haas.
p.   cm. — (The political economy of international change)
Includes bibliographical references.
ISBN 0-231-07012-8
ISBN 0-231-07013-6
1. Water quality management—Mediterranean Sea—International
cooperation.   2. Water—Pollution—Mediterranean Sea.
I. Title.   II. Series.
HC244.5.Z9W324 1990
363.73'94526'091638—dc20   89-25298
                                                                                              CIP

Printed in the United States of America

c 10 9 8 7 6 5 4 3 2 1
p 10 9 8 7 6 5 4 3 2

To Julie

Contents

Contents

Chronology of Major Mediterranean Action Plan Dates

June 1972   United Nations Conference on the Human Environment (Stockholm)

September 1974   IOC/GFCM/ICSEM International Workshop on Marine Pollution in the Mediterranean (Monte Carlo)

February 1975   Intergovernmental Meeting on the Protection of the Mediterranean (Barcelona)

February 1976   Conference of Plenipotentiaries of the Coastal States of the Mediterranean Region on the Protection of the Mediterranean Sea (Barcelona)

February 1977   Intergovernmental Consultation Concerning a Draft Protocol for the Protection of the Mediterranean Sea Against Pollution from Land-Based Sources (Athens)

February 1977   Intergovernmental Meeting of Mediterranean Coastal States on the Blue Plan (Split)

September 1977   Meeting of Experts on Pollutants from Land-Based Sources (Geneva)

October 1977   Second Intergovernmental Consultation Concerning a Draft Protocol for the Protection of the Mediterranean Sea Against Pollution from Land-Based Sources (Venice)

January 1978   Intergovernmental Meeting of Mediterranean Coastal States on the Mediterranean Action Plan (Monaco)

February 1979   Intergovernmental Review Meeting of Mediterranean Coastal States on the Mediterranean Action Plan and First Meeting of Contracting Parties to the Convention for the Protection of the Mediterranean Sea Against Pollution and Its Related Protocols (Geneva)

June 1979   Meeting of Technical and Legal Experts on the Preliminary Draft Protocol for the Protection of the Mediterranean Sea Against Pollution from Land-Based Sources (Geneva)

October 1979   Second Meeting of Blue Plan National Focal Points (Cannes)

February 1980   Intergovernmental Meeting of Mediterranean Coastal States on the Mediterranean Action Plan (Barcelona)

May 1980   Conference of Plenipotentiaries of the Coastal States of the Mediterranean Region for the Protection of the Mediterranean Sea Against Pollution from Land-Based Sources (Athens)

March 1981   Second Meeting of the Contracting Parties to the Convention for the Protection of the Mediterranean Sea Against Pollution and Its Related Protocols (Cannes)

March 1982   Extraordinary Meeting of the Contracting Parties to the Convention for the Protection of the Mediterranean Sea Against Pollution and Its Related Protocols (Geneva)

April 1982   Conference of Plenipotentiaries of the Coastal States of the Mediterranean Region for the Protocol Concerning Mediterranean Specially Protected Areas (Geneva)

March 1983   Third Meeting of the Contracting Parties to the Convention for the Protection of the Mediterranean Sea Against Pollution and Its Related Protocols (Dubrovnik)

April 1984   Extraordinary Meeting of the Contracting Parties to the Convention for the Protection of the Mediterranean Sea Against Pollution and Its Related Protocols (Athens)

September 1985   Fourth Meeting of the Contracting Parties to the Convention for the Protection of the Mediterranean Sea Against Pollution and Its Related Protocols (Genoa)

September 1987   Fifth Meeting of the Contracting Parties to the Convention for the Protection of the Mediterranean Sea Against Pollution and Its Related Protocols (Athens)

Abbreviations and Acronyms

BOD   biological oxygen demand

BP   Blue Plan

CIM   Cooperative Investigations in the Mediterranean

COD   chemical oxygen demand

CROP   Centre de Recherches Oceanographiques et des Pêches (Algiers)

DATAR   Delegation a l'Amenagement du Territoire et à l'Action Regionale (France)

DCs   developed countries

EC/EEC   European Community/European Economic Community

ECE   Economic Commission for Europe of the United Nations

FAO   Food and Agriculture Organization

GCS   Group of Coordination and Synthesis of the Blue Plan

GDP   gross domestic product

GESAMP   Joint Group of Experts on the Scientific Aspects of Marine Pollution (IMCO/FAO/UNESCO/WMO/WHO/IAEA/UN/UNEP)

GFCF   gross fixed capital formation

GFCM   General Fisheries Council for the Mediterranean (FAO)

IAEA   International Atomic Energy Agency

ICES   International Council for the Exploration of the Sea

ICSEM   International Commission for the Scientific Exploration of the Mediterranean Sea (CIESM in French)

IGO   intergovernmental organization

IMCO   Intergovernmental Maritime Consultative Organization

IMO   International Maritime Organization (formerly IMCO)

INFOTERRA   International Referral System (UNEP)

IOC   International Oceanographic Commission (UNESCO)

IRPTC   International Registry of Potentially Toxic Chemicals (UNEP)

IUCN   International Union for the Conservation of Nature

LDCs   less-developed countries

MARPOL   IMCO International Convention for the Prevention of Pollution from Ships (1973)

MEDEAS   Centre d'Activités Environnement-Développement en Mediterranée

Med Plan   Mediterranean Action Plan

Med Pol   Med Plan Coordinated Pollution Monitoring and Research Programme

MNC   multinational corporation

NGO   nongovernmental organization

NIEO   New International Economic Order

OECD   Organization for Economic Cooperation and Development

PAP   Priority Action Programme

PCB   Polychlorinated biphenyl

PCT   Polychlorinated triphenyl

RAC   Regional Activity Center

ROCC   Regional Oil Combating Centre

tonne   metric ton

UN   United Nations

UNCHE   United Nations Conference on the Human Environment

UNCTAD   United Nations Conference on Trade and Development

UNDP   United Nations Development Programme

UNEP   United Nations Environment Programme

UNESCO   United Nations Educational, Scientific and Cultural Organization

UNIDO   United Nations Industrial Development Organization

UNITAR   United Nations Institute for Training and Research

USAID   United States Agency for International Development

WHO   World Health Organization

WMO   World Meteorological Organization

Introduction

If present trends continue, the world in 2000 will be more crowded, more polluted, less stable ecologically, and more vulnerable to disruption than the world we live in now. Serious stresses involving pollution, resources, and environment are clearly visible ahead. Despite greater material output, the world's people will be poorer in many ways than they are today.
— Global 2000 Report to the President *(1980), p. 1*

Great catastrophes may not necessarily give birth to genuine revolutions, but they infallibly herald them and make it necessary to think, or rather to think afresh, about the universe.
— *Braudel (1980), p. 6*

Over the last two decades many people have become concerned about the state of the world environment. Confronted with exaggerated claims in the early 1970s about the approaching collapse of modern society, most people—including diplomats—began to seriously consider the causes and implications of this new range of international issues. Governments were told, as is seen in the quotation above from the *Global 2000 Report* addressed to the president of the United States, that our collective survival may well depend upon governments' ability to manage such complex novel issues. In a related manner, Fernand Braudel offers a bleak observation about the consequences of such putative crises.

How will states respond to such new challenges? Will they cooperate with each other, or will they continue to pursue their own objectives as if they were selfish individuals? Are existing institutions capable of handling such a challenge? Will governments adopt new modes of decision making, will older persistent patterns of behavior prevail, or will some hybrid result? How do governments come to recognize and internalize an acceptance of the interrelationships between issues, and between themselves and their environment? Are patterns of behavior that are shaped by features of international political and economic systems immutable? What role can groups of experts, or epistemic communities—knowledge-based groups of experts and specialists who share common beliefs about cause-and-effect relationships in the world and some political values concerning the ends to which policies should be addressed (this term is elaborated in chapter 2)—play in identifying new problems and proposing solutions? Can scientific or ecological advice be used by foreign policy makers to create more effective policies?

International environmental management, or the management of environmental degradation as it is perhaps more commonly conceived, has only recently emerged as a popular topic of study. The environment is perhaps best characterized as an arena in which many different issues interact: for instance patterns of energy use, industrial practices, and demographic change all play key roles in the understanding of the major dynamics and causes of environmental degradation, and hence its management. Its study resides at the interstices of a number of disciplines, including the natural sciences, technical disciplines, and social sciences.

Social science in general has not been very good at analyzing complex, nonlinear systems such as international environmental issues seem to involve. Social sciences have done relatively well at developing theories to explain periods of order and stability, but have done much less well at explaining the dynamics of periods of change, or identifying possible breakpoints between such persistent periods, as some authors who are discussed in chapter 1 claim the current global environmental "crisis" may portend. Most works have tended to focus on the causes of observed degradation, rather than on the social and political responses which such problems may engender.[1] This book focuses on the latter dimension, and seeks to elaborate emergent international responses to such a perceived transgression of natural limits.

Unfortunately, the record of past responses to systemic challenges does not permit confident predictions about how states will manage shared environmental problems. Western development has been based on innovative adaptations to shifting economic conditions, involving both the recognition of the appropriate dimensions of change and the formulation of expedient strategies. European societies successfully adapted to the massive transformations following the Industrial Revolution, suggesting their resilience when faced with environmental change (Rosenberg and Birdzell 1986). On the other hand, we see all too vividly the archeological detritus of entire civilizations that exceeded the carrying capacity of their environments, and perished. Past behavior thus bids us not to be overly optimistic about the likelihood of adaptive responses. Historically, crises or cataclysmic events have been instrumental in signaling the need for collective responses. Post–World War II economic management relied on the lessons of the Great Depression and the end of a major conflict which eliminated the resources of many economic actors who had played key roles in the past. Yet crises are only identified within the framework of existing expectations. The interpretation of signals of environmental disruption is filtered by prevailing world views.

This book looks at how the international community responded to such alarms of ecological calamity. How did countries recognize, understand, and respond to these recent threats? What does this action imply for international politics as a whole, and for our understanding of international politics? How can one create equitable rules and arrangements for the protection of the environment and nurture the conditions under which they will be respected? Can collective norms and patterns of behavior be developed which do not merely mimic preexisting international political and economic conditions? Is the conduct of international relations becoming informed with a new biologically grounded world view and replacing an instrumental, mechanical one?

To answer these questions, this book describes evolving forms of cooperation for treating pollution, in particular the Mediterranean Sea (the Mediterranean Action Plan or Med Plan). It then evaluates three major theoretically informed explanations in the international relations field to see if such behavior is consistent with our general understanding of international relations. By understanding how common pollution control policies for the Mediterranean were devised, we may gain insights into the broader process by which countries collectively manage problems of marine pollution and environmental protection, and where else such lessons may be fruitfully applied.

Marine pollution is one of the most pressing major contemporary environmental problems. "Over a quarter of the world's people live in coastal areas, up to 90% of the world's currently exploitable living marine resources are to be found in coastal waters, and contamination of the marine environment is generally most severe in semi-enclosed seas and along the world's coasts."[2] These contaminants particularly interfere with such other uses of the sea as fisheries, coastal development, and recreation.

The Med Plan, which was developed under the auspices of the United Nations Environment Programme (UNEP), is widely acclaimed as the most successful example of international environmental collaboration, and serves as a model for arrangements for nine other regional seas in which over 130 states, sixteen United Nations agencies, and forty other international organizations take part.[3] The twenty-three 'regional seas' conventions and protocols adopted under UNEP's auspices all reflect the experience and vision of the Med Plan. All eighteen Mediterranean governments—Albania finally sent two officials from its Rome embassy to an intergovernmental meeting at Genoa in 1985—have negotiated an elaborate package of agreements to control many sources of Mediterranean pollution, and many governments have developed extensive domestic policies to control such pollution as well. It is widely regarded as a success: without it the Mediterranean would be much more polluted than it is now.

Chapter 1 describes the emergence of international cooperative efforts to control pollution (of which the Med Plan is a part) and the political factors that make coordinated pollution control difficult.

Chapter 2 presents three contemporary approaches to explaining cooperation, which will be used to explain the success of the Med Plan. These are neorealism, historical materialism, and a more recent research approach which looks at the role of specialists and knowledge-based communities in articulating state policies under conditions of technical uncertainty.

Neorealism, which deduces state behavior from the international distribution of power resources, suggests that cooperation is likely to be brief and determined largely by the most powerful state actor. At best, states will respond to the new knowledge of new environmental threats and the existence of widespread ecosystemic linkages through the traditional pursuit of state power. Historical materialism, which largely looks at the prosperity and power of smaller developing countries in light of the international distribution of the means of production, sees such efforts at cooperation as either ill-fated partial attempts at minimizing the collateral damage of capitalism or as masking efforts by developed countries to influence developing countries. A lower-level approach looks at the influence of groups of experts, or "epistemic communities," on the reformulation of national objectives, and indicates how states and leaders may realize that new attitudes and political decision-making procedures are necessary to cope with the putative environmental menace.

The Med Plan also offers a "crucial-case study" (Eckstein 1975; Wenger 1975) for the assessment of neorealism and historical materialism because it is a case of relatively successful international cooperation in a setting where few theories would predict it. Of course, one case, no matter how well chosen, cannot falsify a research program or tradition. Yet it can highlight shortcomings in such a program and question its applicability in other areas where it may be growing obsolete.

The setting of the Mediterranean is one where these theorists would least expect extensive cooperation to occur. For neorealists the Mediterranean, as an area beset with deep political animosities, is one in which cooperation is unlikely. The Algerians and the French have been antagonists since Algeria was a French colony; Algeria and Morocco fought wars over the western Sahara; Greece and Turkey are bitter historical enemies; the industrialized and industrializing countries of the region have been at loggerheads over the New International Economic Order negotiations; and the Arab-Israeli differences are legion. Moreover, with a cleanup cost of $US 10–15 billion, this is a costly issue appearing during a recessionary period of generalized government consolidation when few states were willing to sustain such daunting new expenses—expenses that could even impair economic competitiveness and hence security. For historical materialists, the Mediterranean is an area dominated by the industrialized states. Although this is not likely to preclude cooperation, such a setting would be likely to lead to cooperation highly skewed toward the interests of the North.

Chapters 3 and 4 review the development of international pollution control measures for the Mediterranean. Chapter 5 discusses the development of national efforts for controlling marine pollution in the region, and concludes with a review of the role played by the ecological epistemic community in redirecting state interests in marine pollution at both the international and national levels. Chapters 6 and 7 assess the ability of the systemic traditions discussed in chapter 2 to explain the development of such cooperation. Finally, chapter 8 recapitulates how the Med Plan evolved and the theoretical explanation for such actions, and seeks to generalize such a discussion by looking at where else similar behavior occurs, and how the understanding based on the Med Plan may contribute to understanding behavior in other issue areas.

In fact, it turns out that behavior in the area of the environment differs dramatically from traditional forms of international behavior. The punch line is that the Med Plan reflects a broader move afoot in international politics toward a new, more comprehensive political order for the environment. International policies for pollution control are increasingly broad in scope and strength. They deal with a long list of pollutants and sources of pollution that were relatively unknown in international legal circles before 1970. Efforts to control these industrial, municipal, agricultural, and ship-based wastes are increasingly stringent; there are specific lists of materials whose emissions into oceans and the atmosphere are banned and of materials for which permits are required before they may be dumped. Similar shifts ocurred nationally as well as in international treaties. In sum, governments learned to apply new patterns of reasoning to the formulation of environmental policy, which reflected a more sophisticated understanding of the complex array of causal interconnections between human environmental and economic activities.

Such behavior is anomalous for neorealism and historical materialism, as it does not closely follow the systemic forces that pressure states in the Mediterranean. As will be seen, its emergence stems from actors and processes that are commonly neglected by the more orthodox systemic approaches, and a more eclectic, mid-level approach involving epistemic communities is required to theoretically explain the process by which such changes have come about. This latter analysis relates such behavior to the development of new interests by regional governments as they struggle with the extensive uncertainty regarding the causes and extent of regional pollution. These new interests were recognized as a result of the penetration of an "ecological epistemic community" into regional decision making at both the international and national levels, after it was identified and consulted by regional governments because of its authoritative professional claim to being able to reduce the uncertainty about regional pollution. These new actors led governments to recognize and follow new interests in environmental protection, so that they were willing to resist systemic forces that would push them to pursue more constrained and transitory arrangements. International environmental cooperation is generated by the influence wielded by specialists with common beliefs, contrary to conventional approaches which stress the role of interstate power.

In discussing the role of scientific interpretations of pollution, I often refer to the uncertainty underlying scientific observations and the inherent possibilities for political, cultural, or social bias in the recognition, organization, and presentation of such data. However, I am not an utter relativist. I believe that an accessible reality exists independent of human experience, even though our own knowledge of such an entity may only be partial and fleeting. Our understanding and construction of it is influenced by the cultural, psychological, and other baggage that intereferes with perception in general.[4] Nonetheless, I believe that intersubjective consensus about the nature of reality and its representation is ultimately possible. I subscribe to Donald Campbell's perspective on learning, as summarized by Brewer and Collins:

. . . there is an objective reality that can be seen (known) by the perceiver. Let us imagine that there is such a reality of independent objects and relationships among objects and that reality exists separately from the knower. Assume further that knowledge of this reality is neither direct nor infallible, but is "edited" by the objective referent and reflected in convergence of observations from multiple independent sources of learning. (1981:1–2)

Thus, groups' claims to authoritative understanding of the world is not purely arbitrary. In the long run, consensual truth tests, rather than correspondence tests, may be applied to assess the accuracy of such groups' images.

The material presented in this book was gathered from over ninety interviews with officials from Mediterranean governments and from international organizations involved in the Med Plan. Other evidence comes from Med Plan documentation, memos and reports from UNEP and FAO archives, and personal notes taken by UN secretariat members at several intergovernmental meetings. I am grateful to the Regional Seas Programme of UNEP for allowing me to attend the 1983 intergovernmental meeting in Dubrovnik, which provided me with a real sense of the personal interactions that are so important in this type of international policymaking, for letting me listen to tapes of the June 1979 technical and legal meetings in Geneva, as well as for graciously extending me office space in Geneva.

For convenience, throughout I use American forms for the names of individuals and cities. Values are presented in current dollars, except when amounts are for a period of time when the exchange rates fluctuated. Data for oil are usually expressed in metric units (tonnes). The research was greatly facilitated by the access offered by the staff at UNEP's Regional Seas office in Geneva, particularly by Stjepan Keckes and Patricia Bliss-Guest. Other UN officials who were involved with the Med Plan's development were also very generous with their time as well as with their personal notes. My thanks go to Peter Shaw Thacher, Peter Sand, and Dominique Alhéritière. I would like to acknowledge the financial assistance and general support I have received from the following sources: the Albert Gallatin Fellowship in International Affairs, the Institute for the Study of World Politics, the Marine Policy Center at the Woods Hole Oceanographic Institution, and the Harvard Center for International Affairs. For comments on drafts I thank Emanuel Adler, Christopher Joyner, M. J. Peterson, John Ruggie, Eugene Skolnikoff, and an anonymous reviewer for the Columbia University Press. Linda Chatfield helped enormously with page proofs and the index.

SAVING THE MEDITERRANEAN

The very deep did rot . . .
That ever this should be!
Yes, slimy things did crawl with legs
Upon the slimy sea.
                    —Samuel Coleridge
The Rime of the Ancient Mariner

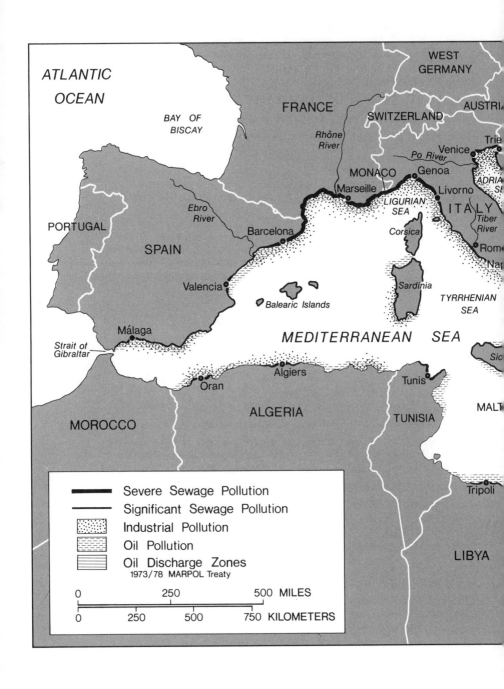

Sources of Pollution in the Mediterranean

Effluents: The Development of International Concern About Environmental Pollution

The 1970s saw mounting international concern about a relatively new international issue: threats to environmental quality. The international community adapted rapidly by devising new collective measures to control transboundary pollution. These efforts were dramatically broad in the range of pollutants that they managed; they recognized multiple channels by which pollutants are transmitted internationally and grew to control an increasingly broad range of sources of pollution. During a decade and a half of collective experience with managing international environmental problems, governments learned to adopt broader policies in a coordinated fashion in order to cope with the interrelationships between a growing range of interdependent environmental problems, despite widespread uncertainty about the nature of these problems and what policies would be most efficacious, and very real political and commercial opposition to such actions. The development of such new and broader forms of cooperation suggests a new international political order for the environment.

This chapter reviews the emergence of international environmental problems; the collective efforts taken to control them; the wide range of different policies that were suggested to manage them; and the political problems that inhibit taking effective international action. In conclusion, it presents the Mediterranean Action Plan as a quintessential case for studying the process by which countries have managed shared environmental pollution. The rest of the book examines how Mediterranean cooperation occurred, and its implications for international politics.

THE HISTORY OF INTERNATIONAL ENVIRONMENTAL CONCERN

A flurry of environmental disasters sparked international concern about the natural environment, which was ultimately understood to threaten sustainable economic growth and overall development. Concern started with the 1959 outbreak of mercury poisoning near Minimata Bay in Japan. The 1962 publication of Rachel Carson's pathbreaking revelation of pesticide pollution in *Silent Spring* riveted attention on the environment, and the problem of marine pollution gained saliency with the 1967 grounding of the supertanker *Torrey Canyon*, which spilled 121,200 metric tons (tonnes) of oil, and the 1968 PCB poisoning in Kyushu (Itai-Itai disease). Twenty million Americans demonstrated on Earth Day in 1970 (Biswas and Biswas 1985). Concern about such problems was periodically reinforced during the next decade by a number of widely publicized environmental disasters, such as the 1976 dioxin leak at Seveso, Italy; the 1978 discovery of multiple toxic substances at Love Canal in the United States; the 1979 nuclear reactor accident at Three Mile Island in the United States; the 1984 methyl isocyanate release from a Union Carbide plant at Bhopal, India; the 1986 fire at a Swiss pesticide factory that led to an extensive and toxic chemical spill in the Rhine River; and the 1986 nuclear reactor accident at Chernobyl in the Soviet Union. People were alarmed to learn that major Third World development projects (largely dam construction) had such unanticipated environmental effects as the spread of waterborne diseases, drastic diminutions in fisheries yields, and heavy riverine siltation (Farvar and Milton 1972).

The effects of environmental degradation were felt not only within the sectors generating pollution but in other interlinked areas as well. For instance:

Rapid population and economic growth stimulate the demand for scarce resources and intensify resource use that leads to, among others, environmental degradation and diminished resource productivity. Loss of land and increased poverty related to population pressures will lead not only to a reduction of the resource base but also to further environmental degradation. Migration flows from mostly rural areas of poor countries to the largest urban areas may create new ecological disruptions and social imbalances. . . .

A specific example is provided by fuelwood, which is the principal source of energy in many developing countries. The effect of rapid population increase and inadequate development of other sources of energy is to intensify the demand for wood, widen the gap between demand and supply and leave more intensive wood cutting as the only alternative for the poor. Given the localized character of wood supply, intensive wood cutting exerts concentrated pressure on tree cover and other woody vegetation that leads to deforestation and therefore decline in agricultural productivity through landslides, flooding, soil erosion and even desertification.[1]

A number of oil spills attracted attention during the decade, although oil tanker accidents account for only 12 percent of global marine oil pollution.[2] Pictures of oil on beaches and oil-smeared birds and fish were images to which people could respond. Those that received the most attention were the 1967 *Torrey Canyon* spill between France and Britain (121,200 tonnes) and the 1978 *Amoco Cadiz* spill off Brittany (228,000 tonnes). Relatively unpublicized were the 1972 *Sea Star* spill in the Gulf of Oman (120,300 tonnes) and the 1983 *Castello de Belver* spill off South Africa (255,525 tonnes) (OECD 1985b:179). The following table shows the frequency and magnitude of major oil spills from 1967 to 1987. Covering over 70 percent of the earth's surface, oceans were felt to be the "most immediately threatened" resource (Ward and Dubos 1972:195).

Evidence of environmental damage resulting from other sources also became clear. With massive industrialization after World War II, a new host of potentially toxic chemicals and other sustances came into frequent use. Barry Commoner notes that "most pollution prob-

TABLE 1.1. Major Tanker Oil Spills, 1967–1987

Year	Number of Spills*	Tons of Oil Spilled
1967	3	146,000
1968	9	128,000
1969	2	60,000
1970	11	183,000
1971	5	124,000
1972	5	215,000
1973	36	84,458
1974	48	67,115
1975	45	188,042
1976	29	204,235
1977	49	213,080
1978	35	260,488
1979	65	723,533
1980	32	135,635
1981	33	45,285
1982	9	1,716
1983	17	387,793
1984	15	24,184
1985	9	79,830
1986	8	5,035
1987	12	8,700
Total	477	3,285,129

Source: Tanker Advisory Center, Inc. (New York), "Trends in Accidental Tanker Oil Spills, Total Losses and Deaths," April 18, 1988, pp. 1–3.

* Data for 1983–1987 is for tankers of 10,000 dead-weight tons (dwt) and over. Data for 1973–1983 is for 6,000 dwt and over. Only three spills of under 3,000 dwt are included.

lems made their first appearance, or became very much worse, in the years following World War II" (1971:125). The production of synthetic chemicals grew from 10 million pounds in 1940 to over 100 billion pounds in 1980 to 225 billion pounds in 1985. Over one thousand new chemicals are introduced every year (White 1986:420–21; Speth 1988:266). Historically high rates of emissions of many heavy metals, which are toxic when present at high levels in human tissue, occurred during the 1970s and accumulated in the environment. Twenty-three percent of all worldwide emissions of cadmium occurred during the 1970s, along with 27 percent of copper, 22 percent of lead, 41 percent of nickel, and 23 percent of zinc (Holdgate, Kassas, and White 1982:43). Increasing atmospheric concentrations of carbon dioxide accompanied the increased burning of fossil fuels for energy, which may result in global warming (World Resources Institute 1986:318, Burch 1970:37). The environmental loading of persistent toxic substances and waste products from industrial production grew with the expansion of production. In the United States, annual outputs grew of such pollutants as phosphates from municipal sewage, nitrogen oxides from automobiles, tetraethyl lead from gasoline, mercury from chloralkali plants, synthetic pesticides, and many new substances such as PCBs, DDT, and synthetic plastics.

Concern also developed about the long distances pollutants can travel. The pesticide DDT was detected in whale blubber in the Arctic as well as in penguins in the Antarctic, far from where it was initially sprayed.[3] Underlying the sustained world economic and industrial growth, concern grew that population growth and international industrialization could lead to the exhaustion of global natural resources and the overall degradation of the global environment.

Technological advances illuminated new international problems. The development of new, more finely calibrated scientific equipment and techniques enabled scientists to study the environment to a much finer degree of resolution, revealing problems that could not be measured with older technology, such as pervasive toxic wastes and the presence of man-made materials in the stratosphere. It is now possible to sensitively monitor global trends from satellites, and gas chromatography and spectroscopy permit technicians to evaluate water quality in parts per billion or even parts per trillion.

A new environmental science gained popularity in the 1970s as well, which provided a new way of viewing pollution. Supported by developments in statistical techniques and computer modeling that facilitated the simulation and understanding of complex systems, ecology developed as a framework science in which multiple environmental interactions could be monitored and understood. Observations could be systematically evaluated, complete with alternative forecasts of what could happen without human intervention, and in conjunction with other global trends (Meadows, Richardson, and Bruckman 1982; Hughes 1985:ch. 1).

It is the integration of traditional disciplines like geology, oceanography, ecology, meteorology, and many more, into the study of the structure and metabolism of the planet, its atmosphere, geosphere, hydrosphere and its living realm, the biosphere, and of the interactions among them. Its emergence comes from the recognition that mankind's activities are now on a scale great enough to affect the planet as a whole, and we must understand these natural systems if we are to live successfully with our new ability to alter them. (Mathews 1988:21)

In part, interest in such an integrated science emerged from concern with possible environmental degradation.The intellectual development of ecology then contributed to the more holistic popular characterization of environmental issues. This new science wasn't perfect, but it offered a way to organize and model the complexity that these events seemed to presage, and hence provided a basis for policies to manage them.

The "Earthrise" photograph of the earth taken from the Apollo 11 spacecraft in 1969 galvanized a conception of a fragile, self-contained ecosystem. Such photographs, matched with the popular phrases of "only one earth" and "spaceship earth" confirmed "what previously could only be grasped intellectually: that earth is indeed small, lovely, unitary, finite and vulnerable."[4] What such photos missed was another reality of life on earth: territorial boundaries, which although created by man rather than natural forces, are no less real for the conduct of international relations.

Problems of environmental pollution certainly existed before the 1970s. Humanity has always profoundly modified the ecosystem. Writers had long expressed concern with environmental degradation and its effects on human activity (see, for instance, Marsh 1864; Glacken 1967; Thomas 1956). However, the effects of many problems are now felt globally, whereas in the past they were felt only locally or regionally (Eisenbud 1978). Although excessive logging and grazing in the third century B.C. led to erosion in Greece and overall deforestation in North Africa (Hughes 1975; Braudel 1976; Thirgood 1981), such practices may now change the global climate (Woodwell 1985). Carbon was found in the lungs of an Egyptian mummy, indicating early air pollution from the burning of coal. In the fifteenth century chimneys were introduced in London to remove irritating coal smoke from within houses (Eisenbud 1978:27–28, 60). Now these problems are much more widespread. The magnitude of potential environmental catastrophes are greater (more people are potentially affected), the effects are more enduring (such as with nuclear wastes), and pollutants traverse greater distances, hence affecting many countries rather than just one. The economic costs of reversing the trends that contribute to environmental pollution are enormous (Eckholm 1982:ch. 6).

The widespread distances which such pollutants travel, their toxicity, and the irreversibility of their effects has irrevocably transformed international life by making countries more ecologically interdependent.

TOWARD A NEW INTERNATIONAL POLITICAL ORDER FOR THE ENVIRONMENT

The international community developed a number of arrangements to manage shared environmental problems. At the international level new institutions were created, and a new body of international law was developed to cope with problems of international pollution. Nationally, many new environmental agencies were established, environmental legislation was passed, and public investment was channeled into environmental protection. In addition, many new nongovernmental groups emerged that attempted to coordinate international efforts for pollution control. In sum, a number of efforts were launched to deal with environmental problems, and, as will be seen below, the scope of these efforts became increasingly broad and increasingly sensitive to multiple environmental interdependencies. Lynton Caldwell observes that "the record of both organized and individual efforts to safeguard the biosphere and the quality of the human environment has been impressive, and the commitment of governments within the last two decades to protection of the biosphere is without precedent" (1984:260).

In the aggregate, this international environmental behavior is remarkably different from generalized international behavior. There is a large amount of international cooperation, and overall behavior— both internationally and nationally—is of a new form. It is more comprehensive, future oriented, and sensitive to environmental interlinkages between issues than has been widely observed in the past and in other issue areas. As such, it constitutes an emergent international political order for the environment. An international political order consists of "the characteristic forms of behavior by which security and change are pursued by states and other international actors."[5]

Traditionally, cooperation within international political orders has been seen to be closely bounded. International orders have traditionally been viewed as being short-sighted, incremental, discrete, fragmented, and ad hoc. Behavior has historically been similarly circumscribed in international environmental issues.[6] Institutional developments have only emerged in pieces, and in response to a crisis (Brooks 1986). Decision makers have commonly acted as if they believed that the world consisted of small problems that could be dealt with discretely, neglecting interlinkages with other issues and externalities that would affect others. Cooperation has tended to be short-lived, and narrow in scope.

The international environmental activities of the 1970s and 1980s mark a significant departure from such past orders. Countries frequently cooperate to manage environmental issues. Moreover, the new political order is broader and more comprehensive than it was in the past. Wider geographic areas are now subject to international cooperative arrangements (such as the global ozone layer and the world's oceans) and arrangements are now more comprehensive in coverage than in the past, covering a variety of new sources of pollution, land-based ones as well as tankers and marine dumping; new channels of pollution such as airborne and riverine transmission as well as pollutants ejected directly into oceans; and pollutants themselves, including oil, chemicals, and agricultural sprays. Many of the multiple interdependencies between environmental issues have been recognized and efforts have been taken to manage them.

INTERNATIONAL EFFORTS TO CONTROL ENVIRONMENTAL POLLUTION

Environmental issues were first popularized internationally at the 1972 United Nations Conference on the Human Environment (UNCHE), and have remained on the international agenda ever since. Proposed by Sweden in 1966, UNCHE was the first world conference that brought delegates together from the North and South to discuss environmental issues; 113 countries attended, although the USSR and Eastern European countries boycotted the conference. The conference adopted a Declaration on the Human Environment, with 26 principles and 109 recommendations for action. Views evolved from the northern view that environmental pollution was a consequence of modern forms of industrial production to include the southern view that pollution was also a result of poverty, when LDCs (less developed countries) could not afford sufficient water treatment and sanitation facilities for their population. Marine pollution was identified as a key problem at UNCHE. Sixteen recommendations covered pollution in general, and

9 more specifically dealt with marine pollution. UNCHE recommendation number 92 urged governments to take early action to adopt "effective national measures for the protection of all significant sources of marine pollution" (United Nations 1973:23). UNCHE also approved the creation of a new United Nations agency to coordinate international efforts for environmental protection (Rowland 1973).

The United Nations Environment Programme (UNEP) was established the following year in Nairobi, Kenya, with a small staff and a budget of $US 16 million. By 1988 it had grown to a staff of 180 and an annual budget of 45 million dollars.[7] It is the first UN agency to be headquartered in a developing country. Its mission is to be "catalytic" and to trigger other organizations to take action for environmental protection. In addition to its Nairobi headquarters, regional environmental offices were established to coordinate activities with the UN regional economic commissions. Since 1973 UNEP has leveraged its own 450 million dollars into 1.2 billion dollars for environmental projects with support from such other international agencies as the World Bank, FAO, WHO, and WMO.[8] In 1973 UNEP's Governing Council designated "oceans" as one of UNEP's priority areas, and subsequently sponsored 23 treaties, through its Regional Seas Programme, to protect ten regional seas from pollution. (Sand 1988:ix).

UNEP has taken an activist role in the sphere of international environmental protection, becoming the environmental conscience of the UN system. Through its Environmental Liaison Center (ELC) in Nairobi, it makes contact with and transmits information to various environmental and scientific nongovernmental organizations throughout the world and keeps such groups in contact with each other, in order to stimulate and sustain interest in the environment and circulate specific environmental and conservation proposals. Its two executive directors, Maurice Strong of Canada and Mostapha Tolba of Egypt, have both served as public spokesmen for the environment, serving a publicity function as well as acting as international civil servants. In addition to individual meetings with heads of state, they frequently made speeches intended to promote international environmental consciousness raising and supported annual celebrations of World Environment Day on June 5 to celebrate UNCHE.[9] In May 1989 Tolba even went so far as to press the UNEP Governing Council to increase the UNEP budget to US$ 100 million over the next three years.

UNEP has been active. In February 1986 UNEP convened a conference of Nongovernmental Organizations (NGOs) in Nairobi. In

November 1984 UNEP joined with the International Chamber of Commerce in sponsoring the World Industry Conference on Environmental Management (WICEM), which brought together 514 representatives from private industry, governments, industrial managers' associations, labor unions, scientific bodies, and intergovernmenal organizations. A center has been established in Geneva to continue such contacts and to disseminate information about industry's efforts to control pollution. A UNEP office in Paris operates to encourage industry to adopt more environmentally sensitive protection, develop and circulate guidelines for disaster response, and to circulate environmental standards. In 1985 the First African Ministerial Conference on the Environment was held in Cairo. It gave rise to biannual African ministerial meetings, at which UNEP stresses the need for intergovernmental policy coordination and more integrated forms of domestic planning which would take into consideration transmission by ecological cycles of pollution externalities from one economic sector to another (UNEP 1987). UNEP has advised twenty-two LDCs on how to establish and enforce environmental legislation, and has trained scientists and technicians in techniques for environmental monitoring, conservation, and pest control methods.[10]

World conferences convened by the United Nations both reflected and reinforced this growing international concern. Subsequent conferences addressed population (Bucharest, 1974), food (Rome, 1974), human settlements (Vancouver, 1976), water (Mar del Plata, 1977), desertification (Nairobi, 1977), science and technology for development (Vienna, 1979), agrarian reform and rural development (Rome, 1979), and new and renewable sources of energy (Nairobi, 1981).[11] Discussions at preparatory meetings and at the conferences contributed to a better understanding of the complex functional interrelationships between environmental issues, and also revealed the diversity of state interests that precluded agreements on resolving such problems.

International law has evolved to cope with many aspects of international environmental pollution. In the early 1970s, in response to growing tanker traffic and the growing size of tankers, the international community developed a number of key pieces of international legislation to cover accidents, operational discharges, tanker construction, operational codes to avoid collisions, and compensation schemes for the costs of cleaning up oil pollution from spills. For example, IMO (the International Maritime Organization, formerly called the Intergovernmental Maritime Consultative Organization) adopted nearly thirty treaties covering the maritime transport of oil since 1959 (Andre 1987:47). It adopted the Convention on the Prevention of Marine Pollution by Dumping of Wastes and Other Matter (the London dumping convention) in 1972. The convention contained two lists of substances whose dumping in the ocean was prohibited (the "black list") or restricted (the "grey list"). A permit is required for the dumping of grey-listed substances. The convention entered into force in 1975. In 1988 the contracting parties agreed to extend the treaty's coverage to include ocean incineration of wastes; they also agreed to end such burning by 1994 unless it is proved to be environmentally safe.[12] All subsequent treaties have utilized the same format of black- and grey-listed substances, although the lists grew longer on successive treaties as governments became more knowledgeable about the variety of toxic pollutants they were seeking to regulate.

In 1973 IMO concluded the International Convention for the Prevention of Pollution from Ships (the MARPOL convention), extending the 1954 IMCO Pollution of the Seas by Oil Convention. MARPOL covers pollution by oil as well as the dumping of noxious liquid substances in bulk, harmful materials carried in bulk, and sewage and garbage generated on board. More stringent pollution standards were set for certain "special areas" which were particularly vulnerable to pollution (the Mediterranean, the Baltic, the Black Sea, the Red Sea, and the Persian/Arabian Gulf). With its 1978 amendments, MARPOL entered into force in 1983. It has been effective. While the total movement of oil by sea fell by 22 percent the amount of oil lost into the oceans from spills fell by over 90 percent, indicating some real international action in controlling oil pollution.[13]

Overall concern about the scope of international environmental problems also grew during the decade. From a common concern with oil pollution and the conservation of species in the early 1970s, countries negotiated treaties governing a wider range of pollutants and sources whose control was more expensive, such as land-based sources of marine pollution and air pollution. In the 1950s and 1960s eight of the nine multilateral environmental conventions signed involved oil pollution. From 1970 to 1985 only thirteen of the thirty-six treaties concluded dealt with oil pollution; 10 covered conservation of species; six were framework agreements encouraging future action; four covered land-based sources of pollution including industrial, agricultural, and municipal wastes; and two dealt with air pollution.[14] The 1983 International Tropical Timber Agreement is the first commodity arrangement to include funding for sustainable development and environmentally sound management of a commodity (Wasserman 1984). The 1985 Vienna Convention for Protection of the Ozone Layer and the 1987 Montreal Protocol for the Protection of the Ozone Layer are the first global treaties to protect the global atmosphere from pollution. The March 1989 Basel Convention on the Control of Transboundary Movements of Hazardous Wastes and their Disposal is one of the first treaties to recognize the links between trade and environmental issues.

Regional efforts progressed in scope as well. The North Atlantic states adopted the 1972 Oslo Convention on the Control of Dumping from Ships and Aircraft. As the governments realized that land-based sources contributed large amounts of pollutants to the North Sea, they adopted the 1974 Paris Convention for the Prevention of Marine Pollution from Land-Based Sources, with a 1986 amendment that included airborne pollutants. The North Sea States intend to eliminate offshore incineration by 1995. The United Nations Economic Commission for Europe sponsored a 1979 framework treaty for transboundary air pollution, followed by a 1984 protocol for atmospheric monitoring, a 1985 protocol limiting emissions of sulphur dioxide, and a 1988 protocol covering nitrogen oxides. It appears successful, as seasonal concentrations of sulphur dioxide in the area fell between 1977/78 and 1983/84 (United Nations Economic Commission for Europe 1987:1–41). The EEC adopted a broad directive for marine pollution in 1976 that contained longer and more detailed lists of banned and regulated substances than any of its previous efforts. The EEC Directive on Pollution Caused by Certain Dangerous Substances Discharged in the Aquatic Environment of the Community banned emissions into rivers and seas of a wide variety of pesticides, herbicides, fungicides, heavy metals, and carcinogenic materials. Twenty metals were included on the grey list; permits are required before substances containing these metals may be discharged into the EEC marine environment. This list of metals contained thirteen more items than any of the previous treaties. Subsequent EEC directives were issued covering a number of other substances (such as cadmium and mercury, in 1983 and 1984 respectively), governing discharges from certain industries (such as the chloralkali electrolysis industry, in 1982), and setting water quality standards for different uses (such as water for swimming and raising shellfish). Few studies have been conducted of compliance with these directives,[15] but it is known that in 1987 only 37 percent of European beaches complied with EEC standards for bathing waters.[16] The EEC has adopted "hundreds" of laws and regulations for environmental protection (Whitehead 1985:30–31). 1987 was the "Year of the Environment" in Europe. The EEC significantly extended its jurisdiction to environmental protection through the 1985 revision of the Treaty of Rome. The EEC now has the authority to implement and enforce common environmental standards throughout the community (Jacque 1986; Rehbinder and Stewart 1988:15–19).

Environmental concern also surfaced in other multilateral forums. In 1969 NATO created the Committee on Challenges of Modern Society to sponsor research on the principally pollution-related problems of the industrialized countries. The 1975 Final Act on Security and Cooperation in Europe (the Helsinki accord) included a full chapter devoted to cooperation regarding the environment. Parties met again in October, 1989 to discuss the environment. The 1982 Law of the Sea Convention has a substantial chapter on marine pollution, developed after the 1978 *Amoco Cadiz* accident. The 1985 Bonn economic summit concluded with a resolution encouraging the participating governments to cooperate in order to anticipate and prevent damage to the environment from transboundary pollution, recognizing that "environmental protection (is) one of the key science and technology areas which relate to economic growth and employment."[17] At the 1987 Venice economic summit leaders proposed to deal "effectively" with environmental problems of worldwide impact.[18] The 1989 Paris summit ended with a call for "decisive action" to "understand and protect the earth's ecological balance" (*New York Times*, July 17, 1989, p. 1). In June 1986 the Organization for Economic Cooperation and (OECD) imposed strict controls on the export of hazardous wastes destined for disposal outside the OECD area, after having adopted the "polluter pays" principle in 1972 aimed at ensuring that pollution control costs are directly borne by polluters and reflected in the prices of their products (OECD 1986b). UNEP estimates that environmental quality improved from 1972 to 1982 in areas introducing measures for environmental protection, notably in cities in developed countries (Holdgate, Kassas, and White 1982: ch. 17).

In 1980 twelve multilateral development banks, including the World Bank, adopted the Declaration of Principles on the Incorporation of Environmental Considerations in Development Policies, Programmes and Projects (Stein and Johnson 1979). These banks committed themselves to include environmental factors in project assessments. In response to concerted pressure from American environmental groups and congressmen concerned that Third World environmental degradation and failed development projects would be the "inevitable result of a tradition of development planning that ignores the interrelationships between economic activity and its biological and ecological underpinnings" (Aufderheide and Rich 1988:302), in May 1987 World Bank president Barber Conable announced a major reorganization of the bank to better evaluate the resource conservation and the environmental aspects of development projects.[19] The Inter-American Development Bank canceled loans for a Brazilian highway due to its role in accelerating the rate of Amazonian deforestation.[20]

Information collection activities were implemented to support global environmental protection. Through its three-part Earthwatch Program, UNEP seeks to assess global environmental conditions and collect and distribute information about them. The Global Environmental Monitoring System (GEMS) collects and disseminates worldwide background and monitoring data on air and water quality from twelve national stations, with an annual budget of $US 2 million. It also coordinates its efforts with networks run by other UN agencies. It started publishing data in 1981. The International Registry of Potentially Toxic Chemicals (IRPTC), created in Geneva in 1976, has created a computer data base on toxic chemicals that is disseminated through a newsletter and to responses to direct requests from governments. It provides users with information on the deleterious effects of chemicals on the environment and in the workplace. A third information referral system (INFOTERRA) serves as a switchboard to direct environmental questions to appropriate international sources. One hundred and twenty-five countries participate in INFOTERRA, giving them access to 5,200 sources of information.[21] INFOTERRA channeled 13,200 inquiries in 1987, up by 500 from 1986. Forty-two percent of the 1987 queries came from Morocco, Indonesia, and the USSR.[22]

National concern with environmental protection has grown as well. At a 1982 UNEP meeting, leaders expressed concerns about a broader array of problems than 10 years earlier, as well as relating environmental issues to many other social and economic concerns (Tolba, 1988). Governmental bodies responsible for environmental protection proliferated wildly during the 1970s. Between 1972 and 1982 ministries or departments responsible for the environment and natural resources were established in 118 countries. In 1972, 15 developed countries and 11 developing countries had such bodies. By 1982, 34 DCs and 110 LDCs had them (Baker, Bassett, and Ellington 1985; vii, ix). Popular concern in Western Europe has shifted to increased concern with quality of life and environmental quality, although it has not been an issue that has successfully mobilized political activity.[23]

Expenditures for pollution control in the industrialized nations rose suddenly in the early 1970s and remained relatively stable thereafter, although they declined in the early 1980s with the second major global recession. Data for France, Germany, Japan, and the United States are presented below. No comparable data exist for developing countries. Fifteen of the 24 OECD countries adopted major environmental laws in the 1970s and 1980s, and all adopted legislation regulating water, air, or solid waste disposal (OECD 1985a:242).

Nongovernmental environmental groups also flourished. In 1982 nearly 15,000 environmental nongovernmental organizations (NGOs) were registered with UNEP's Environmental Liaison Center, 2,230 of them in the LDCs and nearly 13,000 in DCs. About 60% of the LDC NGOs were created in the 1970s, and 30 percent of the DC NGOs (Caldwell 1988:19). Membership in 8 major United States environmental groups soared from 525,000 in 1968 to over 2 million in 1985.[24] Recently there has been an environmental awakening in the Soviet Union as well. The chairman of the State Committee for Environmental Protection announced at the nineteenth Party Congress in July 1988 that the USSR faced grave environmental problems (Sun 1988).

In the LDCs, however, environmental awareness has been stated in different terms than those used to express concern with the preservation of the environment that so prevails in the West. LDC concern was much more with the economic and social impacts of environmental issues. Speaking to the United Nations Conference on the Human Environment (UNCHE) in 1972, Indira Gandhi made the reasons clear: "How can we speak to those who live in the villages and in the slums about keeping the oceans, the rivers, and the air clean when their own lives are contaminated? Are not poverty and need the greatest polluters?"[25]

The process of environmental policymaking has been very different in these two sets of countries as well. In Europe, environmentalism has penetrated mass politics, with the spread of "Green parties" who have left their mark in public elections.[26] Green party members have been elected to national parliaments in Belgium, Finland, Switzerland, Luxembourg, and West Germany; they have also won seats in the European Parliament (Rudig and Lowe 1986:262; Parkin 1989). In the LDCs, however, policies to improve environmental quality have been "at best, grudging" (Leonard and Morell 1981:300). In single-party

Table 1.2. Comparative Expenditures for Pollution Control

	1973	1975	1977
United States			
Public and private expenditures/GNP	1.6	2.0	2.0
Public and private investment/GNP	.37	.45	
Federal Republic of Germany			
federal expenditures/GNP	.		.759
federal expenditures and private investment/GNP		.796	.95
Japan			
Federal expenditures/GNP			.34
federal expenditures and private investment/GNP			.56
private investment/GFCF	.11	.18	.07
France[a]			
environmental expenditures as a percent of GDP			
public sewage treatment/GFCF			
private sewage treatment/GFCF			
total sewage treatment/GFCF			
public sewage treatment/GDP			
private sewage treatment/GDP			
total sewage treatment/GDP			

Source: France, Ministère de l'Environnement et du Cadre du vie (1982–1986); *Donnees Economiques de l'Environnement* International Monetary Fund, *International Financial Statistics* (various years).

Note: Expenditures = investment + operating expenses.

[a] France includes water management for economic uses as well—i.e., irrigation, etc.

states and in countries under military rule policy change has largely been driven by elites and by bureaucratic politics within the executive branch. Enforcement is very difficult due to a lack of environmental monitoring capabilities and small enforcement staffs. Recently, environmental groups have emerged in Mexico (Redclift 1987), India (Bandjopadhyay and Shiva 1987; Agarwal 1985), Thailand, and Malaysia (Asia-Pacific People's Environment Network; Mohan 1987), although these groups have not engaged as extensively in transnational alliance building as have DC NGOs.

1978	1979	1980	1981	1982	1983
1.9	2.0	2.2	1.9	1.8	
.819	.872	.914	.871	.808	
.98	1.02	1.09	1.06	1.03	
.43	.51	.50	.468	.443	
.59	.67	.66			
.05	.05	.05	.05		
1.54	1.64		1.7	1.7	1.7
1.3	1.51		1.85	1.75	1.78
.41	.34		.34	.53	.54
1.71	1.85		2.19	2.28	2.32
.28	.32		.39	.36	.35
.088	.073		.073	.11	.11
.368	.393		.463	.470	.460

WHAT ENVIRONMENTAL PROBLEMS PORTEND

These responses to evidence of environmental degradation occurred despite extensive disagreement about the meaning of the environmental crisis and what policies were called for. Informed by different disciplinary and political perspectives, both academics and
policymakers drew dramatically divergent conclusions from the same
phenomena.[27] They disputed whether environmental problems were
unique, whether they could be resolved by existing practices, or whether
they required governments to learn novel collective forms of behavior. Others went so far as to suggest that the intermeshed nature of
environmental issues would serve as a new determinant of international behavior.

They disagreed about the nature of the problem that they felt
environmental degradation reflected. Did the environmental disasters

of the 1970s reflect a deeper trend, anomalies that required greater attention, or were they merely *sui generis* events with no broader meaning? In the midst of such events the answer could not be determined.

The discussion has still not been resolved. Are all major problems truly global? Is collapse imminent? Is it inevitable? Are all problems equally nondecomposable? Are all effects equally irreversible? Is there truly one interlinked and nondecomposable system in which all behavior takes place? Are remedial efforts sufficient, or must leaders take anticipatory measures for environmental protection even before problems emerge or their effects are felt? May environmental problems be treated independently of the social, political and economic patterns which give rise to them? For example, when presented in 1972 with the discovery of DDT in penguins, observers were unsure whether this constituted a minor anomaly or was evidence of much deeper global disruptions (Thacher 1985:207). Although the unanticipated negative side effects of many large-scale Third World development projects also came as rude shocks to many economists (Farvar and Milton 1972), it is still not clear whether these are a result of naive planning, venal civil servants, or ignorance. They may be the unavoidable concomitants of large-scale projects, and their catastrophic potential may be overdrawn.[28]

We simply do not know if the appropriate systemic metaphor is one of punctuated equilibrium, exponential growth, or catastrophe. If all problems are now somehow interlinked within the global problematique, spaceship earth, or similar metaphors describing a cybernetic self-regulating system surrounding an ensemble of interrelated problems, then coherent integrated action is called for because issues are not analytically decomposable.

But if a more disjointed view calling for more attention to interlinkages—but falling short of requiring a whole new mode of analysis and decision making—is taken, then incremental actions may still be effective for guaranteeing survival. Even if all problems need not be simultaneously managed, policies must be more comprehensive. Plans must be drawn up that are sensitive to the possible effects on other economic sectors, and they must be placed within the context of the ecosystemic forces that may transmit these impacts elsewhere. Effective responses to environmental problems require fairly sophisticated learning about the social and environmental contexts of decisions. Such comprehensive policies must also be coordinated between states so that states may avoid adopting incompatible policies or policies that interfere with each other.

Analysts' characterizations of the extent of problems, as well as their identification of new variables and interconnections that must be controlled, varied according to their beliefs about the underlying holism of such problems. Most of the analysts shared a common concern with global survival, rather than with economic redistribution or poverty alleviation, and hence were less concerned with locating environmental problems within a context of forms of economic production or political domination.

At the extreme, wide-scale environmental deterioration and degradation were posed as profound evolutionary challenges to human survival: "According to the ecological version of doomsday, a vast breakdown in an overloaded natural system would be followed by a new biospheric equilibrium in which there would be no place or role for the human race as we have known it."[29] *Homo sapiens* has altered the world through the biospheric effects of modern industrial civilization, and leaders are now faced with the challenge of adapting to such changes, or creating a new niche in which to live. The problem of pollution control will increase in importance for LDCs as they continue to develop economically (Strong 1984).

In game-theoretic terms, this is truly a vision of a game against nature in the purest sense. Possible misperceptions about the rules of the game or the plans of the opponent may have fatal consequences for the human players. Poor choices in response to natural selection may lead to species extinction. Rice Odell pointed to past precedents in which environmental pressures and sociopolitical failures to deal with them were implicated in the collapse of major civilizations (Odell 1977; Odell 1979).

Many writers believed that the emergence of widespread environmental pollution was merely the tip of an iceberg signifying the deep interconnections between all issues. All human activities were presumed to be intimately interlinked; political and economic interdependence was now combined with ecological interdependence. All human activities interacted with each other, as well as with the physical environment in which they took place. Individual actions were likely to have multiple repercussions in related social activities as well as in the ecosphere. Such authors argued that "new perspectives, orientations, theories, models and designs are urgently needed *now* if most organizations are successfully to adapt to and survive in such turbulence" (De Greene 1982:ix). Because problems cannot be decomposed analytically, incremental trial-and-error policymaking and learning is no longer sufficient when error may mean global extinction (Lustick 1980). Anticipatory action is necessary (Botkin, Elmandjra, and Malitza 1979; Michael 1973). The sources of pollution must be eliminated, they argue, rather than merely controlled. Recently an American diplomat averred that:

> . . . in practice, a new paradigm for international cooperation likely will be needed. . . . Somehow leaders and government processes and budget makers must accustom themselves to a new way of thinking. The scientific issues are complex, interrelating many different scientific disciplines, often at the frontiers of discovery. (Benedick 1986:31, 34)

Donald Michael has argued that "disjointed incrementalism" is insufficient to deal with the complex interrelationships evident between the array of international problems bedeviling decision makers, and contended that states must adopt more integrative and long-range planning styles (Michael 1973; Emery and Trist 1972; Emery 1977). More recently, the International Union for the Conservation of Nature (IUCN) presented its World Conservation Strategy, which is based on the premise that long-term sound economic development relies on integrating environmental factors into development planning (IUCN 1980).

One position, epitomized by the UNEP staff, was that environmental problems should not be viewed simply as negative pollution externalities. Pollution may be the most tangible signal of the transgression of deeper global physical limits. These tensions are distinguished by a wide range of interacting stresses that require *"comprehensive* rather than incremental decisions; synoptic rather than piecemeal outlooks and vision. These policies are characterized by an *indivisibility* in the political commitment and resources they require for success"* (Schulman 1975:1355).

Such writers felt that environmental or other problems should not be dealt with in isolation. Policy required concurrent attention to the sources, channels, and multiple effects of pollutants. The sources were presumed to include the social conditions giving rise to specific polluting habits, for instance demographic, social, and cultural forces that led to crowding along the seashore and hence to coastal pollution. Transboundary pollutants must be controlled by international cooperation, yet UNEP officials also believed that cooperation should embody comprehensive and simultaneous efforts to deal with the deeper forces that gave rise to such polluting practices. Efforts should be made to manage the underlying patterns of economic production and demand that generated the widespread generation of environmental pollutants, while remedial efforts should still be made for the sanitation of contaminated areas. For instance:

> ... environmental management of the Earth's ecosystems de-
> mands an inter-disciplinary evaluation of the world's resources,
> on land, in the seas and in the atmosphere, coupled with an
> assessment of the impacts of technological, agricultural, biolog-
> ical and other practices on these ecosystems and their environ-
> ment. Increase in the world's population, together with higher
> standards of living and limited arable land, increase in soil
> erosion, loss of genetic diversity and the disappearance of pro-
> ductive natural ecosystems, and movement of population from
> rural areas ravaged by drought to burgeoning urban centres
> cause traumatic stress on productive agricultural land, both to
> supply space for housing and to feed those to be housed. In turn,
> malnourished people are compelled to destroy the world's re-
> sources for nourishment and shelter. Land is forced, often by
> unsound agricultural practices and the use of chemicals, to be
> more productive than ever. Also, chemicals find their way to
> man through the food chain, disturb the productivity and natu-
> ral evolution of the ecosystems, and contaminate the seas, lakes
> and groundwater by rain run-off; and often with a devastating
> impact on plant, animal (including marine) and microbial re-
> sources and on human health (UNEP 1986c:39).

UNEP went so far as to design political arrangements for unified pollution control organized around such ecological criteria as river basins or regional seas, rather than more traditional political bound-aries.[30]

Two different sets of conclusions were adduced from the experience of environmental degradation. One group viewed environmental problems within a broad perspective on the interlinkages between all international issues, of which the environment is but one element. The world is made up of a web of intertwined clusters of problems, which they term the "problematique." Environmental degradation is but one of such clusters, which include population growth, economic growth, energy consumption, and the like, and must be understood in relation to the others. The Club of Rome, composed of one hundred prominent Western futurists and industrialists, forcefully argued for seeing environmental pollution within the context of the "global problematique," and commissioned reports on different aspects of the problematique.[31] Aurelio Peccei, the president of the Club of Rome, concluded:

> There are no longer separate economic, technical or social problems, which can be judged fairly well on their own terms and attacked individually, at leisure, one after the other. The dynamics, speeds, energies and complexities of our artificial world are orders of magnitude bigger than anything before—and so are our problems. (Peccei 1977:61)

From such a holistic view, to which UNEP also subscribed, the problematique could only be managed by adopting a new, more integrated way of thinking about the world, one that is sensitive to the complex interrelationships between its social and ecospheric components. Moreover, they regarded the nation-state as obsolete within a global context defined by global forces. Sovereignty was seen as a barrier to effective management of the global problematique and the transboundary flows it embodied. They sought to supercede the nation-state with some form of transnational or global ecomanagement.

Indicative of its holistic vision of interlinkages between issue areas are UNEP's recent efforts to promote global disarmament in order to free up money for investment in environmental protection. Individuals could play an educational role. International organizations could trace the exact nature of the links and estimate the thresholds or "outer limits" beyond which global equilibrium was impossible and the "inner limits" beyond which societies would collapse (see, for instance, Hirsch 1976). Ultimately, governments would have to cooperate to ensure that their activities remained sensitive to the limits imposed by the natural system.

This vision anticipated greatly transformed roles for the modern nation-state. It would become an "environmental intervener,"[32] a particularly contentious role during a period of mounting privatization and deregulation, by creating new national and international institutions that would be responsible for environmental protection and have a comprehensive scope of action.

A slightly different perspective was taken by environmentalists in Western Europe and the United States. They viewed the environment in terms of a relationship between nature and mankind that was in disarray. They offered two sets of proposals. They called for developing a new collection of collective ethics, under which humanity would assume responsibility or stewardship for the biosphere. The laws of ecology would dictate social organization. Thus, collective action would be a result not of politics or of administration, but of morality (see, for instance, Thompson 1987; Seed et al. 1988). The European green movements argued that governments must recognize man's key relationship to nature and integrate such concerns into all public policy (Porritt 1985). Extreme groups rejected the anthropocentric nature of Western development, arguing that all species deserve equal treatment and that the nation-state must be replaced by smaller, self-sufficient bioregions defined by common ecological characteristics, such as watersheds and weather patterns.[33] They found the "spaceship earth" metaphor to be too mechanistic and utilitarian for their ideal of a decentralized system in which *Homo sapiens* lives in harmony with its surroundings.

In more policy-relevant terms, this extreme wing of the environmentalists felt that government planning must be subordinated to ecological principles, similar to some of the views of the Club of Rome. These principles were loosely based on Barry Commoner's informal "four laws of ecology" (1971:29–41):

1. Everything is connected to everything else.

2. Everything must go somewhere.

3. Nature knows best.

4. There is no such thing as a free lunch.

Sociologists have referred to such a new set of beliefs as the "New Environmental Paradigm" (Catten and Dunlap 1978). National and international social planning would have to take account of the systemic limits in which it would take place, implicitly calling for a strong role for international organizations in collecting information about sustainable ranges of activity, monitoring the environment, and developing and disseminating information about alternative modes of production and planning.

Evolutionary theorists (who are seldom political scientists, but are frequently cited by those authors who believe that international relations may be analyzed as a system) saw environmental deterioration as a global-level threat, appropriate for systems analysis.[34] They regarded evolutionary theory as the appropriate method, theory, framework, or metaphor to integrate the relevant social sciences and natural sciences necessary to analyze *Homo sapiens'* responses to global environmental challenges. New policies should balance all of the variables, stocks, and flows that are relevant to the interactions of open environmental subsystems. With arguments grounded in homeostatic models, these writers often saw the world as internally self-adjusting and tending toward a long-term dynamic equilibrium. By neglecting domestic and international political dynamics, such writers generally omitted discussions of how systemic accommodation to more complex environmental interrelationships would occur.

Many authors writing from this approach presumed that the novel, interpenetrated nature of environmental problems would automatically give rise to a holistic collective awareness and more integrated forms of behavior.

> Two qualitatively new dimensions appear. First, the costs of remedial action, and the absence of a source for renewal suggests, for the first time, that the trends may not be reversible. Adaptation to the inevitable might be the only achievable goal. Secondly, the label of "pollution" or "environmental" is no longer appropriate. These are problems not understood simply in terms of industrial or agricultural outputs burdening the air or water. They are fundamentally ecological because they affect processes that link elements of our biological world to global atmospheric and hydrospheric processes. Forests, swamps, and termites become more than resources or curiosities of nature. They are part of a system of sustainability. (Holling 1984)

Cooperation and natural planning would come to echo the natural laws that such authors observed. The novel interdependent nature of environmental problems and the use of holistic scientific methods would be a determinant of international behavioral and cognitive change. John McHale suggested that "accompanying these expansions of the levels of conceptual awareness is a significant recourse to the planetary ecology as a pragmatic framework for their interrelation, with the focus on the role of man as symbiotic agent and disruptive factor."[35] Richard Falk suggested the emergence of a global ecological consciousness, noting

> the integrative trends associated with the many dimensions of an emergent ecological reality. The appreciation of limits and interrelationships on a global scale is giving rise to various forms of planetary consciousness. More and more people everywhere realize that the boundaries of sovereign states are artificial, whereas the unity of the planet is natural. As a consequence, many people who do not know or will not acknowledge

the words, or are bothered by their rootless cosmopolitan reso-
nance, are beginning to feel and act as if they are "planetary
citizens." . . . Naturally, such people also experience a deepening
conflict between their loyalties to the state and their feelings of
human and planetary identity. (1979:x)

Other perspectives were more moderate. Writers suggested that
although the environmental crisis may not be inescapably global and
holistic in scope, most problems were indeed interdependent. A less
apocalyptic prediction was offered by Maurice Strong, who anticipated a sequence of cascading crises resulting from partial attempts
to manage such interrelated issues, pointing out

the prospect of slow but probably accelerating slide into chaos
due to social limits on our ability to cope with the complexity
inherent in a high-technology society. Political, psychological
and institutional limitations could condemn the world to a vi-
cious cycle of interlocking crises, with the institutional structures of society breaking down or becoming paralyzed by the
sheer weight and complexity of problems it cannot handle. And
this could happen well before resource limitations put physical
restraints on man's activities.[36]

Within the sphere of development economics, a number of new
textbooks and primers sprang up to guide Third World planners in
incorporating environmental considerations into their national development plans.[37] They stressed the need for balanced growth between
interlinked economic sectors in order to avoid destroying or exceeding the carrying capacity of the natural environment. Resources might
be finite, contrary to the conventional economic assumptions of infinite and substitutable resources. In effect, economic planners must
adopt new patterns of reasoning to effectively deal with the complex
interplay of issues, although they downplayed the question of the
novelty of the problem.

More optimistic versions were offered by Herman Kahn and Julian
Simon. They did not think that any new behavior was required beyond relying on market forces. They felt that countries and economies
will be able to respond effectively to such systemic transformation
through the judicious recognition of market signals and the efficient
allocation of economic resources as evidence of scarcity appears.[38]
Their views were grounded on a rosy view of the development of new
and efficient technologies, and they generally neglected the real con-

flict of political interests that arises when states attempt to resolve shared problems. Most instances of pollution were regarded as disjointed events that could be treated in isolation through the selective introduction of more effective pollution control technologies and that did not require the type of comprehensive approaches that other authors advocated.

Many writers among the more mainstream analysts of international relations saw environmental problems as a new issue area that required attention but could still be analyzed in terms of conventional concepts and methods and managed through the orthodox channels of diplomacy and international institutions.[39] Effective environmental policy was thus posed as a question of institutional design; these writers pondered the difficulties of using existing organizations to deal with problems that inherently transcend the functional boundaries of those organizations. Most writers concerned themselves with the causes of environmental degradation rather than the political or social consequences of pollution.

Many European Marxists attributed such cases of environmental pollution to the excesses of capitalism, which tolerated and created such externalities (Gorz 1980). However, noting the extensive environmental degradation in centrally planned societies as well, Rudolf Bahro expressed his displeasure with the entire modern form of industrial production.[40]

Lessons were also drawn for how analysts should study the interaction of states, or societies, with their environments. Methodologically, diachronic rather than synchronic study was viewed as necessary to understanding the relationship between behavior and a changing systemic context.[41] Interdisciplinary study was hailed as being necessary to grasp the full variety of pressures operating on the nation-state, and a historical perspective was encouraged to enhance our understanding of the differences between the current international system and that of the past and the casual processes that led to this transformation. Theories of international relations are now probed for their ontological foundations, which neglect the relationships between theories and the historical areas they are designed to explain.[42]

Although disagreeing about the full implications of the emergence of environmental problems and the true extent of their interrelationships, these analysts concurred at least on the need for international cooperation and policy coordination to manage transboundary pollution. In addition, many felt that more integrated policymaking domestically was necessary to recognize and assimilate the interlinkages between issues into development planning.

POLITICAL DIFFICULTIES WITH COORDINATING
POLLUTION CONTROL EFFORTS

International cooperation was the least common denominator of these policy prescriptions for managing transboundary pollution. Yet even accomplishing that end was commonly fraught with political and economic controversy over who would pay for environmental protection and what level of environmental quality was desirable.

The international management of such issues challenges the core of the international legal order, which is grounded on the sovereign right of control over activities within national borders. The Westphalian legal notions that created state control over territorial space were based on a presumption of infinite and unsullied resources (Christy 1975; Schneider 1979; Birnie 1988). Governments are now mutually dependent in a way that was inconceivable to those drafting the legal norms of the present system. This tension is expressed in Principle 21 adopted at UNCHE: "States have . . . the sovereign right to exploit their own resources pursuant to their own environmental policies, and the responsibility to ensure that activities within their jurisdiction or control do not cause damage to the environment of other States or of areas beyond the limits of national jurisdiction" (United Nations 1973:5).

The Mediterranean pollution problem exemplifies these difficulties. The development of the Mediterranean Action Plan (Med Plan), a collective effort to coordinate the marine pollution control practices of all eighteen Mediterranean littoral countries, also highlights how a new environmental order has come about. Under the auspices of the Med Plan Mediterranean governments now seek to coordinate their pollution control practices, jointly conduct monitoring and research, and develop and diffuse actual coastal management practices to reduce pollution. Mediterranean governments have gradually adopted more comprehensive policies in a coordinated fashion in order to control pollution from a growing range of sources, pollutants, and channels.

Different countries wished to use the Mediterranean for different purposes, and hence disagreed about what level of water quality was desirable. Moreover, leaders disagreed about the need for immediate action, the range of pollutants to control, and the fundamental desirability of negotiating with countries that had traditionally been enemies.[43] With a large proportion of their industry and population lying near the coast, many LDCs interpreted efforts to control marine pollution as indirect ways of retarding their attempts at industrialization. With high rates of population growth—after growing by 120 percent from 1950 to 1980, 50 percent of Algeria's population was under age fourteen—a growing economy was seen as key to providing future individual welfare as well as political stability.

Pollutants disperse very slowly in semienclosed seas like the Mediterranean. Most of the water comes in through the Strait of Gibraltar with a renewal time of about eighty years. Because of the virtual lack of tides and the weak coastal currents pollutants tend to linger near the coasts. Pollutants come from industries and cities along the coast, from ships and offshore dredging and mining operations, and from inland sources via rivers. Although largely concentrating along the coast rather than in the open ocean, pollutants do flow from one country to its neighbors, requiring collective action for their management.

With a heavy concentration of population and industry along the coast, much of the pollution comes from the emission of untreated or inadequately treated wastes that flow directly into the Mediterranean. Both organic wastes, which gradually biodegrade in the sea, and inorganic wastes, which do not, are produced. Over 100 million people live in the coastal zone, with a summer influx of another 100 million. These numbers are expected to double by the year 2000. The Mediterranean is also a major navigation route for tankers coming from refineries and pipeline heads in the eastern and southern Mediterranean, as well as those coming through the Suez Canal. Forty percent of world tanker traffic passed through the Mediterranean in 1975 (Saliba 1978:173).

A number of competing uses of the region must be coordinated between countries, as well as within them. Each use generates pollutants of its own while simultaneously receiving pollutants from other uses. Each use also needs a different level of water quality.[44] During the Med Plan negotiations different coalitions composed of scientists and international civil servants formed around each group of pollutants identified.

Coastal cities produce a great deal of pollution. Very few of the fifty-six coastal cities with populations of over 100,000 (or the 228 coastal cities with over 10,000 population) have sufficient sewage treatment facilities, and most of the organic municipal wastes go directly into the sea. Untreated municipal wastes contain microorganisms and bacteria that spread such diseases as typhus, hepatitis, typhoid, paratyphoid, tetanus, cholera, polio, dysentery, and skin infections. These microorganisms can be particularly hazardous when they contaminate seafood. A 1973 hepatitis outbreak in Naples was traced to polluted shellfish. Ironically, for such nutrient-starved areas as the eastern portion of the Mediterranean, municipal wastes may be beneficial for fisheries as they contain nutrients like nitrogen and phosphates. Yet they also contain substances hazardous to fish, such as heavy metals and detergents.

Coastal industries, principally chemicals, iron and steel, petro-chemicals, and refineries, generate heavy metals and other inorganic chemical wastes. They are located principally in Spain, Italy, France, and Greece (Helmer 1977:34). Such substances are often directly toxic to humans and fish. They also accumulate throughout the food chain as they are transmitted from plankton up through large predators. Thus, large fish tend to have higher concentrations of chemicals in their bodies than they would have if they had simply absorbed ambient levels of pollutants through their gills. Radioactive wastes from inland nuclear power plants in Spain, France, and Italy are also transmitted to the sea by rivers. Smaller power plants are in Greece and Egypt.

Through standard operations tankers create oil pollution along the coast as well as in the open sea; they flush their ballast, and clean their tanks with seawater. Four hundred million tonnes of petroleum are unloaded annually in Mediterranean ports.[45] Of the nineteen crude oil–loading terminals in the Mediterranean, only nine have deballast-ing stations. In the ten ports without such facilities, tankers have to discharge their ballast into the sea before entering the harbor. The construction of sufficient facilities would cost $US 145 million.[46]

Although relatively less harmful than other pollutants, oil clots mar the aesthetics of beaches for tourist purposes, and also clog fishermen's nets and the engines of their boats. Freighters and cruise ships also tend to dump their garbage overboard rather than saving it for disposal in port. Dredging operations also generate heavy concentrations of suspended materials in the water, which may interfere with fish spawning.

Agricultural spraying also produces a runoff of organic and inorganic fungicides, biocides, pesticides, and fertilizers which reaches the sea and contributes to the buildup of inorganic chemicals such as organochlorines, organophosphates, and carbamates and leads to eutrophication and the loss of fisheries in areas receiving heavy inputs of phosphorous and nitrogen. Eutrophication is the buildup of nutrients in the water leading to the growth of water plants that fight fish for the available oxygen.

Fishermen and tourists require fairly clean coastlines. Various pollutants are transmitted through the food chain to shellfish and commercial fish, making them unsafe for consumption. Many coastal areas are heavily dependent upon summer tourist income for their existence. Tourism requires clean coastal waters and beaches that are relatively clear of debris, odors, tar balls, and microorganisms. Other users would be content to use the sea as a garbage dump.

The only tangible or visible pollutants are tar balls. Fish may make the existence of pollution manifestly clear because of tumors on their bodies, but these only occur at extremely heavy concentrations or after long exposure. Perceiving and monitoring most toxic pollutants requires the use of sophisticated gas chromatographs and atomic absorption spectrophotometers, which were not widely available in the Mediterranean in the early 1970s. Thus, if most policymakers wished to understand the full range of pollutants they required the expertise of scientists as well as a faith in their equipment to measure the level of pollution.

Because pollutants are transmitted by currents in the Mediterranean, countries must coordinate their policies in order to assure that they pursue common standards and do not impede each other's attempts to improve their environments. For example, if France only chose to control the industrial emissions of heavy metals, yet the Italians focused on municipal wastes, neither problem would be effectively controlled. France would still suffer from the presence in its waters of Italian heavy metals transmitted by currents, and Italy would suffer from French sewage. Moreover, Italian industries that did not invest in pollution control technology would gain a competitive advantage over French firms through lower production costs. As a Greek researcher wrote in 1984:

> Greece has come to realize that there is no way in which it alone can have clean beaches if those of the rest of Europe, and especially of the Mediterranean, are not clean as well. And if all the European beaches are to be clean and suitable for tourism, the environmental policies of the Governments of all the states which have these beaches should be aimed in the same direction, which is to provide meaningful protection for the coastline.[47]

Collective decision making was inhibited, as it is regarding most environmental issues, by the large degree of uncertainty about pollution. Scientists did not fully understand the way in which these pollutants were transmitted through the ecosystem, the related issues or economic sectors in which effects might be felt, or the long-term and possibly irreversible effects of pollution. The identity of individual pollutants is often not known or unclear. The behavior of specific substances and their interaction in the environment is often only poorly understood. Projections are shaky at best. Tolerable environmental thresholds for pollutants are seldom known, and the dynamics by which pollutants are absorbed in the environment and are transferred to other media are often unclear. "The links among the natural systems of air, water, land, and the living biota are often global. Disturbing any one of them can have unexpected results that are remote in both space and time" (World Resources Institute 1987:1). In sum, demonstrating the effects of putative pollution problems can be proved to everyone's satisfaction only by "performing the experiment" on the real (natural) system (Schneider and Thompson 1985:412), as their causes and behavior are too uncertain to usefully apply computer modeling or conventional heuristic policy approaches.

Although assessing challenges to environmental quality is difficult, evaluating alternative pollution abatement strategies is just as hard. The costs of different behavior, such as control measures and shifting to alternative substances, are commonly incompletely known and disputed. Actors' values and preferences conflict. Tradeoffs between incommensurate objectives, such as short-term economic development in order to alleviate poverty versus environmental protection, are poorly defined. Objectives are difficult to achieve, and the long causal chains operating in the biosphere commonly lead decision makers to favor instrumental reasoning over substantive decision making, particularly when facing pressing deadlines. Thus, analyses of environmental degradation and pollution control policies are often based on the marginal analysis of recently encountered problems rather than on perspectives that relate problems of pollution to broader patterns of development. Pollution control policies commonly treat symptoms of environmental decay rather than its causes, and are reactive rather than anticipatory.

Efforts for collective responses to environmental threats and broader policy initiatives are further inhibited by conventional institutional design. Governments and international agencies are seldom organized to cope with issues that cut across traditional functional or spatial boundaries. They are designed according to geographic or functional logics, and thus are insensitive to recognizing or managing natural resource and environmental quality issues that transcend or cut across such institutional boundaries. At the national level, policies are oriented toward the mission of the sponsoring agency. Most international attempts to manage pollution vary by the type of pollutant (e.g., oil and radioactive wastes) or the method of introduction into the marine environment (ocean dumping, routine tanker operation), or its spatial location (territorial waters, contiguous zone, high seas), or the institutional framework for its management (Pearson 1975:41). Moreover, the partial and incommensurable approaches of scientists working on the problem make coherent policymaking even more difficult. Few people are trained or capable of thinking holistically about the type of synergistic and feedback relationships that are often involved in such environmental issues.[48]

Such coordinated policy virtually calls for new industrial policy. Pollution controls must be installed in coastal industries. Sewers and sewage treatment plants must be constructed. Agricultural spraying must be supervised. Regionally coordinated planning is necessary to assure that heavily polluting coastal industries are not adjacent to waters used for shellfisheries or tourism. In effect, even managing shared problems of marine pollution calls for adjusting well-entrenched habits of domestic consumption and production.

If leaders wish to anticipate the need for constructing sewage treatment plants, then comprehensive estimates of population growth, economic growth, and demographic trends need to be incorporated into national economic planning. Conversely, economic planners must integrate environmental externalities into their projections in order to more effectively plan for the future. If fishery yields are to grow to feed a burgeoning population and employ coastal populations, then navigation, coastal industrial emissions, agricultural spraying, and municipal sewage must all be included in both domestic and international planning.

A study of the Med Plan cuts to the core of understanding the dynamics by which countries respond to shared environmental problems. Such an analysis illustrates the new environmental order, and sheds light on how it develops.

TWO

Influence: Explanations of International Environmental Cooperation

Protecting the Mediterranean in the 1970s from pollution required regional cooperation. Environmental cooperation, as in other international issues, means that different parties accommodate their actions in accord with the desires of their partners. Robert Keohane writes that "intergovernmental cooperation takes place when the policies actually followed by one government are regarded by its partners as facilitating realization of their own objectives, as the result of a process of policy coordination" (1984:51–52).

Such cooperation may take a number of forms. Specific cooperative arrangements vary by scope, strength, and duration.[1] *Scope* refers to the range of coverage of arrangements; from narrow efforts to control narrow problems, such as individual pollutants or sources of pollution, to comprehensive efforts that address multiple pollutants, their sources, and channels of transmission and that may even seek to integrate environmental considerations into entirely discrete issue areas. Developing a series of treaties that progressively cope with more types and source of pollution would indicate a move toward more comprehensive scope, as would the utilization of environmental impact assessments in planning economic development. The *strength* of an arrangement relates to the extent to which the arrangements' injunctions actually bind state behavior: whether they are weak or binding. Are there specific measures with which parties abide? The *duration* of an arrangement relates to its persistence. Arrangements may be enduring or transitory.

Cooperation in international politics is difficult. Writers from a number of different traditions in international politics offer contradictory interpretations of the conditions under which cooperation in the Mediterranean is likely to occur, and its form. Realism, and its most recent version, neorealism, is concerned with the relation between state power and order, generally in the area of security affairs and the political economy of the advanced industrialized societies. Historical materialism is concerned with international equality and the distribution of economic resources, often in North-South relations. A concern with knowledge-based communities and the interpretation of uncertainty offers a third set of explanations involving the groups of specialists that are responsible for articulating policies and identifying the national interest. As new patterns of cause-and-effect relations are recognized and accepted, forms of international behavior may change accordingly.

Realism, neorealism, and historical materialism are predominantly systemic approaches, because they explain international behavior in light of the overarching and enduring international political or economic circumstances in which policies for environmental protection are formulated. Each seeks to explain behavior in terms of the context in which actors operate, rather than in terms of factors internal to the parties. Patterns of behavior and cooperation are explained by more profound systemic features, which determine or shape the range of effective alternative choices for different actors. For realists and neorealists, the principle of national sovereignty within an international setting of anarchy dictates how power is likely to be deployed, as well as the determinants and form of international cooperation. For historical materialists, the unequal international distribution of forms of economic production and unequal terms of exchange within a global context of capitalism make the South politically weak and economically dependent on the North. Thus, states' motivations and bargaining outcomes can be predicted based upon the characteristics of the political or economic system in which they arise.

Just because they are systemic does not mean that they do not pay attention to actor's perceptions. Sophisticated authors within each tradition do address this issue, although both presume that such perceptions will be shaped or conditioned by the circumstances in which they occur.

Cooperative arrangements that fail to match the theoretically informed expectations of authors from the contending systemic traditions would seriously challenge these traditions' ability to fully explain the dynamics of cooperation in that case. If the Med Plan's causes and forms are sufficiently different from the expectations of each research tradition, one may question the theoretical ability of these research traditions to explain cooperation in this area.

REALIST AND NEOREALIST EXPLANATIONS OF COORDINATED MEDITERRANEAN POLLUTION CONTROL

Realist and neorealist writers believe that environmental cooperation will be driven by enduring patterns of international behavior. Neorealism is the most recent version of classical realism in international relations. Descended from Thucydides' *History of the Peloponnesian War*, Machiavelli's *The Prince*, and Hobbes' *Leviathan*, realist authors have an overriding concern with state security. For such authors, states are the major actors in world affairs; they may be analyzed as rational, unitary actors; and, in the absence of an international authority, states interact in a context of "anarchy." Under such conditions, Morgenthau said that statesmen "think and act in terms of interest defined as power."[2] Thus, even when negotiating pollution control arrangements, states will seek to obtain military and economic resources that allow them to directly and indirectly control the actions of other countries.

Realists also regard states as rational actors. States are presumed to have full information about world events, and calculate the costs and benefits of proposed actions and choose the courses of action closest to their fixed preferences. For realism, these preferences are the acquisition of power. Different neorealists, discussed below, disagree on the particular articulation of such preferences.

Issues of national security get top billing. Hence, environmental issues, which have not been seen as pertaining to such matters of state, are relegated to the back burner (Morgenthau 1985:122). Indeed, a climate of high politics persisted throughout Med Plan negotiations. In 1983 a Greek research vessel was challenged by Turkish naval ships and forced to leave Turkish waters, because the Turks suspected that the Greeks were mapping the continental shelf as well as monitoring surface pollution. It is less clear how lower-saliency issues will be resolved, whether they will merely receive less attention or be resolved by other means. Thus, realism is ambiguous in suggesting how states will manage shared environmental problems.

Recently, a critique has been offered: that the realist notion of security is inappropriate for environmental issues. Environmental degradation may truly be a threat to international security, even though it has not been traditionally seen in that light (Ullman 1983; Brown 1977; Matthews 1988). The notion of "security" should be extended to focus on issues that threaten public health, the integrity of society, and economic well-being, and the security of borders, such as would be raised by extensive coastal pollution. Serious environmental degradation may also give rise to "environmental refugees," and hence reinforce existing international tensions and contribute to instability. Critics argue that such political notions of security myopically focus on issues of political import rather than on background conditions that may undermine such stability.[3] If environmental issues were cast in this light, would they be more or less likely to be resolved collectively? It is not clear for under such circumstances states might still subordinate environmental concerns to the defense of conventional powers, as seen in the Greek-Turkish example.

Hedley Bull, who shared many realist assumptions, expresses dismay about the likelihood of mustering sufficient international will to deal coherently with "global problems" of pollution. He believes that the Westphalian states system is capable of coordinating policies: "acceptance by independent political communities of one another's right to independent existence, subject to observance of certain rules of coexistence, is a device for providing some element of order where otherwise one may be possible (Bull 1977:294; Morgenthau 1985:122). However, effective short-term management of the multiple dimensions of the environmental crisis, which transcend purely national borders, is extremely unlikely:

> In the long-run it [sic] unlikely that action at the purely state level will be sufficient to cope with environmental dangers, and

the functionality of the states system, or of any other form of universal political order, will depend upon the emergence of a greater sense of human cohesion than now exists. . . . The states system provides the present structure of the political organisation of mankind, and the sense of common interests and values that underlies it—meagre through it is and inadequate as it is likely to prove in relation to long-term challenges to world-order —is the principal expression of human unity or solidarity that exists at the present time, and such hopes as we may entertain for the emergence of a more cohesive world society are bound up with its preservation and development. (Bull 1977:294–95)

At best, realists expect environmental cooperation to be extremely narrow in scope. Mediterranean pollution control would be obscured by states' efforts to obtain or extend political leverage over their neighbors.

Neorealism

Neorealists have formalized these notions about international relations by appropriating concepts and methodologies from game theory and microeconomics to provide rigor for their analysis of how states behave under anarchy.[4] These structural analyses give rise to hypotheses about both state motivations and outcomes which result from bargaining between states. Although there are extensive differences between neorealist writers, as will be revealed soon, they do adhere to a common systemic level of analysis; a common treatment of states as the most important actors; and a methodological affinity for deducing state motivations from their systemic position, and hence analyzing all behavior in light of the circumstances surrounding the actors.[5] Modified neorealists expanded notions of actors, goals, and rationality.

Neorealists accept anarchy as the prevailing international condition that affects state foreign policy making. Kenneth Waltz characterizes this as a "self-help" system. Ultimately, states have no other recourse in times of duress other than their own capabilities or alliances that they are able to forge. The fundamental problem of world politics, then, is the uncertainty of reciprocity. This concern is most severe in security issues, but persists in all issues where countries resist having to rely on possibly irresponsible partners. The larger the number of parties, the less likely it is that cooperation will be reciprocated because of the difficulty of monitoring compliance. Countries are inhibited from cooperating out of fear that possible partners may not reciprocate, leading to a generalized unwillingness to commit to collective action because of the risk of being a "patsy."

Because states are presumed to accurately perceive and represent the anarchic nature of international politics, they realize that if they do not act to protect their own autonomy they are doomed to perish. Natural selection contributes to such motivations, for if states do *not* act to protect their own autonomy they risk elimination. Competitive behavior is thus built into all forms of collective actions, including environmental protection.

Yet even under anarchy writers distinguish between behavior in issues that directly confront national security and issues that are not security related. One may distinguish between fundamental and instrumental objectives. The fundamental objective of all states under anarchy is security. How this is to be achieved varies by issue. In areas that directly pertain to state survival, it is most easily accommodated by the instrumental pursuit of power and wealth.[6] Under such conditions countries are not likely to cooperate, because this would inhibit their pursuit of power and expose them to possible influence by other countries.

However, in areas in which survival is not at risk, or after survival has been guaranteed, such as in some economic and environmental relations, state motivations are less clear. More cooperative outcomes are possible in such issues, because the costs of unreciprocated concessions are less as state survival is less at stake. However, states are likely to attempt to preserve their autonomy over policy choices in order to reduce their potential vulnerability to decisions made elsewhere. Under such circumstances neorealists presume that states will still continue to seek to maximize their autonomous (or sovereign) latitude of policymaking. Wealth and power are instrumental means to such ends.

International environmental problems pose a curious paradox for such theories. As low-profile issues they are subject to being ignored. Yet, the more pressing environmental problems become, the more they assume the trappings of realist security concerns, and the less likely it is that they would be effectively resolved.

Also, the resolution of such shared environmental problems as Mediterranean pollution pits contending instrumental state objectives against one another. States wish to protect public health and amenities, which require coordinated policy action with neighbors.

Concurrently, they seek to insulate themselves from decisions made abroad. State survival can only be obtained at the price of sacrificing policy autonomy. Policy autonomy may only be preserved at the cost of endangering national survival.

Kenneth Waltz offers the starkest neorealist explanation of cooperation, and captures the gist of the problem of Mediterranean pollution control for neorealists. For Waltz, the collective goods nature of the problem of all types of shared pollution problems strongly inhibits any collective efforts for their management.[7]

Presumably, all would benefit from a clean environment. However, the actual distribution of costs to be sustained for the cleaning of the environment, and how clean the environment should be, are extremely controversial choices, and shift the nature of the negotiations from a positive-sum case to a zero-sum one. With already polluted coastlines, Europeans hoped for promoting a cleaner Mediterranean. On the other hand, with coastlines that were still relatively pristine, North Africans hoped to normalize standards that would require Europeans to control their emissions, yet allow themselves to continue to pollute up to a higher threshold. In effect, Europeans were being asked to stop polluting, whereas LDCs were being asked to forgo polluting. Too clean an environment would subordinate LDC preferences; standards that establish too dirty a baseline would bother DCs. With concerns about the additional production costs that pollution control will entail, each group has a strong incentive to defect to offer its coastal producers a comparative advantage over their regional competitors with higher production costs resulting from the introduction of pollution control equipment. Thus, although all may benefit in some fashion from a cleaner sea, there are real differences about how clean a sea should be collectively pursued.

Waltz notes that under such circumstances (he discusses the general case of environmental cooperation, not just the Mediterranean) cooperation is unlikely to occur. With a large number of actors whose activities need to be coordinated, the monitoring of national compliance is difficult, and where none can be excluded from enjoying the benefits of others' unreciprocated pollution control efforts, collective action is deemed extremely unlikely.[8]

The systemic condition of anarchy gives rise to state motivations regarding Mediterranean pollution control. For Waltz, the appropriate environmental instrumental objectives will be the preservation of state autonomy, as direct security is not at stake. State attachment to autonomy will never permit serious incursions on that autonomy in order to realize other goals, such as environmental protection, the enhancement of amenities, or public health. Since few governments had yet introduced comprehensive pollution control measures by the early 1970s, they would act to avoid having to impose such new restrictions. They would ignore the problem and hope it would go away.

Most developing countries would continue to pursue the goal of economic development, which satisfies both the instrumental and fundamental goals of weak states within the international system: that is, the goals of reinforcing the state relative to its society and of insulating the country (and the state) from external influence.[9] Furthermore, with little guarantee of reciprocity, countries would strongly value their policy autonomy and ability to regulate domestic industry, and be loathe to commit themselves to collective arrangements to which others' commitments were dubious.

The specific commons nature of Mediterranean pollution gives rise to propositions about the form of arrangements. If countries did cooperate, such arrangements would be extremely fragile and transitory, as states would constantly be strongly tempted to defect. They would also be very narrow, and cover very few pollutants, sources of pollution, or channels of transmission, as states would be acting to preserve their limited latitude of policymaking authority. Uncertainty about the extent of pollution would further inhibit cooperation, by further discounting the value of future benefits from a cleaner environment.

Hegemonic Stability

The hegemonic stability school of neorealism suggests that cooperation is most likely to occur when it is imposed by a dominant state[10] or a "hegemon" with a "preponderance of national resources" that include "control over raw materials, control over sources of capital, control over markets, and competitive advantages in the production of highly valued goods" and the willingness to use them (Keohane 1984:32). Robert Gilpin concludes that, ultimately, hegemony is grounded on the capacity of the hegemon's economy to respond flexibly to international market shifts (Gilpin 1987:77), while more recently hegemony has been defined in terms of "superiority in the possession of information and in the ability to inflict costs on others" (Alt, Calvert, and Humes 1988:447). Such a strong actor would be able to compel or induce other states to overcome their resistance to cooperation.

France is the most powerful state actor in the Mediterranean, as is elaborated in chapter 6. It serves as the most likely candidate for hegemonic leadership to coordinate Mediterranean pollution control efforts. Under French leadership coordinated pollution control would be most likely to occur.

Yet there are two distinct schools of hegemonic stability theory. They differ regarding the likely motivations that would influence French leadership, how closely the scope of the pollution control arrangements would follow French interests, the extent to which other participants benefit from such collective arrangements, and their duration. Which pollutants would France seek to control, how would it exercise its leadership, and how tolerant would France be should other countries continue to pollute? Specific French concerns about which pollutants, sources of pollution, and channels of pollution to control will be elaborated in subsequent chapters. The intent here is to lay out illustrative propositions about the form and dynamics of pollution control arrangements that such authors would expect.

These two versions—a benign and a malevolent one—differ most fundamentally in their basic presumption about the extent of conflict that exists in international relations. This orientation bears on whether or not they believe that all states will benefit from hegemonic cooperation. The benign version tends to view the nature of the issue being managed in collective goods terms, thus evoking the possibility that once institutions for cooperation are provided all will benefit from participating. The malevolent one sees instead the cooperative arrangements themselves as public goods; hence they will only be provided by a powerful state if the arrangements coincide with the interests of that state (Snidal 1985).

The benign version, presented by Robert Keohane and Charles Kindleberger, is based on a presumption that many cases of international cooperation are positive-sum games, and that all states may benefit from cooperation, even though they are leery about initially participating, out of fear of nonreciprocity.[11] In this benevolent view of leadership, the hegemon pursues its own long-term objectives; however, because of the nature of the issue, all benefit from such arrangements.

These authors make no assumptions about the motivations of the hegemon or smaller states. The hegemon rationally pursues its given interests, and the nature of the circumstances in which hegemony is deployed to create cooperative arrangements dictates whether all benefit from such action or not. Fundamental state interests still involve the preservation of sovereignty and autonomy, but in particular cases the instrumental means to accomplish such ends may be unclear, or even vary by issue-area.

Hence, in the Mediterranean France would promote a program for regional pollution control. The scope of the arrangements would reflect French concerns with specific pollutants, sources of pollution, and channels of transmission. To the extent that most countries suffer from the same pollutants, French objectives are beneficial for other countries as well because all benefit from environmental protection. France would be tolerant of occasional lapses or delays in compliance on the part of other governments. The strength of the arrangements would be a function of French willingness to reward compliance. In fact, smaller countries could benefit more than the hegemon, because they are reaping benefits for which they do not have to pay.

However, cooperation is likely to be transitory, passing with the demise of the hegemon. Should French power diffuse, cooperation is likely to decay as well, although it may only erode slowly. Because smaller states are benefiting from the arrangements it will take them a while to realize the gains possible from defection and will allow their coastal industries to pollute while others bear the additional production costs from pollution control and lose comparative advantage.

The dark side of hegemony is suggested by Robert Gilpin and Stephen Krasner (Gilpin 1975; Gilpin 1981; Krasner 1976). They see all international relations as being inherently conflictual, because all states seek to gain control over other states. Gilpin believes that states persistently pursue economic and military power (Gilpin 1981). Krasner suggests that state interests are systemically generated: large successful states support and impose existing rules, and smaller states cheat (Krasner 1976). Thus, all of world politics is a zero-sum game, as one state's acquisition of power and wealth may only occur at another's expense. Gilpin and Krasner both argue that because outcomes depend entirely on the leadership of a dominant party and that party's willingness to compel other parties to comply, coordinated arrangements will occur in terms favorable to that party. Coordinated policies will reflect the short-term interests of the hegemon, rather than the more generous, longer-term ones proposed by Keohane and Kindleberger. Gilpin and Krasner think that cooperation will only be transitory: that, in fact, the possibility that resources and power will be redistributed as a result of faithful adherence to cooperative goals will in part deter full hegemonic support out of each country's fear of losing its control over other countries (Gilpin 1975).

Because cooperation reflects the hegemon's interests, and the smaller states do not want to comply, they must be compelled to do so. The hegemon must devise a system of sanctions against those who do not cooperate, and rewards for those who do. However, because in essence countries are being forced to cooperate against their wills, in the absence of hegemony they will defect like rats fleeing a sinking ship. Negotiations will be dominated by competition over relative gains, thus in effect making the context a zero-sum game. A more refined notion of power, such as that offered by the historical materialist writers discussed below, adds that part of a hegemon's true arsenal of power resources is its ability to make other countries think that cooperation is in their interest, when it may not truly be.

Thus, the malevolent version suggests that the scope of Mediterranean pollution control arrangements will reflect France's interests, possibly at the expense of other countries who are compelled to participate. If French hegemony is widely based (i.e., a hegemon strong in multiple issue–areas), then environmental issues may be linked to others, so as to allow France to exercise its power most efficiently and gain returns to scale, as it were. If hegemony is limited to one or only a few issues, then the scope of cooperation will be correspondingly narrow. As a heavily polluting advanced industrial society, France would be interested in assuring regionwide treatment of the pollutants that were present on French beaches, as well as covering the sources that produce them and the environmental channels that transmit them to French beaches. France would be acting to compel other countries to reciprocate what France already had to do as the dominant state with one of the most heavily polluted coasts. The scope of the Med Plan would largely reflect such French concerns, possibly at the expense of pollutants that concerned other countries.

Since states disputed which pollutants to control, these arrangements would reflect French preferences, possibly at the expense of others. Thus, the specific environmental standards that the program adopted would be stronger than desired by many of the weaker LDCs.

The strength of other countries' efforts at pollution control would covary with France's regional hegemony, as would the duration of collective agreements. Because the arrangements reflect immediate French concerns, with the diminution of French regional power the entire arrangement would collapse. The decay of such arrangements would be likely to follow more rapidly than in the benign view, because states are cooperating against their wills.

Cooperation Under Anarchy

Yet another tradition of neorealism suggests that limited cooperation is possible in the absence of hegemony, or in its aftermath to
prevent countries from reneging on previous commitments. By relax-
ing some of the more rigid realist rationality assumptions, writers
have suggested that countries will cooperate in order to acquire a
number of informational resources that are commonly unavailable
within anarchic relations (Keohane 1984; Keohane 1983a; Keohane
and Axelrod 1986). Although believing in the need for powerful actors
to intervene to create coordinating institutions, they believe that a
number of factors may lead states to continue to respect their agreements past the waning of hegemony.

These writers reject the realist assumption of perfect information
and complete information processing by considering forms of bounded
rationality that include imperfect information, limited search procedures for alternatives, and variable actor preferences. Facing incomplete information, and lacking the time or ability to fully evaluate
and compare all alternative actions, decision makers satisfice and
value arrangements that enable them to acquire information in a
relatively prompt and inexpensive manner (Keohane 1983a, 1984: ch.
7; 1986:12–13). The absence of international authority may in part be
compensated by an actor's reputation for responsibly adhering to its
obligations, or for consistently imposing sanctions on others who
violate them.

The cooperation under anarchy school identifies a number of factors that may promote cooperation in the absence of hegemony. They
may be objective features of an issue being managed, or they may be
designed by the architects of such institutional arrangements. Once
in place the benefits of such arrangements may become so manifest
that actors choose to comply with them without coercion, or past the
decline of the hegemonic actor responsible for their establishment.
Thus, a watered-down form of pollution control for the Mediterranean
would be likely to include these elements.

Because anarchy impedes the full circulation of information, states
would value cooperative arrangements that facilitate access to otherwise scarce information. In the absence of good information, or if
such information is controlled by a few actors, other parties will
cooperate in order to obtain new information. Without cooperation,
this information would be unavailable to them. Information about
pollutants and possible methods for their control and about how

pollutants are transmitted throughout the region, and the costs of regulation, would make such arrangements attractive to states and would encourage their support. Monitoring and publicizing other countries' efforts to control pollution would compensate for the informational weaknesses of anarchy, and hence reinforce states' commitments to the Med Plan, as it would minimize the possibility of imposing costs on one's coastal industries that were not reciprocated by other Mediterranean states. Likewise, arrangements that establish state diplomatic channels through which states may regularly coordinate their activities, monitor others' actions, and exchange information would be viewed as desirable by states, as they would enable them to overcome the transaction costs associated with developing diplomatic arrangements as new problems emerge.

These writers offer some other propositions as well. Institutional arrangements that spread out the number of interstate interactions (an "iterated game" with multiple plays) will be an effective organizational form, because they will increase the likelihood of concessions and persistent cooperation through the possibility of future reciprocity. Thus, states would be likely to continue to cooperate through such a framework. Similarly, if actors think that they will be interacting for a prolonged period (the "shadow of the future") they will be more likely to cooperate with hopes for future benefits. A smaller number of actors facilitates surveillance, and hence improves the likelihood of further cooperation. Side-payments made in complementary negotiations will also facilitate continued cooperation, and cooperative arrangements will also be desired because they facilitate such actions (Keohane 1983a).

In special cases, such as issues with high "issue density" or multiple interlinkages with other issues, of which the environment is such a case, arrangements will be more "extensive" to cover the associated issues (Keohane 1983a:155–57, 1984:99; Ruggie 1972). Hence the scope would be fairly comprehensive to reflect the broader range of information that decision makers require about the interlinkages between environmental pollution and other issues. However, due to uncertainty about the sources and extent of Mediterranean pollution, as well as the costs of cleanup, cooperative arrangements would principally provide information about pollution and pollution control, or insurance against pollution emergencies, rather than being regulatory and specifying ways of controlling state behavior (Keohane 1983a:167–70). Administrators would have to take care to guarantee the quality of such information, for if there is doubt about the information's accuracy or possible bias, smaller parties may be unwilling to participate (Keohane 1984:92–96).

Again, the liberal assumptions about human nature that are evident in the benign form of hegemonic stability theory recur in the formulation of cooperation under anarchy. Thus, the institutional design demands for cooperation are much less than what is suggested by the malevolent school, since actors presumably want to cooperate and merely need arrangements that will assure them that their partners will not renege on their obligations. As such, cooperation and most forms of international relations may be positive sum, since all actors pursue objectives that will make everyone better off. Essentially, it is presumed that actors want to cooperate, and they merely need reassurance that they will not become "patsies." This is very different from the malevolent neorealist perspective, which presumes that all states are simply waiting to defect, and must be compelled not to.

The cooperation under anarchy school offers a number of relatively optimistic hypotheses about the causes and forms of cooperation. So long as there are many iterative negotiations for coordinated pollution control and information about Mediterranean quality and states' actions are forthcoming, states will cooperate for Mediterranean pollution control. The scope of pollution control will be comprehensive, although limited to the informational sphere. Cooperation may persist so long as states are able to gain real information about the overall environment and others' actions from the arrangements.

The Assessment and Evaluation of Neorealism

In short, few neorealist authors are sanguine about the development of new forms of cooperation to deal with environmental threats to the Mediterranean. All states will be unwilling to accept any limitations on their compass of policymaking. Cooperative arrangements are likely to be developed and maintained by France. The existence of cooperative arrangements would covary with the concentration of systemic power. With the waning of its power, France would become increasingly loath to support such arrangements, and other states will probably be unwilling to continue to comply with their commitments as well. In special circumstances such cooperation may persist, given the provision of information about other countries' pollution control practices, environmental quality, and instructions for monitoring. The scope of any arrangements is likely to be narrow, and to the extent that France promotes such cooperation, it will closely resemble either French environmental concerns or broader French foreign policy ambitions in the region. The strength of such arrangements will depend upon France's commitment to enforce them. Their durability is unlikely to persist past the decline of hegemony. To the extent that such arrangements develop without French support, or endure past French hegemony, they will be largely informational.

Such formal approaches neatly capture the structural inhibitions to cooperation. Indeed, they successfully stress the relative infrequency with which such actions occur, and the types of issues for which they do occur. They stress the enduring strength of the nation-state, and provide a parsimonious explanation for why conflict appears endemic in the international political system and for the frequent recourse to the exercise of power to mediate interstate differences.

Such approaches are not optimistic about the emergence of new patterns of behavior to deal with such new challenges as those that the environment may conjure up. Because they assume that political orders are determined by systemic conditions, and that structures such as anarchy are rigid and basically invariant over time, they view new political orders as extremely unlikely: without changing the underlying principle of anarchy, enduring and comprehensive cooperation is virtually impossible.[12] Gilpin writes:

> Ultimately, international politics still can be characterized as it was by Thucydides: the interplay of impersonal forces and great leaders. . . . World politics is still characterized by the struggle of political entities for power, prestige and wealth in a condition of global anarchy.[13]

HISTORICAL MATERIALISM

In contrast to this analysis of persistent patterns of coerced or infrequent collaboration, the historical materialist tradition sees a world of enduring political and economic exploitation of Third World states by European and North American states, occurring at multiple levels of interactions, as well as the domination of elites over nonelites.[14] The world is divided into three spheres according to the international division of labor. Highly industrialized Western countries are in the core, industrializing countries are in the semiperiphery, and the periphery consists of developing countries that export raw materials (Wallerstein 1979). When effective interstate collaboration does occur, it is on the terms of the North, or serves to reproduce the systemic principles of world capitalism, which permits persistent outcomes to be determined according to the logic of the international division of labor. Historical materialists posit a more fundamental and deeply rooted inegalitarian nature of international political and economic relations than do the neorealists. In this view, relations with the industrialized North are part of "a more complex, post-colonial dependency of the peripheral countries, in which foreign capital (international corporations), profit repatriation, adverse changes in the terms of trade (unequal exchange) all play a role in confining, distorting or halting economic development and industrialization" (Sutcliffe 1972:172). Whereas neorealists generally define structures according to the distribution of political and military resources, or in terms of sensitivity to market shifts, historical materialists' structures reflect the distribution of productive capability.

Grounding their analysis on a constitutive principle of unequal exchange, historical materialists believe that capitalist exchanges with the North, or attempts to collectively manage such side effects of capitalist development as marine pollution, will operate to the disadvantage of the developing world. The scope of arrangements would reflect northern experiences, and would possibly make LDCs pay for problems that do not affect them. Direct arrangements with Europe would inhibit North African industrialization, and reaffirm and reproduce old colonial linkages (Flory 1974:64). Even the distribution of benefits from participation in the Med Plan—research contracts, positions on the secretariat, and the like—are likely to go disproportionately to the North.[15] Alternatively, agreements to control pollution will serve to extend the penetration of European corporations in North African economies by encouraging the North Africans to "purchase expensive, sophisticated (pollution control and monitoring) equipment from the north—equipment they could ill afford,"[16] and deepen commercial dependence on the North.

The deep persistence of such structural determinants of outcomes penetrates to the formation of interests and inferences as well. States' interests, as well as knowledge, are derived from the global division of labor. Concepts that have been articulated in international relations and economic development have been framed by the northern experience. Relatively little attention has been paid to the conditions endemic in the LDCs, which may differ profoundly from those found in the North. Thus, commonly accepted modes of discourse will either serve to legitimate systemic principles and the interests of the North, or they will serve to exclude southern interests from the agenda. Historical materialists expect technical discussions between the North and South to be either warped by northern notions, full of gaps regarding southern objectives, or serve the function of eliminating concepts that challenge the legitimacy of capitalism or its most obvious features, the division of labor and comparative advantage. Collective pollution control arrangements would impose Western development styles and models on LDCs. Technical advice would mask northern interests in extending the LDCs' dependence on the North.

Underlying such an analysis is the view that countries' and individual experts' views and perspectives on environmental issues are conditioned by social and economic factors. These views and perspectives may be conditioned in two ways: directly from current structures, and as historically received from past structures. The current structural argument is that ideas will be concomitants of the short-term political interests of those articulating (or using) them. The historical argument is less pernicious, recreating intellectual history to determine whether certain concerns have been systematically eliminated from a discipline that is used to shape the policy discourse and that is historically transmitted. This historical focus looks to the antecedent social shaping effects on agendas to determine whose interests get expressed within the legitimate research ambit identified by a scientific discipline and whose get excluded. As such the historical argument is less deterministic than the historical one, and more sensitive to historical nuance.

Many historical materialists analyze the way in which elite interests in the Third World are conditioned by the inherent *systemic bias* within the structure of the international economic order. Thus, they argue, LDC leaders may not know their own objective interests; "an individual's subjective interests are not merely *given*, or *randomly* generated, but rather are systematically determined by the way in which his life-chances are objectively affected by objective conditions."[17]

Even with regard to technical issues such as the environment, systemic sources influence the determination of authoritative policy proposals. Authority consists of the untested acceptance of another's judgment. Dennis Wrong identifies authority as a device that shapes outcomes: "leaders whose judgement is trusted on grounds of character or expert knowledge emerge and are able to obtain the compliance of others to their directives" (Wrong 1979:249). Essentially this is the power to deem what is and what is not relevant knowledge, such as what forms of collective measures are necessary to control marine pollution.

The ability to control what is deemed relevant information gives an actor potent control over outcomes and establishes on whom the burden of proof rests:

> In the absence of political institutions endowed with an effective monopoly of legitimate violence, political action proper can be exercised only by the effect of official action, and thus presupposes the *competence* (in the sense of a *capacity socially recognized in a public authority*) required in order to manipulate the collective definition of the situation in such a way as to bring it closer to the official definition of the situation and thereby to win the means of mobilizing the largest possible group, the opposite strategy tending to reduce the same situation to a merely private affair.[18]

As baseball umpire Bill Klem is reputed to have said, "It ain't nothing till I call it." Sociologists of science Barnes and Edge contend that "in modern societies, science is near to being *the* source of cognitive authority: anyone who would be widely believed and trusted as an interpreter of nature needs a license from the scientific community" (1982:2).

Michael Mann writes:

> We cannot understand (and so act upon) the world merely by direct sense perception. We require concepts and categories of *meaning* imposed upon sense perceptions. The social organization of ultimate knowledge and meaning is necessary to social life. . . . Thus collective and distributive power can be wielded by those who monopolize a claim to meaning. (1986:22)

Indeed, Robert Cox warns that "the language of consensus is a language of common interest expressed in universalist terms, though the structure of power underlying it is skewed in favor of the dominant groups" (1977:386).

Thus, authority may come from two sources. It may lie in the historical capture of a scientific discipline by a social group, so that the subsequent application of that discipline will generate policies amenable to its patrons and exclude competing interests from the political agenda (Foucault 1972, 1980). Johan Galtung proposes that bias may also lie in the social shaping of scientists' behavior through their graduate training or professional aspirations: "Concretely, this means that when negotiations take place between Center and Periphery, the former may have the best representatives among the delegates from the latter. It facilitates negotiations in the interest of the Center tremendously when their interests are represented at both ends of the table" (1980:120–21). For instance, LDC scientists attending Med Plan meetings and advising their own governments, may actually express the regionally dominant French interests.

Jürgen Habermas proposes a second, deeper social penetration of knowledge. He argues that such a construction of reality is subordinated to the instrumental purpose to which society will put such knowledge, and that it isolates instrumental reasoning from reasoning addressed to achieving ultimate values (Habermas 1970, 1971:301–17). Science, in this view, will be used by decision makers to extend technical control over the environment rather than to accommodate public policy to the objective facts of limits imposed by the sustainability of natural ecosystems. Also, such efforts would be likely to exclude alternative arguments about the fundamental causes of environmental problems, which would question the legitimacy of such deep-seated concepts as capitalism. Inappropriate models of development will ensue from the application of such models developed in the North.

In either view of the structural penetration of perceptions and cognition, historical materialists argue that authoritative policy prescriptions will inherently embody northern preferences. Southern preferences will either be eliminated or disingenuously associated with northern preferences.

Historical materialists focus attention on the underlying structures that promote cooperation. Such writings lead one to ask the valuable question of what is not dealt with and, in addition, cause one to look at what is treated cooperatively.

Historical materialists predict a fair amount of environmental cooperation in the Mediterranean. However, such cooperation will be subordinated to the broader economic and social factors operating in the region. Historical materialists are not sanguine that the LDCs will benefit from environmental cooperation. Cooperation will be imposed by the North, and its scope will cover issues of concern to the North, not the South. Moreover, it may even serve to distract attention from problems that would underscore the inappropriateness for the South of models of economic development devised in the North, by promoting reforms instead of questioning the overall viability of such projects and deepening LDC dependence on the North. The duration of cooperation will correspond to the North's continued domination over the South, and its strength will be whatever is necessary for the North to compel southern planners to continue to be reliant upon northern resources.

EPISTEMIC COMMUNITIES AND ENVIRONMENTAL COOPERATION

Responding to such recent features of international politics as complex interdependence and advances in science and technology, a third explanatory approach in international relations is concerned with the effect of experts and knowledge-based communities on governmental learning and the development of new state objectives. Such an approach looks at the conditions under which behavior may change based upon a new understanding of the causal relationships in the world. Writers from this tradition look at policymaking in terms of such nonsystemic variables and actors as ideas, knowledge, beliefs, experts, and scientists. Arguing that structural analysis alone overpredicts interstate conflict and underpredicts cooperation, such writers rely on insights from organization theory, policy sciences, social psychology, the philosophy and history of science, the sociology of knowledge, and international relations to explain the choice of state ends to which resources will be deployed and the preconditions for and forms of international cooperation.

This approach proceeds from an epistemological warrant. Epistemologically, there is no such thing as a "brute fact." All interpretations come from a prior framework erected to organize experience, from which certain phenomena are identified as facts and set into a given causal framework that will denote the implications of such "facts" (Anscombe 1958).

Because the understanding of reality through the organization of our experience is "developed, transmitted and maintained in social situations" (Berger and Luckmann 1967:13), one must study how events are recognized and interpreted by actors. Reality is not directly accessible, and our interpretation of events is processed through filters, including those of prior experience and expectations.[19] Thus, responses to environmental change may have little to do with any objective factors.

Responses to changes are often lagged, as well. Studies have demonstrated that actors' recognition of their circumstances may be inaccurate, or may change over time.[20] Concluding from rational actor models that are applicable to state behavior, individuals tend to resist recognizing anomalies, and generally move incrementally toward new policies. Even in the economic case of firms recognizing market change, adjustment is not simultaneous since market disequilibrium is not immediately apparent (Nelson and Winter 1982:24–26). States often simply follow habitual patterns of behavior out of inertia (Rosenau 1986; Jervis 1988) and also because policy responses are influenced by domestic and bureaucratic politics (Allison 1971).

Environmental changes themselves are not immediately apparent, beyond the superficial appearance of some contaminants. Their implications for action depend, in part, upon the cognitive frameworks of those who are held responsible for formulating national policies to identify and respond to such problems. For instance, the identification of pollutants requires faith in scientists and techniques. Heavy metals are invisible; policymakers must accept scientists' assertions that equipment readings accurately represent heavy metal concentrations and that they truly threaten public health.

Even floating feces in the Mediterranean did not induce equal repugnance in all observers. A journalist recounted a story to the author of swimming in the southern Mediterranean with his wife and a Moroccan friend, and seeing fecal matter floating around them. His wife was repulsed and returned to shore, but the Moroccan was unperturbed and continued swimming. The journalist was amused by the disparate reactions.

Responses evoked by polluting smokestacks in the early 1970s also varied. In the West they were regarded as polluting and therefore bad, but in the developing world they were seen as symbols of modernization and industrialization, and hence good. LDC leaders resented the DC position, which they saw as denying their countries the middle-class pleasures that the North enjoyed. In the absence of coercion, the collective definition of meaning must precede coordinated responses to environmental degradation. Leaders or governments may learn about new causal connections to the environment and choose to alter their behavior despite structural inhibitions.

The ability to symbolically represent physically imperceptible phenomena confers great influence on those deemed to be authorities. How states respond to instances of environmental degradation will depend upon who is chosen to articulate the causes of such degradation and to propose policies for its management. Those chosen will determine what events signify. At their most influential, they would also influence which events decision makers choose to regard as significant. Hence they would be responsible for identifying anomalies from prevailing patterns of behavior and articulating the need for new patterns of behavior to be assumed in response.

Under conditions of uncertainty, leaders are likely to consult experts to help them identify their own interests and policies. Uncertainty in this regard will exist in cases where probabilities of alternative outcomes cannot be accurately estimated due to a lack of information or understanding of the nature of the problem (Elster 1983:185). Crises would serve as good triggers to alert decision makers to the existence of such uncertainty. Thus, policymakers are likely to consult experts when they are confused about anomalous policy results in the world and uncertain about the technical dimensions, causes, or political consequences of such problems. As discussed in the previous chapter, such conditions are widespread in environmental issues.

Governments may confer increased authority on those scientists and experts who are better able to understand the complex causal interlinkages between issues and propose policies for their management (Wilensky 1967; Benveniste 1977). For decision makers to mitigate uncertainty while defending their own autonomy, they commonly resort to scientists for information and policy advice (Holdgate 1982:6–7). In addition to enabling one to reduce uncertainty, resorting to expert advice is valuable domestically as a political device that helps one avoid or postpone short-term conflict by shifting policy responsibility to the experts, even though experts often lack sufficient information to propose fully bounded and coherent policy.

Some writers have looked at the impact of such groups of experts. In international secretariats, William Ascher found that in the World Bank uncertainty about what objectives are feasible and what procedures will best accomplish them resulted in top-level officials conferring decision-making authority on groups able to "absorb uncertainty."[21] Operating in several governments concurrently, during the Great Depression groups with an authoritative claim to policy-relevant knowledge contributed to a "transnational [Keynesian] language of discourse" guiding common European policy responses (Weir and Skocpol 1985:149). Within individual governments such groups have also been influential, such as with the United States' decision to "go off" gold in 1971 (Odell 1982; see also Adler 1986).

In the Mediterranean, confronted with evidence of coastal pollution but ignorant of the full extent of regional pollution, leaders would be likely to turn to regional scientists to gain policy advice and resolve the dissonance between expectations of environmental quality and experiences with pollution. If the group spoke with one voice, it would be likely to have a significant influence on the scope, duration, and strength of policies that countries adopted. Although sharing with some historical materialists a concern with the source of authority in advanced industrial societies and in technical issues beyond the scope of the layperson, this approach does not automatically assume that such groups will confer a systemically derived bias to areas regarding which they provide advice.

Such a knowledge-based group is an "epistemic community."[22] An epistemic community is a professional group that believes in the same cause-and-effect relationships, truth tests to assess them, and shares common values. As well as sharing an acceptance of a common body of facts, its members share a common interpretive framework, or "consensual knowledge," from which they convert such facts, or observations, to policy-relevant conclusions.[23] They identify problems in the same manner and process information similarly. They also share a common vocabulary, common political objectives to which such policies should be addressed, and a common network in which findings are exchanged and shared concerns are formulated. Although members of an epistemic community may be drawn from different scientific disciplines, all will share some common world view and concern about the same subject matter. Although they concur on appropriate methods for validating their knowledge, they need not be positivist. Many of these conditions may be adduced from accepted exemplars, such as textbooks.

An epistemic community need not have a monopoly on relevant knowledge, but it must share a common approach to understanding. Scientists split on causal knowledge cannot be members of an epistemic community. Presented with incomplete or ambiguous evidence, members of an epistemic community would draw similar interpretations and make similar policy conclusions. If consulted or placed in a policymaking position, they would offer similar advice. Individuals who were not members of the same epistemic community would be much more likely to disagree in their interpretations. Unlike an interest group, confronted with anomalous data they would retract their advice or suspend judgment.

An epistemic community's power resource, domestically and internationally, is its authoritative claim to knowledge. Presented with observations, it may convert them into common policy by drawing common inferences. To the extent that its members can penetrate the walls of government and maintain their authority, new orders of behavior are possible. Insofar as members' policy proposals are accepted, they exercise unobstrusive control. By heeding an epistemic community's advice, governments may come to identify new policies or new policy objectives.

An epistemic community would influence Mediterranean pollution control through several channels. If its members were present in an international secretariat, that secretariat would be able to identify problems for public treatment; specify pollutants, sources of pollution, and channels of transmission for regulation; provide information; draft proposals; and monitor and publicize national activities. It would be responsible for selecting desirable levels of water quality and deciding, implicitly, who would have to pay for environmental protection. Such a group would delimit the dimensions of policy at international conferences by establishing the boundaries within which actual policies would be considered[24] and the range of discourse; it would also propose specific quality standards. It would be able to create transnational and transgovernmental coalitions of individuals and groups holding similar views in the Mediterranean countries; such coalitions would engineer or guide simultaneous and congruent action by their governments by identifying possibilities for mutual benefit that had not been previously recognized or by developing entirely new policy objectives.[25]

When invited to fill administrative positions in governments, the group's members would encourage common policies in their respective governments and push for their enforcement. When present in national environmental ministries or the relevant regulatory bodies, such groups would then be directly responsible for enforcing such measures and providing advice to other members of their governments. Serving as advisory scientists on delegations, they would be able to provide specific bits of advice regarding the scope of collective arrangements under consideration. To the extent that policymakers in several states receive similar advice, they may adopt convergent policies and learn of the need to cooperate in order to coordinate those policies. Meetings at which an epistemic community is well represented would be more constructive than those in which it is not. The most environmentally concerned countries will be the countries in which the epistemic community is best represented.

The specific beliefs of individual secretariat members would make a significant impact on the scope of the arrangements that such an organization supports. As seen in chapter 1, the precise expression that new environmental norms took in the 1970s and 1980s reflected the mandate of the body that articulated them: the harmonization of trade in the EEC, free trade in the OECD, the problems the industrialized countries presented for NATO, and the promotion of holistic patterns of environmental protection through UNEP.

The scope of Mediterranean pollution control arrangements would depend upon how comprehensive were the beliefs of the epistemic community and how long the epistemic community was able to insinuate itself into policymaking. For instance, a group informed by the writings of the Club of Rome or E. F. Schumacher would have proposed a much more comprehensive set of arrangements than would one grounded in the writings of Herman Kahn and Julian Simon.

Fisheries management practices have shifted recently with the popularization of "large marine ecosystems" as a conceptual tool for managing fisheries, as a more comprehensive idea which considers ecological principles linking multiple species within a given region. By applying such principles it is easier to apply to maintain sustainable yields. In the absence of such ideas informing fisheries management, greater overfishing would occur (Morgan 1987).

The concept of ecosystemic management, and the need to manage many species sharing a common habitat, rather than one species in isolation, was key to the conclusion of the 1980 Convention on the Conservation of Antarctic Marine Living Resources (CCAMLR). The ecosystems approach means that when limits are set on fishing, the regulators must also consider the impact on populations of other animals which may rely on the species for their own food (Lyster 1985:158).

The strength of cooperative arrangements will be determined by the domestic power amassed by members of the epistemic community within their respective governments. So long as they remain firmly embedded in their national policymaking process, they will encourage strong international commitments and the adoption and enforcement of common policies in line with their shared world view. The strength of countries' commitments will thus vary by the epistemic community's retention of its domestic power, which is achieved through its own intellectual solidarity and through repelling challenges by interest groups. A fracturing of its shared causal understanding of the world through the invalidation of its causal beliefs would lead to a weakening of its authoritative position, as its authoritative claim to common understanding would be eroded and it would no longer be able to reduce uncertainty.

The duration of such cooperative arrangements would similarly be determined by the continuing access of an epistemic community to its own government. Cooperation will persist as long as the epistemic community is able to retain power within most of the participating governments.

However, a diminution of influence by such groups may well be lagged, as governments will not be immediately aware of the collapse of intellectual solidarity. This may be thought of as one effect of the "elasticity of demand for advice" (Blau 1967: ch. 7). Governments need scientific input when there is uncertainty, but will only be likely to search for more advice if new problems appear. As governments have only limited resources, they will concentrate on whatever issues are most pressing. They will only be alerted to the need for replacing an epistemic community once there is external evidence, such as subsequent crises, of its inability to manage uncertainty. Without new crises, other governmental bodies would be unaware of the collapse of an epistemic community's knowledge base.

Governments have different elasticities of demand for scientific input. Larger, better-staffed governments are better able to consider multiple questions, and hence would be more likely to become aware of an epistemic community's internal collapse. A smaller bureaucracy that was stretched thin would be much less likely to reconsider past choices, and would be less aware of changes in an epistemic community's power base. In a related vein, cooperation is also likely to continue if there are sufficient crises in other issue areas to distract the attention of the foreign ministry officials or top political officials. This will be particularly likely in small ministries or executive staffs where officials lack sufficient time or resources to stay abreast of many issues. Consequently, epistemic communities might have the most long-term influence in the LDCs surrounding the Mediterranean.

Ultimately, epistemic communities may contribute to policy change made in response to new causal understanding, or governmental learning. Learning is "increased intelligence and sophistication of thought, and of increased effectiveness of behavior" (Etheredge 1979:4). Herbert Simon concurs with such a definition, writing that "learning is any change in a system that produces a more or less permanent change in its capacity for adapting to its environment."[26]

Talking about learning is a useful way to describe the manner in which decision makers adopt new styles of environmental policymaking. Such styles would reflect new patterns of reasoning. The types of learning discussed below also serve as a scale with which to measure the influence of an epistemic community on the collective ratiocination of the Mediterranean governments as they adopt new styles of environmental policymaking.

There need not be a progression along this scale of reasoning patterns.[27] The appropriate form of decision making may well be different for different types of issues. A priori it is impossible to determine what would be the "correct" form for a specific issue, as such a determination would vary by the perspective of the observer. Nonetheless, we may use the scale below to determine the pattern of reasoning which Mediterranean decision makers acquired. The variety of responses to the environmental crisis reviewed in chapter 1 ran the whole gamut from adopting new means to a reformulation of world views. Which style is adopted will be a function of the shared beliefs of the epistemic community that prevails in the struggle to explicate uncertainty.

It is unclear whether this learning is a psychological process, occurring as individuals or groups are persuaded by new information and analysis offered by an epistemic community; a generational one as an "old guard" dies off or retires and is replaced by "young Turks" with a new set of beliefs; or a political process, as an epistemic community vies with bureaucratic contenders for control over policy (Odell 1982). It may be either, depending on the type of policymaking process into which an epistemic community is invited. At international conferences, where its members must interact with delegates over whom they have no leverage, their impact may depend upon their ability to persuade (Haas 1980; Haas, Williams, and Babai 1977). However, if members are present on the secretariat they may have a subtler shaping effect by identifying possible policies for countries to pursue collectively. Nationally, rather than convincing others of the need for new policies, they may use their claims to better understanding to usurp control over policymaking within those areas. Rather than contributing to learning through persuasion, they would promote learning by capturing the relevant machinery for making and enforcing environmental policy. In either case, learning will only occur after an epistemic community has established its channels of communication to governments. Such policy changes could be reversed after an epistemic community loses its influence.

The simplest learning consists of merely pursuing new policies (means) in order to accomplish given objectives within the same framework of cause-and-effect relationships. More sophisticated learning entails adopting new objectives (ends). Even more sophisticated learning entails the acceptance of entirely new cause-and-effect relationships and reasoning patterns. The most sophisticated learning could be seen as a type of transcendental learning, quite uncommon among governments, consisting of a recognition of historical rupture and the development of an awareness of historical differences between eras, from which states would adopt new fundamental objectives.

Policymakers may learn that new methods must be adopted to achieve existing objectives. They may imitate what works elsewhere to obtain given objectives.[28] This is basically tactical learning, changing behavior to achieve given goals. Basically, it is a process of trial-and-error learning, as errors are incrementally detected and corrected.[29] Steinbruner writes:

> The learning experience which would characterize the cybernetically operating organization manifests itself in terms of changes in behavior rather than changes in outcome calculation. The organizational decision-making entity is assumed to have a limited repertory of action patterns (programs). . . . Such learning is of the kind commonly known as *instrumental learning*. The cycle of adjustment in this learning pattern tends to be slow relative to causal learning, and instead of being a consistent process it occurs only sporadically—when the established action sequence is inappropriate enough to result in substantial disruption. (1974:78–79)

Typically, the stimulus for this kind of learning has been seen to be information that an outcome is dissonant vis-à-vis expectations, such as lower fishery yields than anticipated. Governments would merely adopt discrete pollution controls for isolated problems as they appear. It would not lead to the adoption of very comprehensive environmental policies.

This simplest form of learning is that which is implicitly assumed by neorealists and historical materialists: persistent behavior, influenced by calculating the most efficient way of accomplishing the objectives of wealth and power maximization. Learning is limited to recognizing the new instrumental objectives that most effectively promote fundamental state goals. Leaders would respond to knowledge of the impact of new pollution problems and of the need for their coordinated treatment in traditional ways. If anything, foreign policy makers learn of Thucydides', or Marx's immutable truths, or of clever diplomatic ploys to promote state interests. Because many neorealist authors use game-theoretic techniques in their analysis, they are unlikely to consider the possibility of learning that recognizes and transcends the limitations of the game being played. Few historical materialists consider more sophisticated modes of learning because they presume them to accompany changes in the distribution of economic production.

In a slightly more sophisticated form of learning, governments can learn to pursue new objectives. Errors are detected and corrected in ways that involve the modification of an organization's underlying norms, policies, and objectives.[30] Officials may recognize that they have competing values that cannot all be achieved simultaneously. Rather than being able to maximize discrete objectives, they are forced to simultaneously optimize them, or reject old objectives for new ones that may be more tractable. Such learning could be based on a better understanding of the fates of pollutants in the sea, or on a better understanding of the transfer of pollutants between the air and sea, leading governments to accept slower rates of industrial growth as investment is diverted to installing pollution controls and forcing them to adopt the notion of environmental protection into avowed national goals.

In a third, even more sophisticated mode of learning, policymakers adopt entirely new patterns of reasoning. This may occur in two ways. Statically, policymakers may accept the existence of new causal mechanisms and adopt new frameworks for policy analysis that are better adapted to the context of the time. In the environment, this would be the recognition of tradeoffs between short-term economic development and longer-term environmental protection, leading to a new form of policymaking that considers more variables and more links between them.

Dynamically, they may recognize that the context in which policy is made has changed, and alter their reasoning process accordingly.[31] Events come to have new meanings for decision makers. The recognition of previously ignored environmental externalities and attempts to internalize them may be an example of this form of learning.

Piaget offers an example of this form of learning as well:

> ... a false finding is inspired not by a well-defined inferential coordination, but by coordinations that include lacunae or that are too global. For example, the surface of water in a container

may be "observed" not to be horizontal because horizontality is thought to depend only on the position of the water relative to the container, and not on relations between external interfigural reference points. In this case the erroneous observation is not directly deduced from an erroneous idea. It is wrong because it is situated within a framework that does not apply to the situation in question. Water is judged to be horizontal not in terms of its relationship to a container, but relative to external referents. (1985:38–39)

The recognition of the appropriate context constitutes learning. Although complete understanding of a prior system is not necessary, or even possible, actors realize that pursuing obsolete decision rules after circumstances change will not lead to desired outcomes. Thus, if a deep global rupture contributing to systemic change has occurred, learning would consist of pursuing new strategies more consonant with the presumed nature of the new system, such as Francis Bacon's dictum that "Nature, to be commanded, must be obeyed."

An example of this last form of learning would be if southern planners realized that mimicking Western development styles and policies may have different and unintended effects in their societies, or that direct foreign investment will have different effects in peripheral societies than in the core because of the operation of the international capitalist system. They may come to call into question frameworks that identify problems or suggest responses or question characteristics of the international system that shape national policy choices (see, for instance, Cardoso and Faletto 1979). The hermeneutically identified aspects of collective discourse that marginalize challenges to the legitimacy of the more powerful may be called into question. Systemic organizing principles will be recognized and targeted for reform. The recognition that the Donation of Constantine was fraudulent demonstrates this type of learning. Such an identification recognized that the present was not isomorphic to the past. In a contemporary vein, many argue that it is no longer possible, as it was until 1973, to pursue economic development based on low-price energy sources.

Officials of the United Nations Environment Programme and many environmentalists promoted this last type of learning on the grounds that it is the only type of learning that would enable societies to manage the environmental crisis. They felt that new attitudes and more comprehensive decision-making practices were necessary to deal with environmental issues and to manage the tradeoffs between discrete objectives that such problems create. Leaders must come to recognize that cooperation, coordinated policymaking, and more integrated domestic policy was necessary to manage and relate the multiple interdependent forces involved in environmental protection.

The most sophisticated form entails the shift to extreme new conceptions of cause-and-effect relationships, which could even be called a shift of "consciousness." It is most commonly analyzed by writers discussing environmental issues. Actors would adopt systems thinking rather than reductionist thinking. Actors would recognize their position within a system, and treat problems as they interrelate rather than as distinct cases. For instance, policymakers may come to view humanity as being in constant balance with nature, rather than in opposition to it. Accommodations must be made to perturbations in the surroundings. Key "leitmotifs" of new views of nature are "non-linearity, instability and fluctuations."[32] When the world is viewed in terms of connections, policies may be framed in terms of responsibilities rather than rights.[33] Policies will be increasingly coherent and integrated. Only here will policies be in anticipation of expected environmental changes. All other types of learning require some signal of failure from the environment in order for leaders to question their policies, objectives, or frameworks.

All of these are types of learning in which governments may engage as a result of political involvement by an epistemic community. Which form of learning results is probably a consequence of the type of knowledge base that the involved epistemic community shares. If its members have a broad and integrated view of the world, such as ecologists do, then they would contribute to more comprehensive forms of learning. If they have a narrow view, then their involvement will lead only to the adoption of new means or ends for policy. Facing governments familiar with lower levels of learning, it will take an epistemic community a long time to successfully instill higher levels of policymaking.

CONCLUSION

This chapter has reviewed three alternative views of cooperation. Their explanations for the causes of cooperation, its effects, and its forms are summarized in the following table. All offer analyses of different forms of influence. Each offers different explanations for how

Table 2.1. Comparisons of Explanations of Mediterranean
Cooperation for Pollution Control

	Realism/Neorealism
Conditioning systemic features	anarchy
Process of cooperation	Hegemonic (French) leadership
Forms of cooperation Scope	pollutants encountered by France, may extend to other issues of concern to France
Strength	covary with French power; may focus on provision of information (cooperation under anarchy) about pollution
Duration	vary with French power, or availability of information
Effects of cooperation	• consolidate French regional influence • diffuse French power • mutual benefits for all participants

cooperation is likely to occur, and its form. Realists and neorealists
relate cooperation and its forms to the distribution of power between
states. Historical materialists explain cooperation in terms of the
systemic control of powerful industrialized capitalist states over weaker
ones. The epistemic community approach offers suggestions for more
resilient cooperation that is broader in scope than that anticipated by
realists, neorealists, and historical materialists. Its primary actors are
bureaucrats, technocrats, scientists, and specialists. If an epistemic
community is able to retain the authority conferred on it by governments—both in terms of disciplinary solidarity and access to governmental decision making—it may lead governments to adopt new
policymaking styles encompassing new means, ends, or patterns of
reasoning. The epistemic community may also lead the national governments in which it is strongly entrenched to adopt convergent pol-

Historical Materialism	*Epistemic Communities*
capitalism and unequal exchange	uncertainty
imperialism by the North	bargaining and learning
unclear, will divert challenges to capitalism and reinforce areas in which the North is preeminent	as defined by the epistemic community
vary with Northern domination	vary with domestic alliances and involvement of epistemic community
vary with domination	vary with involvement of epistemic community
• impose alien ways of thinking on LDCs • impose undesirable forms of development on LDCs • foreclose development alternatives to LDCs • North will get relatively more benefits than South • deepen LDCs' commercial dependence on the North	• lead to convergent governmental pollution control policies • reinforce cooperation within range delimited by epistemic community • instill new patterns of comprehensive environmental policymaking in Mediterranean governments

lution control policies and support rigorous efforts at coordinated pollution control. Foreign and domestic policies may both be affected.

Looking at epistemic communities supplements the analysis of neorealists and historical materialists. A concern with epistemic communities provides the dynamic element that these two approaches lack, because it addresses the issue of variable state perceptions and interests. At the least, this approach can identify the source of state interests. At the most, it can aspire to explaining how states may replace limited efforts at environmental management with more holistic, ecological schemes, and can supplement fundamental national security objectives with interests in environmental preservation. The ability of each of these approaches to explain the Mediterranean Action Plan is examined in the following chapters.

THREE

The Origins of Awareness of Mediterranean Pollution and Early Negotiations for the Mediterranean Action Plan

The Mediterranean states confronted evidence of pollution in the 1960s. In 1972 Lord Peter Ritchie-Calder alerted the world that:

> The Mediterranean Sea is sick. It needs intensive care, day and night nursing. By nature it has always been delicate but its condition has grievously deteriorated in recent years. The short term prognosis is obvious: on present trends, things will get worse because the effects will be multiplied and magnified by the increase in industrial activity. Recreational beaches will be tarred and ordured. The sea will be out of bounds for bathers. Seafood will be a health hazard. In terms of epidemic diseases, the Mediterranean can become a biological time bomb. The trees will be dying around the coasts, suffocated or poisoned by polluted sea winds.[1]

The coastal area and harbors had always been polluted by industrial growth,[2] but the increasing tanker use of the sea in the 1960s greatly exacerbated the problems. There were now tactile tar balls on many Mediterranean beaches. Lacking any real information about the extent of pollution, the Mediterranean states requested the United Nations Environment Programme (UNEP) to develop a program for evaluating the extent of the problem, determining its sources, and controlling them. In 1975 sixteen Mediterranean governments approved the Mediterranean Action Plan (Med Plan). Twelve years later a greatly expanded program is in place "to take all appropriate measures . . . to prevent, abate, and combat pollution . . . and to protect and enhance the marine environment."[3]

The Med Plan consists of an interconnected set of of four components: regional treaties; coordinated research and monitoring; integrated planning; and administrative and budgetary support. Beginning in 1976 with seven pilot monitoring and research projects, a protocol banning marine dumping, another protocol urging cooperation in case of oil spills, and a framework convention, the participating states have now developed a far more comprehensive program. They completed the first phase of studying pollution in the region, and established the monitoring program as a continuing institution supported by governments rather than by international organizations. They established regional centers to coordinate oil spill management actions, the preservation of species, integrated development planning, and studies of development projects of specific interest to developing states. A coordinating headquarters unit was established in Athens, with a Mediterranean staff supported by annual contributions from all the Mediterranean countries. Governments meet biannually to review the program. The parties adopted legal agreements that establish marine parks to preserve endangered marine species and to ban pollution from land-based sources.

The Land-Based Sources Protocol, which was signed in 1980 and entered into force in 1983, is the most important part of the Med Plan, as it sets limits on industrial, municipal, and agricultural emissions into the Mediterranean, as well as controlling wastes transmitted by rivers and through the atmosphere. Politically, the adoption of this protocol is the capstone of the Med Plan, as it was the most contentious issue negotiated between the developing (LDCs) and developed states (DCs). Controlling land-based sources directly influences industrialization policies, about which the LDCs are extremely sensitive. The protocol's adoption without significant alteration, and its subsequent ratification by Algeria and Egypt, who initially opposed it, demonstrates a dramatic change from considering environmental protection and economic development as incompatible goals to accepting an uneasy balance between them.

These Med Plan efforts at marine pollution control have become more comprehensive over time. By 1982 many more pollutants were covered by the protocols than were included initially. The sources of pollution that were regulated grew from oil pollution from tankers to land-based emissions from industry, municipal sewers, and agricultural spraying. Initially treating only pollutants that were dumped directly into the sea and transmitted by Mediterranean currents, the Med Plan came to cover pollution that is transmitted by major rivers to the sea and blown through the atmosphere. Its strength grew from an exhortatory framework convention in 1976 to a set of controls over specific substances by 1983.

Governments learned that environmental problems were more extensive than coastal pollution resulting from tanker traffic and untreated sewage and that they required more coherent policymaking, including industrial restraint, for their control. Although short of a radically new mode of reasoning, the Med Plan's development does reflect governments' acceptance of a much broader spectrum of interconnected pollution problems that must be managed in tandem.

SOURCES OF MEDITERRANEAN POLLUTION AND NATIONAL INTERESTS

In the early 1970s countries faced a variety of pollution problems. Four sets of actors, with different sets of interests, were involved in the negotiations to control regional pollution.

Foreign ministry officials led delegations to Med Plan meetings and were generally responsible for articulating their countries' positions on regional pollution control, subject to their own broader foreign policy concerns. They hoped to control only the pollutants produced in their countries. All states suffered from oil on beaches. But their common concern about Mediterranean degradation was overwhelmed by specific disagreements over which pollutants to control and who would have to bear the costs for their control.

In addition, regional marine scientists, the UNEP staff, and secretariat members from other specialized agencies whose mandates included some dimension of environmental protection sought to promote collective arrangements that would reflect their concerns with which pollutants, sources, and channels of pollution required collective attention. Officials from foreign affairs ministries participated in negotiations on the legal components, integrated planning, and review meetings of the entire Med Plan. UNEP coordinated meetings and drafted background documents. Other specialized agencies convened and participated in early meetings dealing with regional problems falling within their purview. UNEP served as a broker in the negotiations, playing on the dynamics between these other groups in order to focus discussions on a broader range of issues that it preferred.

Table 3.1 shows the sources and types of Mediterranean pollution. Most of it is carried to the Mediterranean by rivers. The pollutants that individual countries hoped to control correlate closely to their stage of development. The more industrialized states with energy-intensive production suffered from industrial pollution (metals, phenols). States at lower levels of development and with large populations faced problems of untreated municipal wastes (organic matter, deter-

Table 3.1. Types and Sources of Mediterranean Pollution
(in percent)

	Organic Matter	Nutrients[a]	Specific Organics[b]	Pesticides	Metals
Region					
1	40.7	43.1	21.8	30.0	35.8
2	28.1	31.6	19.8	22.3	38.0
3	10.8	6.8	27.5	21.9	6.4
4	3.8	4.7	9.0	10.1	5.2
5	16.6	13.0	19.9	15.7	14.4
Total	100.0	100.0	98.0	100.0	99.8

1 = Spain, France, Italy (northwestern basin and Tyrrhenian Sea).
2 = Italy, Yugoslavia, Greece (Adriatic and Ionian Seas).
3 = Morocco, Algeria, Tunisia, Libya (southern coast).
4 = Lebanon, Israel, Egypt, Libya (south Levantin Sea).
5 = Greece, Turkey, Cyprus, Syria, Lebanon (central and Aegean Sea).

Source: Calculated from UNEP (1984), annex 2.

[a] Nutrients are phosphorous and nitrogen.

[b] Specific organics are detergents, phenols, and mineral oils.

Table 3.2. Major Economic Indicators, 1978

Country	GNP (at Market Prices; $US Billions)	GNP per Capita (in $US)
France and Monaco	473.0	8,800
Libya	19.8	7,210
Italy and San Marino	260.9	4,600
Spain	146.9	3,960
Israel	13.7	3,730
Greece	32.4	3,450
Cyprus	1.7	2,580
Malta	0.8	2,310
Yugoslavia	46.1	2,100
Algeria	25.7	1,450
Turkey	53.9	1,250
Tunisia	6.0	990
Syria	7.8	960
Morocco	12.9	680
Egypt	16.9	420
Lebanon	—	—

Source: World Bank, *1980 World Bank Atlas;* United Nations, *Statistical Year Book, 1981.*

gents, and nutrients), as did many developed states with old cities without sewage systems. All states faced the problems of agricultural runoff (pesticides and nutrients), and oil on beaches. Table 3.2 presents the economic profiles of the Mediterranean countries. It also illustrates the great disparity in economic resources in the region.

Many officials thought that pollution was a commons problem, and thus required coordinated action throughout the region. They assumed that currents transferred the pollutants fairly freely among countries. UNEP officials were well aware that currents were not sufficiently strong to transmit pollutants across the Mediterranean Basin—if they were that strong the whole sea would have been dead —but they hoped to complete an agreement, so they just smiled and nodded when others characterized Mediterranean pollution as a commons problem. Only later did studies reveal to marine scientists that currents were too weak to fully exchange the wastes between the northern and southern shores; regional pollution was not a true collective good, and could be managed bilaterally or subregionally, al-

Average Real Growth in GNP Per Capita 1970–1978 (in %)	Per Capita Energy Consumption (in Kilograms of Coal Equivalent per Capita)	Population in Millions (mid-1978)
+3.1	4,174	53.3
+2.6	1,967	2.7
+2.0	3,039	56.7
+3.1	2,154	37.1
+1.6	2,220	3.7
+3.8	2,043	9.4
+1.4	1,706	—
+11.2	1,197	—
+5.0	1,949	22.0
−2.6	1,582	17.6
+4.1	712	43.1
+5.7	554	6.1
+6.0	763	8.1
+3.9	286	18.9
+6.3	—	39.6
—	922	3.1

though this fact was never fully appreciated by foreign ministry officials, who continue to accept pollution as a regionally shared problem. This false perception actually facilitated the resolution of the problem, as the fact that the problem was thought to have a collective nature provided the weaker North African states with leverage: they could threaten to refuse to comply if Med Plan arrangements did not satisfy them. Leaders also feared the political costs of unilateral action. Voters threatened to recall the mayor of Genoa after he closed unsafe beaches during the tourist season.[4]

Political antipathies exacerbated the problem of managing such a collective good. A common aversion to oil pollution and a shared fear of being taken for a "patsy" masked deeper-seated disagreements. Foreign ministries had other objectives besides cleaning up pollution. French and Italian delegates sought to promote regional environmental legislation compatible with international law, particularly EEC directives. LDCs hoped to receive equipment to monitor pollution and get training in oceanography and pollution control. Environmental concerns also seemed like a good pretext for establishing diplomatic linkages between such otherwise hostile countries as Algeria and France and Israel and the Arab countries. Greece and Spain, returning to democratic governments, also hoped to use environmental cooperation as a lever to assert an open foreign policy.

More profoundly, LDCs were concerned that attempts to control pollution would divert resources from economic development. Their principal objective was to improve the welfare of their populations by developing economically. The costs from controlling pollution, particularly from the manufacturing sources to which they looked to drive their development efforts, would retard the rate of industrialization. The Algerian Ten Year Plan (1972–1982) expressed that country's aspirations to be fully industrialized by 1980, anticipating three hundred major projects from 1970 to 1973 to diversify to manufacturing from primary extractive industries.[5] The effect on the manufacturing sector and on national economies of controlling land-based sources of pollution is significant. The manufacturing sectors principally responsible for land-based pollution in 1976 account for 56 percent of gross fixed capital formation in Egypt, 28 percent in Greece, and 40 percent in France.[6]

In the early 1970s Algerian president Houari Boumedienne was actively antagonistic to environmental protection. He announced: "if improving the environment means less bread for the Algerians, then I am against it" (NOVA 1980). The Algerian representative to UNCHE stated that Algeria "will not sacrifice development at the altar of the environment."[7] Boumedienne was a leading figure in the Non-Aligned movement during the early years of the New International Economic Order discussions, and along with many LDC delegates questioned the very desirability of cooperating with the North. Following Boumedienne's death in 1979, President Chadli Bendjedid continued Boumedienne's emphasis on autonomy in economic decision making, along with a commitment to cooperation among LDCs to reduce dependence on the North.[8]

LDC and DC policymakers also differed on how rapidly to develop pollution controls and on how strong these controls should be. The DCs, suffering more heavily from pollution, hoped to introduce strong pollution controls immediately. The LDCs, still industrializing and with relatively cleaner coasts, preferred waiting until they had industrialized and the problem was more noticeable. With coastal waters that were still much more pristine than European waters, the LDCs wanted much weaker water quality standards than the Europeans, as they were willing to tolerate much more pollution in the short run in order to industrialize.

France was the most forceful negotiator. France and Italy sent the largest delegations to meetings; delegates were drawn from a wide variety of ministries but were controlled by the delegates from the foreign affairs ministries. Among the LDCs, the Algerians had the strongest delegations, and often took vigorous positions in opposition to the Med Plan.

Other countries and actors were not involved in Med Plan negotiations. The United States decided, after having attended early meetings, that its interests would not be affected by the Med Plan. The EEC, although a signatory party to the Med Plan, played only a minor role in the negotiations, as LDCs were extremely sensitive about the presence of a nonnational authority. Multinational corporations were also absent. Their sole involvement was in 1981, when the European Center of Silicon Manufacturers unsuccessfully approached the Med Plan secretariat in order to remove organosilicons from a list of substances for which permits must be obtained from national authorities before they could be released into the Mediterranean.

Few countries had pollution specialists, so they resorted to scientists who were trained in monitoring techniques and knowledgeable about substances that might be pollutants. Marine scientists' views were solicited by governments and international organizations to explicate the variety of Mediterranean pollution problems. National marine scientists participated in scientific and monitoring exercises. Scientists came from all of the disciplines that study the use of the oceans: marine biology, marine geology, physical oceanography, microbiology, and marine chemistry; public health officials were also included. Each group was principally interested in studying and controlling pollution as it applied to its own domain of marine science. For instance, marine biologists who study life in the oceans were concerned with pollutants that affect fishery yields. Marine geologists and physical oceanographers studying the physical behavior of the ocean and its effects were interested in tracing currents and the flow of pollutants. Chemists were more concerned with heavy metals and industrial compounds. Microbiologists were concerned with the organisms in municipal sewage. When drafting reports and identifying potential pollutants that required monitoring, scientists from these disciplines tended to stick closely to these concerns.

Many of these scientists operated independently of their foreign ministries when they served as delegates to Med Plan meetings; they participated either as individual experts or as representatives of their environmental ministries. Scientists from Algeria, Egypt, and Greece did not receive instructions from their foreign ministries, and had a fairly free hand. French scientists, however, received detailed instructions from the French Foreign Ministry and at times had to check back with Paris to ensure that their position at technical meetings was consistent with the Quai d'Orsay's objectives.

Specialized international organizations were involved in the Mediterranean and sought to coordinate activities falling within their organizational purviews. The Food and Agriculture Organization (FAO) and its General Fisheries Council for the Mediterranean (GFCM) were responsible for fisheries and living resources. IMCO and its successor, IMO, were responsible for tankers and navigation. The World Health Organization (WHO) dealt with public health. The International Oceanographic Commission (IOC) and the International Commission for Scientific Exploration of the Mediterranean (ICSEM) were concerned with marine research. Other organizations had more peripheral concerns: the World Meterological Organization (WMO) monitored the airborne transmission of pollutants; the United Nations Educational, Social and Cultural Organization (UNESCO) was involved with protecting national landmarks and cultural heritage; and the International Atomic Energy Agency (IAEA) studied radioactive emissions. Coastal industrial practices fell under the mandates of the United Nations' Economic Commission for Europe (ECE) and United Nations Industrial Development Organization (UNIDO).

Each group had only a partial grasp of the full range of Mediterranean pollutants. De facto alliances grew up between specialized agencies, scientists, and foreign ministry officials who shared concerns about specific pollutants. UNEP attempted to integrate all of these activities under its broader rubric to develop a program dealing with all forms of Mediterranean pollution.

UNEP officials had an overriding ecological orientation that encompassed the specific concerns already mentioned. Created in 1972 with a "catalytic" and crosscutting mandate, UNEP was primarily a coordinative UN agency, without the staff to conduct fully integrated projects. It took a more integrated focus than the existing international agencies operating in the region, which had narrower sectoral and project-oriented focuses. Members of UNEP's senior staff were interested in creating a new program to enhance their position within the universe of United Nations agencies, and wanted to control a broad range of sources of Mediterranean pollution and incorporate environmental considerations into national economic planning.

UNEP's leadership consisted of members of an epistemic community. They shared an abiding belief in ecological principles and were committed to preserving the physical environment, which they thought was threatened by pollution. Other individuals around the basin shared their perspective. The epistemic community included members of the Greek government, French modelers and systems scientists, UNESCO bureaucrats, FAO lawyers, and individuals in the Israeli, Spanish, and Egyptian governments. These members of the ecological epistemic community had varied professional training, although each accepted ecological tenets that relate problems to one another. Few of the active ecologists in the region actually had formal training in the field of ecology. They commonly had advanced training in other disciplines, but were attracted to the ecological framework because of their discontent with what they saw as the narrow and parochial nature of their own disciplines. They key individuals within the upper echelons of UNEP were Maurice Strong, a Canadian international businessmen who was its first executive director; Robert Frosch, an American theoretical physicist; Peter Thacher, an American career civil servant; and Stjepan Keckes, a Yugoslav marine biologist. Midlevel members of the epistemic community who were not in UNEP were engineers and social scientists who were sympathetic to environmental arguments. They approached the issue with fervor, referring to their allies as "true believers" and "converts."

The epistemic community shared a set of causal beliefs about the interdependence of environmental problems. They were motivated by an ecological viewpoint.

> The holistic viewpoint, as a philosophy of science, is both a confession of faith and a goal to be pursued; and as such it has great significance. In describing Nature as one integrated system it reveals the scientists' faith in a universe of cause and effect relationships, the whole of which is capable of being made intelligible to the normal mind. At the same time it points to the essential unity of science with respect to its problems and its ultimate goal. (Hawley 1950:9–10)

Ecology as a discipline is a fairly recent development. It was only popularized after World War II, although the term was coined by Haeckel in 1866 to mean:

> the body of knowledge concerning the economy of nature—the investigation of the total relations of the animal both to its inorganic and to its organic environment; including above all, its friendly and inimical relations with those animals and plants

with which it comes directly or indirectly into contact—in a word, ecology is the study of all those complex interrelations referred to by Darwin as the conditions of the struggle for existence.[9]

Ecology is more a way of organizing experience than a predictive science. It is a cognitive framework that calls attention to an interlinked set of relationships, a "synoptic approach that addresses those interdependencies directly" (Clark 1986:7). Ecologists believe in the need for interdisciplinary studies and multidimensional analyses, although ecologists take pains to emphasize that the field is more than simply a global or holistic approach (di Castri 1984). Ecology textbooks seek to appropriate existing disciplines within a synthetic framework (see, for example, Odum 1975; Ehrlich, Ehrlich, and Holdren 1977). Ecologists share a professional and intellectual stance which attempts to relate populations to their environmental settings and to balance populations to the capacity of their environment in some form of dynamic equilibrium (Sears 1954; Worster 1977; McIntosh 1985). The field is inherently integrative, focusing on the interaction between large components, which are often regarded "as functional wholes" (Odum 1977:1289) rather than reductionist units that may be studied and understood in relative isolation from one another.

They also share a set of political values that complement their ecological beliefs. Their broad vision implies that they hope to subordinate traditional national foreign policy objectives to comprehensive efforts at environmental protection, and to reorganize political arrangements to better recognize the interlinkages between ecosystems. They hope to reorient state interests and transform the way in which states formulated environmental policies in the 1970s. They hope to transform the Mediterranean governments into environmental interveners, with international organizations serving to coordinate their activities and monitor nationally adopted data and quality standards.

UNEP's leadership envisioned and masterminded an entire interlinked program for broadly defined environmental protection; the program would control the full gamut of pollutants, sources of pollution, and channels of pollution, while promoting more comprehensive forms of economic planning that would include environmental and other factors in its models. They were interested in promoting holistic analyses of international problems and dealing with the social causes of environmental degradation, rather than promoting remedial coordinative efforts for isolated issues.[10] They hoped to design a program for the Mediterranean to achieve efficient management of their coastal resources on a *sustainable* basis. They admit the need for truly comprehensive plans reflecting the idea that for the effective protection and development of a marine region, all factors, maritime and land based, affecting their ecoregion should be taken into account when formulating development strategies for their individual nations. In other words, rather than addressing only the problems which appear to be consequences of poor resource management and environmentally inappropriate development practices, the key to a successful protection of and development within an ecosystem lies in proper and sustainable resource management and careful application of development practices which are consistent with the health of the environment. (Thacher 1983:2)

Mostapha Tolba, an Egyptian microbiologist who replaced Strong as UNEP's executive director in 1975, still talks of "development without destruction" and "environmentally sound management." Members of UNEP saw pollution as a visible "canary in the miner's helmet" signifying what they thought happens when planners omit ecological interlinkages from their planning. By supporting efforts to standardize methodologies for marine pollution monitoring, they hoped to generate results that would prove compelling to the Mediterranean government about the full extent of pollution and its variety of sources and channels. By interesting states in controlling some sources of marine pollution, they hoped to further steer them down a "slippery slope" to controlling land-based sources, more specific pollutants, and riverine and atmospheric transport, and ultimately to inculcate leaders and planners with a new pattern of thought about integrated economic development. In addition to promoting environmental assessment, UNEP also aspired to encourage environmental management: "to assist the Governments in taking environmentally sound decisions about development and to improve their ability to make rational choices among various options concerning alternative patterns of development and allocation of resources."[10] UNEP hoped that by developing a concern with marine pollution they would lead the region to an overall reassessment of coastal land use practices, giving rise in turn to a concurrent consideration of ecological, demographic, social, cultural, and economic forces operating in the littoral zone and of their role in shaping aggregate demand for uses of the Mediterranean.

In short, UNEP and its ecological colleagues was seeking to promote very sophisticated learning. Maurice Strong repeatedly asserted: "The process is the policy" (Thacher 1983:2).

As early as February 1971, Dan Serwer, a consultant to the United Nations Institute for Training and Research (UNITAR), and Peter Thacher (seconded to Maurice Strong's staff for the preparation of UNCHE from the U.S. Department of State, later to be director of the Geneva Regional Office supervising the Regional Seas Programme, and ultimately deputy executive director of UNEP) identified marine dumping and land-based sources as key areas that were not covered by international legislation. With Strong, they realized that regulating land-based sources was an unrealistic goal at that time because of the cost of regulation and its contentious nature, but hoped to control them later. At UNCHE they encouraged delegates to recommend the prompt adoption of a dumping treaty: what became the London dumping convention.

UNEP's broad viewpoint enabled it to form transnational alliances with marine scientists and nongovernmental organizations who shared complementary, if narrower, views. These alliances were cemented with the provision of research funding, monitoring equipment, and training in its use. Together they led governments to accept a broader international agenda and to support more comprehensive domestic policies.

CONFLICT RESOLUTION

UNEP played a two-level game. Internationally, it promoted a more comprehensive program through the use of political compromise and technical consensus. This international level activity alerted governments to the need for developing familiarity with problems facing them at home. At the national level, UNEP forged transnational alliances with regional scientists who then provided advice to their governments consistent with UNEP's own preferences.

Political compromise kept everybody involved in the negotiations. Without the political compromise, the process would have broken down as countries left the talks, and UNEP would have been unable to establish alliances with scientists for each nation. By using information that was accepted by all of the regional scientists, UNEP was able to demonstrate the need for treating more sources of pollution by encouraging recognition of more interlinkages and moving negotiations toward a more comprehensive focus. In conjunction, political compromise and technical consensus laid the groundwork for members of the epistemic community and for marine scientists to gain access to decision making within their countries and ultimately guide domestic decision making toward convergent, broader policies regionwide. Once in position in their own governments, they urged compliance with the Med Plan and pushed their governments to adopt and enforce more comprehensive pollution control policies.

UNEP's ideology was not shared by national foreign affairs officials, nor by most of the scientific community. The foreign policy officials participated because they hoped to achieve their environmental foreign policy goals, and most of the scientists hoped for research support. UNEP managed to adroitly wed these interests in a broad enough program that satisfied everyone's short-term interests, while incrementally promoting a more all-inclusive program. Ultimately, Algerian and Egyptian foreign policy officials came to support the Med Plan not because they shared UNEP's holistic vision, but because they felt that land-based sources of pollution now required treatment, and because they benefited materially from participation in the other Med Plan projects.

UNEP promoted political compromises in order to ensure that foreign ministry representatives would continue to attend meetings and fund the Med Plan. UNEP adopted the principle of "geographic distribution" to reward countries for participating. Regional Activity of Centers (RACs) were developed to assist UNEP and coordinate projects of the Med Plan Coordinated Pollution Monitoring and Research Programme (Med Pol). Thus, each project was delivered to an institution in a Mediterranean country to supervise. RACs were established in France, Yugoslavia, Tunisia, Malta, and Greece. Spain was the temporary legal depository, until the Athens office was established. Prestigious lead laboratories for monitoring and research were set up in Algeria, Egypt, France, Italy, Malta, Turkey, and Yugoslavia. The nationalities of the Athens headquarters staff are regionally mixed. Even the equipment that UNEP distributed was American, rather than French. The Athens unit has WANG computers, much to the dismay of the French, who attempted to create contracts for French firms. Monitoring stations use equipment manufactured by VARIAN, an American company. But the geographical principle has its costs; only two of the seven lead laboratories performed up to snuff.[11] Countries that were initially opposed to negotiating were mollified by these rewards of laboratories, funding, training, and prestige. Although they weren't sufficiently large to overcome opposition to the Med Plan, they were sufficient to guarantee continued attendance at meetings.

The countries that did not actively participate did not receive any tangible rewards. Libya and Syria failed to eke out any form of gain from their infrequent attendance. Although Israel did not receive any direct benefits from its involvement, it was able to participate in a forum with Arab states, and hence gain some legitimacy in international discussions.

UNEP also built alliances with domestic marine scientists. The marine scientists then demonstrated the need for a broader international agenda, and encouraged their own governments to develop pollution control measures. These alliances were developed in a number of ways.

Stjepan Keckes, a Yugoslav oceanographer who in 1975 was named the director of the Geneva Regional Seas Office of UNEP that was responsible for administering the Med Plan, firmly believed that governments would only respond to scientific information generated domestically, and that scientific studies conducted by a team from an international organization or from selected countries would be sterile in generating national compliance with the Med Plan. He believed in self-reliant science. Faced with a paucity of capable institutions in the LDCs, UNEP elected to improve them, even though the quality and efficiency of their work would be less than if the work were contracted entirely to France, and the work would take longer. UNEP made a deliberate choice for a "moderate" program with universal participation over a "high-quality" program in order to ensure LDC participation. Although other agencies opposed the idea of using LDC laboratories, UNEP insisted.

Keckes recognized the value of including domestic scientists in this network: "you don't have to wait until the infrastructure is well-developed to use it. You have to make the infrastructure grow through the Program."[12] By using a number of LDC institutions as lead laboratories for the Med Plan monitoring projects, he was able to attract their allegiance to UNEP away from their own governments, who were not forthcoming with research funds (Thacher 1977:311).

Many scientists became dependent upon UNEP to fund their research. For instance, 20–25 percent of the costs of Yugoslav pollution monitoring has been supported by UNEP. The director of the principal Yugoslav oceanography institution—the Rudjer Boskovic Institute, of which Keckes had been deputy director from 1971 to 1975—estimated that without UNEP's role Yugoslav pollution monitoring and research would be impossible, or dramatically constrained.

Through UNEP and the Med Plan, these LDC institutions received research funding and new equipment, and were provided with maintenance and training in its use. Research projects were designed calling for multiple indicators of pollution in order to appeal to the diverse collection of marine scientists that UNEP was wooing. During periods of budget shortages Keckes had to distribute funds equitably among the marine scientists to retain their allegiance. Measurements taken with the monitoring equipment (gas chromatographers and atomic absorption spectrophotometers) distributed by UNEP gave the scientists tangible support for their contentions with their own governments.

UNEP also fostered an ambiguous nongovernmental role for participating scientists by inviting them to technical meetings in their individual professional capacities rather than as governmental representatives. UNEP conducted biannual workshops with ICSEM and the IOC on pollution in the Mediterranean to further involve regional marine scientists in developing knowledge about pollution in the area. From 1972 on the workshops met biannually to compare papers on data, methodology, and general findings about conditions of the Mediterranean. By broadening personal ties between scientists, the meetings served to band the scientific community together, to disperse information about the degree of Mediterranean pollution, and to deepen the ties between the secretariat and the scientific community. By publicizing scientists' findings at home, UNEP further enhanced their domestic reputation for expertise.

In addition to forming a coalition with national scientists, UNEP sought to reach out directly to the general population of the Mediterranean states by publicizing the program whenever possible. UNCHE's planners had devised a similar strategy to involve universities, NGOs and the public (Johnson 1972:88). The Geneva UNEP staff included a full-time public relations officer who was to promote the program to the media and develop close contacts with national nongovernmental organizations. When meeting with heads of government, UNEP executive directors would stress the need to participate in the Med Plan and to comply with Med Plan protocols.

Contact with different ministries and other international organizations smoothed UNEP's acquisition of data. For instance, the French Foreign Affairs Ministry, the formal focal point by which pollution data would be transferred to UNEP, was reticent to provide data on emissions of radionuclides, because the French felt that they would be pinpointed as the principal regional culprits for such pollution. UNEP managed to get this information by getting the French Public Health Ministry to provide the data to WHO. Similarly, the Egyptian

Fisheries Ministry yielded pesticides data that the Agricultural Ministry would not divulge.

UNEP's actions were constrained by the need to retain credibility with the foreign affairs community. UNEP rejected offers by France and the EEC to draft the Land-Based Sources Protocol. UNEP also rejected a 1974 French offer to conduct all of the monitoring and an offer from the USSR to provide a research vessel for monitoring open waters. The secretariat was able to offset rambunctious delegates at negotiating sessions by proposing them for positions as officials at the meetings (i.e., as chairmen or rapporteurs). UNEP was committed to ensuring that the quality of its scientific studies was as high as possible, so as not to tarnish their publicity value in generating continuing attention to pollution.

UNEP served as a buffer between the North and the South. LDC officials respected UNEP's unbiased position, so that UNEP's documentation was generally accepted as authoritative, whereas such material submitted by the French would have been suspect.

The most successful aspects of the Med Plan are those where UNEP's epistemic focus combined with the interests of marine scientists. The Med Plan's failures are distinguished by the absence of extensive domestic alliances or the lack of access of members of the epistemic community or its allies to governments.

EMERGING CONCERN WITH MARINE POLLUTION

When Mediterranean officials first expressed concern about marine pollution in the late 1960s uncertainty prevailed, and governments looked for ways to gain information about the sources, types, and degree of pollution and about what could be done to improve the quality of the Mediterranean. It was an era of unfocused anxiety. Lacking detailed scientific studies of marine pollution, concern was dominated by the most visible type of marine pollution: tar balls from tanker operations, which accounted for annual emissions of 300,000–500,000 tonnes.[13]

The global furor accompanying the preparations for UNCHE had resulted in a number of partial initiatives for pollution control in the Mediterranean. Italy convened the International Conference on Oil Pollution of the Sea in Rome in October 1968, followed by the International Conference on the Protection of the Sea in Milan in April 1969. These meetings found that information was generally scanty, and that various studies of the Mediterranean were not comparable with each other. Pollution from a variety of sources, including coastal industries and municipal wastes, seemed to be widespread (International Conference on Oil Pollution of the Sea 1968).

Decision makers were ignorant about the sources and extent of pollution. Many countries also lacked indigenous capabilities to assess their own pollution. Scientists concluded at a scientific meeting in February 1974:

> The attention drawn to the impact of pollution on marine communities is too recent and, as a result, data is still too spare for it to be possible to draw an overall picture of the situation. Furthermore, the word "pollution" is used to cover very different attacks, both in kind and in intensity and pollution may rightly be considered to include thermal effluents just as much as the discharge of excavation waste, industrial waste, and urban effluents.[14]

Besides the visual evidence of widespread oil clots, there was no hard evidence of secular environmental deterioration. However, popular scientific accounts were very effective at increasing concern about pollution. Jacques Cousteau was active in attracting publicity. He spoke before the United States Congress and United Nations General Assembly, and was widely cited in the regional press. He announced:

> In the Mediterranean shore-life has practically disappeared. It was very abundant when we started diving [30 years before], and today you can barely see a fish three inches long and very rarely. Sardines are very rare and only in the area of Gibraltar. The factories are closing down. The price of lobster is skyrocketing because it is almost impossible to find.[15]

The *Economist* jumped on the bandwagon, reporting that: "[the Mediterranean's] ecological balance was not seriously disturbed until the early 1960s. Now overpopulation, the tourist boom, industrial development and maritime irresponsibility are combining to turn it into a dead sea."[16] In October 1973 the Italian delegate to IMCO warned that "if draconian measures were not taken at the earliest possible moment, the Mediterranean would become a source of desolation and death."[17]

Beaches were closed. In 1971 Naples closed twelve beaches as health hazards when 18 percent of tourists were found to have contracted typhoid or infectious hepatitis.[18] In 1972 four miles of prime

French beaches were closed at Hyeres due to high bacteria counts.[19] In 1974 Genoa closed thirty-eight of its eighty beaches. A swimmer in the Mediterranean had a one in seven chance of getting a skin infection or catching a disease.[20]

Fishermen in Bastia, Corsica rioted to protest the Italian chemical firm Montedison's practice of dumping titanium dioxide wastes from its factory in Scarlino into the sea outside territorial limits between Tuscany and Corsica. The Italian consulate was bombed.[21]

Most developing countries lacked the equipment and trained personnel to evaluate their water quality. Keckes, touring Mediterranean research institutes in late 1974 as a UNEP consultant, concluded:

> Only a few of the institutions and laboratories visited could as yet fully participate in the recommended programs, as these required a complex of field samples, facilities, analytical techniques, and other laboratory facilities, and the expertise necessary for a critical evaluation and interpretation of the data obtained. . . . A general lack of scientists trained for pollution research was a serious obstacle to the full participation in the recommended coordinated programmes of most of the scientific institutions and laboratories visited. . . . With the exception of a few well-equipped environment centres, there was a general lack of good and up-to-date analytical equipment in most of the scientific institutions and laboratories visited.[22]

Table 3.3 illustrates the limited scientific capability of the Mediterranean marine science institutions at this time. Of these institutions, the only ones with relevant facilities to test for heavy metals and pesticides—atomic absorption spectrophotometers and gas chromatographs—were in Egypt, France, Greece, Israel, Italy, Lebanon, Spain, and Yugoslavia. Egypt and Lebanon were the only LDCs with domestic monitoring capabilities. Other countries were unaware of the degree of their coastal pollution. Algeria was so opposed to controlling industrial pollution that a United Nations Development Programme (UNDP) consultant's demonstration of the extensive pollution of Algerian harbors was denied by the government.[23] It was only after Algerian marine scientists with access to the government could produce similar evidence were its implications accepted, and Algeria came to support the Med Plan.

The data in this table point unequivocally to the limited and differentiated scientific capability of the states outside Western Europe. The quality of such capability in different countries is of course extremely difficult to discern.

Table 3.3. Scientific Capabilities, 1974

Country	Number of Marine Research Centers	Number of Marine Scientists with a B.A. or Higher Equivalent Degree
Italy	31	–
France	28	433
Greece	17	–
Israel	13	59
Spain	8	91
Yugoslavia	7	–
Tunisia	6	–
Turkey	6	74
Egypt	5	–
Morocco	5	–
Algeria	3	11
Libya	3	–
Malta	3	10
Cyprus	2	8
Lebanon	2	–
Syria	1	–

Source: UNEP (1977); FAO (1977).

A listing of the countries' research fleets in table 3.4 presents a similar story of weak research capability outside France and Italy.

Prior to 1974, few studies of pollution had been conducted by the Mediterranean countries. Table 3.5 shows the number of studies on different pollutants conducted by different national laboratories, and the difference in focus depending upon economic development of the country. DCs studied the pollution problems associated with affluence, such as pollution by heavy metals from industrial emissions. LDCs studied problems associated with poverty, conducting, for example, microbiological studies of water polluted by municipal wastes.

There was no data available demonstrating the existence of widespread pollution from sources other than oil. Fishery yields had declined slightly in the eastern Mediterranean from 1968 to 1969, but this was generally viewed to be a result of widespread overfishing.[24] Algeria and Lebanon were the only Mediterranean countries reporting increases in the incidence of typhoid and paratyphoid.[25] Tourism revenues increased yearly during the 1970s, despite fears of polluted beaches.[26]

Table 3.4. Surface Research Vessels, 1977

Country	Number of Ships	Gross Tonnage
France	24	837 (5)[a]
Italy	18	184 (9)
Yugoslavia	8	416 (3)
Turkey	7	239 (5)
Egypt	4	692 (3)
Spain	4	
Cyprus	3	39 (1)
Morocco	3	−
Greece	2	45 (1)
Israel	2	139 (2)
Monaco	2	69 (2)
Tunisia	2	90 (1)
Algeria	1	−
Lebanon	1	−
Malta	1	−
Syria	1	−

Source: Borgese and Ginsburg (1980), pp. 162–64.

[a] Numbers in parentheses are numbers of ships included in the gross tonnage figure.

In response to mounting but unfocused concern, states proposed a number of regional arrangements. At a preparatory meeting for UNCHE in London in June 1971, Algeria, Cyprus, Egypt, France, Malta, Morocco, Spain, Turkey, and Yugoslavia, following Italian leadership, urged a regional agreement to control Mediterranean pollution from all sources.[27] At a subsequent meeting in November, Spain submitted a list of principles to control dumping from ships that was not discussed due to lack of time.[28] Delegates at the July 1971 *Pacem in Maribus* Conference in Malta also raised the problem of Mediterranean pollution. Although scientists discussed a draft Mediterranean agreement to control pollution prepared by Elisabeth Mann Borgese, they did not think that its acceptance by Mediterranean governments was likely at that time.

In September 1970 the IOC's Group of Experts on Long-Term Scientific Policy and Planning identified the Mediterranean, along with the Baltic, the North Sea, the Gulf of Mexico, and the Sea of Japan as areas that were potentially severely threatened by pollution.[29] In 1971 the IOC launched a joint research program called Cooperative Investigations in the Mediterranean (CIM) which was rejected by a major-

Table 3.5. Studies of Pollution Through 1974

SOURCES AND TYPES OF POLLUTION STUDIED

Country	Metals	Inorganic Wastes	Pesticides	Bacteria	Oil and Organic Wastes	Nutrients	Total
France	10	4	9	7	11	7	48
Yugoslavia	8	3	0	6	6	5	27
Spain	5	1	6	4	6	4	26
Italy	4	4	0	2	1	5	16
Israel	3	1	0	2	4	1	11
Greece	2	1	0	1	1	2	7
Egypt	2	0	0	0	1	3	6
Turkey	0	1	0	0	1	1	3
Lebanon	0	0	1	1	0	0	2
Cyprus	1	0	0	0	0	0	1
Tunisia	0	0	0	0	0	1	1
Total	35	15	16	22	31	29	148

Source: FAO/GFCM, "Research and Monitoring Facilities of Institutes in the Mediterranean Region," submitted to UNEP/IOC/GFCM/ICSEM, International Workshop on Marine Pollution in the Mediterranean, September 1974, pp. 13–26.

ity of Mediterranean coastal states as "symptomatic of an attempt by outside powers to use marine scientific research as a cover for resources exploitation and intelligence gathering" (Boxer 1982:328). In other words, they suspected that the CIM was a front for the Soviet Union or United States to gain data about the ocean floor that could be used for hiding submarines.

By 1972 Italy and France were promoting their own proposals for controlling regional oil pollution. In April 1972 Algeria, France, Spain, Italy, Libya, Malta, Monaco, Morocco, and Tunisia, as well as five non-Mediterranean states, met outside Paris and approved a French draft treaty to control oil pollution. The agreement divided the Mediterranean into longitudinal strips, and required states to inform their neighbors in case of oil spills and to offer assistance (Saliba 1978:175; Moore 1976:629–30; de Yturriaga Barberan 1976a:63–64). The French were interested in applying the Bonn Agreement for Cooperation in Dealing with Pollution of the North Sea by Oil to the Mediterranean, particularly to the Italians, who were not party to the Bonn agreement; they also wanted to start some form of action for cleaning up the Mediterranean. In July 1972 the Italians convened a meeting in

Rome to discuss the Criteria and Principles for Discharges of Matter or Energy Into Coastal Waters.

Both of these initiatives were overtaken by broader FAO and UNEP proposals. The French and Italian attempts broke down when subsequent scientific investigations revealed that they were too narrow in their focus on just oil, and that effective pollution control required participation by the entire region. The developing countries were suspicious of initiatives unilaterally developed by major regional powers.

In March 1973 Italy, Libya, Malta, and Tunisia met in Malta to discuss cooperation in the central Mediterranean, including the establishment of a surveillance system to prevent oil discharge from tankers (Saliba 1978:175). Concern was also increasing at subnational levels. In June 1973 the United Towns Organization, representing 132 Mediterranean cities and towns, adopted the "Beirut Charter" that urged governments to adopt a regional antipollution code. Oil pollution was frequently mentioned as a common pollution problem, and some French and Tunisian city representatives focused on the need to treat municipal waste.[30]

The Inter-Parliamentary Union, convened at the request of Italy, met in Rome in March and April 1974 for a special session on Mediterranean pollution. Participants mainly stressed oil pollution, and adopted recommendations urging member parliaments to sign and ratify existing IMCO marine pollution conventions.

Collective responses really began in 1972 with the presentation of the first systematic collection of information on the sources and extent of Mediterranean marine pollution. Such technical consensus moved the scope of concern from oil pollution and fisheries to a much broader range of sources and channels of pollution. The identification of specific pollutants to be controlled did not occur until protocols were negotiated several years later.

This overview emerged from a study commissioned by FAO's General Fisheries Council for the Mediterranean (GFCM). Its membership consists of fisheries directors from all the coastal states but Albania. Not surprisingly, the fishery directors were principally concerned about depleted yields of Mediterranean fisheries and the effect of pollution on living resources. At its tenth session in December 1969 in Rome the GFCM approved a questionnaire on pollution of the Mediterranean, in response to a request from the 1968 Rome Conference on Oil Pollution of the Seas. The Review on the State of Marine Pollution in the Mediterranean Sea[31] was presented to the eleventh session of the GFCM in March 1972 in Athens. Several of the consultants later appeared as delegates at Med Plan meetings.

The report's scope greatly exceeded GFCM's concern with living resources because it was drafted by consultants whose expertise included all forms of marine pollution. GFCM's concern with fishery depletion and overfishing would have mainly covered dumping from ships in open waters: land-based sources would have been of secondary concern. The report included a number of sources of pollution that could also possibly harm public health. The study included chapters on pollution from domestic sewage, industry, oil, pesticides, radioactive substances, heat, floating materials, suspended matter, and PCBs; it also summarized relevant national and international legislation. The study concluded that pollution in the Mediterranean had "reached a critical level." Principal sources of pollution were untreated and inadequately treated sewage and industrial effluents, as well as to oil pollution from tanker traffic. Principal channels of transmission for sewage and industrial wastes, in addition to marine dumping, were found to be rivers, marine outflows, and pipelines.

Different areas suffered from different pollutants. Most widely affected by domestic sewage were the northwestern basin (from the River Ebro in Spain to the River Arno in Italy) and the Lebanese and Israeli coasts. Industrial wastes affected the northwestern basin, the northern part of the Adriatic (Yugoslavia and Italy), the Tyrrhenian Sea (Italy), the Sea of Marmara (Turkey), and parts of the Aegean and the Levant Basin (Greece and Turkey). The report found that pesticides were not a major problem, and that most pollution was largely caused by—and affected—the industrialized countries of the northern basin.

The LDCs saw that talking about pollution would be a good way to resolve their concern with oil pollution; it was also a way to lay the blame for overall pollution on the northern countries. The FAO secretariat shelved discussion of land-based sources because it was too sensitive a topic, given the LDCs' opposition.

The GFCM report provided the only scientific information about the extent of pollution in the Mediterranean for the next five years. It identified the pollutants for subsequent discussions about pollution control, and provided the framework for debate.

After reviewing the report, the GFCM states called upon the FAO to take action for a "convention to control the discharge into the sea of pollutants that would affect its living resources, bearing in mind the economic effects of such control,"[32] as well as to develop pilot projects for monitoring pollution. The GFCM was still largely concerned only with fisheries and living resources. The FAO secretariat circulated a letter to governments in September 1972 asking what they wanted the convention to cover. The FAO fisheries and legal secretariat began to draft a treaty in February 1973. Regional consultations were held in December 1973, February 1974, and May 1974 to discuss the FAO "Guidelines Which Could Serve as a Basis for the Drafting of a Framework Convention on the Protection of the Marine Environment Against Pollution in the Mediterranean."[33]

This document was drafted by members of the FAO legal office, who lacked specific knowledge about the technical problems of marine pollution. In fact, they believed that ships were the principal source of Mediterranean pollution. They realized from the outset that effective regional treatment of pollution in the Mediterranean was outside the FAO's limited purview of living resources. They were members of the ecological epistemic community, however, and expressed, as individuals, their concern with environmental degradation and their belief that holistic measures were necessary to respond to or manage such degradation, even if they exceeded the jurisdictional boundaries of their own organization. They wanted to draft a comprehensive agreement that treated more than just threats to fisheries.

In forty-eight hectic hours in room B368 of the FAO building in Rome, they drafted principles that drew extensively from previous international treaties, supplemented by language controlling land-based sources of pollution. Their draft framework convention contained principles that extended far beyond their formal mission to protect living resources from oil pollution. They extended the coverage of the treaty to include the entire range of sources and channels of pollution. Their draft principles called for the control of pollution caused by dumping from ships and aircraft, pollution from ships, pollution resulting from the exploration and exploitation of the sea bed, and pollution from land-based sources, and asked for cooperation in dealing with emergencies and for the monitoring and exchange of information and technical assistance.

The states already involved in regional pollution control exercises tried to influence the draft. Italy and France argued that the draft should be consistent with their own regional pollution control initiatives. Libya wanted the convention to cover every conceivable discharge. Tunisia was interested in covering radioactive sources. In short, lacking specific information regarding the scope of the problem at the national or the international level, foreign ministry officials argued for including problems that they were already committed to dealing with domestically, or problems about which they had read, but about whose effects they were unsure.

The FAO initiative had absorbed all other Mediterranean pollution control efforts by mid 1974. From the GFCM report, countries were convinced of the need to act cooperatively, but also believed that the range of problems exceeded the FAO's narrow focus on living resources (Saliba 1978:175). UNEP, with its catalytic mission and comprehensive approach, was just the organization to conduct such an enterprise.

At the May FAO consultation France, Italy, and Spain suggested that the scope of the problem was too broad for the FAO's expertise, and should be entrusted to UNEP. Italy and Spain had been in contact with UNEP since the 1971 preparatory meetings for UNCHE with regard to creating a regional pollution control agreement. The North African states preferred staying within the FAO's jurisdiction, as the FAO's fisheries focus mirrored their concerns (de Yturriaga Barberan 1976a:66).

In August 1974 UNEP informed the FAO that UNEP, after receiving a formal proposal from Spain, had decided to convene a meeting of government representatives in December 1974 or January 1975 to discuss the preparation of a framework convention, based on the FAO consultations. The FAO thus lost the leadership and coordination of Mediterranean pollution control to UNEP, although the FAO continued to invite countries to meetings on monitoring and principles. The pace of preparations accelerated under UNEP leadership. This loss generated some lasting resentment among the FAO secretariat, although some of it was ameliorated because many of the key drafters of the FAO guidelines continued to work with UNEP in preparing the Action Plan, and FAO retained responsibility for many of the subsequent monitoring projects.

UNEP's first move was to mobilize scientific support for the exercise, and to elaborate the FAO's early efforts at devising a pollution monitoring program. In September 1974 UNEP cosponsored, with the GFCM, IOC, and ICSEM, the International Workshop on Marine Pollution in the Mediterranean. This technical meeting served to set the agenda for all subsequent pollution discussions. By getting agreement on an extremely comprehensive list of sources and channels of pollution, UNEP was free to later develop controls for a comprehensive list of pollutants.

Forty marine scientists from ten Mediterranean countries attended the meeting; they represented all of the marine sciences. The meeting identified the following pollution problems: the lack of domestic sewage treatment and subsequent disposal leading to high biological oxygen demand (BOD) and eutrophication; the lack of industrial discharge treatment leading to inorganic and organic pollution, primarily transmitted by rivers; pesticides, largely DDT, transmitted by runoff and atmospheric fallout; oil pollution from ships; and pathogenic organisms consumed by man (IOC 1975). The fundamental conclusion was familiar. Inadequate information existed to properly evaluate the extent of pollution in the Mediterranean, although participating scientists expressed the view that land-based sources and ships constituted the most important sources requiring control. Open waters were fairly unthreatened, but coastal waters "should be considered as being badly polluted."

This full list corresponded to UNEP's own belief that multiple sources and channels of pollution required regulation. It provided regional scientific consensus to present to the foreign ministries, thereby justifying UNEP's desires for an extremely comprehensive program for Mediterranean pollution control. Without making compromises on the determination of necessary monitoring and research projects, the attending scientists' consensual support for such a full range of sources and channels would not have been forthcoming.

The scientists also proposed a list of three monitoring studies and four research projects. The marine scientists agreed on the need for the following seven studies, but they were unable to order them by importance, because of competition between the disciplines for projects.

1. Baseline studies and monitoring of oil and petroleum hydrocarbons.

2. Baseline studies and monitoring of metals, particularly mercury.

3. Baseline studies and monitoring of DDT, PCBs, and other chlorinated hydrocarbons in marine organisms.

4. The effects of pollutants on marine organisms and their populations.

5. The effects of pollutants on marine communities and ecosystems.

6. The coastal transport of pollution.

7. A coastal water quality control project to correlate pollution of the sea and the pathogenic infections in seafood with public health.

This selection of studies reflects a compromise between different alliances at the meeting. The chairman, Stjepan Keckes, was the only one present with a coherent project in mind, which he had drafted beforehand. He had to balance a number of competing interests while seeking to infuse his own interests into the program. He wished to support studies of pesticides and heavy metals based on his own sense of what the major Mediterranean pollutants were. Having worked with radionuclides for much of his seventeen year professional career, he felt that they were not a serious problem at the time.[34] In addition, he was opposed to studies of coastal transportation of pollutants, believing that most problems were localized and could be monitored by local observations.

Keckes had to satisfy other interests as well. These interests were promoted by coalitions of scientists acting to obtain research funding for their disciplines; international organizations, whose missions overlapped with the focus of scientific disciplines; and foreign ministries. Although the foreign ministries were not represented at the meeting, their positions were well known to Keckes, who tried to incorporate them and also to keep everyone satisfied by the monitoring program. The coalitions formed around a concern with the effects of pollutants on living resources, public health, and amenities. Keckes satisfied all of the coalitions by including their research interests on a broad list. Ultimately, he had to include interests that he did not consider justified—the coastal transport of pollutants—in order to reach consensus.

Following his success in leading his peers, and with recommendations from advisors close to Peter Thacher, UNEP hired Keckes as a consultant to help develop the Med Plan. The following discussion describes the different groups at the 1974 meeting, and shows how each was satisfied.

Concern with living resources linked the FAO, national fishery directors, and marine biologists. This informal group was only interested in monitoring pollutants with adverse effects on fishery yields, such as some metals and organochlorine substances resistant to biological breakdown (pesticides and PCBs) coming from industry, agriculture, and tanker wastes. They were not seriously concerned with other industrial wastes, agricultural sprays, or organic wastes with possible public health effects. This group was satisfied by plans to study marine organisms and ecosystems (#4 from the above list) and marine communities and ecosystems (#5).

A public health approach linked WHO, the Egyptian foreign ministry, public health officials, and microbiologists. This group focused principally on pollutants that affect public health, such as organic wastes that contain microorganisms and salmonella, and that could contribute to illnesses resulting from eating tainted seafood, to infections, and to communicable diseases contracted in recreational waters. A public health approach also included concern with inorganic industrial wastes, whose ingestion could pose a threat to public health. This group looked at industrial and municipal sewage as the sources of pollution, and promoted the construction of sewerage and sewage treatment plants as a solution. This group was satisfied by plan to study coastal water quality (#7).

A concern with amenities, or the appearance of the seashore, united foreign ministries and IMO. Monitoring coastal oil pollution appealed to this group, as oil on beaches had elicited regional concern in the first place. This group's policy concerns lay with regulating tanker traffic, and plans for the study of oil and hydrocarbons (#1).

Other interests present at the meeting were voiced by marine chemists and by a broad group concerned with currents and the regional transport of pollutants. The marine chemists were interested in heavy metals in seawater. Although coming from all around the basin, their disciplinary interests in heavy metals coincided with the interests of the French and Italian foreign ministries in controlling industrial and municipal wastes. They naturally gravitated to Keckes' own position, and were satisfied by the commitment to study heavy metals and pesticides (#2 and #3), which Keckes detailed indirectly through designing a broad structure of monitoring studies satisfactory to the other groups. Keckes did not want to include studies of the coastal transport of pollutants, but a group consisting of marine geologists, physical oceanographers, and the IOC did. Unable to sell the whole program without appeasing them, Keckes incorporated their concerns into plans to study the coastal transport of pollutants (#6) and to do some work with oil on beaches (#1).

UNEP later cemented these diverse approaches and interests by adopting a broad definition of pollution, developed by the Joint Group of Experts on the Scientific Aspects of Marine Pollution (GESAMP) in 1969, which incorporated everyone's interests:

"Pollution" means the introduction by man, directly or indirectly, of substances or energy into the marine environment resulting in such deleterious effects as harm to living resources, hazards to human health, hindrance to marine activities including fishing, impairment of quality for use of sea-water and reduction of amenities. (United Nations 1971:53)

Although this definition may be "unscientific" (Tomczak 1984; McIntyre 1985) insofar as it does not provide objective standards by which to recognize deleterious effects, hazards, or hindrances, it effectively combined the competing interests of the developing countries in health effects and oil pollution, of the developed countries in amenities and oil pollution, and of the existing FAO initiative on living resources. It even includes thermal and radioactive discharges from nuclear power plants. UNEP's own ecological outlook enabled it to offer such a broad definition. UNEP pushed the definition at the 1975 Barcelona conference to adopt the Med Plan, where it satisfied all parties, although Algeria wished to add "abusive fishing" to the list of causes.

CONCLUSION

Concern about the implications of Mediterranean pollution mounted between the late 1960s and 1974. Initial concern was focused on oil pollution resulting from tanker traffic. Subsequent studies and conferences demonstrated the need for managing a more comprehensive range of sources and channels of pollution, including land-based sources, agricultural runoff, and marine dumping, as well as pollution transmitted by rivers and through the atmosphere. The legal office of the Food and Agriculture Organization drafted a treaty in 1974 that included this broad coverage. Later in 1974 UNEP was invited by the Mediterranean governments to direct regional efforts to coordinate marine pollution control. Soliciting input from forty of the region's marine scientists, UNEP developed seven monitoring and research projects which encompassed a comprehensive set of sources and types of pollution. UNEP also developed pilot projects that would demonstrate the need to control a wide range of pollutants from multiple sources: then transmitted through the atmosphere and by rivers as well as those dumped directly into the Mediterranean. A broad definition of pollution cemented a comprehensive approach to Mediterranean pollution control.

FOUR

The Adoption of the Mediterranean Action Plan and the Development of More Comprehensive Measures To Control Pollution

Following its preemption of the Med Plan adoption proceedings, UNEP proceeded to develop a program that was much broader in scope than prior efforts. UNEP added more environmental assessment, legislation, and integrated management directed at ensuring the long-term protection of the Mediterranean and seeking to develop an "environmental consciousness" in the region. Under UNEP's guidance, the Med Plan grew in scope over the following ten years.

In October 1974 UNEP convened a high-level task force, composed of high-ranking Mediterranean government officials acting in their individual capacities and representatives from the FAO, IMCO, and WHO, to assist in designing the program. The government representatives were to provide advice concerning national preferences and to promote the program at home. France and Italy were represented by ambassadors from their foreign ministries; Algeria, Egypt, Lebanon,

Malta, and Yugoslavia provided oceanographers or public health experts.

The task force considered the desirability and feasibility of preparing additional protocols on land-based sources, pollution from ships, marine dumping, cooperation in cases of emergencies, seabed exploration and exploitation, and research and monitoring. They agreed that, although scientifically justified, protocols for land-based sources and dumping were too politically sensitive to get the quick approval that UNEP desired for the launching of the program. Seabed exploration was delayed pending the completion of work on the Law of the Sea. Pollution by ships was already covered by IMCO's 1973 MARPOL convention, so oil pollution was largely left to IMCO (M'Goningle and Zacher 1979:70–71). IMCO was asked to draft a protocol for oil spill emergencies. The FAO was already drafting a framework convention. WHO began to draft general principles for a protocol on land-based sources, although it would not be discussed for several years. Spain was asked to continue preparing a draft protocol on dumping, which it had presented to the UNCHE preparation meetings. Other agencies were consulted for the development of seven monitoring and research projects, in keeping with the guidelines developed at the September 1974 workshop.

The Med Plan was adopted at Barcelona in February 1975 by sixteen governments.[1] Designed by UNEP, the action plan is a framework that establishes areas in which countries may develop projects to control various aspects of pollution. It grafted UNEP's comprehensive approach and desires onto the existing regional initiatives. All of the littoral countries' interests were still represented in the Med Plan, as were additional components relating to UNEP's desire to promote integrated economic planning to regional planners. The Med Plan has four components, meant to be mutually reinforcing:

1. The integrated planning of the development and management of the resources of the Mediterranean Basin.

2. A coordinated pollution monitoring and research program in the Mediterranean.

3. A framework convention and related protocols with technical annexes for the protection of the Mediterranean environment.

4. Institutional and financial implications of the action plan.

The integrated planning component emerged from UNEP's holistic focus, and was closest to the designers' hearts. It was intended to relate problems of marine pollution to patterns of land use and long-term demographic and economic forces in the littoral countries. Senior UNEP officials hoped to use this section to encourage Mediterranean economic planners to incorporate concern with environmental consequences of development projects into their economic planning. Most Mediterranean officials were mystified by this component, however, and they criticized the project document for being excessively abstract and conceptual. They were more interested in the direct causes and effects of pollution. France was the only country that expressed interest in integrated planning, or understood its use, due to its own experiences with prospective planning. Satisfied with the rest of the Med Plan, the delegates at the Barcelona conference were willing to accept this idiosyncratic proposal of UNEP's.

The assessment component (monitoring and research) was included in order to generate data on the actual state of pollution in the region. As such, it was more a monitoring proposal than a research proposal, although later it came to include more research. The projects adopted at Barcelona were the same seven proposals accepted the previous September. This assessment component, called Med Pol, received the greatest support by governments, as most states did not know the state of pollution in the Mediterranean, and their greatest priority was ascertaining the degree of pollution before adopting concrete measures for controlling it.

The legal components were intended to support the already ongoing drafting exercises under UNEP's supervision. The parties endorsed the need for legal arrangments for regional pollution control, including the FAO's preparatory work for a draft framework convention as well as the IMCO and Spanish drafts to control pollution by oil and marine dumping.

Countries disagreed about the thrust of the program and about what would constitute appropriate supporting institutional arrangements. At Barcelona, LDCs argued for a program that would enhance their marine science capabilities. They wanted a regional operational center that would perform both a switchboard function for the transmission of information and coordination and other executing functions, as well as actually providing technical assistance and transferring pollution monitoring equipment to the LDCs. They also supported the development of comprehensive regional arrangements for pollution control which would be legally binding on the participants. Spain, Italy, and France, already possessing effective marine laboratories, wanted only minimal, flexible, and mostly subregional cooperation schemes, and preferred a weak organization that would only facilitate information exchange. They thought that further responsibilities should be purely voluntary and bilateral. As a result of these disagreements, the meeting approved stronger monitoring and assessment proposals than the DCs wished, but the supporting administrative arrangements remained unspecific. UNEP was charged with devising some administrative supports for the action plan, and with overseeing and coordinating the projects within each component of the plan.

Mostapha Tolba averted conflict between Arabs and Israelis by extracting a promise from the Arab states that they would not challenge Israel, in exchange for Israel delegates maintaining a very low profile. Both groups have since abided by these ground rules. The PLO was not invited to the meeting. The United States attended as an observer, but did not attend any subsequent meetings after being convinced that the Sixth Fleet would remain unaffected by Med Plan arrangements.

Certain tacit rules of diplomatic behavior prevail at official Med Plan meetings, which have diffused traditional sources of interstate conflict in the Mediterranean. The Turkish delegation commonly submits a letter to the UNEP secretariat protesting the Greek presence on Cyprus, which the secretariat duly lays out on a side table, and is ignored by all parties. Syria ratified the 1976 Barcelona Convention with the qualification that their ratification did not constitute a recognition of Israeli sovereignty. No delegates have criticized other countries' polluting habits, in part due to an implicit recognition that all are guilty, in part due to the future oriented nature of the negotiations, which have sought to gather information about the quality of the Mediterranean and to develop pollution control measures, rather than to allot blame.

Certain political considerations prevailed over efforts to control pollution. Unwilling to have an effective USSR presence through the participation of the Black Sea states of Bulgaria and Rumania, delegates eliminated the Black Sea and rivers flowing into the Mediterranean from the area covered by the agreement. The Mediterranean was defined as the area between the Strait of Gibraltar and the southern limits of the Strait of Dardanelles between the Mehmetcik and Kumkale lighthouses in Turkey. Such a definition excludes nonlittoral states with rivers that feed into the Mediterranean from compliance with the convention, such as Portugal, Switzerland, and the Sudan, and thus fails to manage some sources of pollution, including the heavily polluted Gulf of Izmit and the Sea of Marmara. Greek and Turkish

delegates opposed locating any institutions in each other's countries.
The components developed at different paces. Each will be discussed individually, and their interplay will be noted in passing.

MONITORING AND RESEARCH

The assessment component (Med Pol) got underway quickly after the first Barcelona conference. The seven projects were already being designed and coordinated with eight other specialized agencies. Actual studies were conducted by laboratories nationally. Virtually no joint studies were undertaken, although there were numerous scientific exchanges in order to train scientists and technicians to conduct common styles of pollution monitoring. The lead laboratories consolidated these nationally generated findings into reports, with support from international agencies. Day-to-day coordination of the Med Pol projects was carried out by the FAO, WHO, and IOC. UNEP hoped to complete the monitoring program in two years, but it took five years to complete, and even then the results were mixed. After the completion of the first phase of monitoring in 1981, states undertook a second phase of monitoring and research, to be completed by 1991.

This component contributed to the perpetuation of the Med Plan in a number of ways. It sealed the alliance between UNEP and marine scientists, it rewarded governments for participating in the separate legal discussions by providing a symbolic recognition of their scientific stature through the choice of lead laboratories, and it created a scientific consensus which demonstrated the need to treat a broad range of sources, channels, and types of pollution. UNEP has taken care to cater to the interests of the region's marine scientists. Thus, research has been as important an element as pollution monitoring. The quality of findings may be poor, but participation is fairly active, and this feeds back into support by the marine scientists and their governments for other components of the Med Plan. UNEP's greatest difficulty in this regard is managing competition for projects between scientists from different disciplines.

Adding to the seven projects conducted under Phase I of Med Pol, six other projects were approved after the 1976 Barcelona meeting. Only two of them were completed.[2] A study of land-based sources (Med X) was completed in conjunction with the discussion on the Land-Based Sources Protocol, and intercalibration exercises were conducted between the national institutions participating in Med Pol.

The contracting parties later approved biogeochemical studies of selected pollutants in the open waters of the Mediterranean, studies of the role of sedimentation in polluting the Mediterranean, studies of the input of pollutants from the atmosphere, and the modeling of marine systems. None of them were completed due to their complexity and the lack of money for their support. France blocked funding for studies that would generate data that might undercut its position at ongoing meetings on the Land-Based Sources Protocol regarding which pollutants should be covered and the pathways by which they are transmitted.

Med Pol's greatest impact may have come from the Med X report. It compellingly demonstrated the need for dealing with land-based pollutants and pollution transmitted by rivers. It set the agenda for the following years, and reinforced UNEP's own contentions for the need to control land-based sources of pollution. In this case, scientific consensus overcame unwillingness by the foreign ministries to deal with the more expensive and politically more contentious land-based sources.

In September 1977 UNEP presented a report on pollutants from land-based sources in the Mediterranean to the Med Plan parties, the first of the scientific studies of the extent of pollution in the Mediterranean to provide concrete data about land-based sources. The report was necessarily haphazard. All information was drawn from secondary sources. Researchers had been unable to find national data on industrial emissions, so they approximated levels of production based on scanty production and employment figures and extrapolated emissions based on figures for specific Western industries, where economists had already calculated pollution loads from certain industries producing at given levels of output. Nonetheless, the evaluating experts from governments concluded that the study reduced the degree of uncertainty about the state of pollution in the Mediterranean from three orders of magnitude to one.

Med X was coordinated by WHO under contract from UNEP. Its purpose was to inventory all major sources of pollutants in the coastal area, to assess their nature and quantity, to assess the nature and quantity of river-transmitted wastes, and to review current waste disposal and management practices. WHO solicited reports from WHO, ECE, UNIDO, FAO, UNESCO, and IAEA on different components of pollution in the area.

Med X produced four findings of major importance which guided subsequent activities of the Med Plan. It demonstrated that industrial and municipal wastes exceeded oil pollution as the principal problems in the Mediterranean; 85 percent of all pollutants in the Mediterranean were found to originate on land; 80–85 percent of land-based pollutants were transmitted to the Mediterranean by rivers; and over 80 percent of all municipal sewage entering the Mediterranean was untreated. In fact, it was discovered that much of the oil in the Mediterranean comes from automobile owners who drain their oil pans into municipal sewers.

Rivers were found to transmit the majority of monitored pollutants: 40 percent of biological oxygen demand (BOD), 35 percent of chemical oxygen demand (COD), 81 percent of phosphorous, 75 percent of nitrogen, 70 percent of detergents, 90 percent of mercury, 58 percent of lead, 50 percent of chromium, 67 percent of zinc, 100 percent of organochlorine pesticides, 84 percent of tritium radioactivity, and 37 percent of other radionuclides.[3] Furthermore, the principal polluters, as everyone had already suspected, were the industrialized states in the northwestern basin: Italy, France, and Spain. The northwestern basin, drained by the Rhone (France and Switzerland), Ebro and Llobregat (Spain), and Arno (Italy), was found to contain 29 percent of the Mediterranean's total organic matter, 36 percent of nutrients, 25 percent of detergents, 31 percent of phenols, 25 percent of mercury, 28 percent of lead, 36 percent of chromium, and 21 percent of zinc. The Adriatic, serving largely as a refuse area for Italian industry in the northeastern valleys drained by the Adige River, held 20–25 percent of the Mediterranean's organic matter, 25 percent of nutrients, 27 percent of detergents, 13 percent of phenols, 32 percent of mercury, 30 percent of lead, and 35 percent of zinc. None of the other regions exceeded 15 percent of the total pollution load of the Mediterranean, and most fell below 10 percent.

Although there was pronounced pressure from the agencies involved in producing the Med X report to control land-based sources of pollution, delegates from foreign ministries at the meeting to approve the report were concerned that the release of such data would harm their exports of fish products and their tourism appeal. Scientists attending the meeting as delegates had been advised to avoid allowing their countries to be clearly identified as major sources of pollution. Consequently, they amalgamated the national findings into ten regions based on FAO fishery presentations, so that no individual country could be targeted as a major polluter. The data was also presented using pie diagrams for logarithmic data, which made it virtually impossible to visually differentiate between the relative amount of pollution in different regions. Thus, the scientists deployed their technical consensus to commit their governments to controlling yet another source of pollution, while avoiding pointing the finger at any particular country as the source of such pollution.

Given the fact that countries had already committed themselves to doing something about Mediterranean pollution by ratifying the Barcelona convention, the scientific evidence firmly placed land-based sources of pollution on the agenda. LDC foreign affairs officials could no longer ignore the issue at international meetings, although they were not about to change their domestic positions about controlling industries and agricultural spraying. In June a group of sanitary engineers concluded at a WHO workshop in Athens on coastal water pollution control that "the total expenditure necessary for the construction and operation of facilities for the collection, treatment and disposal of liquid wastes in the Mediterranean region is likely to be not less than the equivalent of US $5,000,000,000 over the next 10–20 years" (WHO 1977:7). Keckes estimated that it would cost two to three times as much to include industrial waste, so that thereafter the number of $US 10–15 billion was widely bandied about as the likely cost for complying with the needs for cleaning up the Mediterranean. It is very doubtful that any countries had any other idea of how much it would cost. Because the Med X study identified rivers as the principal sources of Mediterranean pollution, the costs of cleaning up the Mediterranean would be spread over the entire territory of littoral states, rather than just the coastal region.

Med Pol Phase I

Phase I was a qualified success. The only project to yield results consistent with the goals of Med Pol—to promote the progress of a program on controlling pollution in the Mediterranean—was the coastal water quality study, which helped set emission standards for shellfish and bathing waters. The first two years were spent organizing: distributing necessary equipment and training personnel. It took one year to begin producing results, as UNEP had to teach many LDC scientists how to use the equipment, how to incorporate it into their labs, and how to keep it properly maintained. Intercalibration exercises revealed that many results were not statistically useful.[4] In 1981, evaluating the first phase of Med Pol, executive director Tolba identified three remaining difficulties preventing the full understanding of the state of pollution in the Mediterranean: it was not known if the areas successfully monitored during the first phase were representative of the rest of the Mediterranean; "present intercalibration exercises did not yet lead to fully satisfactory quality control of data"; and many reports from the first phase were filed too late or in the wrong format.[5]

Few studies were completed. What reliable findings did emerge did not reinforce the initial concern about the Mediterranean, leading Tolba to recant slightly the earlier gloom-and-doom prophesies. In 1978 he stated:

> The Mediterranean Sea is neither dead nor dying—but the slow, progressive deterioration of the environmental quality of the whole Mediterranean Basin, provoked by man's ever-increasing and often ill-timed activities, could only result in a situation which finally had to be confronted by a cooperative effort of all Mediterranean countries.[6]

Preliminary analysis of the Med Pol Phase I results indicated that the Mediterranean was not dying, as anticipated by ecologists in the early 1970s, but was merely on a decaying trend.

In 1984 the FAO released a study of mercury concentrations in the Mediterranean which revealed that the overall population was not in danger of mercury poisoning; only fishermen and their families were potentially at risk.[7] WHO studies of bathing waters, shellfish, and shellfish-growing waters found that a very high percentage of monitored shellfish demonstrated some form of microbial pollution.[8] Roughly 80 percent of monitored beaches were deemed satisfactory for recreational purposes.[9] Although hard data were absent, pollution from sewage was presumed to be extensive. Such findings undermined the sense of urgency imparted by earlier studies.

Med Pol did yield some positive results. Through 1987, forty-six technical manuals detailed reference methods for subsequent monitoring and research were produced and distributed, largely in English. Although these were valuable, the senior scientists involved in their drafting were distracted from conducting research. The LDCs received sophisticated equipment, as well as extensive training in its use and in standardized analytic procedures, which satisfied the foreign ministries' desire for technology transfer. Direct benefits for the Mediterranean states are presented in table 4.1.

Egypt and Algeria did extremely well. Eighty-four laboratories from sixteen countries participated, with many in LDCs. The total cost of Med Pol Phase I was estimated at $US 17.4 million: $3.5 million from UNEP, $1.4 from other UN agencies, and the rest from the national institutions, although mostly in staff time rather than equipment.

Med Pol Phase II

A second phase was initiated in 1981. Whereas the first phase of monitoring was supposed to ascertain the degree of pollution in the Mediterranean, the second phase aimed at determining the effects of Med Plan measures and generating findings directly relevant to setting standards for the control of land-based sources. Focus shifted from general environmental assessment to the provision of specific information relevant to the implementation of established rules. To satisfy its marine science constituency, UNEP developed projects with more research including more indicators than in Phase I. In 1984 countries also allocated $US 180,000 to study "jellyfish invasions" of Mediterranean beaches.[10]

The topics for research and monitoring in the second phase were:[11]

1. The development and testing of sampling and analytic techniques for monitoring marine pollutants.

2. The development of reporting formats required by the Dumping, Emergency, and Land-Based Sources Protocols.

3. Formulation of the scientific rationale for the environmental quality criteria.

4. Epidemiological studies related to environmental quality criteria.

5. Guidelines and criteria for the application of the Land-Based Sources Protocol.

6. Research on oceanographic processes.

7. Research on toxicity, persistence, bioaccumulation, carcinogenicity, and mutagenicity.

8. Research on eutrophication and concomitant plankton blooms.

9. The study of pollution-induced ecosystems modifications.

10. The study of the effects of thermal discharges on coastal organisms and ecosystems.

11. The study of biogeochemical cycles of specific pollutants, particularly those relevant to human health.

Table 4.1. Distribution of Benefits from Med Pol Phase I
(1975–1982)

Country	Total Assistance from Med Pol to Participants (in $US)	GC[a]	AAS[b]
Yugoslavia	249,616	2	2
Egypt	201,566	2	1
Turkey	186,657	2	2
Algeria	129,905	1	1
Israel	128,275	1	0
Malta	107,883	1	1
Italy	80,700	0	0
Greece	80,621	1	0
Cyprus	77,925	1	1
Tunisia	54,505	1	0
Morocco	53,585	1	1
Spain	49,113	0	1
Lebanon	38,210	0	1
France	25,560	0	0
Monaco	6,635	0	0
Syria	0	0	0
Libya	0	0	0
Albania	0	0	0

Source: UNEP/WG 46/3, updated to 2/81 with figures from the Athens headquarters unit.

[a] GC = gas chromatograph.

[b] AAS = atomic absorption spectrophotometer.

[c] Other = other instruments worth more than $5,000 apiece.

12. The study of pollutant transfer processes (a) at river/sea and air/sea interfaces, (b) by sedimentation, and (c) through the straits linking the Mediterranean with other seas.

Monitoring in Phase II was to be supported virtually entirely by national research institutions, at an annual cost of $US 10 million. The Med Plan provided $627,650 between 1982 and 1984 for research projects. By the end of 1984, 102 research projects had been carried out by 70 research centers in sixteen Mediterranean states. Many countries were slow to identify institutions to participate, but by 1988 most countries were actively participating.[12]

Other[c]	Trainees Sent to Other Labs	Number of National Institutions in Med Pol Projects	Number of Research Contracts Signed Between UNEP and National Institutions
5	21	5	23
1	20	2	12
2	21	5	12
1	3	1	4
1	7	7	12
2	5	2	8
0	8	17	19
2	15	13	24
1	4	1	5
1	11	3	5
0	5	3	5
0	10	8	13
2	7	1	4
0	0	12	15
0	0	1	1
0	0	1	0
0	0	0	0
0	0	0	0

All in all, although providing only limited information about the actual quality of the Mediterranean, the assessment component served to transfer much monitoring technology to the LDCs and to train many LDC technicians in monitoring and research techniques. The Med X report of 1977 provided consensual support for UNEP's efforts to develop more comprehensive efforts at pollution control.

LEGAL COMPONENT

The legal component of the Med Plan was underway by February 1976 in Barcelona, as twelve states signed the umbrella Convention for the Protection of the Mediterranean Sea Against Pollution (the Barcelona convention), the Protocol for the Prevention of Pollution of the Mediterranean Sea by Dumping from Ships and Aircraft (the dumping protocol), and the Protocol Concerning Cooperation in Combating Pollution of the Mediterranean Sea by Oil and Other Harmful Substances in Cases of Emergency (the emergency protocol). With the Med Plan itself, the Barcelona convention served as the framework for subsequent pollution control efforts.

The Barcelona Convention and Protocols

The Barcelona convention laid out states' general commitment to protect the Mediterranean from pollution and specified forms of pollution that countries would seek to control. It commits states to a continuing program encompassing the development of future legal agreements to control pollution by dumping from ships and aircraft, from discharges from ships, and from land-based sources; to cooperate in dealing with oil spill emergencies; and to control pollution from the exploration and exploitation of the continental shelf and the seabed and its topsoil. It further provides for scientific monitoring and research and scientific and technological cooperation.

The emergency protocol commits states to notify each other in case of an oil spill and to cooperate in the cleanup. The Regional Oil Combating Centre (ROCC) was established in Malta to coordinate action in case of oil spills, conduct seminars on ways to control oil spills, and disperse information on new technologies. Turkey unsuccessfully contended for the ROCC headquarters, but lost out to a well-planned Maltese campaign which included distributing a pamphlet testifying to Malta's ideal location and credentials for hosting such a center. The countries also adopted a resolution encouraging states to ratify the 1973 MARPOL convention, which forbids tankers from releasing oily wastes into the sea. Countries are to install deballasting facilities to accept oily wastes from tankers using the ports, at an estimated cost of $US 145 million for the region (IMCO 1979).

The dumping protocol commits states to ban the dumping of certain substances (the "black list") and issue permits for the dumping of less hazardous substances (the "grey list"). Spain's draft list of substances and the formulation of two lists of substances that were to be controlled reproduced the style and list used in the 1972 Oslo and London dumping conventions. At the Barcelona meeting the delegates agreed to add acid and alkali compounds to the draft black list, and selenium, antimony, and synthetic organic chemicals to the grey list.

Its adoption was fairly amicable, as was the adoption of the Barcelona convention and the emergency protocol. There was only one hitch with the dumping protocol. At the time of the meeting France and Italy were involved in a vituperative exchange concerning the control of titanium dioxide wastes that the Italian chemical manufacturer Montedison was dumping off Corsica. The Italian consulate in Bastia, Corsica was bombed by French activists. France wanted these emissions banned, while Italy opposed their inclusion on either list. A compromise was reached by omitting any direct reference to titanium dioxide or wastes from the aluminum or paint industry, and referring instead to acid and alkaline compounds. The vague phrasing of "compounds in such composition and in such quantity that may seriously impair the quality of sea-water"—an evaluation which could not be made at the time—was used for the black list. France and Italy agreed to refer the problem to the EEC, which subsequently issued the Directive on the Emissions of Titanium Dioxide Wastes.

In 1979 states developed standardized forms for issuing dumping permits as well as an annual reporting system to report on the number of permits issued and the amount of wastes dumped annually. Through 1984 only France, Israel, Italy, Monaco, and Yugoslavia had submitted reports to the Med Plan secretariat.[13]

At the Barcelona conference, Morocco proposed the creation of an Interstate Guarantee Fund to compensate states for the costs of cleaning up in case of emergencies. France fiercely opposed this proposal, maintaining that it would be difficult to determine whether countries would deserve to be compensated for deliberate, accidental, or background cases of pollution. Rather than being included in the framework convention, the Interstate Guarantee Fund was adopted by the conference as a resolution, with the reservation of France (de Yturriaga Barberan 1976a:88).

The European Economic Community (EEC) was accepted as a signatory state after a long contentious debate between EEC members France and Italy, and Yugoslavia and the Arab states, who opposed their acceptance. The LDCs did not want the EEC to participate as a supranational actor. Having used up many diplomatic resources to achieve signatory status, the EEC only played a minor role in subsequent discussions.

The states quickly ratified the Barcelona convention and protocols, which entered into force in February 1978. By this time work was underway on the monitoring and research projects, providing an input of accepted scientific knowledge that stimulated action on protocols to control more sources of pollution. UNEP played a minor role in the Barcelona discussions, as states were dealing with relatively uncontentious forms of pollution. As they came to deal with the more difficult land-based sources, UNEP's influence in the form of agreements grew as it authorized the drafting of the protocol and supplied information to delegates in order to persuade them to support it.

The Land-Based Sources Protocol

With the Land-Based Sources Protocol, the Mediterranean countries directed their attention to controlling a new and important source of pollution. The treaty came to cover the entire gamut of land-based pollutants, banning a number of agricultural compounds used as fungicides, biocides, and pesticides (organohalogens, organophosphorous compounds, and organotins); it also covered some industries (various heavy metals and industrial compounds), thermal pollutants from energy generation, and municipal wastes. The protocol also came to include pollutants transmitted by rivers and through the atmosphere, and added many pollutants to the ones already regulated on the grey list of the dumping protocol. By supporting this new treaty countries agreed to adopt new industrial and agricultural practices, as well as building sewage systems.

UNEP was largely responsible for determining the range of pollutants covered by the protocol and the channels by which they are transmitted. Allocation of the cost of their control was accomplished through political compromise, although UNEP also played a significant role in suggesting the specifics of such compromises.

UNEP had commissioned WHO to draft a treaty governing land-based sources of pollution. In keeping with UNEP's own desires, the draft treaty was very comprehensive. The draft consisted of a legal text and technical annexes. The text discusses the range of application of the agreement, while the annexes identify specific substances. Agreement on the two parts progressed by different processes and included different actors. The legal text was developed from precedents of international agreements governing land-based sources of pollution, and was discussed by legal representatives from foreign affairs ministries. The technical annexes were discussed by scientists at concurrent meetings, which went much more smoothly than the political talks, as the marine scientists resorted to technical consensus to determine whether specific pollutants were hazardous to human health and how long it takes them to degrade in the environment.

Negotiations took three years. Countries first considered the draft protocol at a meeting in Athens in February 1977. Delegates were initially very leery about the principles, and, without the attention generated by the Med X report, would have been unlikely to continue the exercise. Legal discussions occurred in October 1977 in Venice, in January 1978 in Monaco, in June 1979 in Geneva, and at the final May 1980 Conference of Plenipotentiaries in Athens.

LDCs and DCs had recurring disagreements. Disputes revolved around the question of which channels of transmission would be covered; whether the protocol would cover new or existing installations; and whether pollution would be regulated by ambient or emission standards.

From the outset France and Italy were committed to following the existing EEC directives, which specified which emissions required treatment and the substances whose emission was banned. Officials from the Italian Ministry of Foreign Affairs' Office of International Organizations and the French Foreign Ministry met biannually to coordinate their positions. Greece, knowing that it would soon enter the EEC, essentially followed their position. Because Greek delegates had little influence from their foreign ministry, they were able to act as a broker between the conflicting parties during negotiations. The LDCs were initially extremely suspicious that the protocol was merely a ruse to constrain their economic development by introducing additional production costs to their industrialization plans. Turkey and Algeria were sensitive to the added possibility that the protocol would serve as a nontariff trade barrier. At the meeting of the contracting parties in Monaco in February 1978 Algeria slowed discussions by objecting to every paragraph and forcing delegates to justify compromises they had made at two previous meetings.

WHO's 1976 draft suggested the inclusion of the transport of pollution by rivers and through the atmosphere under its scope and geographic coverage, following the 1974 Convention on the Protection of the Marine Environment of the Baltic Sea Area. The draft also suggested that a subsequent annex be developed to deal with the airborne transmission of pollutants, although it acknowledged the difficulty of controlling it. France and Italy were opposed to the inclusion of atmospheric transmission because they felt that insufficient data existed about this problem, and that scientific knowledge was inadequate to identify sources that might be thousands of miles away, in the territory of nonparticipating states. Having the largest industrial sectors, these countries would also be the largest producers of pollutants emitted through smokestacks. Yugoslavia and Tunisia argued for the inclusion of this annex at the 1977 Athens meeting, and Malta, in a letter to UNEP in 1978, expressed its support for the inclusion of atmospheric transport. They argued that the protocol's coverage would be incomplete without reference to atmospheric paths of transmission, especially from petrochemical industries and agricultural spraying. They felt that the necessary findings would come from Med Pol studies.

France and Italy also opposed the protocol's coverage of rivers, as the Rhone and Po are major sources of Mediterranean pollution. Technical consensus also extended to resolve some political difficulties. French and Italian opposition to the coverage of river-transmitted pollutants was untenable in the face of the 1977 Med X findings of the extensive pollution transmitted to the Mediterranean by rivers.

UNEP ensured that discussions could continue on an annex for atmospheric transport, in spite of French opposition. In 1979 France rejected funding studies of the airborne transmission of pollutants, so there could be no technical basis for such an annex. In turn, UNEP submitted the exercise to GESAMP's Working Group on the Interchange of Pollutants Between the Atmosphere and the Ocean, which later produced the report titled "Atmospheric Transport of Contaminants Into the Mediterranean Region."[14] In this instance UNEP was able to offset state power through the use of international institutional channels.

The draft protocol contained articles applying to existing sources (Article 3) and to new installations (Article 6). The industrialized countries thought that this distinction was indispensable; it required different timetables for compliance for new installations and older ones. The DCs, which had older facilities, argued that many of these should be excluded from regulation, or should at least be subject to a more lenient schedule for compliance, since they would soon be decommissioned due to their inefficient production. The LDCs felt that such a distinction would give unfair competitive advantage to older European firms that would not have to immediately face the retrofitting costs sustained by plants under construction in LDCs. Delegates and the UN agencies were also unable to agree on a definition of a new installation, as it was necessary to differentiate between factories that were planned or contracted for, or for which construction had actually begun.

The biggest point of dissension involved how the substances should be controlled: by emission controls, as preferred by the Europeans, or through the ambient standards advocated by the South. The crux of the protocol lies in Articles 5 and 6, which committed the parties to "eliminate pollution" by the substances listed in Annex 1 (the black list) and to "strictly limit pollution" by the substances listed in Annex 2 (the grey list). The LDCs, sensitive to the possible economic effects of banning the emission of a number of substances from their industries, argued that their coasts, because they historically had experienced less industrial pollution, were better able to assimilate emissions; hence the protocol should make reference to the capacity of the receiving environment to assimilate wastes. The industrialized countries, with greater coastal pollution, advocated the adoption of emission standards rather than the ambient standards supported by the LDCs. France and Italy were already committed to following emission standards under the EEC Directive on Pollution Caused by Certain Dangerous Substances Discharged Into the Aquatic Environment of the Community.[15]

Agreement on which substances would be covered in the annexes was reached earlier in the negotiating process, by recourse to accepted scientific information, which was supplied by UNEP. Substances were chosen by their "toxicity, persistence and bioaccumulation." Hence, the drafters—marine scientists and ecologists—were entirely responsible for choosing the parameters by which pollutants would be identified. Whereas many problems in the text were not resolved until the actual Conference of Plenipotentiaries, the technical annexes were effectively completed at the June 1979 Geneva meeting because the scientists could agree relatively easily based on these criteria.

The WHO draft had drawn its list of substances for the two annexes from the existing EEC directives and the 1974 Paris Convention for the Prevention of Marine Pollution from Land-Based Sources. In an attempt at simplicity, WHO initially listed only the six elements contained in the Paris convention. However, at the insistence of France, Italy, and Spain that the annex be compatible with the EEC directive, the list was rapidly expanded to ten and then to the full twenty elements covered by the EEC directive. Organosilicons were listed on the most-dangerous-substances lists by the Paris convention and EEC directive. They were initially put on the black list by WHO, but were transferred to the grey list by common agreement. Carbamates were dropped from the original WHO draft because they decompose rapidly, so they do not conform with the criteria for hazardous materials. Other compounds containing organohalogens, organophosphorous, and organotins, used widely in agriculture in pesticides, fungicides, and biocides, were retained on the black list. "Crude oils and hydrocar-

113

bons," WHO's original terminology, was changed to "used lubricating oils," because of the heavy metal content of these oils, and the remainder of crude oils and hydrocarbons were moved to the grey list.

Several additions were made to the EEC list, despite French efforts at limiting the coverage to only those pollutants on the EEC list. Radioactive substances were added to the black list over French objections; French nuclear reactors are the principal sources of radionuclides in the Mediterranean. LDCs also added teratogenic and mutagenic substances to the black-listed carcinogenic substances. After losing on this point, France stopped providing data to UNEP on radionuclides. Acids and alkalis were retained from the dumping protocol over Italian objections. The relatively noncontentious pathogenic microorganisms and thermal discharges were added to the EEC grey list, because UNEP stressed their importance.

LDC delegates were generally unaware of the actual chemical content of their industrial waste or of the health effects of these substances, but were afraid that these restrictions would impose unknown costs on them. For instance, Tunisia opposed placing fluorides and phosphorous on the grey list, because it thought that they were associated with phosphate mining, which Tunisia conducts along the Mediterranean coast. In 1978 UNEP had presented a comprehensive two-volume profile of the substances listed in the technical annexes (IRPTC 1978). In the face of such overwhelming technical support for the potential harm from such substances, LDC scientists accepted the need for their control, and convinced their foreign ministry counterparts to accept their inclusion in the protocol.

Political compromises were struck at Geneva as well, although many difficulties were not fully resolved until the conference of plenipotentiaries the following May in Athens. A major goal of the LDCs had been for technical assistance. Initial phrasing in Article 10 committed the contracting parties to provide assistance to developing countries "particularly in the fields of science, education and technology." At the 1979 meeting Lebanon, Libya, Morocco, Tunisia, and Turkey successfully added the terms "and implementing" to the phrase "formulating . . . programs of assistance to developing countries," although France converted Morocco's proposal for technical assistance "provided on a favorable financial basis" to the provision of "appropriate equipment on advantageous terms to be agreed upon among the Parties concerned."

The parties finally included the atmospheric transport of pollutants as an area of control, but deferred specific action on it until an unspecified point in the future "under conditions to be defined in an additional annex" (Bliss-Guest 1981), which is due to be completed in 1989. The problem of existing or new installations was resolved by eliminating references to new or existing installations in the final version of the protocol in 1980. Rather, it included a new qualification: "The programmes and measures . . . shall be adopted by taking into account, for their progressive implementation, the capacity to adapt and reconvert existing installations, the economic capacity of the Parties and their need for development," thus fudging the issue to everyone's satisfaction (Dobbert 1980:112–13).

The emission/ambient disagreement was finally resolved at the Conference of Plenipotentiaries. Both sides had been adamant in adhering to their positions; the industrialized states were already committed to emission standards, and the LDCs staunchly refused to accept emission standards. The secretariat preferred emission standards because of their ease of application. Finally, at the Conference of Plenipotentiaries, the countries finally agreed to compromise by applying emission standards for the black list and ambient standards for the grey list, based on suggestions by the UNEP secretariat. The LDCs also insisted on reference to "the economic capacity of the Parties and their need for development, the level of existing pollution and the real absorptive capacity of the marine environment" in connection with the guidelines for the development of standards regulating the emission of the covered materials.

LDCs, who in 1977 were concerned that the protocol would be used to retard their economic development, were appeased by the differentiation between ambient and emission standards. These concessions by the Europeans effectively gave LDC industries a comparative advantage over their European competitors. Because the North African coast is not as polluted as the southern European coast, the application of ambient standards means that the LDC factories do not have to introduce pollution controls immediately for grey-listed materials, whereas European factories will.

The protocol was quickly ratified or acceded to by Algeria, Egypt, France, Monaco, Tunisia, Turkey, and the EEC. It entered into force in June 1983. Since then Cyprus (1987), Italy (1985), Greece (1987), Morocco (1987), and Spain (1986) have ratified it. Further work remains to be done for the protocol to become fully operational. Water quality and emission standards must be adopted based on Med Pol studies. Specific compounds and products that contain the banned substances have to be identified. Interim ambient standards for mercury and environmental quality criteria using microbiological indicators for bathing waters and for shellfish and shellfish-growing waters were adopted at the 1987 Meeting of the Contracting Parties, based on studies completed by the FAO and WHO from Med Pol projects. The contracting parties hope to have the Land-Based Sources Protocol fully operational by 1995, calling for the development of over fifty measures specifying water quality and emission standards for each of the banned substances, and for different possible uses of the water (UNEP/WG. 125/6).

The substance of the treaty—the actual pollutants that are controlled—was adopted by scientific consensus. Its conclusion was eased by political compromise, in which UNEP also had a hand.

In the case of the technical annexes, foreign ministry officials deferred to the authority of the region's marine scientists, who were responsible for its negotiation. Convinced by data provided by UNEP's epistemic community, these scientists accepted the urgency of managing a wide variety of pollutants. The scientists were able to conclude relatively quickly an amicable agreement on the range of pollutants to be covered by the treaty, making it more difficult for the foreign ministry delegates to delay too long on the legal texts. In turn, persuaded by the arguments of the ecological secretariat, the makers of foreign policy acceded to suggestions for emission standards for the more urgent and toxic black-listed substances. The original topics chosen for inclusion in the protocol, such as pollutants transmitted by rivers and through the atmosphere, as well as the initial candidates for the technical annexes, came from the WHO and UNEP drafters, who were members of the ecological epistemic community. Thus, much of the agenda of the key Land-Based Sources Protocol was set by the ecological epistemic community, with subsequent confirmation and additional persuasion coming from the marine scientists present on their national delegations.

Within these parameters, the Land-Based Sources Protocol was completed by political compromise. The LDCs were assured that atmospheric transport and river transport of pollution, radioactive wastes, and technology transfer would be covered by the protocol, and that some ambient standards would be included. The DCs were satisfied by a full list of substances in the annexes that were largely consistent with EEC obligations, even though France had to accept some ambient standards and some controls exceeding those laid out in the EEC directive.

Specially Protected Areas

The Mediterranean states also signed a new protocol in April 1982 which was outside the scope of the program as it was initially anticipated and set out in the Barcelona convention and in the Med Plan. Nine states of the sixteen attending the Conference of Plenipotentiaries signed the Protocol Concerning Mediterranean Specially Protected Areas, which encouraged the creation and development of marine parks to preserve regionally endangered species, in particular the Mediterranean monk seal. Three other states signed later. The protocol entered into force in March 1986, following ratification of accession by Algeria, Egypt, Italy, Tunisia, Yugoslavia, and the EEC. Cyprus, France, Greece, Israel, Malta, Spain and Turkey later ratified it.

Although outside the formal parameters of the Med Plan, and hence indicating that a broader array of pollution-related issues had been learned about, the extent of actual compliance with the protocol suggests that a qualified assessment be made. UNEP is still in the process of gathering information about existing and planned marine preserves, and is identifying areas and species in need of protection. A Regional Activity Centre in Tunis began operations in November 1985. Israeli attendance at its meetings must be finessed; Tunisia does not admit formal Israeli governmental representatives, so delegates are ushered through customs as consultants to the center.

The protocol does reinforce the process of collective policy coordination. Peter Thacher declared that "it maintains the momentum created in Barcelona in 1975 with the adoption of a Mediterranean Action Plan . . . [and] does create another link in the cooperative chain that has been forged by 17 countries."[16]

Other Legal Efforts

Other objectives identified in the Barcelona convention have not been met or even actively pursued. In December 1978 UNEP and the International Juridical Organization convened the Meeting of Experts on the Legal Aspects of Pollution Resulting from Exploration and Exploitation of the Continental Shelf and the Seabed and Its Subsoil in the Mediterranean. At subsequent meetings the contracting parties have not authorized funding for any more meetings, although UNEP has drafted a treaty to regulate offshore oil and gas drilling. No work has yet been undertaken on the Interstate Guarantee Fund.

Overall, the legal scope of the Med Plan has grown from treating only oil pollution to controlling land-based sources of pollution as well as conserving species. Its strength has grown from broad exhortations in the Barcelona convention to specific guidelines for selected substances, with more to come.

INTEGRATED MANAGEMENT

Integrated management is the Med Plan's least successful component. Countries were more interested in other components, and it has taken the longest time to develop the integrated planning projects, many of which are still only in nascent forms. This was never as well understood or accepted as other components. Negotiations lacked the group of scientists actively advocating compliance and demonstrating the need for action that moved debate along on the other components. After floundering around until 1977, this component was separated into a visionary integrated modeling exercise and a set of concrete projects to study and distribute environmentally benign technologies.

In March 1975 UNEP accepted a French offer to prepare a "Blue Book" to operationalize the integrated planning section of the Med Plan. Although this focus matched UNEP's vision of holistic planning, UNEP officials were initially suspicious that the French were attempting to control it. France has long used the Amenagement du Territoire (regional management) approach of siting industries around population centers. With a tradition of prospective planning founded by Gaston Berger and Bertrand de Jouvenal, such conceptual planning exercises were also popular in French universities (for example, see Sachs 1974). UNEP officials satisfied themselves that the French offer was not merely an attempt to control the program, and allowed the French to draft an operational document for the integrated management component. Other states evinced little interest in the project, and the French were able to effectively capture the integrated management component through drafting the document, and later by supporting the RAC for the integrated planning component. France coordinates and supports the integrated management projects from the Centre d'Activités Environnment-Développement en Mediterranée (MEDEAS), a federally funded research institute in Sophia-Antipolis, outside Cannes. The government gives it 700,000 francs yearly for Med Plan–related work.

French interest in integrated management came solely from the director of the Research Division of the Environmental Ministry, Serge

Antoine, whose concern was with "anticipatory planning." French Foreign Ministry officials knew nothing of the details of the program, nor did they care. They were willing to promote the project because of the Environmental Ministry's interest, but did not relate the project to any of their own Med Plan objectives. The Blue Book was drafted by Serge Antoine, with assistance from two other planners who had been involved with OECD's Interfutures project: Paul-Marc Henry and Jacques Lessourne. They envisaged a systems analysis of the interrelations between different terrestrial and marine economic processes around the Mediterranean, in order to provide regional planners with a variety of "prospective studies" describing regional development trends under a number of different hypothetical growth patterns of population and economic sectoral growth, to help them choose between alternative development plans. They were interested in designing studies to assist planners in designing national strategies for fulfilling the demands of rapidly growing coastal populations. In 1976 a UNEP officer, accompanied by a French official funded by France, visited Mediterranean countries to promote the project. President Giscard d'Estaing had it on his agenda for discussions with the heads of state during his 1975 visits to Algeria, Tunisia, Morocco, and Greece.

The French first draft was discussed with UNEP representatives in Geneva in July and September 1975. The team finalized its work in December, and the operational document, dubbed the "Blue Plan," was transmitted to UNEP in early 1976. Following its discussion at meetings in January and May 1976 that were attended by national experts, the Blue Plan was submitted to governmental representatives in Split, Yugoslavia, in February 1977.

Throughout this procedure, Serge Antoine was the only one to have a clear idea of what the Blue Plan would be. At the 1976 meetings participants shared a basic focus on safeguarding renewable resources while meeting the fundamental demands of growing populations. There was general consensus that the Blue Plan should consist of a number of cross-disciplinary sectoral studies, to incorporate development concerns with their environmental consequences, identifying as many interlinkages as possible. Discussions failed to suggest how to choose sectors, or how to later integrate them. The consultations proposed the following studies, although the experts were unable to list them in any order of priority: fisheries and aquaculture, water, energy, urban industrial ecosystems, agriculture and rural development, human migration, industrialization, health, tourism, navigation and leisure craft, social projects, and resource management. "Urban ecosystems" was put on the list at the behest of Israel and Malta, who were particularly concerned with the potential long-term damage to shorelines, underground water supplies, and natural areas from inadequate sewage and solid waste disposal.

On the eve of the Split meeting, Mostapha Tolba decided that there were two diverse groups of interests in integrated planning. The French were avidly interested in the abstract Blue Plan, and the Italians were interested to a lesser degree. However, the LDCs found the Blue Plan too abstract, and were interested in much more concrete projects that would be directly applicable to their development efforts. Tolba broke up the Blue Book into a more theoretical, integrated management approach following the French proposal (the Blue Plan), and the more concrete Priority Actions Programs (PAP) that was set up to study projects of immediate interest to the delegates. The Blue Plan is future oriented, aimed at developing a systematic view of the region for the years 2000–2025. The PAP looks at projects that may be adopted immediately. At Split, fifteen governments approved both components.

The Blue Plan

The Blue Plan's concern was with an overarching environment and development problematique, and was not necessarily limited to just the Mediterranean coastal zone or pollution. Its designers were fond of stating that "the Blue Plan is neither Blue nor a Plan." Cooperation was intended to create a pool of information for regional planners, rather than a unique plan that could be used by national decision makers to choose between alternative modes of development and to sensitize them to the interlinkages between sectors:

> The programme envisaged under the "Blue Plan" should contribute to the promotion of economic and social development of the whole Mediterranean region in a manner which will safeguard the natural systems on which sustained development depends . . . the objective of the Blue Plan is to place at the disposal of decision-makers and planners in the different countries of the Mediterranean region information enabling them to formulate plans for optimum socio-economic development on a sustainable basis without environmental degradation. . . . to assist the governments of the coastal states . . . to gain a more accurate

insight into the common problems they face both in the Mediterranean Sea and in its coastal zones, to assist these governments in reaching appropriate decisions that would promote rational management of resources and sustainable development in the Mediterranean region.[17]

Indeed the Blue Plan was not blue, although its planners may have become so following its weak reception by governments. As formulated at MEDEAS (Centre d'Activités Environnment-Développement en Mediteranée), it had very little to do with pollution or even the Mediterranean. It extended to the entire country, not just the coastal zone, and was conceived as a modeling exercise for the Meditereranean region to produce alternative regional scenarios based on economic and demographic trends.

At Split, delegates approved eighteen "surveys."[18] They proposed five inventories of biological resources (water, soil, marine flora and fauna, air, flora and fauna of the littoral), two of mineral and energy resources (the seabed and continental shelf or the littoral), seven studies of human activities (industrialization, urbanization, agriculture, fisheries and aquaculture, maritime transport, tourism, and soft technologies), and four studies of "man" (demography and health; social and cultural environments, standard of living and quality of life; training, information, and documentation; and transfer of appropriate technologies and experimentation). The work was to be synthesized through a three-stage process over four years at a cost of $US 1.5 million. First would be broad exploratory work within each survey for a year, then a consolidation of the surveys over one and a half to two years to identify interrelationships, according to an overarching structure that would emerge during the first stage, and finally a one-year synthesis of the studies and the formation of alternative future scenarios for use by government planners.

The first phase of the Blue Plan was not approved until October 1979 at Cannes, with the choice of a new director of the program and his rewriting of the operational document. The first director, René Bourone of France, was replaced by Ismail Sabri Abdalla, a former Egyptian minister for planning (1971–1978) and the chairman of the Third World Forum. Under Bourone countries were unwilling to fund the studies because they were unsure of their focus. Sabri Abdalla had been selected by Tolba and the French and approved by the other Mediterranean states over three Italian candidates and an Algerian. He rewrote the project document for the Blue Plan to reflect the plan's interdisciplinary focus on interlinked problems, which had been absent from the document drafted at Split. As a neo-Marxist economic planner, his own interests were with the economic and demographic forces in the region, which he felt contributed to the problem of marine pollution. He revised the list of proposed studies, asking for twelve "consolidated diagonal" studies of:[19]

1. Land-marine systems and subsystems.

2. Water resources: competitive uses and human priorities.

3. Industrial growth: industrialization strategies and services related to the environment and the utilization of subsoil resources.

4. Old and new sources of energy.

5. Health, population, and population movements.

6. Space use, urbanization, and rural development.

7. Tourism, space use, and the environment.

8. Intra-Mediterranean economic relations.

9. Transport and communication.

10. Cultural heritage and cross-cultural relations.

11. Environmental awareness and value systems.

12. The impact of non-Mediterranean influences on the Mediterranean Basin.

Due to funding delays, work didn't begin until September 1980. The twelve studies were delegated to twelve teams of consultants, each composed of one expert from an industrialized country and one from a developing country, an arrangement intended to balance the viewpoints represented in the studies. Their work was coordinated by MEDEAS, in relative isolation from any Mediterranean government's supervision. The Group of Coordination and Synthesis (GCS) was established in 1980 to assist Sabri Abdalla in the development of the Blue Plan. It was composed of economic planners and mathematical modelers from Algeria, Yugoslavia, France, Greece, Morocco (later replaced by Tunisia), and Spain, with a French executive secretary (Antoine 1985). Phase I was finally completed in April 1984.

Phase II was to be completed in 1987, and was actually concluded in 1988, although it was largely ignored by the participating states. Governments had become confused and suspicious about the projects; they were uncertain whether the projects were directed by UNEP or by MEDEAS. In addition, UNEP grew disillusioned with MEDEAS and the Blue Plan, because it appeared that Sabri Abdalla's intentions distracted from the environmental thrust of the Med Plan. Delegates were loath to fund the various phases of the Blue Plan. For Phase II they replaced the GCS with a steering committee drawn from national institutions who had been involved with the Phase I projects of the Blue Plan (the "focal points"). These institutions would presumably be more accountable to governments, so that they would be able to reassert control over the Blue Plan.

The Blue Plan's findings were generally ignored by governments, who were slow to approve the Blue Plan budgets, and even then often slashed their requests. Without the broad scientific coalition that exists in other Med Plan components, governments had no reasons to support a program that they did not understand. UNEP continued to defend its existence because of its hopes that it would encourage leaders to consider more thoroughly the social and economic causes of Mediterranean pollution, although they also became increasingly disillusioned and dubious about its success or relevance to the Med Plan.

The Priority Actions Programme

Six priority studies were selected at Split for the PAP from the shopping list of Blue Plan surveys. Following polling of the delegates by UNEP officials, soil protection, water resource management, fisheries and aquaculture management, human settlements, tourism, and "soft" energy technologies were selected for further study. Yugoslavia subsequently hosted the RAC for the PAP in the Town Planning Institute in Split; this did not become operational until 1980.

This selection of projects was a compromise amalgam of all of the countries' concerns voiced at the Split meeting. The soil study was selected by eleven of the fifteen government representatives. Greece, Italy, Malta, and Monaco failed to choose it. The water resources study was selected by thirteen representatives. Italy and Monaco did not choose it. Eleven states chose aquaculture. Israel, Italy, Libya, and Spain did not. Eleven chose soft energy technologies. They were not chosen by Cyprus, Italy, Turkey, or Yugoslavia. Ten went for human settlements. Those not selecting human settlements for study were Egypt, France, Monaco, Morocco, and Yugoslavia. Nine opted to study tourism; Algeria, Cyprus, France, Greece, Lebanon, and Turkey did not. Several other subjects were selected by a small number of countries, although not by enough countries to be designated priority projects. Yugoslavia also suggested that food be studied. Greece, Malta and Turkey urged public health studies. Studies of natural disasters were suggested by Cyprus, Italy, and Turkey. Marine parks were promoted by Algeria, Monaco, and Tunisia. Marine parks were subsequently included in the Specially Protected Areas treaty. Historical monuments were suggested by Spain and Yugoslavia. Israel suggested environmental impact assessment, land use planning, and ecosystem protection studies. Turkey suggested the study of the transmission of pollutants between countries.[20]

Table 4.2 shows which states were satisfied and which were frustrated by the PAP selections. The French and the North Africans were the most satisfied, getting all of their preferred studies, whereas the states in intermediate levels of development were more frustrated.

There was no money for the PAP until 1980, when countries began to contribute to the Med Plan's budget. Progress in the first few years

Table 4.2. Satisfaction of National Desires by the PAP

	Number of Projects Indicated as Priorities	*% of Priority Projects That Were Adopted*
Morocco	6	100
Libya	5	100
France	4	100
Spain	7	86
Tunisia	7	86
Algeria	6	83
Cyprus	5	80
Greece	5	80
Malta	5	80
Italy	4	75
Monaco	4	75
Israel	9	67
Yugoslavia	6	67
Turkey	7	57

Source: Compiled from UNEP/IG 5/7, annex 1. Column 1 shows the number of projects indicated as priorities by delegates. Column 2 shows the proportion of these priorities that were adopted as PAP projects.

was hindered by funding disagreements between UNDP and UNEP. Projects and seminars did not get going until late 1984. Initial seminars on the projects were not held until late 1984.

In the subsequent years additional PAP projects were approved. These projects largely cater to the LDCs' concerns with developing methods for coping with urban poverty, alternative inexpensive energy sources, and technology transfer. PAP projects now include integrated planning and management of the coastal zones, the rehabilitation of historic settlements, land use planning in earthquake zones, and solid and liquid waste disposal. The PAP has really just begun its activities.

Institutional Arrangements

Following the Barcelona convention's entry into force in February 1978, the Mediterranean states developed an institutional structure to support Med Plan operations. Coordination had originally been run out of UNEP's Geneva Regional Seas Office, but by 1979 UNEP had created similar projects for other regional seas elsewhere, and the UNEP executive director was under fire from UNEP's Governing Council for committing excessive funds to the Mediterranean region. From 1973 to 1975 7.2 percent of UNEP's Environment Fund resources had gone to the Mediterranean. The states approved the Mediterranean Trust Fund, which was to be supported by contributions from the Mediterranean states; they also approved the creation of a small Med Plan secretariat, called the Coordinating Unit.

The Trust Fund was established in July 1979 to finance the Med Plan's activities. States pledged amounts proportional to their overall UN schedules, leaving France responsible for 48 percent of the governments' contributions. From the Med Plan's inception through 1986, UNEP contributed $US 7.8 million, and other UN agencies added another 6.6 million dollars, while the seventeen participating governments gave 13.3 million dollars (UNEP 1986a). The EEC provided $US 2.2 million.[21] Before the Trust Fund's creation, the Med Plan was supported almost entirely by UNEP, with some early support from France. Since 1979 UNEP has reduced its financial involvement in the Mediterranean and increased national support. The budget is presented in table 4.3. UNEP takes a 13 percent cut of the budget as a management fee. Governments have unsuccessfully searched for alternative management arrangements for the Trust Fund, and have tried to get UNEP to reduce its fee.

From 1979 to 1982 contributions from governments lagged while

Table 4.3. Med Plan Budget
(in $US thousands)

1978	1979–80	1981	1982	1983	1984	1985	1986	1987
2,465	4,720	3,500	3,822	3,445	3,462	3,768	4,020	4,183

Source: UNEP/BUR 18, table 1; UNEP/IG 56/5, annex 8, p. 1.

governments approved the necessary domestic agreements to commit the funds. Through discretionary control over the allocation of the budget, UNEP was able to continue to maintain its alliance with scientists by channeling scarce money to Med Pol projects that would reinforce domestic constituencies, while allowing the Blue Plan, PAP, and the Regional Oil Combating Centre (ROCC) to survive at very low levels of support. UNEP had to be careful, however, to spread the money around sufficiently to avert distributional conflicts between marine scientists from different disciplines. Through 1981 65 percent of Med Plan expenditures went to Med Pol, with 17 percent going to the ROCC, 15 percent to the Blue Plan, and 2 percent to PAP.[22] By the end of 1982 contributions began to flow in, but operations were further delayed by the physical transfer of the Coordinating Unit to Athens.

A small bureau of four representatives from Mediterranean states was created to oversee the short-run operation of the Med Plan. The French initially opposed the creation of such a small bureau, encouraging instead a bureau with full representation from all of the Mediterranean countries in order to ensure that French interests were not overlooked. Their proposal was soon found to be unworkable because it would be no different from the annual intergovernmental review meetings. Bureau members serve two-year terms and meet four to six times a year. The president comes from the country hosting the meeting at which the bureau is elected. Following UNEP's principle of geographic distribution, the four seats are equally distributed between developing and developed countries, although the developed-country delegates generally have better attendance records. The composition of the bureau is presented in table 4.4.

The headquarters unit was transferred to Athens in 1982. Since 1978 France had urged that the headquarters be moved from Geneva to a Mediterranean location, finding it impossible to control the UNEP staff in Geneva. At a number of intergovernmental meetings, dele-

Table 4.4. Membership on the Med Plan Bureau

Offices	1979–1981	1981–1983	1983–1985	1985–1987
President	Tunisia	Italy	Yugoslavia	Spain
Vice-president	Spain	France	Egypt	Morocco
Vice-president	Greece	Algeria	Spain	Syria
Rapporteur	Malta	Lebanon	Tunisia	Turkey

Source: UNEP/BUR 18; UNEP/IG 56/5.

gates considered Barcelona, Madrid, Monaco, Athens, and Beirut. Beirut was soon rejected as a result of the civil war in Lebanon, and Monaco was suspect because it was too closely linked to France. Finally, at the Second Meeting of the Contracting Parties at Cannes in March 1981, the states voted to transfer the headquarters to Athens, following an "auction" at which the Spanish and Greek representatives bid for the headquarters unit. Greece finally won with an offer of $US 450,000 per year. Spain was appeased by getting the senior scientist slot for the first five years.

A new secretariat was recruited to staff the new offices. Professional members are drawn from Mediterranean countries. The coordinator is an Italian who had already worked for UNEP who was selected over French, Spanish, and Algerian candidates. The staff consists of six professional-level positions and twelve support positions. WHO and the FAO each provide a scientist as well. Although formally autonomous, the secretariat retains close ties to UNEP's Regional Seas Programme (RSP), which is run by Keckes. The RSP's active support for the Med Plan has flagged since 1985, when it was transferred from Geneva to UNEP headquarters in Nairobi. Its activities were hindered by the need to hire an entirely new staff of professionals, as none of the Geneva staff wished to follow Keckes to Nairobi, and because of a year-long internal reassessment of UNEP's performance after fifteen years, called by Tolba.

RECENT CHANGES

In 1988 the Med Plan secretariat "refocused" the direction of the Med Plan to give "greater emphasis to environmentally sound coastal zone planning and management in the region."[23] UNEP has provided advice and sent consultants to Mediterranean governments in order to support such objectives. For instance, consultants were sent to Libya to assist the government in developing a plan to manage coastal oil pollution, and to Yugoslavia to assist in cleaning up Castela Bay.[24] With financing from the World Bank and the European Economic Community, UNEP is also encouraging governments to install oil reception facilities in their major ports, and to construct sewage treatment plants. Due to the relative absence of offshore mining and oil and gas development in the region, there was little need for the development of addition protocols to control such activities. Arrangements are ongoing to develop the necessary environmental standards to operationalize the Land-Based Sources Protocol.

SUMMARY

Since its adoption in 1975, the Med Plan has become dramatically more comprehensive. Protocols grew to cover land-based sources of pollution as well as marine dumping and oil spills from tankers. Moreover, they came to include pollution transported by rivers and through the atmosphere as well as that dumped directly into the sea. The list of specific pollutants covered grew as well. Environmental assessment evolved from seven to twelve monitoring and research projects. The plan's strength has been enhanced as well. Interim standards were developed in 1987 for levels of mercury and for the quality of recreational waters and areas used to raise shellfish. Mediterranean scientists estimate that the Mediterranean is less polluted than it would have been without these measures. [Greenberg 1985:41]

FIVE

Evolving National Measures for Pollution Control

Throughout the 1970s and 1980s national efforts at marine pollution control and environmental protection in general became more comprehensive and were enforced with greater vigor. Governments adopted increasingly more comprehensive pollution control legislation, and many of their control practices focus on broader and more stringent forms of control than before the Med Plan was adopted. Most governments now control a broader range of marine pollutants and sources of pollution. They came to control land-based sources as well as oil pollution, and several countries now require environmental impact assessments for all new development in the coastal zone.

In short, domestic as well as international efforts for environmental protection have grown in scope and strength. States actually comply with their Med Plan obligations. In particular, the Med Plan's Regional Oil Combating Centre (ROCC) directly gave rise to domestic environmental efforts to control oil pollution. The first half of this chapter discusses the evolution of domestic marine pollution control practices throughout the Mediterranean. The second half relates the Med Plan to domestic practices and illustrates the role played by the epistemic community and allied marine scientists in leading countries toward more comprehensive domestic pollution control measures and support for the Med Plan. The degree to which domestic policy changed varies by country, but, as will be seen, in general the countries with the strongest and broadest pollution control policies are those in which the ecological epistemic community had established access to national policymaking through a regulatory environmental authority. These countries also became the strongest proponents for a comprehensive Med Plan. Those countries in which the epistemic community was less able to consolidate its bureaucratic influence were less supportive of the Med Plan and adopted weaker domestic pollution controls.

Direct evidence of changed water quality is weak. No synoptic data are available on Mediterranean water quality, nor are there time series data.[1] In the absence of direct measures of water quality, one must measure compliance with the Med Plan by the development of pollution control measures, for "the scientific and conceptual basis of environmental regulation is so precarious, the empirical evidence so ambiguous, that most regulatory decisions can only be evaluated and legitimated in terms of procedural, rather than substantive rationality—by process, not by outcome" (Majone 1982:307).

Anecdotal evidence points to some success in alleviating regional pollution. Ten years ago about 33 percent of Mediterranean beaches were unsafe for swimming. By 1986 only 20 percent were unsafe.[2] The biggest advances have been in the construction of sewage treatment plants. Such facilities have been built or are under construction in such major cities as Barcelona, Marseilles, Nice, Toulon, Genoa, Naples, Venice, Salonika, Athens, Istanbul, Aleppo, Beirut, Tel Aviv, Alexandria, Tripoli, Tunis, and Algiers,[3] although many are still overwhelmed by additional wastes from summer tourists. At least 30 percent of municipal sewage is now treated (Ress 1986:267). Between 1982 and 1984 Spain lowered the number of contaminated beaches from thirty-six to eight.[4] Between 1972 and 1980 France substantially reduced pollution in the Berre Lagoon, which receives wastes from the industrial zone of Fos, at a cost of $US 96 million.[5] Toxic emissions into the Rhone were reduced by 44 percent during the 1970s, and mercury emissions dropped sevenfold.[6] Nationwide, the quality of French beaches improved from 1976 to 1984. In 1976 73 percent of the beaches were of "good and average quality." By 1984 80 percent were good or average.[7] With UNEP's encouragement, ballast reception facilities are under construction or planned in ports in Egypt, Greece, Tunisia, Turkey, and Yugoslavia.[8]

Although impossible to confirm, regional scientists frequently assert that the quality of the Mediterranean is better than it would have been without the Med Plan. They feel that the level of pollution has remained roughly constant over the last decade, even with the rapid growth of coastal industry and population. Thus, efforts have kept the sea at the same level of quality, despite the production of more pollutants.

NATIONAL ACTIONS

Following the Med Plan's adoption, national pollution control practices converged around more comprehensive marine pollution controls. From a baseline in 1972 of few or no measures for pollution control, many have been introduced. A 1971 USAID survey found

> little evidence of awareness of environmental problems among the peoples of developing countries, or among their government administrators. ... Many countries are preoccupied with the development of their natural resources, and to the extent that concern does exist for the environment, there appears to be apprehension that social and economic costs of environmental protection may very well out-weigh the benefits.[9]

By 1985 almost all Mediterranean governments had created environmental ministries or agencies. Most adopted pollution control legislation (except for Morocco, Cyprus, Lebanon, Albania, and Syria). Some states even increased pollution control expenditures. Table 5.1 presents the measures that governments took to control Mediterranean pollution.

As the table indicates, most countries' adoption of more coherent domestic and international marine pollution control policies follows the creation of regulatory national institutions responsible for controlling marine pollution. Generally, these institutions were staffed by members of UNEP's epistemic community and by marine scientists allied with UNEP. Some individuals in the ministries were members of the ecological epistemic community who tried to control as

Table 5.1. Measures for Mediterranean Pollution Control

	Creation of National Authorities	
Country[a]	*Coordinative*	*Regulatory*
France	1970	1974
Israel	1973	1976
Greece	1976	1980
Algeria	1974	1979, 1983
Egypt	1980	1982
Italy	1973, 1983	1986
Libya	1981	none
Spain	1972	1978
Morocco	1974	none
Tunisia	1975, 1980	none
Turkey	1979	none
Yugoslavia	1974, 1982	none

Note: LBS = land-based sources; EIA = environmental impact assessments.

[a] Little or no data is available for Malta, Cyprus, Lebanon, Albania, Monaco, and Syria.

wide a range of pollutants and sources of pollution as possible. Others were simply members of the UNEP's transnational alliance, who encouraged their governments to ratify Med Plan protocols as well as to adopt and enforce domestic pollution controls. Both groups conveyed congruent advice to their governments, and policies began to converge. This process is laid out in greater detail later in this chapter.

In table 5.1, countries are ranked according to the strength and breadth of their measures, determined by the adoption of legislation or policies dealing with a broader range of pollutants: either explicitly through new laws for previously uncontrolled sources of pollution, or through requiring environmental impact assessments in order to weigh the environmental consequences of development projects. Countries' policies converge most closely where the UNEP—marine scientists' alliance was strongest, and the scientists were able to consolidate their foothold in governmental policymaking by endowing their newfound ministries with regulatory authority.

Existing government stances were reinforced in France, Italy, Greece, and Israel. In Algeria and Egypt stronger national stances followed the elevation of those institutions to regulatory status, which itself was a result of the scientists' empowerment through participation in

Introduction of Marine Pollution Control Legislation		When Delegations Became More Supportive at Med Plan Meetings
General (Oil, Dumping)	*More Effective (LBS, EIA)*	
1964, many after	1976/1977	1975–1976
1971, 1983	1982	1975
1975, 1977	1981, 1986	1975
1983	1983	1979
1982, 1983	1983	1982
1976, 1982	none	1977
1976	none	seldom attended
1977, 1982	none	low profile
none	none	low profile
1975	none	1979
1983	none	low profile
1965, 1976	none	1975

the Med Plan. Following the consolidation of the marine scientists' bureaucratic power, their governments adopted more comprehensive environmental legislation and policies and became more constructive at Med Plan meetings. Elsewhere, with the absence of strong pollution control partisans within the government, efforts to control marine pollution were much weaker.

The Creation of National Institutions

Most countries began with broadly focused, interministerial bodies which were intended to coordinate national policymaking among such ministries as those for agriculture, industry, the merchant marine, and mining in order to avoid excessive environmental harm from their activities. Without clear-cut administrative mandates or sufficient budgets, and with relatively small staffs, these bodies were generally unable to convert into effective policy ministers' concerns with limiting pollution. Such bodies were soon replaced or matched with dedicated environmental ministries with their own budgets and regulatory responsibilities. With this greater political clout, members of the ministries were better able to translate their concerns into national policy.

Regulatory bodies are more centralized than are coordinative bodies. With their own staffs and budgets and clear mandates they are able to directly regulate and control pollution. Coordinative bodies, although more consistent with the holistic conception of environmental problems, lack both the funds to pay for pollution control activities in other ministries and the power to compel them to incorporate environmental considerations into their own activities.

The Med Plan was not, of course, the only force responsible for such mounting environmental awareness. In most states some institution building preceded the Med Plan. Only in Egypt, Libya, and Turkey did governments create environmental institutions after becoming involved in Med Plan discussions. UNCHE had done much to start such concerns nationally, as had, for its members, EEC directives, which were later incorporated into national legislation and decrees.[10]

The individuals staffing the environmental authorities took advantage of such mounting sentiments to justify their own consolidation of power within their governments. The Med Plan strengthened the new bodies by publicizing Mediterranean pollution problems and reinforcing their legitimate responsibility for pollution control. This process of building an environmental interest took longer in the LDCs than in the DCs, as the environmental bodies commonly had fewer resources: a lower budget, fewer trained staff, and less equipment. Many of them still have difficulty enforcing the policies they have introduced.

France has had the longest experience of the Mediterranean countries with governmental environmental institutions. On July 30, 1970 President Pompidou established the advisory High Commission for the Environment to coordinate ministerial environmental efforts.[11] On January 7, 1971 President Pompidou created the Ministry for the Protection of Nature and the Environment, with a staff of three hundred, to which the secretariat of the High Commission reports. The new ministry was entrusted with the protection of natural sites and with preventing, controlling, or reducing all forms of environmental pollution. Its inspectors closed thirty polluting factories in 1971.[12] It originally focused on the protection of natural sites, but its mission was enlarged in 1974 to cover the overall quality of life as the Ministry for the Environment and Quality of Life. In subsequent cabinets it has been directed by ministers and secretaries of state. In 1981 the "quality of life" was omitted, and its head was elevated to full ministerial rank.

Since its inception, the Ministry for the Environment's role in the government has eroded in terms of its share of the federal budget. In absolute terms, the budget of the ministry, as well as all of the environmental budget lines in the federal budget, grew between 1972 and 1986, as may be seen in table 5.2. However, the environment's share of the federal budget fell from 2.19 percent to 1.10 percent during this period.

Under the Ministry for the Environment's aegis, France developed a number of coordinative interministerial committees. The International Action Committee for Nature and the Environment (CIANE) was created in February 1971, chaired by the prime minister. A fund, called the Fonds d'Intervention pour la Nature et l'Environement (FIANE), was established to subsidize private investment in pollution control equipment. On August 2, 1978 the Interministerial Committee on the Sea was created to control the protection of coasts and seas, fishing, hydrocarbon research, the Mediterranean Action Plan, a 200-mile maritime zone and fishing issues, and the general exploitation of maritime resources.[13] At its first meeting in February 1979 the committee approved a program to prevent Mediterranean pollution by oil from tankers and from shipping accidents.[14]

River pollution is regulated principally by six River Basin Agencies, established in 1966, as well as by the Interministerial Commission on Water and the Ministry of the Environment's National Committee on Water. From 1972 and 1977 contracts to limit pollution were concluded and implemented with the metal plating industry, the pulp and paper industry (calling for an 80 percent reduction in emissions), the chemical industry, and five food-processing subsectors.[15]

In Israel the primary governmental institution responsible for environmental protection is the Environmental Protection Service (EPS). Originally established in 1973 as a separate government agency in the prime minister's office, with a staff of thirty-six (of whom thirty were professionals), the EPS deals with all aspects of natural resource management, including pollution control, noise abatement, solid waste management, land use planning, environmental protection, and education. Its budget for 1982–1983 was $US 3.5 million (Baker, Bassett, and Ellington 1985:140–41). The EPS was intended to coordinate its activities with the National Planning and Building Board and to advise the board on environmental aspects of planning, design a system for environmental impact assessment, and collect data on environmental quality. In 1976 the EPS was transferred to the Ministry of the Interior, and its authority and responsibilities were expanded, making the EPS the central coordinating body for environmental protection.[16] In 1989 it was elevated to full ministerial rank.

The EPS' first enforcement unit—the Marine Pollution Section—

Table 5.2. French Environmental Budget
(in Millions of Francs)

	1972	*1973*	*1974*	*1975*	*1976*
Budget of Environmental Ministry	159	201	238	268	278
"Environmental" budget for all ministries	971	1,080	1,353	1,355	1,486
All environmental budgets as a percent of federal budget	2.19	2.26	2.48	2.21	2.11

Source: *Le Monde*, February 24, 1982, p. 30; October 8, 1986, pp. 35–36.

began operations on July 1, 1983. It is responsible for enforcing Israeli coastal standards and the 1983 National Dumping Law to control oil spills and preventing land-based sources of pollution. It inspects 25 percent of the ships visiting Israeli ports and monitors the Mediterranean and Gulf of Elat coastlines.[17]

Greece also developed a structure with concentrated regulatory authority. The Ministry of Culture and Science was selected as the locus of environmental policymaking in December 1974. Environmental responsibilities were spread among a number of uncoordinated ministries and special government agencies, including the Ministry of Coordination and Planning, the Ministry of Culture and Science (national heritage), the Ministry of Industry, the Ministry of Social Services (health protection), the Ministry of Public Works (master plans), the Ministry of Transport (automobile emissions), and the Ministry of the Merchant Marine (protection of the sea). In 1976 the National Council for Physical Planning and the Environment (NCPPE) was established within the Ministry of Coordination. Chaired by the prime minister, the NCPPE was the national body responsible for environmental protection, composed of the ministers of coordination, finance, agriculture, sciences and culture, industry and energy, social affairs, public works, and the merchant marine, supported by a small technical secretariat. In May 1980 Greece established a new Ministry of Regional Physical Planning, Housing and the Environment, which was responsible for environmental policies at all levels of government and was intended to work in close cooperation with the Ministry of Industry. Following the election of the PASOK government in 1982,

1977	1978	1979	1980	1981	1982	1986
254	344	353	387	541	417	616
1,272	1,266	1,389	1,538	1,365	1,624	
1.66	1.53	1.47	1.42	1.24	1.10	

environmental responsibilities were gradually transferred from the NCPPE to the new centralized ministry.

Algerian institutionalization was stimulated by UNCHE. On July 12, 1974 the Committee for the National Environment was created "for the purpose of studying the problems of improving the environment and conditions of life, of preserving and recreating biological resources, of pollution and nuisances of all kinds, and more generally, of all the positive and negative aspects of man's environment."[18] The committee had representatives from most ministries, as well as its own permanent secretariat. It provided a liaison, exchanged information between ministries with relevant programs, coordinated the preparation of measures and programs involving more than one ministry, and provided advice on all studies concerned with the environment. The committee was charged with developing a national code for the protection of nature and the environment. The Ministry of Hydraulics, Land Development and Environmental Protection was established in 1975. In 1979 the Committee for the National Environment's responsibilities were transferred to the newly formed Secretariat of State for Forests and Land Development, formed from the Ministry for Hydraulics. After 1983 its mandate was expanded within the Ministry for Hydraulics, Environment and Forests. In July 1983 the National Agency for Environmental Protection was formed.[19]

Egyptian institutions were put in place following the Med Plan. Before 1980 there was virtually no environmental policymaking machinery, and most attention was focused on environmental research. Almost all environmental research was conducted by the Environmental Research Council within the Academy by Scientific Research and Technology. Some marine studies were also carried out by the academy's Institute of Oceanography and Fisheries in Alexandria. In September 1981 the academy created the permanent National Environmental Committee, with a mandate to recommend policy, prepare legislation, and evaluate new international agreements for possible accession, such as the Land-Based Sources Protocol. The committee was established to evaluate whether Egypt should ratify the Med Plan and to decide what appropriate follow-up actions would be.

In late 1980 President Sadat created the interministerial Ministerial Committee for Environmental Affairs to discuss policies, coordinate legislation, and formulate a uniform pattern for action based on existing legislation. In December 1982 President Mubarek issued a presidential decree creating a more centralized and permanent Environmental Affairs Agency to serve as a link between the prime minister's office and all agencies and ministries concerned with the environment, within the office of the prime minister, with a technical staff of ten people and an annual budget of $US 8 million (Baker, Bassett, and Ellington 1985:175). In January 1985 the staff was expanded to twenty-one full-time professionals (Talaat Alou Saada 1987:7).

Through their participation in these committees, the Egyptian ministries of agriculture, industry, health, and petroleum became more interested in environmental problems as they affected their own sectoral responsibilities. The Ministry of Industry also pursues an environmental project to promote investment in capital equipment for increasing economic productivity, personnel training, environmental protection, and pollution control, supported by $US 153 million from USAID's Industrial Production Project.

Less active environmental governments lack such centralized regulatory governmental authorities. Italy did not create its environmental ministry until 1986. Formerly marine pollution control was principally the reserve of the Merchant Marine Ministry, along with thirteen other ministries. The Ministry of the Environment (without portfolio —lacking staff or budget) was established in July 1973, but was soon combined with the Ministry of Cultural Property in March 1974.[20] The Ministry of Ecology, again without portfolio, was created in the summer of 1983, and was severely criticized by environmental groups for its lack of power (Reich 1984:386). In July 1986 the Ministry of the Environment was created, along with an advisory National Council for the Environment, with a budget of $US 7 million for 1986 and a staff of sixty. Its initial mission was to promote environmental impact studies and to develop a report on the state of the environment.[21]

Spanish environmental policymaking generally emerges from the interministerial Commission for the Protection of the Environment (CIMA) of the Ministry of Public Works. The commission was created in April 1972 with a staff of 120 (20 of whom are professionals), following national preparations for UNCHE, to encourage the development of overall environmental legislation, public education, and the coordination of environmental activities of other agencies. Its authority was expanded in 1978. Its 1982–1983 budget was $US 10.3 million (Baker, Bassett, and Ellington 1985:122). Other environmental offices were established in the Ministry of Industry, the Ministry of Agriculture, and the Superior Council of Scientific Investigations. In addition to the CIMA, the Subsecretariat of the Merchant Marine has been responsible for marine water quality. Under the subsecretariat, the General Navigation Office is responsible for ship-based pollution; the General Office of Maritime Fisheries is responsible for controlling coastal pollution; and the General Inspectorate of Ships and Naval Construction is responsible for pollution control technology.[22]

Elsewhere, environmental institutions were established, but they were merely coordinative and never significantly affected state policies. In 1981 Libya created the National Commission for Environmental Protection within the Secretariat of Foreign Affairs. In 1974 Morocco created the National Committee for the Environment and the Regional Committees for the Environment. The National Committee's responsibilities include assessing environmental problems and assisting in drafting legislation to resolve them; there is, however, no evidence of such action (Kuwabara 1984:90). In Tunisia, the Agriculture Ministry's Office of Environmental Affairs is responsible for environmental protection, research, and management, liaison, and the coordination of all national and international environmental affairs; it is also responsible for ensuring that the environmental effects of development projects are considered. The National Environmental Board was established to presidential decree in 1978; chaired by the prime minister, the board's membership includes a number of governmental agencies, nongovernmental environmental organizations, unions and political parties (USAID 1981:42–44). Offices for the environment were established in the Ministry of Industry and Commerce in 1980 (Kaak 1987:202).

Turkey also has only a weak coordinative environmental body. In 1979 the Office of the Undersecretary for the Environment, with a staff of eighty, was established in the prime minister's office. Staff size was cut by 20 percent in 1984. The undersecretary coordinates actions with other agencies to control air and water pollution, and establish pollution standards (Ural 1987:189). Other environmental problems are dealt with by the relevant ministries: the Ministry of Village Affairs for soil and the Ministry of Health and Social Assistance for solid waste disposal.[23] Formerly environmental issues were supervised by the Ministry of Reconstruction. The Office of the Undersecretary for the Environment also supports the interministerial Supreme Environmental Council, established in 1983, which has only met once since its creation (Ural 1987:186, 193).

Yugoslavia's ability to create strong federal environmental institutions is limited by the Republics' substantial autonomy and self-governance. In addition to environmental institutions at the level of the republics, the Yugoslav federal government has the Permanent Commission for the Protection of the Sea and Inner Waters from Pollution. The commission formulates proposals for other authorities and acts as a liaison with international organizations. Yugoslavia created the Federal Council for the Environment in 1974, which was replaced in 1982 by a lower-level Coordinating Committee for Environment, Physical Planning, Habitat and Public Utilities (OECD 1986:18). Eighty-five percent of Yugoslavia's coastline is in Croatia, so most coastal water quality decisions are made by Croatia's Ministry of the Environment. Research and policy analysis is provided by the Zagreb-based Rudjer Boskovic Institute and its Center for Marine Research in Rovinj and by the Republican Town Planning Institute in Zabreb.

The Development of National Legislation to Control Marine Pollution

The Mediterranean countries have also been developing domestic legislation to control marine pollution. Most of this legislation covers oil pollution and offshore dumping. France, Greece, Algeria, Egypt, Spain, and Yugoslavia went on to cover land-based sources of pollution. France, Greece, and Israel also require environmental impact assessments for coastal development, and Algerian and Egyptian legislation implies that these countries may develop such a process in the future.

These efforts, however, are not closely compatible. Provisions vary widely by country. For instance, Yugoslavian laws establish ambient quality standards spanning over two hundred parameters that are effectively impossible to monitor or enforce. Greek and Italian laws use emission standards. Egyptian and Algerian legislation refers to the future determination of appropriate standards, which are likely to follow World Health Organization guidelines laid down in its *Technical Report* series, as has much environmental legislation in many LDCs. Countries use different indicators for microbiological quality standards for recreational waters.[24] In the absence of such guidelines, authorities have had to rely on sectoral regulations to protect public health and fisheries. Legislation is often more exhortatory than regulatory, and environmental impact assessment is now widely practiced. The form to be taken by environmental impact assessments is seldom indicated, nor is the procedure widely understood.

Legislation in the DCs and LDCs developed on different schedules. General legislation in the DCs often accompanied or preceded the creation of environmental ministries. Specific marine pollution controls in France, Italy, and Greece followed the introduction of EEC standards for a number of uses of coastal waters outlined in the 1976 EEC directives. Following Greek entry into the EEC on January 1, 1981, Greek authorities requested a two-year extension to implement EEC directives on water quality. Sadly, in 1986 Greece was sued before the European Court of Justice for failure to comply with four EEC water quality directives.[25] Legislation in the LDCs follows the institutionalization of environmental interest groups within the government: once these were in place, their ministries sought to draft legislation, allocate sufficient funding to enforce it, and lead their governments toward more constructive Med Plan policies.

This pattern is not surprising. In parliamentary democracies legislation is much more likely to follow popular concern, whereas single-party states are much more likely to adopt policies following the creation of new constituencies within the government.

France has been the leader in developing marine pollution controls and environmental legislation in general. From 1960 to 1981 France adopted twenty-seven major items of environmental legislation. Starting with the protection of nature and controls for marine and freshwater pollution, France progressed to controlling the more costly and technically complicated problems of air pollution, land-based sources of pollution, and solid waste disposal.[26] Table 5.3 demonstrates the progression of French environmental legislation.

Following the adoption of a broad range of laws, the French turned in 1981 to their enforcement. Since 1977 all coastal developments have required the approval of environmental impact assessments. In 1978 704 such assessments were submitted for the Mediterranean region.[27]

The basic French law covering coastal and freshwater discharges is

141

Table 5.3. Major French Environmental Legislation, 1960–1981

National Parks/ Preservation of Nature	Air Pollution	Marine Pollution/ Maritime/Littoral
1960	1961	1963
1976	1980	1975
		1976 (3)
		1977
		1979 (2)
		1981 (2)

Source: France, secretariat d'etat aupres du premier ministre (1983), annex 3.

Law No. 64-1245 of December 16, 1964. Licenses are required for "any discharge, drainage, outfall, or deposit of wastes, in particular industrial or radioactive wastes liable to cause harmful effects to public health and to the aquatic environment, or detrimental to the economic and tourism development of coastal regions" (Kuwabara 1984:81). Law No. 64 also calls for a full inventory of pollutants to be completed every five years. The laws and decrees issued from 1973 to 1977 facilitate the licensing procedure for specific substances—including toxic substances and heavy metals—for a variety of different types of receiving waters by establishing water quality and emission standards.[28]

Article 24 of the new Greek constitution of 1975 committed the government to protect the physical and cultural environment. Subsequent Greek marine pollution controls reside in Law No. 743 of 1977 for the Protection of the Marine Environment. The law prohibits dumping from tankers, the dumping of sewage, and emissions from coastal installations, and requires that coastal industries wishing to discharge pollutants into the sea obtain permits. Presidential Decree 1180 of 1981 carries the act further, and requires environmental impact assessments for all major industrial installations (OECD 1983:61). In February 1983 a new housing law was passed in Greece banning the construction of any buildings within 50 feet of the high-tide mark. The 1975 constitution requires the state to protect the natural and cultural environment. The Framework Law on the Environment (Law No. 1650 of 1986) was adopted in October 1986. A number of 1965 national sanitary regulations specify water quality standards for water intended for swimming, raising shellfish, and fishing. The trade and

Freshwater Pollution	*Solid Wastes/ Nuclear Wastes*	*Other*
1964	1975	1976 (2)
1973	1976	1977 (4)
	1980	1979
		1981

use of a number of pesticides (including DDT, Dieldrin, Heptachlon, Isone, and Endrin) are prohibited (Kuwabara 1984:96, 102). Ministerial decisions by the Ministry of the Merchant Marine made from 1978 to 1986 prohibit the dumping of chemicals in the sea, pollution by hydrocarbons, and emissions from other sources. In 1986 Greek law was brought into conformity with EEC directives.[29]

Twenty-seven violations of Law No. 743 were reported in 1978, leading to fines totaling over $US 35,000. In 1981 153 violations were detected, yielding fines exceeding 2.2 million dollars. Between 1978 and 1981 nineteen fines totaling approximately 200,000 dollars were imposed on oil refineries. (OECD 1983:61). Law No. 743 led to the building of reception facilities for oily residues from tankers at the ports of Corinth, Syros, Piraeus, Salonika, Elefsis, and Kavala and to the purchase of $1.25 million worth of specialized equipment for combating oil spills. Facilities are planned for five more ports as well (OECD 1983:64–66). During 1981 seventy-six ships were prosecuted for violating national laws and international conventions within Greek territorial waters, and fines amounting to $2.7 million were imposed and paid (OECD 1983:65).

Israeli regulations cover marine pollution from oil (adopted in 1936, with amendments in 1966, 1972, 1977, and 1980) and from dumping (1983). The Act for the Prevention of Sea Pollution from Land-Based Sources was passed in 1988.[30] Since 1982 the Ministry of the Interior has required environmental impact assessments for all coastal development, although there are no standards for different coastal uses of the water (Kuwabara 1984:88–89, 97).

Algeria and Egypt have only recently adopted environmental legislation. Algeria promulgated Law No. 83-3 in 1983, which sets out a broad framework for the development of environmental policy.[31] Although failing to specify water quality standards, it does recognize, in Article 3, the need for a balance between the imperatives of economic development, environmental protection, and the quality of life. The decree creates a corps of environmental specialists to draw up procedures for environmental monitoring and assessment and specify techniques and physical, chemical, biological, and bacteriological criteria for their implementation. The National Agency for Environmental Protection is responsible for drawing up a list of hazardous substances that should be covered by the legislation and establishing emission standards. Since 1979 all industry has been required to treat industrial wastes, although enforcement, however, has been weak.[32]

Egypt seeks to control most of its marine pollution through Law No. 48 of 1982 for Protecting the River Nile and Other Bodies of Water from Pollution, which supercedes the unenforcable Law No. 93 of 1962. It covers emissions from "houses, shops and tourism, industrial and trade establishments as well as sanitary drainage plants." The ministers of health and irrigation are responsible for setting water quality standards and issuing licenses for emissions. Ministerial decrees were issued in 1982 and 1983 regulating emissions from the pharmaceutical industry and the cement industry. The minister of industry and mineral wealth and the minister of electricity and energy required ministerial review of the availability of pollution control technology before new construction, and called for retrofitting all factories, power plants, and mines with pollution control equipment. The prime minister issued a directive necessitating the drawing up and reviewing of environmental impact assessments before new factories are built. In January 1983 President Mubarek announced that water quality and sewage treatment was a primary national policy, and called for an investment of 3.4 billion Egyptian pounds to develop water resources and control water pollution.

Elsewhere legislation is more haphazard. Lacking concentrated regulatory agencies for the environment, few countries have the institutions to push for legislation covering pollution from a variety of sources and to set water quality standards. Libya and Tunisia have a number of draft water pollution laws, but none of them seem to be in force and all require the subsequent formulation of appropriate emission and dumping standards (Kuwabara 1984:87, 90). Malta, Morocco, Lebanon, Syria, and Cyprus have not yet established major legislation regulating domestic or industrial coastal discharges.

Spain has pursued a disjointed approach to pollution control, favoring legislation for general environmental protection and the conservation of nature over specific pollution control measures. This progression may be seen in Table 5.4. Spain adopted a "comprehensive approach to the control of land-based pollution" that "defines effluent characteristics requiring regulation, treatment requirements, and technical standards for the planning of submarine outfalls" under the Order of April 29, 1977 (Kuwabara 1984:83–84).

Italy and Turkey have started to develop legislation but, with only incipient institutional support, have been unable to pass it or enforce it. In Italy, Law No. 319 of May 10, 1976 (the "Merli law") provides comprehensive provisions for the management and control of coastal and inland water resources and quality. A schedule of emission standards is introduced for heavy metals, pesticides, organic compounds, acids and alkalies, nutrients, and microorganisms, and licenses are required before factories may discharge wastes (Kuwabara 1984:85–86). The implementation of this law has been postponed repeatedly, although the new Ministry of the Ecology, which was created in 1986, has expressed its interest in enforcing it.

For comprehensive legislation for the protection of marine environmental quality, the Italian Parliament adopted Law No. 979 of December 31, 1982, which detailed provisions for the protection of the sea. The Ministry of the Merchant Marine is charged with drawing up a general plan for the protection of the sea and of the marine coastline against pollution. The new law establishes a network for monitoring coastal waters, strengthens the means for intervention in case of pollution emergencies, and creates twenty protected marine areas, with a budget for staff and new equipment of $US 180 million.[33] A fleet of forty-three ships, supply vessels, and tugs costing about $38 million to operate was set up in 1987 to patrol Italy's coast.[34]

Turkey passed its first environmental law in August 1983. Law No.

Table 5.4. Major Spanish Environmental Legislation

General	Maritime	Inland Waters	Air	Conservation of Nature and National Parks
1978	1980 (2)	1982	1972	1978
1979	1984 (1)		1979	1979 (4)
1981 (4)				1980 (2)
1982 (7)				1981 (2)
1983 (5)				1982 (5)

Source: Spain, Commission Interministerial del Medio Ambiente (1984), pp. 340–50.

2872 imposes stiff penalties on factories that pollute, and includes provisions for industrial and agricultural growth and plans for green areas and parks to be built in cities. It lays the groundwork for including environmental considerations in Turkish development policies (Baker, Bassett, and Ellington 1985:128; Ural 1987:185).

Yugoslavia has a set of extensive controls for coastal water quality. The Federal Decree of March 15, 1965 and its enabling regulations of December 24, 1965 (No. 53-2181) contain quality criteria for a number of uses of coastal water. Amendments adopted in 1976 establish further water quality criteria for the Adriatic (Kuwabara 1984:84–85; Ercman 1977:118–21). However, too many parameters exist for such standards to be enforced efficiently, and administrative support is weak (OECD 1986:95).

Oil Pollution Control

States may have been most active in controlling oil pollution by ships. The Barcelona convention and the emergency protocol call for the control of oil pollution from spills and accidents. The Regional Oil Combating Centre (ROCC) in Malta established an emergency communications network to notify national oil pollution control authorities in case of oil spill emergencies and to coordinate action. National and bilateral oil spill contingency plans have also been developed, with strong guidance from the ROCC. Emergency reporting is particularly important since most of the slicks reported to ROCC between 1977 and 1983 were reported by pilots flying over the area or other observers, and prompt effective actions from governments are required to respond to information from nongovernmental sources. Tests of the network have shown national authorities to be very slow in responding to alerts, due to the reliance on public telephone systems and delays in processing information and generating responses at the national levels, as well as the failure to transmit alert messages in an official language.[35]

ROCC has been most successful at getting states to develop oil spill emergency plans. In 1976, before the entry into force of the Barcelona convention or the emergency protocol, only four states had oil spill contingency plans (France, Greece, Israel, and Italy), and Spain was in the process of preparation. In response to national requests, ROCC technical consultants went to Malta (1977), Tunisia (1978), Algeria (1981), Morocco (1981), Libya (1982), and Yugoslavia (1983) to help formulate such plans (Le Lourd 1983a:10). With ROCC encouragement and assistance, by 1983 three more states (Monaco, Spain, and Turkey) developed contingency plans or at least a text indicating actions to be taken in case of an emergency. Six other coastal states were in the process of preparing their plans (Algeria, Cyprus, Malta, Morocco, Tunisia, and Yugoslavia), and four others (Egypt, Lebanon, Libya, and Syria) were considering drawing up such plans. Algeria, Cyprus, and Morocco were to complete and adopt their plans in 1984. After six years of the Med Plan, only Albania has failed to begin to prepare contingency plans for an oil spill emergency (Le Lourd 1983b:1–3), although most states lack the necessary pollution containment equipment.

ROCC has also encouraged the development of subregional contingency plans. France and Italy developed such plans, as did Italy, Yugoslavia, Greece, and Italy. As of 1980, agreements were under preparation between France and Spain for the northwest Mediterranean and the Bay of Biscay, and between France and Italy for the Tyrhennian and Ligurian seas.[36]

The number of Mediterranean oil spill alerts has declined since 1981, and the size of spills is smaller than in the past. The following tables present the number and size of accidents and oil spills reported in the Mediterranean from 1977 to 1985. There were probably fewer spills before 1977 because tanker traffic in the Mediterranean from 1967 to 1974 was greatly reduced due to the Suez Canal's closure.

Table 5.5. Number of Oil Pollution Cases in the Mediterranean

	Accidents Reported[a]	Slicks Reported	Total Alerts
1977	16	8	24
1978	8	3	11
1979	7	3	10
1980	8	4	12
1981	14	8	22
1982	8	3	11
1983	10	7	17
1984	8	2	10
1985	11	4	15

Source: ROCC and *ROCC News* (Winter 1983), no. 12.

[a] Accidents include wreckage or grounding (24), fire or explosion (21), collision (12), and other (21). Numbers for 1977 are adjusted for a full year from data on the last quarter.

Table 5.6. Size of Oil Spills (in Metric Tons)

	1977	1978	1979	1980	1981	1982	1983	1984	1985
Unknown	4	6	1	1	5	1	1	0	0
Under 50 tonnes	0	1	1	2	6	1	1	0	1
50–500 tonnes	0	1	1	2	6	1	2	2	1
500–1,000 tonnes	4	1	0	2	1	1	0	1	1
500–1,000 tonnes	0	0	1	1	0	0	0	0	0
1–5,000 tonnes	0	0	1	1	0	0	0	0	0
5–10,000 tonnes	8	0	2	0	0	0	0	0	0
Over 10,000 tonnes	0	0	1	2	1	0	0	0	0

Source: Regional Oil Combating Centre.

The frequency of oil spill alerts peaked in 1981, although the amount of oil transported through the sea continued to grow, demonstrating that maritime oil management in the Mediterranean is improving. The magnitude of spills also dropped after 1981, and there were no spills reported over 1,000 tons.

Other Regional Efforts

Outside the Med Plan, countries have also been pursuing subregional efforts at pollution control. These are weaker than the Med Plan, however; they deal with coordinating research rather than coordinating pollution control policies.

The RAMOGE (St. RAphael, MOnaco, GEnoa) Project was adopted in May 1976 by the governments of France, Italy, and Monaco. It seeks to enhance contacts between French, Italian, and Monagesque scientists and officials in order to coordinate antipollution efforts along the Riviera for the Ligurian Sea. The program includes the measurement of pollution loads using common procedures, technical rationalization of industrial and domestic waste water treatment, and monitoring to assure the maintenance of common environmental quality standards. It entered into force in 1981 (Boxer 1982:333–34).

In February 1974 Italy and Yugoslavia signed the Agreement on Cooperation for the Protection from Pollution of the Waters of the Adriatic Sea and Coastal Areas (the Adriatic Agreement). The agreement created a joint commission charged with reviewing programs of the two states, proposing and coordinating research and other programs, and proposing measures for combating pollution, including draft international regulations to implement the general provisions of the agreement. Subcommittees were established for scientific research, protection from oil pollution, and legal matters. In 1979, under the auspices of the Federation of Institutions Concerned with Studies of the Adriatic, the governments started a joint Multidisciplinary Program on the Investigation of Pollution in International Waters of the Adriatic Sea, including monitoring of the entire Adriatic, creating a data bank, studying the effects of pollution on marine life, and modeling the Adriatic marine system by twelve laboratories (Accerboni and Jeftic 1980; Boxer 1982:334; Kuwabara 1984:74).

The Italo-Greek Agreement on the Protection of the Ionian Sea was signed in Rome on March 6, 1979. Following the format of the Adriatic agreement, the agreement calls for cooperation between the governments and the creation of a joint commission to provide advice on joint research and pollution control programs (Kuwabara 1984: 74–75).

A number of Mediterranean countries ratified the 1973 MARPOL convention with its 1978 amendments. The convention entered into force in 1983, with France, Greece, Italy, Lebanon, Monaco, Tunisia, and Yugoslavia as contracting parties. In June 1982 the Union of Greek Shipowners and the Panhellenic Seamen's Federation created the Hellenic Marine Environmental Protection Association (HELMEPA) to monitor oil spills and provide information and training to shipowners, captains, and crews about cleaning bilge and ballast tanks, in order to facilitate compliance with MARPOL.[37]

Expenditures for Pollution Control

The best indicator of states' commitment to such new pollution control efforts, and of their enforcement, is whether they spend money on them. Data are inconsistent on actual expenditures for marine pollution control. Although the construction of new municipal sewage treatment plants and sewerage systems is underway all around the region, and may constitute, with oil spill contingency plans, one of the brightest points of the Med Plan's influence, data on investment to control other forms of marine pollution is haphazard. Only France publishes systematic data, and it only began collecting data in the mid-1970s. Most data for the region are only presented as overall environmental protection. Little data is available for expenditures by the private sector.

France leads the region in environmental expenditures. During the

1970s, increasing resources were directed to environmental protection. As table 1.2 showed, from 1978 to 1983 total public and private investment in sewage treatment grew from 1.71 percent of GFCF to 2.32 percent, and from .368 percent of GDP to .46 percent of GDP. Total nationwide environmental expenditures grew from 1.54 percent of GDP to 1.7 percent of GDP. During the 1970s more than 6,000 sewage treatment plants were put into service, so that there were about 10,000 plants operating by 1980.[38] The French population served by sewage treatment plants grew from under 40 percent in 1975 to 60 percent in 1983 (OECD 1985a:54).

In the clearest indication of policy derived from the Med Plan, on June 16, 1980 the minister for the environment and quality of life, Michel d'Ornano, announced that a new ten-year $US 380 million program for the construction of sewage treatment facilities along the Riviera was a direct response to the recently concluded Protocol on Land-Based Sources.[39] The Marseilles sewage treatment plant—the world's largest subterranean plant—was inaugurated in November 1987.[40]

French investment in environmental protection was higher from 1976 to 1980 than it had been from 1971 to 1975. This increase follows the 1976 adoption of the Med Plan and the EEC Directive on Emissions Into the Coastal Environment. On a per capita basis, public investment in all forms of environmental protection grew during the second half of the decade, as may be observed in the following table. Investment in the Mediterranean region exceeded the national average.

During the 1970s total public investment in the environment grew by over 250 percent from around 3.75 billion francs in 1970 to over 14 billion francs in 1980. Investment in pollution control during the decade grew from about 1.25 billion francs to 6 billion.[41] The environment's share of total public investment grew from 14.6 percent in 1967 to 17.9 percent in 1981.[42] This is a significant mobilization of public resources during a recessionary period, for it exceeded the rates of growth for the decade for total public investment (139 percent), as well as for federal budgetary allocations to agriculture (121 percent), veterans' benefits (193 percent), and commerce and industry (236 percent).[43]

Private sector investment in pollution control grew as well during this period. Between 1969 and 1979 the industrial sector invested 4,888 million francs in controlling water pollution. This was 1 percent of the total investment for the ten most polluting industries (chemicals, pulp and paper processing, food processing, metal finishing) and .4 percent of overall private investment for the decade (OECD 1985c:74). Thirteen percent of this investment occurred in the Mediterranean region.[44]

Israeli public expenditures for environmental protection grew as well. Expenditures from 1971 to 1983 are presented in table 5.8. Despite severe inflation in 1982–1983, expenditures grew in real terms by 2 percent from 1981/82 to 1982/83. About half of these expenditures were for services associated with pollution prevention.[45] From 1976 to 1985 Israel conducted a National Sewage Project to provide at least secondary treatment for all municipal waste water.[46]

Greece has also shown an increasing annual public investment in pollution control since the early 1970s. The 1972–1987 Perspective Development Plan called for an annual investment of 306 million drachmas, accounting for 1.7 percent of GFCF.[47] The 1983–1987 Five Year Plan calls for a massive increase to 6 billion per year.[48] Construction of sewage treatment plants has begun in Salonika, Volos, Larissa, Kavala, and Athens.

Egypt is constructing sewage treatment plants in Alexandria and Cairo. A billion-dollar sewage treatment plant in Alexandria is slated for completion soon, and work is underway for much-needed sewerage construction in Cairo to supplement its aged system. Most Cairene wastes are pumped into the Nile, which flows into the Mediterranean. More than $US 4.6 billion ($2.46 billion by USAID, $2.2 billion by Egypt) has been spent since 1977 for constructing treatment facilities in Cairo, Alexandria, five secondary cities, and many small towns and villages (Talaat Abou Saada 1987:7). Indicative of Egyptian movement to stronger pollution control efforts and a broader conception of environmental issues is officials' insistence on a design for the Alexandria treatment plant that calls for land-based disposal, so that wastes may be recycled as fertilizer, rather than the less expensive method recommended by USAID consultants, which utilizes long pipes to diffuse the emissions into the Mediterranean.[49] As part of the USAID-supported Industrial Production Project, the Ministry of Industry plans to spend $US 31 million to retrofit pollution control devices in existing public sector industries, it also plans to establish an industrial pollution laboratory (Talaat Abou Saada 1987:7). The 1987–1992 Five Year Plan calls for an ambitious £Eg580 million to be spent on environmental pollution, largely directed at controlling emissions into the Nile (£Eg500 million) and for the protection of the marine environment (£Eg80 million).[50]

Table 5.7. French Investment in Environmental Protection During the Sixth and Seventh Plans (per capita in 1979 French Francs)

	DEVELOPMENT OF NATURAL AREAS		SEWAGE TREATMENT	
Region	*1971–1975*	*1976–1980*	*1971–1975*	*1976–1980*
Mediterranean				
Languedoc-Roussillon	152	190	63	88
Provence-Alpes-Côtes d'Azur	101	133	55	95
Corse	174	186	45	90
Rest of France				
Ile-de-France	35	32	60	75
Champagne-Ardenne	124	78	78	69
Picardie	66	75	48	75
Haute-Normandie	68	69	64	98
Centre	109	140	65	96
Basse-Normandie	122	132	42	79
Bourgogne	132	125	51	76
Nord-Pas-de-Calais	42	40	57	82
Lorraine	55	63	87	64
Alsace	48	49	76	89
Franche-Comte	94	101	72	85
Pays-de-la-Loire	130	148	49	86
Bretagne	172	169	77	86
Poitou-Charentes	121	151	66	99
Aquitaine	153	136	87	90
Midi-Pyrenees	176	134	62	58
Limousin	200	174	56	99
Rhone-Alpes	131	118	63	94
Auvergne	158	186	55	85
National Average	100	103	63	83

Source: France, Ministère de l'Environnement et du Cadre du Vie (1982–1986), *Edition 1982*, p. 16.

With the establishment of the new Italian Environmental Ministry, in 1986 Italy allocated $US 846 million for new water purification plants; 559 million for river decontamination; and 184 million for the construction of waste disposal plants.[51]

Although Spain has shifted toward greater environmental concern, actual commitments remain low. The environment came to play a

SOLID WASTES		NATIONAL PARKS AND QUALITY OF LIFE		TOTAL	
1971–1976	*1976–1980*	*1971–1975*	*1976–1980*	*1971–1975*	*1976–1980*
13	15	16	34	244	327
16	34	13	30	185	292
26	27	42	96	287	399
10	17	10	20	115	144
7	9	6	11	213	167
8	9	6	7	128	166
19	11	5	9	156	177
16	11	6	14	196	261
19	12	4	11	187	234
11	14	5	14	199	229
19	17	5	12	123	151
15	8	7	9	154	144
14	9	7	8	145	155
22	25	14	20	202	232
17	14	6	10	202	258
8	14	8	12	265	281
7	13	5	9	199	272
13	16	11	19	264	261
13	9	12	15	263	216
9	8	20	24	285	305
12	19	12	22	218	253
4	12	14	37	241	320
12	16	9	18	184	220

minor role in the Spanish federal budget, running between 5 and 6.8 percent of the federal budget from 1975 to 1981 (Castillo 1982:65). Public and private investment for pollution control remained under .5 percent of GFCF, far lower than for France. Of the 190 municipalities along the Mediterranean coast, 77 have sewage treatment plants, and plans have been approved or plants are under construction in 36 more.[52] From 1975 to 1985 Spain spent nearly $US 200 million on water supply, sanitation, and sewage networks for the Mediterranean

Table 5.8. Total Public Expenditures for Environmental Protection, 1971–1983 (in millions of Israeli pounds through 1977, in scheckels for 1981–1983)

	1971	*1972*	*1973*	*1974*
Total	337	452	594	879
National government	18	25	40	47
Local authorities	291	394	511	766
Nonprofit institutions	28	33	43	66
As percent of GNP (in current prices)	1.46	1.53	1.58	1.62
Percentage of change on previous year at 1977–1978 prices				

Source: UNEP, "Handbook on National Environmental Institutions and Legislation," unpublished document; UNEP Regional Seas Programme Israel files; Israel, Central Bureau of Statistics, "Public Expenditure on Environmental Protection, 1982/83," Monthly Bulletin of Statistics No. 7. Supplement (1985).

Note: 1971–1977 are calendar years; 1981/82 and 1982/83 are for periods from April to March.

coast. Between 1983 and 1985 $US 40 million went for beach protection or improvement, resort access roads, pedestrian paths, and other projects to support the carrying capacity of the coastal environment.[53] The conservation of marine species has been a very small element of Spanish environmental protection. The federal budget called for only $5,000 for protecting marine waters in 1978, $3,400 in 1979, $5,000 in 1980, and $8,875 in 1981. (Castillo 1982:64).

Many governments received external concessionary financing for their sewage treatment efforts. Most of Egypt's foreign exchange is provided by USAID. The World Bank extended large loans to Algeria ($US 82 million), Israel (30 million) Greece (36 million), and Tunisia (54.5 million) for installing sewage systems and constructing treatment facilities. The EEC's European Investment Bank has also supported the construction of a $US 115 million dollar biological treatment station outside Athens, a 15-million-dollar sewerage expansion project in Aleppo,[54] as well as floating oil reception facilities for major ports.

1975	1976	1977 (est)	1981/82	1982/83
1,291	1,629	2,252	3,934	9,122
63	81	111	661	1,613
1,122	1,400	1,935	2,891	6,554
106	148	206	380	854
1.71	1.71	1.68	1.3	1.3
			4	2

THE ROLE OF EPISTEMIC COMMUNITIES IN PROMOTING STRONGER NATIONAL POLLUTION CONTROLS

Although there has been mounting concern in the Mediterranean about pollution control, actual efforts to control pollutants have been strongly stratified. One group, consisting of France, Israel, Greece, Algeria, and Egypt have developed broader and stronger measures for controlling marine pollution and have become more active supporters of the Med Plan through taking more constructive positions at Med Plan meetings. A second group, consisting of the rest of the Mediterranean states, has pursued less comprehensive domestic measures and has been a much more tepid supporter of the Med Plan.

This variance may be explained by the presence of the epistemic community. The countries who have come to adopt the strongest environmental protection standards, and who became the stronger supporters of the Med Plan at international meetings, are those countries in which the epistemic community is strongest. Countries that were less active internationally and have not moved to take a more comprehensive approach to pollution control have not had as active an involvement of the epistemic community. In outlying Tunisia an outspoken member of the small delegation to Med Plan meetings was strongly interested in the Specially Protected Areas Protocol and in attracting its regional activity center to Tunis, but had virtually no political base within the administration for altering national policies.

The experience of the five states with the strongest shift to controlling marine pollution reveals a common process by which they came to comply with the Med Plan and adopt more comprehensive measures for pollution control. The epistemic community was active in the domestic bargaining process in each of these countries after it had consolidated its bureaucratic power in regulatory environmental ministries. From this base it influenced domestic and foreign environmental policymaking. As will be seen in the following sketches, in France, Israel, Greece, Algeria, and Egypt, members of the ecological epistemic community, allied with marine scientists, led their governments toward more comprehensive marine pollution control. The marine scientists promoted the control of specific pollutants, but were relatively uninterested in adopting new patterns of development planning. When serving on delegations to Med Plan meetings, representatives from the environmental ministries also encouraged their foreign policy colleagues to support ever more comprehensive efforts. Table 5.9 shows Med Plan intergovernmental meetings from 1975 to 1984 that were attended by delegations from foreign and environmental ministries and demonstrates the extensive number of potential interactions in which these groups could make themselves felt.

Facing evidence of environmental degradation, fearing the impending "death" of the Mediterranean, and pressured by UNCHE preparations, governments established environmental ministries to alleviate the uncertainty surrounding the causes and effects of Mediterranean pollution and to develop measures to control it. Uncertainty led governments to pursue new sources of advice domestically as well as internationally. The institutions were staffed by scientists sympathetic to UNEP's cause. In France, Greece, Egypt, Israel, and Yugoslavia high-level officials in these ministries were members of the ecological epistemic community. In Algeria the marine scientists were members of UNEP's transnational coalition.

Algerian officials had always asserted the primacy of industrial development over environmental protection. In the early 1970s Algerian leaders opposed any measures that might impede or retard economic development. Algeria did not attend the 1976 Barcelona conference, and only acceded to the Barcelona convention and protocols in 1981. Following the inclusion after 1975 of the marine science community within the administration, pollution control was elevated to a more equal footing with economic development by 1980. Algerian officials approved the draft Land-Based Sources Protocol in 1979, which they had previously stridently opposed; ratified it in 1983; and adopted national environmental legislation in 1983. In 1985 they ratified the Specially Protected Areas Protocol. The 1983 legislation was broader in scope than any of their prior statements had indicated. By including the control of industrial wastes in domestic policy, the Algerian position changed from one of refusing to accept constraints on economic development to imposing them.

Governmental policy did not change until the early 1980s, with domestically produced analyses of marine pollution and the entrenchment of marine scientists in the government. The Algerian scientific community originally obtained access to the government through its national committee for the environment and its subsequent institutionalization within the Hydrologic Ministry, the Secretary of State for Forests and Development, and the National Agency for Environmental Protection.

Policy advice also came from scientists in the Centre de Recherches Oceanographiques et des Pêches (CROP) in Algiers. Charged by the government in 1975 to study the causes of anticipated diminished fisheries yields, CROP began monitoring coastal pollution in 1975. UNEP gave CROP scientists a gas chromatograph and atomic absorption spectrophotometer to monitor industrial and agricultural wastes and also provided them with training in their use. With this new equipment, the Algerian assessments of levels of oil and other industrial wastes were consonant with those in other countries around the Mediterranean Basin. In 1978 Mostapha Tolba visited Algeria for three days and tried to convince Boumedienne of the value of the Med Plan.

In 1979 and 1980 CROP published its first reports describing the industrial and public health dimensions of Algerian coastal pollution.[55] These reports generated concern within the government and among elites. The information provided by CROP supported the broader policies that the Hydraulic Ministry encouraged. The importance of marine pollution was finally accepted by the early 1980s, and policies were changed. Broad pollution control legislation was adopted in February 1983, along with a new agency to administer it.

The Algerian position also became much more constructive at Med Plan meetings after 1979. Delegates from CROP and the Hydraulic Ministry accompanied foreign ministry officials to these Med Plan meetings, and in 1978 a recalcitrant delegate was replaced with more

Table 5.9. Attendance at Major Med Plan Intergovernmental
Meetings, 1975–1984

	Date of Meeting					
Country	2/75	2/76	2/77	2/77	10/77	1/78
France	x	x	x	x	x	x
Greece	x	x	x	x	x	x
Israel	x	x	x	x	x	x
Italy	x	x	x	x	x	x
Spain	x	x	x	x	x	x
Tunisia	x	x	x	x	x	x
Yugoslavia	x	x	x	x	x	x
Algeria	x		x	x	x	x
Egypt	x	x	x	x		x
Lebanon	x	x	x		x	x
Turkey		x	x	x		x
Libya	x	x	x	x		x
Syria	x	x				x

ᵃ Meeting of experts.
Full names and locations of meetings are presented in the chronology, pp. xi–xii.

constructive ones from the Hydraulic Ministry. Although foreign ministry officials retained control over decision making, they invited greater policy input from the scientific community, and scientists gained a stronger voice within the government. Although the CROP scientists did not appear to share UNEP's holistic viewpoint, they did hope to study and control a broader range of marine pollutants than was currently controlled. Thereafter, they urged government officials to adopt more comprehensive policies and to encourage their foreign affairs colleagues at Med Plan meetings to do the same.

There had been extensive domestic evidence of coastal pollution from Algerian industry before CROP's reports were completed. The coastal population in Algeria became alarmed by localized fish kills, discoloration of the water, and the appearance of tar balls on beaches. Zinc electrolysis at Ghazouet led to death of shellfish from heavy metals in 1975, and pulp and paper production at Mostaghanem led to local fish kills in 1976. There were also cases of pollution from phosphate fertilizers at Annaba and from petrochemical production at Arzew and Skikda. Despite this evidence in the mid-1970s of coastal industrial pollution, "pollution" was still taken to mean the poisoning

2/79	6/79[a]	2/80	3/81	3/82	2/83	4/84	Total (of 13)
x	x	x	x	x	x	x	13
x	x	x	x	x	x	x	13
x	x	x	x	x	x	x	13
x	x	x	x	x	x	x	13
x	x	x	x	x	x	x	13
x	x	x	x	x	x	x	13
x	x	x	x	x	x	x	13
x		x	x	x	x	x	11
x	x		x	x	x	x	11
x	x		x	x	x	x	11
x	x	x	x	x	x	x	11
x	x		x	x	x		10
x		x				x	6

of the environment, but it always affected someone else (Abbas 1981: 3–8).

Thus, changes in government policy did not directly follow from the observation of coastal pollution. This new awareness did not come only from an objective change in environmental quality. In Algeria changed policies awaited the identification of an authoritative expert community and its bureaucratic entrenchment within the government to promote and enforce such policies. Foreign observers had reported the same evidence of pollution in the early 1970s, when the Algerian Foreign Ministry was deaf to outside advice.[56] Nor was the new behavior a response to new information, as it lagged the Med X Report by four years.

The gradual involvement of the epistemic community also transformed Egyptian environmental policy. Scientists were initially isolated from the government, having access only to the National Academy for Scientific Research and Technology. During Med Plan negotiations the Foreign Ministry focused on encouraging the transfer of technology on concessionary terms, but did nothing substantive with regard to specific sources or types of pollutants to control. Delegates expressed an ambivalence about pollution control that verged on lack of interest. However, scientists were consulted in the early

1980s, as the government convened commissions to determine whether Egypt should adopt the Land-Based Sources Protocol and to anticipate the domestic implications of ratification.

The scientists had a good sense of the variety of pollution problems facing Egypt. Egypt has a tradition of strong marine science competence (El-Wakeel 1976, 1984; El-Kassas 1981). Scientists' attention had been attracted by evidence of pollution in the late 1960s and early 1970s. An 85 percent drop in the fish catch in Lake Maryut led the National Academy for Scientific Research and Technology to fund monitoring of the quality of the lake by oceanographers in 1972–1973, and to create the Environment Research Council. Scientists at Alexandria University studied summer typhoid epidemics, which were related to the inadequate treatment of municipal wastes that were pumped into the sea through outfalls near the most popular beaches (El-Sharkawi and Hassan 1979). In 1971 the deaths of 1,300 water buffaloes in the delta town of Quatour from the pesticide Phosvil alerted scientists to the hazards of widespread and unregulated pesticide spraying.

Scientists studied the problems of highest concern to the academy, which was oriented toward applied research relevant to expanding industrial production, commercializing new technologies, and improving public health (Zahlan 1980). They monitored microorganisms that threatened public health rather than the more expensive and technically demanding monitoring of heavy metals emanating from industrial sources, even though local oceanographic institutions possessed the necessary equipment. Studies found extensive pollution in Lake Maryut from industries, municipal wastes, and agricultural spraying.

Administrative reforms from 1980 to 1982 established the Environmental Affairs Agency within the prime minister's office, and the National Academy for Scientific Research and Technology established committees charged with developing environmental policy and determining whether Egypt should ratify the various Med Plan treaties. Chaired and lobbied by individuals who were members of UNEP's epistemic community, the committees, not surprisingly advocated immediate compliance with the Med Plan norms and with all other international environmental treaties. Two prominent Egyptian scientists played key roles. Mostalpha Tolba, a microbiologist who had been president of the Egyptian Academy of Scientific Research and Technology and headed the Egyptian delegation to UNCHE, and was then executive director of UNEP, urged ministers to support the Med

Plan. Mohammed Kassas, a botanist and an ardent environmentalist who was then director general of the International Union for the Conservation of Nature, chaired the academy's policy review committee.

Already sensitive to the variety of pollution problems facing Egypt, once invited into the policy arena the scientists encouraged policy that would treat the whole gamut of pollutants and sources of pollution. In 1982 the government introduced Law No. 48 to protect the Nile, as well as a number of ministerial directives aimed at controlling pollution. In 1983 it ratified the Land-Based Sources Protocol and the Specially Protected Areas Protocol. Recently the Environmental Affairs Agency has pushed for a more thorough enforcement of measures to protect the Nile and the coastal areas.

In Greece, both domestic and foreign environmental policy changed following the incorporation of the epistemic community into the administration. Greece had always had a highly competent marine science community, but it lacked access to the government. Its advice was deliberately misconstrued or ignored by policymakers until the 1974 return to civilian rule. In fact, "in certain cases, the military regime of the late 1960s tried to refute the reliability of actual measurements of pollutants and even put pressure against some scientists who published alarming reports" (Gerakis 1981:163). The Office of International Organizations of the Foreign Ministry was concerned with marine pollution, and in 1975 entrusted negotiations for the Med Plan to the environmentalist staff of the National Council for Physical Planning and the Environment (NCPPE) in the Ministry of Coordination. In addition, the NCPPE was instructed to be "pro-environment," in essence making the Greek delegation an active environmental lobbyist as the scientific constituency within the government was given a free hand to formulate and pursue policy. The NCPPE was staffed by individuals who considered themselves ecologists and who were members of the ecological epistemic community. With the NCPPE as a springboard, the staff drafted new domestic environmental legislation for Parliament, handed down decisions identifying marine species for preservation and specifying the creation of marine parks,[57] and served as an "honest broker" to mediate between conflicting positions at Med Plan meetings.

The Israeli experience also conforms to this process of growing environmental protection shaped by UNEP and domestic marine scientists. Israeli environmental policy was developed by a small group of scientists with ecological views in the Environmental Protection

Service (EPS), cut off from the rest of the government and national politics. An observer writes that "pressure to establish a governmental agency concerned with environmental matters came primarily from the academics and scientists serving on the National Council for Research and Development."[58] This small, closely knit group shared an interest with UNEP in environmental impact assessment. The director of the EPS headed the Israeli delegation to Med Plan meetings and spearheaded attempts to make Israeli policies agree with the Med Plan. Med Plan support for environmental impact assessment also strengthened and legitimated his own efforts to introduce such measures at home. He continually supported Med Plan cooperation in a low-key manner befitting Israel's low-profile role among the Arab delegations.

France provides the limiting case for the extent of an epistemic community's influence. Although the epistemic community consolidated its power in the French Ministry of the Environment and was able to redirect domestic planning policy, it was relatively weak in influencing foreign environmental policy, as the Quai d'Orsay would not cede authority to it. Thus, although the epistemic community explanation is generally confirmed by other countries, it is less effective for countries in which the epistemic community's claims to authority are not respected elsewhere in the government. Conventional theories of state power are more appropriate for such cases, where calculations of state power remain preeminent.

As has been seen, domestic French environmental policy became stronger and more comprehensive under the auspices of the environmental ministry during the 1970s and 1980s. The Med Plan did reinforce part of this effort, as Minister d'Ornano indicated earlier, by leading France to construct sewage treatment plants along the Riviera. The growth of comprehensive pollution control efforts was largely a consequence of the complementarity of environmental interests between the staff of the Environmental Ministry and UNEP's own ecological staff, however, rather than the result of any active efforts at coordination on the part of UNEP. Marine scientists in France were not as closely tied to UNEP as were scientists in the other countries which were active environmental managers. With extensive domestic resources and activities, the French scientists had much less interest in the Med Plan than did their colleagues from other Mediterranean countries. Nor did UNEP try to attract them, sensing that its efforts would be more widely received in needier countries.

The domestic allies of the epistemic community's influence on any of the Mediterranean countries' foreign ministries was weakest in

France. The French Foreign Ministry had definite aims in the Mediterranean to which the Med Plan was subordinated, and kept the scientists on a close rein, so that they had little role in France's policy with respect to the Med Plan. At the final meeting for the Land–Based Sources Protocol delegates from the Ministry of the Environment had to call back to the Quai in Paris to authorize their decisions. As seen in chapter 4, their advice was only heeded with regard to the Blue Plan, about which the Foreign Ministry was uninterested. Delegates from the Foreign Ministry were reluctant, even though the Environmental Ministry supported them, to accept the provisions in the Land-Based Sources Protocol that covered riverborne and airborne transmissions of pollutants and that banned the emission of radioactive substances. Although the Environmental Ministry had gained in bureaucratic power relative to many ministries over the 1970s, it did not gain relative to the Foreign Ministry.

In all of these cases the development of national environmental programs and movement toward more constructive foreign environmental policies followed the domestic empowerment of marine scientists. Less extensive evidence from other countries confirms this experience. In table 5.1, the countries without strong environmental institutions failed to take broader pollution control measures. In countries where marine pollution control efforts and support for the Med Plan are weaker, there are no members of the epistemic community or scientists allied with UNEP, or the scientists lack linkages to their governments. The importance of scientific access to governments is underscored by the Italian experience. With a deeply entrenched and experienced scientific community including many individuals who firmly believed in UNEP's message, but without an active environmental ministry to help them channel their concerns, Italian domestic policy did not change until these concerns were embedded within a regulatory ecological ministry in 1986.

Controlling marine pollution and supporting the Med Plan has been basically an elite-driven process. Domestically, issues of marine quality were not highly politicized, following their initial popularity, and remained the purview of a small group of elites and technocrats. In general, the saliency of pollution issues was sufficiently low so that the Environmental Ministry's authority over pollution control was not challenged by industrial groups or by commerce ministries. In France, where the scientists were most closely supervised by the Foreign Ministry, they had less influence over foreign environmental policy than did their colleagues in the region.

Citizen response was generally too weak and too delayed to influ-

ence the decision to control marine pollution. Although public acceptance of "environmental values," at least in Western Europe, was on
the rise (Inglehart 1977; Milbrath 1984) such support did not extend
to marine issues. The coverage of "environmental" issues in France
from 1973 to 1975 overwhelmingly focused on energy issues and on
the preservation of cute animals.[59] Public opinion surveys in 1974 and
1981 revealed that 90 percent of the population was "concerned" or
"rather concerned" about environmental degradation, and distrusted
unbridled technological growth, but very few expressed concern about
marine pollution. Membership in French environmental associations
grew by 70 percent from 1979 to 1985.[60] However, concern was largely
limited to solid waste, urban congestion, and air pollution.[61] The
Green movement, although receiving as much as 3.9 percent of the
national vote in the 1981 presidential elections, is organized around
issues of distrust of modern technocratic society rather than specific
marine issues.[62]

The situation in Greece was similar. Environmental deterioration
did not emerge as a popular issue until 1982, when it was briefly
regarded as country's second most pressing problem—behind inflation yet ahead of unemployment; and then it was as a response to a
severe episode of Athenian air pollution (the *nefos*).[63] Very few citizens
expressed concern about the quality of the Mediterranean, although
in the mid-1970s an environmental group successfully opposed the
construction of several factories in enclosed gulfs. The group went
bankrupt in 1982. In Israel, environmental protection appeared on
the Knesset's agenda before it appeared in the popular press.[64]

CONCLUSION

Mediterranean states' domestic efforts grew in strength and breadth
from 1970 to 1985, years in which comprehensive measures for pollution control were increasingly adopted internationally through the
Med Plan. New institutions and legislation were developed to control
a broader array of marine pollutants. Most governments adopted or
are in the process of devising contingency plans for responding to oil
spills. Many governments are constructing sewage treatment plants.
Expenditures for environmental protection grew. The most extensive
efforts were taken in countries in which UNEP's ecological epistemic
community has its closest ties, and in which they had the strongest
bureaucratic power base.

SIX

Assessing Neorealist Explanations of Cooperation

For realists and neorealists, the Med Plan, as with all forms of international cooperation, is subject to explanation in terms of general patterns of international behavior that are dominated by state power. Realists propose that states will resist any efforts to encroach on their autonomy, and that such resistance to environmental cooperation may only be surmounted through a strong country's leadership.

Hegemonic stability theorists suggest that cooperation is only likely to exist and persist while there is a hegemon to support it. Their analysis revolves about the motivation of the hegemon and its power over other actors to compel them to cooperate. The scope of arrangements will reflect the range of concerns and power of the hegemon, and the strength and duration of such arrangements will vary with the concentration of power in hegemon. These authors argue that cooperation will diminish as hegemony ebbs.

However, the malevolent and benign schools are split about whether the hegemon will promote its own short-term objectives at the expense of smaller states, or collective long-term interests from which all benefit; whether smaller states will cooperate as a result of coercion or rewards; and whether the benefits from cooperation will accrue to all participants or states will fight over the relative distribution of such benefits. They also disagree about the rapidity with which cooperation will dissolve. The benign version of hegemonic stability theory expects cooperation to endure longer than does the malevolent version, although both expect that eventually countries will become unable to resist the temptation to ride freely.

In order to assess these explanations, this chapter addresses the basis of French hegemony, French motivations, French behavior and the form that the Med Plan took, and smaller state behavior. Finally, it analyzes the impact of some of the other dimensions of the Med Plan that would make its scope and persistence intelligible in light of the analysis of the cooperation under anarchy school, which considers general conditions that may contribute to cooperation, either in the absence or aftermath of such a concentration of power. The years 1972 to 1980 were the height of French hegemony, and hence would be the apogee of the Med Plan's scope and strength. Analyzing the period following the relative decline of France's regional preeminence after 1980 will shed light on how France and the other Mediterranean countries behaved in the aftermath of hegemony when negotiations were conducted, if not between equals, between states with fewer power disparities.

Mediterranean states' attachment to autonomy made them resist incursions on it. Power and control were prominent concerns for the Mediterranean governments. Both large and small states voiced concern that their economic comparative advantage could be jeopardized by participating in the Med Plan, as they required their industries to introduce costly pollution control equipment which would inhibit their ability to compete internationally by adding to their costs. They did not want to be made vulnerable to possible external control over their national economic activities and choices, which for many developing countries were a major security consideration—both as a symbol of modernity and independence and as a source of employment for their rapidly growing populations. As neorealists observe, each government needed reassurance that the program would truly reflect its own preferences for which pollutants would be controlled, that it would not sustain costs while other states rode freely, and that its economy would not absorb unacceptable costs in complying with the arrangement.

French leadership helped overcome such recalcitrance, although UNEP's provision of training, equipment, and information helped overcome state resistance as well. By publicizing the problem of marine pollution UNEP helped to persuade Mediterranean governments of the importance of accepting the new goal of environmental protection, and even making nominal economic sacrifices to accomplish it. Subsequent arrangements did successfully assure states that their neighbors would not make "patsies" of them, but in so doing they also led to the reformulation of state goals.

Many aspects of the Med Plan elude explanation by neorealist writers. Although much of early collaboration was a result of French leadership, the scope, strength, and duration of Mediterranean pollution control exceeds neorealist expectations. Pollution control was more comprehensive than the neorealist myopic norm. It endured past the limited erosion of partial French hegemony, and was broader in scope than expected by authors from the cooperation under anarchy persuasion.

THE DISTRIBUTION OF POWER IN THE MEDITERRANEAN

France was the most powerful state in the region through the 1970s. Although short of global hegemony, France was the regionally dominant state actor. It did monopolize the relevant "capabilities that can be used to entice or compel others" (Krasner 1976:322) in the issue area of the Mediterranean environment for most of the 1970s. Other important state actors, such as the United States and the Federal Republic of Germany, were simply not involved in Med Plan discussions. Germany was only indirectly represented through the EEC, and the United States had satisfied itself in 1976 that no crucial state interests or security concerns were at stake for it.

France's dominance was grounded on its large share of regional economic, scientific, and diplomatic resources. In 1978 France's share of regional GNP was 42 percent, nearly twice that of Italy, whose share was the second largest. By 1984 this fell to 37 percent (see table 3.2). France was also the principal trading partner of the major parties negotiating the Med Plan. Although the United States and the Federal Republic of Germany slightly exceeded France's importance as a trading partner for some Mediterranean states, neither one was interested in influencing the Med Plan. For the purpose of controlling Mediterranean pollution, France was hegemonic. By the end of the decade the distribution of these resources had gradually diffused around the region, and French hegemony ebbed slightly.

France's role as a major trading partner of the Mediterranean countries, without itself being dependent upon the other economies for a large proportion of imports or exports, gave France significant leverage over the other countries. All delegates were aware of the strong tacit influence over them that France possessed, for other countries would be certain to suffer economically if France elected to resort to unilateral measures for controlling Mediterranean pollution. France was relatively insensitive to the trade effects of unilateral environmental policies implemented elsewhere, whereas its trading partners were much more sensitive to policies made in France. If France were to unilaterally impose emission controls on French manufacturers, the cost to importers of French goods would rise. If France were to introduce product or quality standards for imports, such as controls on the pesticide content of agricultural imports, North African export earnings would decline. Thus, French preferences implicitly established the baseline for Mediterranean environmental quality standards.

Being widely recognized as the major Mediterranean polluter (although the actual pollutants and their amounts were unknown) gave France an economic edge that allowed it to seek to compel other states to conform with its preferred pollution control policies. Without active French participation, no efforts to clean up the Mediterranean could hope to succeed. Since the developing countries were more dependent on French trade for contributions to their GNP than France was dependent on trade with them, French negotiators were in a better position to coerce compliance from the LDC diplomats by way of tacit threats of unilaterally implementing new policies to control pollution. Thus, France could expect to create pollution control arrangements which would satisfy French concerns.

Table 6.1 presents the proportional trade dependence for the Mediterranean countries, and consequently their sensitivity to decisions made by their major trading partners. It only lists countries with more than 1 percent of their trade dominated by the four countries listed. Although only being truly "hegemonic" over Algeria, in the sense of being able to severely affect Algerian policy through unilateral action, France was well insulated from actions in other Mediterranean countries. Such a table overlooks the possibility for substitution between commodities provided by specific countries, but it does provide an overview of the general trade sensitivities of the area. Hirschman underscores the strategic importance of reliance on trading partners for key imports as well as for markets; hence proportions of overall trade provide a good indicator of external economic dependence (Hirschman 1980). The following discussion of imports and exports confirms the pattern of trade sensitivity presented in table 6.1.

Table 6.1. Trade Sensitivity

		Algeria	*Egypt*	*France*	*Greece*	*Italy*	*Spain*	*EEC*
Algeria	1971	–	.3	31.7	–	8.1	3.3	67.2
Algeria	1973	–	–	27.6	.3	8.9	7.1	66.0
Algeria	1975	–	.3	26.7	.4	9.5	3.1	59.6
Algeria	1979	–	–	15.9	.4	9.1	3.8	48.9
Algeria	1980	–	–	17.3	.3	8.3	4.1	49.0
Algeria	1984	–	–	25.1	.3	11.1	3.7	55.7
Egypt	1971	.3	–	4.1	1.1	4.3	1.4	17.6
Egypt	1973	.4	–	5.2	1.1	4.6	2.1	22.2
Egypt	1975	.5	–	8.3	.6	5.5	.7	28.1
Egypt	1979	–	–	6.1	2.3	14.6	1.6	45.8
Egypt	1980	–	–	7.0	2.5	15.2	2.1	41.7
Egypt	1984	–	–	8.2	1.2	12.7	4.9	40.4
France	1971	1.7	.2	–	.2	10.3	2.1	54.6
France	1973	1.7	.3	–	.6	10.2	2.5	54.6
France	1975	2.5	.5	–	.6	9.1	2.5	48.7
France	1979	1.5	.5	–	.5	10.6	2.8	51.4
France	1980	1.7	.6	–	.6	10.4	2.8	47.2
France	1984	2.8	.8	–	.3	10.1	3.3	48.7
Greece	1971	–	.6	7.9	–	9.0	1.5	51.3
Greece	1973	.2	.3	7.2	–	9.2	1.1	51.6
Greece	1975	.5	.5	6.4	–	8.2	2.0	44.7
Greece	1979	.4	3.7	6.3	–	9.5	1.1	45.2
Greece	1980	.4	5.3	6.6	–	8.9	.7	42.8
Greece	1984	.6	1.5	7.4	–	12.2	1.0	51.8

Source: International Monetary Fund, *Direction of Trade Statistics Yearbook* (1978, 1985).

Note: Reading across gives row country's trade with column country as a proportion of total row trade; i.e., in 1971 31.7 percent of Algeria's trade was with France, whereas 1.7 percent of France's trade was with Algeria. Such a disparity indicates greater Algerian sensitivity to French environmental policy affecting trade than vice versa, and hence indicates potential French power over Algeria.

In the region, France is the principal trading partner of the participants in the Med Plan. France is Algeria's major trading partner. France and Italy are the major partners for Egypt and Greece. France is far and away Algeria's largest source of imports, at nearly twice the level of Italy and the Federal Republic of Germany. On the other hand, France is only dependent on the Mediterranean states for a very small proportion of its foreign trade, with the slight exception of Italy.

France's preeminence in regional trade declined from 1971 to 1979, although it revived in the early 1980s when the price of oil collapsed, and Algeria reverted to its former dependence on France for trade. Algerian reliance on French trade declined from 31.7 percent of all of Algerian trade in 1971 to 15.9 percent of its trade in 1979, and in 1979 Italy replaced France as Egypt's largest regional trading partner. France would still be less affected by trade perturbations resulting from unilateral action on the part of its trade partners than would be its partners by French action. French trade partners diversified their dependence, so that their sensitivity to possible French unilateral action was reduced.

The analysis of import sensitivity in table 6.2 tells a similar story of France's declining regional dominance. Algerian dependence on imports from France declined during the 1970s, dropping from 37.7 percent of all Algerian imports in 1971, to 34 percent after the 1973 Middle East war and oil price hikes, and to 18.4 percent in 1979. Egyptian reliance on French imports oscillated between 5 and 10 percent during the 1970s. France relied most heavily on imports from its EEC trade partners, and was relatively free from sensitivity to Mediterranean states' policies regarding imports.

In the area of exports (presented in table 6.3) a decline in French regional sway is also evident. Algeria nearly halved its dependence on the French market for the purchase of Algerian goods during the 1970s.[1] In 1971 23.5 percent of Algerian exports went to France. By 1980 this had fallen to 13.4 percent. Following the renewal of ties with the West, Egypt expanded its exports to Italy from 2.8 percent of Egyptian exports in 1971 to 29.4 percent of their exports in 1984. France's share grew from 1.6 percent of Egyptian exports in 1971 to 11.2 percent in 1984.

Algerian sensitivity to price perturbations from the French market fell through a reduction in reliance on the French market for Algerian exports. Exports to France fell from 6.0 percent of Algerian GNP in 1973 to 4.0 percent of GNP in 1980. French dependence on the Algerian market for exports remained at 0.4 percent of French GNP for the

Table 6.2. Import Sensitivity

		Algeria	Egypt	France	Greece	Italy	Spain	EEC	*Principal Partner*
Algeria	1971	–	–	37.7	–	8.5	2.8	67.0	France
Algeria	1973	–	–	32.0	–	8.4	5.1	66.8	France
Algeria	1975	–	–	34.0	.4	10.0	3.4	62.9	France
Algeria	1979	–	–	18.4	–	12.6	5.3	63.2	France
Algeria	1980	–	–	23.1	–	11.8	5.2	62.6	France
Algeria	1984	–	–	28.8	–	8.3	3.5	58.4	France
Egypt	1971	–	–	5.2	1.0	5.6	–	23.7	USSR
Egypt	1973	–	–	8.6	1.1	4.7	1.0	29.9	U.S.
Egypt	1975	–	–	10.7	–	5.9	–	33.8	U.S.
Egypt	1979	–	–	7.7	1.9	8.5	2.0	40.6	U.S.
Egypt	1980	–	–	10.2	2.2	6.7	2.4	39.5	U.S.
Egypt	1984	–	–	7.2	1.4	7.3	4.7	34.6	U.S.
France	1971	1.1	–	–	–	9.9	1.7	55.3	FRG
France	1973	1.3	–	–	–	9.0	2.1	54.6	FRG
France	1975	1.4	–	–	–	8.8	2.3	49.1	FRG
France	1979	1.0	–	–	–	10.1	3.0	50.4	FRG
France	1980	1.3	–	–	–	9.4	2.9	46.3	FRG
France	1984	2.7	–	–	–	9.9	3.4	50.4	FRG
Greece	1971	–	–	7.4	–	9.2	1.1	50.9	FRG
Greece	1973	–	–	7.6	–	9.1	1.2	50.1	FRG
Greece	1975	–	–	6.0	–	8.2	2.1	42.5	FRG
Greece	1979	–	3.7	6.4	–	9.4	1.4	43.7	FRG
Greece	1980	–	6.6	6.2	–	8.5	.9	39.9	FRG
Greece	1984	–	–	7.5	–	10.9	1.1	51.1	FRG

Source: International Monetary Fund, *Direction of Trade Statistics Yearbook* (1978, 1985).

Note: Reading across gives row country's imports from column country as a percentage of its total imports.

entire period of the 1970s. French trade supremacy was on the up-surge again by 1984, but French hegemony had by then declined along scientific and diplomatic dimensions.

France also had the greatest scientific prowess in the region, as tables 3.3 and 3.4 demonstrated. France was the only Mediterranean country to have an operating pollution monitoring network in place. Italy and Israel also had strong reputations in regional marine science, but did not take a leadership role at Med Plan talks as France did. With more equipment and better-trained scientists France was

Table 6.3. Export Sensitivity

		Algeria	Egypt	France	Greece	Italy	Spain	EEC	Principal Partner
Algeria	1971	–	–	23.5	–	7.5	4.0	68.0	FRG
Algeria	1973	–	–	22.0	–	9.5	9.5	65.0	France
Algeria	1975	–	–	15.5	–	8.4	2.0	53.0	U.S.
Algeria	1979	–	–	13.7	–	6.1	NA	36.7	U.S.
Algeria	1980	–	–	13.4	–	5.9	NA	39.8	U.S.
Algeria	1984	–	–	21.8	–	13.4	NA	53.4	U.S.
France	1971	2.4	–	–	–	11.0	2.4	54.1	FRG
France	1973	2.0	.5	–	.9	11.5	2.9	54.7	FRG
France	1975	3.6	.8	–	.8	9.5	2.7	48.4	FRG
France	1979	1.9	.9	–	.95	11.1	2.7	52.4	FRG
France	1980	.2	1.1	–	1.0	12.0	2.7	49.8	FRG
France	1984	2.8	1.0	–	.8	10.4	3.1	46.8	FRG
Egypt	1971	.3	–	1.6	1.1	2.8	.6	10.4	USSR
Egypt	1973	.6	–	2.4	1.0	4.4	3.0	16.0	USSR
Egypt	1975	1.6	–	1.5	.5	4.5	.6	11.8	USSR
Egypt	1979	–	–	2.8	3.1	27.4	.7	53.6	Italy
Egypt	1980	–	–	1.7	2.9	28.6	1.6	45.6	Italy
Egypt	1984	–	–	11.2	.3	29.4	5.4	58.4	Italy
Greece	1971	–	1.5	9.4	–	8.6	.3	53.0	FRG
Greece	1973	.3	.9	6.6	–	9.5	1.1	54.8	FRG
Greece	1975	1.0	1.4	7.3	–	8.3	1.8	50.0	FRG
Greece	1979	1.5	2.4	6.1	–	9.8	.7	49.1	FRG
Greece	1980	1.2	1.7	7.3	–	9.7	.6	48.0	FRG
Greece	1984	1.8	3.9	7.3	–	14.6	.9	59.1	FRG

Source: International Monetary Fund, *Direction of Trade Statistics Yearbook* (1978, 1985).

Note: Reading across gives row country's exports to column country as a percentage of its total exports.

dominant in marine science institutions in 1974. Other countries depended upon French research and monitoring to assess the quality of the sea, even though many of them were suspicious of the objectivity of such findings, which demonstrated that they may be partly responsible for such pollution. French scientists had the most authoritative voice in the technical sphere. By 1980, through Med Pol, other Mediterranean countries' scientific capabilities were enhanced as they acquired more equipment and training for their scientists. Many other states were now able to conduct their own scientific investigations.

The vast disparity in scientific capability between France and the other countries, although still large, was diminished. By 1980 Algerian and Egyptian foreign officers were able to rely on indigenous scientific advice on marine pollution, which they had been previously unable to do.

Diplomatically, France sent large and diversified delegations to Med Plan meetings. Italy also sent large delegations, drawn from a variety of ministries, but they were much less vigorous than the French. Large delegations drawn from a variety of pertinent ministries ensured that the heads of delegations would be up to date on domestic developments and would effectively represent their aggregate national interests. Senior French diplomats wined and dined other delegates and visited high-ranking secretariat members in order to press the French position. The LDCs were generally well represented by small but capable delegations. Algeria sent small delegations, but individuals were familiar with the issues because they attended each meeting. By 1980 LDC delegates had become more experienced at negotiating pollution control issues.

Some of these shifts in the distribution of power occurred as a result of global processes. Others were a direct result of the Med Plan. Increasing OPEC commodity control led to a diversification of Algerian trade and, as a consequence, to a decline in Algeria's sensitivity to French action. This occurred outside the strict boundaries of the issue of pollution control. On the other hand, Med Plan projects facilitated the transfer of scientific resources to the developing countries, thus adding to France's partial hegemonic decline.

FRENCH MOTIVATIONS

French leadership was addressed to the pursuit of two sets of goals. French foreign policy was interested in asserting a broad and assertive presence in the region. More specifically, the French Foreign Ministry also hoped to harmonize regional pollution controls with existing international regulations to which France was already committed.

French leaders were concerned with extremely broad foreign policy goals in the region. In addition to controlling pollution, French leaders consistently wanted to extend France's sphere of influence in the Mediterranean. Under De Gaulle and Pompidou, France sought privileged relations with Third World governments in order to extend its influence. De Gaulle and Pompidou pursued various strategies intended to achieve the following goals (Kolodziej 1974:51, 490–91):

1. Disalignment with Israel and alignment with the Arab position in the Middle East conflict.

2. Continued French assertion of a big-power role in the settling of the conflict and the insulation of the area from superpower contention.

3. Regrouping the western Mediterranean states around French leadership.

In the closing months of De Gaulle's administration a Mediterranean policy was launched to strengthen French bilateral ties throughout the Mediterranean. France was interested in expanding its access to the Third World, and Algeria had always been seen as the door. Historically, French ties to North Africa were closest with Algeria. Jean de Broglie, French Secretary of State for Algerian affairs, stated in 1964:

> Certainly, while pursuing her policy of cooperation with Algeria, France defends certain interests and strives to counterbalance the tendency of this country to slide towards communism. But Algeria is also and especially the "narrow door" through which we are penetrating the Third World. ... A falling out with Algeria would go beyond the limits of Franco-Algerian relations and would peril the efforts of our diplomacy in the whole world.[2]

France had a strong foreign policy interest in taking a dominant role in the Mediterranean. A common expression among the French concerning the geographic range of immediate French interests was "France, from Dunkirk to Tamanrasset" (Sanson 1974:55). (Tamanrasset is in southern Algeria.) This focus on the Mediterranean was reinforced by journalistic references to the Mediterranean as the *"Mare Nostrum* of France" (Kolodziej 1974:514). French policymakers regarded the Mediterranean as France's historical backyard, or wading pool. France was always interested in assuring a continuous flow of North African energy (Hager 1974; Lieber 1980). In addition to its broad, although not clearly articulated, aim of extending its influence in the region, France had more specific goals for pollution control. Specifically, French delegates hoped to apply the provisions of international environmental law, to which they already adhered, to the Mediterranean. Giscard d'Estaing had Mediterranean pollution control on his personal agenda of items that he raised with Mediterranean heads of state he visited in 1975.

These motivations amounted to a limited scope for pollution control, however. The French were not interested in controlling the full range of Mediterranean pollution, but only those aspects to which they were committed by previous treaties. France and Italy were bound to extensive EEC directives on the quality of the environment that presaged many of the materials included in the protocols to the Barcelona convention. France was already party to the 1972 London dumping convention and to international agreements governing marine pollution in the northeast Atlantic; the 1972 Oslo convention for the Prevention of Marine Pollution by Dumping from Ships and Aircraft, and the 1974 Paris Convention for the Prevention of Marine Pollution from Land-Based Sources (Oslo and Paris Commissions 1984). Thus, many of France's coastal activities were already covered by international statutes. With respect to oil pollution and dumping from ships, all of the Mediterranean states were nested in agreements made under the auspices of the International Maritime Organization[3] and the 1973 MARPOL convention, which bans the dumping of oil in the Mediterranean.

French motivations were for a circumscribed list of pollutants and sources of pollution. France was solely interested in controlling the pollutants and channels to which it was already committed, and uninterested in extending such coverage to any other pollutants or channels that might be peculiar to the Mediterranean, such as radioactive substance, or rivers. Thus, French motivations seem closer to the malevolent vision of hegemonic leadership than to the benevolent vision, as they were directed to broader foreign policy considerations and narrow, short-term environmental considerations. Although the French pursuit of its own absolute gains by way of a cleaner coastline would also generate absolute gains for other Mediterranean states, the overlap of interests between French aims and an objective collective good of a cleaner Mediterranean encompassing a full range of sources, types, and channels of pollution, was much narrower than the benign version would have it.

In addition, France hoped to appropriate as many benefits from such arrangements for French firms as possible. This did not appear to be a major foreign policy aim for the French, however, as they continued to support the Med Plan despite UNEP's persistent successes at hampering such efforts by the French.

FRENCH BEHAVIOR AND THE MED PLAN

Hegemonic stability theorists presume that France would take a leadership role while it was hegemonic, and then tire of such a position once its concentration of power diffused. Moreover, they presume that the scope of the ensuing arrangements would reflect French motivations. Still, the benevolent and malevolent versions differ in their expectations of whether France would lead by rewards or through compellance. Motivated by an interest in extending its preexisting commitments to other countries, France took a leadership role in the Med Plan. However, it was consistently frustrated by UNEP in its efforts to impose its own preferred scope on the arrangements and to eke out relative gains from the Med Plan.

Because of its dominant position, France was able to take, and did take, a leadership role in the early phase of the Med Plan. France underwrote many of the expenses of the Med Plan during its formative years. During the early years of the program the greatest national contributions came from France; without this support the program would not have gotten off the ground. In addition to direct budgetary support, France contributed $US 20,000 in 1976 to pay for early Blue Plan preparations, and continues to fund MEDEAS.

France continues to pay the lion's share of countries' support for the Med Plan. Table 6.4 shows national contributions to the Med Plan Trust Fund. France's declining proportional financial contribution to the Med Plan is a result of France's proportionate decline in global GNP relative to other Mediterranean states.

Other states were content with this distribution of payments; the Algerians frequently asserted that the biggest polluters should pay the most for the support of the Med Plan. On the other hand, the Algerians were well aware that France expected a quid pro quo for its support and regarded the Blue Plan as France's just reward.

With the diffusion of regional power by 1980, French support for the Med Plan waned briefly. At the Third Meeting of the Contracting Parties in 1983 France announced that it would freeze its annual support at $US 1 million, and would not contribute to the 5 percent annual increase approved by the other states. This threat would have reduced France's annual share to 43.44 percent.

Despite momentarily surrendering to the temptation to withdraw support from a program it could no longer control, France overcame this hegemonic malaise, and continued to support the Med Plan.

Table 6.4. National Contributions to Med Plan Trust Fund
(as a percentage of total national pledges)

	1979–1981	*1981–1982*	*1983–1985*
France	48.91	46.48	45.85
Italy	23.29	27.04	26.33
Spain	12.89	12.24	13.57
Yugoslavia	3.37	3.20	3.23
Greece	2.95	2.80	2.81
Turkey	2.52	2.40	3.25
Israel	1.94	1.84	1.61
Libya	1.35	1.28	1.81
Algeria	0.84	0.80	0.91
Egypt	0.67	0.64	0.49
Morocco	0.42	0.40	0.35
Lebanon	0.25	0.24	0.14
Syria	0.17	0.16	0.22
Tunisia	0.17	0.16	0.22
Cyprus	0.08	0.08	0.07
Malta	0.08	0.08	0.07
Monaco	0.08	0.08	0.07

Source: UNEP/IG 23/11, annex 10; UNEP/IG 49/5, annex 5; UNEP/IG 56/INF 3, annex 2.

Note: Does not include host country contributions to Regional Activity Centers or to the headquarters unit.

Pressured by delegates from the Ministry of the Environment, French delegates from the Foreign Ministry did not live up to their threat to put a ceiling on annual French contributions, and continued France's leadership role by accepting assessments calculated directly from its General Assembly budgetary assessment. France ratified the Land-Based Sources Protocol in 1982, and remained the strongest proponent of the Blue Plan, arguing strongly at the 1983 meeting for its retention and continued funding through subsequent stages; France also continued to finance the Blue Plan center in Sophia-Antipolis. Along with most other governments, France was slow to designate laboratories to engage in Phase II of Med Pol.

France continued to comply with the Med Plan, too, even after its hegemonic decline. It began construction of sewage treatment facilities along the Mediterranean coast, "in compliance with the Athens Protocol to the Barcelona Convention," in the words of Minister of the Environment Michel d'Ornano,[4] and increased the budget of the Environmental Ministry by 76 percent from 1980 to 1982 and another 47 percent in 1986 (see table 5.2).

Why did French leadership not decay as predicted? For one thing, French behavior in the Med Plan was constrained by prior commitments made in other organizations. The Mediterranean pollution control policies preferred by the French Foreign Ministry are nested within the policies formulated for marine pollution control in other bodies to which France belongs,[5] so France could not renege at will from the Med Plan. Furthermore, the truculence of the French Foreign Ministry was tempered slightly by the Environmental Ministry's advice for more concerted efforts at pollution control.

As leader, France made few demands on other parties. No measures were taken to sanction parties who were slow to ratify treaties or who failed to develop domestic measures in support of international treaties. Nor did France make any overt efforts to link Med Plan discussions to other issues, other than occasionally falling prey to the temptation to obtain contracts for French businesses from Med Plan operations. France was commonly stymied by UNEP in these efforts, but continued to support the Med Plan nonetheless. Although smaller parties were rewarded for participation, these rewards came from UNEP rather than France. Countries received some research support, monitoring technology, and training for participating in the Med Plan; they were also awarded regional activity centers. UNEP was responsible for much more linkage: adding research, monitoring, and integrated planning to the initial efforts for pollution control.

Despite its leadership, France could not appropriate the benefits from the Med Plan. Leadership did not pay as well as was expected by theorists of the malevolent school of hegemonic stability theory. Even at the peak of French dominance in the early 1970s, France was unable to corner the immediate benefits from the Med Plan, or to dictate its terms. The Med Plan secretariat was able to defuse such efforts. UNEP deterred French efforts to draft the Land-Based Sources Protocol by referring it to WHO, which shared many of UNEP's concerns. UNEP arranged for regionwide research and monitoring funded through the Med Plan, rather than acceding to France's offer to provide it. UNEP offset French efforts to attract UNEP contracts for French technical equipment by using non-French manufacturers. Lastly, Tolba repelled French efforts to appoint a Frenchman director of the headquarters unit by selecting an Italian already working in UNEP. Although succeeding in pressing the contracting parties to move the coordinating unit from Geneva to Athens, France was unable to determine the new site or to control its activities. France also made many concessions at the negotiations for the Land-Based Sources Protocol.

In fact, all benefited from the Med Plan during the 1970s. The benefits from Med Pol, as was illustrated by table 4.1, did not accrue to France. As was seen in chapters 3 and 4, most of the benefits from Med Plan participation were widely distributed, and reflected broader interests than just France's. Smaller states benefited more than the hegemon did. Similar points are treated in greater detail in chapter 7.

Contrary to the expectations of benign hegemonic stability theorists, even though there was ample opportunity for a country to acquire some absolute gains from components of the Med Plan and from a cleaner coastline, negotiations were more often characterized by fights over relative gains from pollution control and over who must pay most for its provision. Also, such disputes were resolved by UNEP rather than by the hegemon. The degree of cleanliness from which all would benefit was not agreed upon: the DCs argued that the entire sea should be cleaned and all littoral states must contribute to create a cleaner sea, whereas the LDCs felt that they could tolerate a dirtier sea than could the North, and that the DCs should pay more for its protection, having been more responsible for its pollution. Thus, squabbles over marginal gains prevailed over the pursuit of absolute gains for all. By accepting the distinction in the Land-Based Sources Protocol between emission and ambient standards for the two annexes, France forfeited any marginal triumphs, as the DCs had to control the grey-listed pollutants more stringently and rapidly than did the LDCs. UNEP's intervention at the Conference of Plenipotentiaries, rather than French dominance, shaped the distribution of benefits from cooperation.

France certainly tried to take a malevolent leadership role. However, France was consistently frustrated in its efforts to dominate the Med Plan's evolution through UNEP's intercession in negotiations. Yet, despite its inability to fulfill its objectives, France continued to support the program, contrary to the expectations of theorists of the malevolent version. This support, however, seems due more to France's prior commitments than to a sense of altruism or a concern with protecting the sea.

Moreover, many Med Plan outcomes did not closely resemble French preferrences. The scope of the Med Plan exceeded that desired by France.

France strove to shape the scope of the Med Plan to areas in which

French interests were expressed: conformity with other areas of international law where the French were concerned, and sources of pollution that others were responsible for as well as France (heavy metals, pesticides, and oil). France had no interest in controlling pollutants for which it was solely responsible, as such actions would entail a loss of its economic comparative advantage or lead to increased costs for the industries producing them. France endeavored to limit the scope of the plan to make it conform to its previous commitments, going so far as to veto funding for Med Pol projects that could develop data on river and airborne transmission of pollution. France also refused to provide data on emissions of radioactive substances in the region, for which France was largely responsible.

However, the Med Plan's scope came to include radionuclides as well as pollutants transmitted by rivers and through the atmosphere. The more comprehensive scope came from the involvement of UNEP and the epistemic community, who consistently drafted treaties to include as diverse a range of pollutants and sources of pollution as possible, despite French opposition. The opposition of the dominant state proved ineffective in the face of the common front presented at international meetings by the epistemic community allied with regional marine scientists.

Thus, French leadership behavior and the form of the Med Plan outcomes are dissonant in relation to many hegemonic stability expectations. French leadership persisted longer than expected because of France's hegemonic position. Although France did reward other countries for participating, their participation was motivated to a large extent by UNEP's involvement and by domestic influence from the epistemic community. Nor was hegemony as rewarding as neorealists presumed. And the scope of the arrangements are also greater than was expected.

Even though hegemonic support helped start the Med Plan, it could not have done so unilaterally. Initially, France was unable to impose a French-drafted treaty on the suspicious North Africans. Early French efforts failed, and it was only UNEP's presence that led to a more comprehensive program in which the North and South could both participate. By serving as a buffer between the North and South, as well as taking an activist part on its own, the UNEP staff tempered the French capacity to dominate negotiations, and promoted outcomes that would reflect smaller parties' concerns.

Moreover, the Med Plan has endured longer than such theorists would expect cooperation to persist. Such writers expect cooperation to flag with the loss of hegemony, and hegemonic support to evaporate. However, the Med Plan continued well past the weakening of French hegemony, as both France and smaller countries continued to support the Med Plan. Although the benign school of hegemonic stability theory would not find this surprising, the actual growth in strength of the Med Plan after 1980 does significantly challenge their proposition about the duration of cooperation.

THE BEHAVIOR OF SMALL STATES

Hegemonic stability theorists presume that the behavior of small states is driven by an enduring temptation to eliminate external influence and to pursue marginal benefits in excess of the hegemon's. Small states' support of the Med Plan would occur only if they were rewarded or compelled by external parties; with the passing of hegemony they would reject their commitments. They would have little influence on the Med Plan's form.

Although the smaller states were willing to allow France to pay the piper, they were very sensitive to which dance steps they would follow. They were aware that they faced great potential economic costs and opportunity costs if they supported pollution control without due consideration. French financial support amounted only to the inclusion of France's concern with the Blue Plan in the Med Plan's integrated planning component; it did not include the identification of specific sources of pollution or pollutants. In fact, the smaller states had to force France to accept the inclusion in the Med Plan of control of river-transmitted and airborne pollution.

Other states also continued to collaborate after the ebbing of French hegemony. Even with the decline in France's ability to compel compliance, smaller Mediterranean governments resisted the temptation to defect from the obligations that France had effectively subsidized earlier. The Land-Based Sources Protocol was amicably adopted in 1980, and the Specially Protected Areas Protocol was adopted in 1982. Med Pol was extended and expanded in 1982. Many domestic policies were adopted to enforce Med Plan objectives.

Contrary to the hegemonic stability thesis of cooperation, the Med Plan has endured beyond the era of limited French hegemony. Despite the diffusion of power in the Mediterranean area and the weakening of France's ability to compel coordination, both strong and weak parties have continued to abide by the Med Plan, meet biannually, and contribute their shares to the Trust Fund.

In fact, cooperation became stronger as states developed more binding arrangements than they had during the first phase of power distribution in the region. Algeria, Tunisia, Turkey, and Egypt rapidly ratified the Land-Based Sources Protocol, and Algeria and Egypt began to develop comprehensive domestic pollution control legislation. Algerian and Egyptian negotiating positions became more constructive after French hegemony ebbed, and continued after its brief reacquisition in the mid-1980s. By 1985 countries' contributions to the Mediterranean Trust Fund were being steadily provided, and fewer countries were in arrears on their obligations than in 1980.

This behavior actually moves in the opposite direction of the behavior that would be expected based on a study of the distribution of regional power. In the waning of hegemony, neorealist analyses unequivocally argue for a diminution in collective support by other parties. Yet Algeria and Egypt elected to support Med Plan initiatives and implement stronger domestic control measures at precisely the time when structural incentives for defection were strongest.

Smaller states also engaged in linkage politics. The LDCs successfully pressed for the transfer of technology to them on concessionary terms, despite French opposition, in return for their support for controlling a broader range of pollutants. The scope, duration, and strength of the Med Plan has exceeded the expectations of hegemonic stability theorists. Moreover, successful cooperation came from rewards rather than sanctions. Furthermore, cooperation persisted beyond French power.

The epistemic community attenuated the hegemon's influence, and even in the aftermath of French hegemony it continued to press for countries to abide by the Med Plan. Cooperation continued after French hegemony had dwindled because governments' interests had been transformed. The Med Plan's durability has been a result of the shift in governments' interests toward dealing more comprehensively with a broad array of interrelated sources of marine pollution, rather than a result of the structural forces that shape governments' choices. As has been argued earlier, the structural forces that neorealists frequently identify served to keep governments in the negotiating process, during which time an epistemic community penetrated the governments and led them to reformulate environmental policies, so that state resources came to be more persistently deployed toward controlling marine pollution, even in the face of strong temptations to cease. The epistemic community was influential in both the larger and smaller states, so that compliance continued past the diffusion of power, and even continued in a more forceful manner than allowed for by the hegemonic stability theorists—or by the cooperation under anarchy school, which is treated in the following section.

OTHER BENEFITS OFFERED BY THE MED PLAN

The Med Plan did offer many scarce resources to the participating states. The cooperation under anarchy school of neorealism argues that cooperation is possible without hegemony if arrangements offer benefits that are not otherwise available to the international community. Situational dimensions may influence states' proclivity to cooperate. Clearly, the state interests were not sufficiently mutual for the countries to cooperate, as France and the LDCs at first fundamentally disagreed about whether the benefits to be derived from the Med Plan consisted of a clean environment or an unfettered economy.

Other factors that may facilitate cooperation have to do with the future: these include such factors as long-time horizons, reciprocity, the regularity of stakes, reliable information about others' actions, and quick feedback about others' actions (Keohane and Axelrod 1986). Presumably, access to information about the quality of the environment that would otherwise be unavailable would be a strong incentive to cooperate as well. Improved transparency of actions generated by smaller numbers of actors and other countries aware of each other's actions would ease cooperation. Lastly, international arrangements that create diplomatic channels between countries otherwise unable to communicate would provide states with strong reasons to support arrangements, regardless of their substantive nature.

The forms that such arrangements would be likely to take would be largely informational or based on the necessity of providing insurance against emergencies. The array of information could be very extensive, as the environmental issue is interlinked with so many other diverse issues.

These cooperation under anarchy writers are correct in identifying a number of factors that modify international structural inhibitions to cooperation. States did come to appreciate the value of information and diplomatic channels established by the Med Plan, and cooperated in areas in which such benefits were made available. Iterated plays, reciprocity, and side-payments served as facilitating factors for the creation and perpetuation of the Med Plan. But these factors are inadequate to explain the Med Plan's full scope and duration. Although these factors do serve as key elements of the Med Plan, they do not tell the full story. Cooperation occurred and continued in areas very different from those projected by these neorealist analyses.

These factors did facilitate agreement. Repeated intergovernmental meetings and the vast number of Med Plan projects allowed governments to think that they would achieve future benefits from the Med Plan; they also allowed the secretariat to dole out a number of short-term plums in exchange for continued collaboration. Developing countries and mid-level industrialized states, such as Turkey, Yugoslavia, and Israel, received lead laboratories for the Med Pol monitoring projects, as well as training and state-of-the-art pollution monitoring equipment. Tradeoffs between the Med Plan components allowed for side-payments leading to continued cooperation, such as support for Greece's offer to house the headquarters unit in return for future support for the lead laboratory for a Med Pol project. In addition, national experts were hired as consultants for the Blue Plan studies, and negotiators could hope for future jobs in the secretariat.

Negotiations were broken down into iterated games. The progressive development of the various Med Plan components through a process of a great number of meetings and interim agreements provided participating states with gradually increasing competence and confidence in the negotiating process, as well as greater familiarity with the subject matter. Besides the payments they received from participating, delegates stood to gain in future exchanges as well. UNEP deliberately set out to lead the Mediterranean states down the slippery slope to more binding environmental commitments, and Mediterranean leaders would probably not have been willing to accept the Land-Based Sources Protocol without experience in negotiating the other protocols or in coordinating the monitoring of pollutants. About twelve governments usually attended Med Plan meetings, so that over time delegates were able to develop a familiarity with each other's positions and needs. A UNEP official who was active in the early years of the Med Plan observed that

> the negotiation of separate protocols contributes to the delicate task of building a consensus. A history of cooperation and, perhaps, favorable technology transfer, create a pattern and expectation of future success. Parties' self-assurance increases with the conclusion of each successive agreement. (Bliss-Guest 1981:279)

In short, nothing succeeds like success.

The Med Plan also served to reduce transaction costs between governments. Holding annual intergovernmental meetings and more frequent expert meetings reduced transaction costs between states and helped to channel information to governments. Algerian and French delegates mentioned that during its early years the Med Plan provided a backchannel for communications between the French and Algerian foreign ministries during an era when tensions were high at the United Nations. As national scientific capacities improved and North-South tensions in the Mediterranean eased, the need for continuing low-profile linkages would presumably ebb accordingly, and reduce the value of such reasons for collaboration after 1981. It also provided a venue for Israeli and Arab delegates to talk face to face, although Israeli delegates generally maintained a low profile at meetings and did not interact with their Arab colleagues. Med Pol also established a way for marine scientists in different countries to exchange information, which was valued by the scientists, if not by the rest of their governments. Such linkages facilitated the transmission of information about Mediterranean pollution and its control, and sped up the rate of its diffusion.

States have strongly supported joint arrangements that provide information. States participating in the Med Pol projects received information about Mediterranean environmental quality and training in pollution monitoring, which they could not otherwise obtain. Governments got information about the quality of the Mediterranean as it became available. ROCC provided information on combating oil spills. UNEP provided advice to governments on actual standard setting as well. The headquarters unit also attempted to provide information about countries' actual pollution control activities, and hence to effectively guarantee for governments the predictability of their neighbors' pollution control actions. However, Algeria and the more obdurate LDCs doubted the accuracy of information that was not generated by their own researchers, suspecting such information as being biased or incomplete. Their primary interests were in receiving new equipment and training in its use, rather than receiving information.

Cooperation also persisted in different areas than those identified by the cooperation under anarchy writers. Information and insurance are no longer the Med Plan's key elements. Countries were extremely dilatory in identifying institutions to participate in Phase II of Med Pol, and have provided little monitoring or research data to the headquarters unit. Even though Med Pol is designed to generate increased data about Mediterranean quality and distribute information about forms of controlling pollution, support for it is weak. Collective support is also absent from the aspects of the Med Plan that shed light on the dimensions of terrestrial practices that give rise to marine pollution; this is associated with "increased issue density," which Robert Keohane sees as a condition under which states will cooperate to exchange information. Support for the Med Plan was weakest for the integrated management component that provided information on managing coastal development. Morocco's Interstate Guarantee Fund, which would have served to insure coastal states against the cost of cleaning up coastal pollution, has been a virtual "dead letter."

Even though these functional benefits exist, collaboration has progressed to include substantive efforts to regulate marine pollution, as countries take steps to implement the goals of the Land-Based Sources Protocol through the development and introduction of common regional pollution control standards, supported by common legislation and policies at the national level. Attention has shifted from providing information about Mediterranean water quality to actually regulating pollution.

In particular, the strength and scope of Algerian and Egyptian collaboration is striking, as it is well in excess of that expected by these writers. The cooperation under anarchy school assumes that states will act rationally, even if such rationality is bounded. Thus, although countries may value the resources made available by the Med Plan, cooperation would be unlikely if the costs of cooperation still exceeded the value of those benefits.

Algerian and Egyptian actions exceed the strength that would be expected based solely on rational calculations by those two states. By 1983 France had unilaterally committed itself to controlling its pollution of the Mediterranean. Other countries could easily have ridden freely by letting France unilaterally implement the Land-Based Sources Protocol, its prior EEC obligations, and various domestic policies. But Algerian and Egyptian annual contributions to the Trust fund continued, even though there was no compelling reason for the small states to contribute to the Med Plan, since they could garner an equal marginal benefit without having to do so. It did not seem likely that without timely payments they would lose the benefits of technical assistance or monitoring information. Moreover, they both moved to introduce more comprehensive and binding domestic pollution control legislation, and ratified the Land-Based Sources Protocol.

But in light of earlier behavior by both Algeria and Egypt such positive actions could not be rationally justified in terms of the benefits made available by the Med Plan. Egypt had been silent at inter-governmental meetings in the 1970s and at negotiations for the Land-Based Sources Protocol. Boumedienne's early hyperbolic expressions of Algeria's national interest, and Algeria's role in international politics, made it appear that Algeria stood to gain more by continuing to pollute rather than by cooperating with the Med Plan.

Many of the putative benefits of cooperation were not compelling for Algeria, and hence would have little effect in swaying Algeria from opposition to the Med Plan. Environmental protection was a very low priority for Algeria, and Algerians were dubious about the quality of externally generated scientific data. Side-payments and reciprocity held little appeal for them. With a high political profile in the Med Plan and NIEO negotiations, short-term concessions would be viewed as political defeats. It would be embarrassing for Algeria, as a speaker for the Non-Aligned movement, which is associated with radical demands for global reordering, to be seen making concessions to France. In general, side-payments may only purchase parties who are not strongly committed to prior positions. Early Algerian expressions of interests were so strong that they would be unlikely to be overcome by such marginal tactics.

The provision of equipment and training worth on the order of, at most, several hundred thousand dollars is inadequate to offset Algerian and Egyptian decisions to embark on far more costly national pollution control programs that would cost on the order of a billion dollars. Those were costs that they were unwilling to bear, according to Boumedienne's statements and Egyptian silences.

Thus, the reversals in Algerian and Egyptian behavior from antipathy or indifference to active support of the Med Plan may not be explained within the rationality framework adopted by the cooperation under anarchy school and other neorealists. The calculation of benefits by unitary state actors, and the value of the payoffs themselves, are inadequate to explain such behavior. Such changes could only result from a redetermination of national interests rather than the impact of factors that would mitigate the constraints of international anarchy.

All of the factors that the cooperation under anarchy school identifies as contributing to cooperation were present to some extent in the Med Plan. They provide a partial explanation of Med Plan cooperation. However, they do not account for the full extent of the Med Plan. Its scope remains more comprehensive than anticipated; national commitments are stronger, and cooperation is more enduring. In addition to these factors, the transnational alliance between the ecological epistemic community and national marine scientists led governments to redefine their interests, so that they accepted a collective program that was increasingly comprehensive, and complied with such arrangements domestically.

Even these persuasive factors were superceded as weaker Mediterranean states came to reformulate their interests. The processes identified by the cooperation under anarchy scholars contributed not only to the persistence of the Med Plan, as they would have expected; they also contributed to the entire transformation of the international political environmental order. The activities empowered a new group of transnational and transgovernmental actors who, with support and coordination by UNEP, led their own governments to recognize and adopt new policies for controlling marine pollution. Thus, they moved to implement broader policies than neorealist deductions based on anarchy would suggest.

CONCLUSION

Many neorealist approaches for cooperation explain French motivations and some static aspects of the Med Plan. Yet they do not fully explain the complete range of cooperation. The Med Plan's scope is more comprehensive and its duration and strength greater than neorealists hypothesize. In the face of temptations to defect, which neorealists commonly deem overwhelming, governments stuck to their commitments to deal more comprehensively with controlling marine pollution.

The conventional neorealist explanation of this pattern fails to fully explain the maintenance of the Med Plan following the decline of French hegemony. French support for the Med Plan continued, and Algeria and Egypt actually increased their support for the Med Plan, rather than riding freely or only moderately participating in activities relating to the distribution of information. Side-payments, reciprocity, and iterated plays kept states in the negotiations, although they were inadequate to explain the dramatic Algerian and Egyptian reversals of pollution control policy and the persistence of widespread support for a strong Med Plan past the waning of French hegemony.

With their systemic approach, neorealist analysts are insensitive to the possibility of a change in the interests motivating national action. Such transformations have commonly eluded neorealist inquiry because of neorealist writers' preoccupation with parsimonious structural analysis. They look at the distribution of power, but not the aims for which power is actually used.

Through the process of negotiating the Med Plan, new groups were introduced to national decision making who succeeded in redefining the national interest, so that states, particularly the weaker ones, came to support the Med Plan despite strong structural incentives to cease their collaboration. Ultimately, the Med Plan exceeds the expectations of neorealist writers because of the ability of states to reconfigure their interests. In response to UNEP and epistemic community involvement, Mediterranean states came to pursue a set of collective arrangements well in excess of the narrow scope and temporary nature anticipated by most neorealist writers based on presumptions of stable interests held by unitary states. Many state inhibitions to cooperate were overcome by UNEP and the epistemic community. By focusing most heavily on the strongest parties, these writers neglect the role played by nonstate actors and ignore the possibility that states, especially small states, may recalculate their interests in light of new information, or as they are penetrated by new groups. Thus, following such involvement, governments were able to overcome the domination of stronger states, and smaller states recognized the need to protect the Mediterranean.

SEVEN

Assessing Historical Materialist Explanations of Mediterranean Cooperation

The Med Plan also circumvented the influences on behavior emanating from the regional distribution of productive resources to which historical materialists attribute recurrent patterns of deeply embedded inequities resulting from North-South interactions. They argue that this pattern is perpetuated and reinforced by a number of partially independent and multidimensional forms of exchange. The structure of dependency leads to a pattern of outcomes unfavorable to the LDCs. Just as a focus on the texts or stories of the Thousand and One Nights obscures the fundamental reason for Scheherazade's recital—her survival—so, analogously, historical materialists argue that such efforts to limit pollution as the Med Plan serve a deeper purpose of exploiting North African states and perpetuating their dependence on Western Europe.

In fact, since 1971 many LDC spokesmen have expressed concern that the new environmental issue area would reproduce the historical materialist patterns of political and economic dependency on the North, which they were seeking to reverse (Founex Report 1972). In the Mediterranean, LDC officials and analysts voiced a number of fears. The problems treated collectively would only be those of the DCs. They thought that their trade would be adversely affected as DCs adopted more stringent product standards, affecting LDC export possibilities. The high cost of environmental cleanup and protection might significantly detract from the money available for industrialization. The infusion of sophisticated pollution control technologies would worsen the problem of inappropriate technologies in the Third World countries.

The LDCs saw many of their problems as the result of poverty, in contrast to the DC problems, which were a result of managing the externalities of affluence (Tomassini 1980). Many LDC leaders felt that concern with environmental protection obscured the historical lesson that the industrialized countries had reached a position of global dominance by ignoring the environmental consequences of industrialization during the Industrial Revolution.[1] More fundamentally, they suspected that the entire notion of concern for ecology and of balanced growth to reduce pollution externalities was merely a conscious or unconscious method of controlling LDC development and maintaining existing patterns of dependence. Technical pollution control advice would merely reinforce such patterns by transmitting an inappropriate or biased perspective to LDCs.

In the Med Plan, however, many of these outcomes were averted. The North did not appropriate most of the benefits provided by the Med Plan; the Med Plan's components do not reflect or impose French objectives on the LDCs; they do not significantly deepen commercial dependence on the North; and the entire Med Plan does not subtly shape or inhibit LDC industrialization choices. Nor did the technical advice offered to LDC governments reflect such systemic conditioning.

The recapitulation of an exploitative international order anticipated by historical materialists was avoided by a number of factors. The Med Plan's designers deliberately avoided reproducing regionally dependent ties. The LDCs' bargaining techniques enabled them to stall until they had developed domestic evaluations of their pollution problems. By virtue of delay, LDC officials were able to recognize the structural implications of imposed agendas. Over time, they developed a familiarity with marine pollution problems, fueled by indigenous research, and learned to deal more comprehensively with problems of regional marine pollution. The integrative nature of ecology avoided the excessive tilting of the agenda toward northern conceptions of pollution problems and solutions.

Nonetheless, certain deeply rooted economic structures persisted. LDCs were unable to alter the deeper relations of production in the region, nor did they even question their legitimacy. The LDCs still largely rely on the North to provide the necessary equipment for monitoring and controlling marine pollution.

Historical materialists ascribe such recurrent patterns of behavior to a dominant northern state's influence. France's dominant role in the region makes the North African states dependent upon France. Their dependency spans a number of dimensions: the provision of key imports, technology, capital, markets for their exports, and expertise (Sideri 1970:10–11; Caporaso 1978:25–26). Many of these dimensions are common to France's regional hegemonic role but they penetrate down to the decision-making processes in the dependent states as well. Commonly:

1. A large share of the dependent state's needs are supplied externally, and principally from one dominant economy.

2. A large share of the dependent state's markets are foreign.

3. There is a large ratio of foreign to domestic capital, technology, production facilities, etc.

4. Exports and employment are concentrated in one or two primary products.

5. Technology in the periphery lags behind that in the core.

The Maghreb (Morocco, Algeria, and Tunisia) states export primary commodities to Europe in exchange for manufactured products.[2] The Maghreb and Mashreq (Libya and Egypt) states principally export crude oil, phosphates, fruits and vegetables, textiles, and labor to Western Europe, in return for capital, processing facilities, manufactured goods, sophisticated technologies, and know-how. For Algeria in 1980, 98.4 percent of exports were hydrocarbons (82.38 percent crude oil, 9.23 percent petroleum products, 7 percent other fuels) and 64 percent of imports were manufactured goods.[3] In contrast, 66 percent of French exports were manufactured goods, and all primary commodities (agricultural raw materials, fuels, ores and metals) accounted for less than 17 percent of exports.[4] The agricultural sector employs over half of the economically active population in Algeria and Morocco, and 45 percent of the population in Tunisia. The Maghreb states are integrated into the Western European economy along the lines of the standard international division of labor (Robert 1980; see also Schlaim 1976; Schlaim and Yannopoulos 1976). As seen in the previous chapter, France alone accounts for a large proportion of Maghreb and Mashreq exports to Europe.

With respect to the Med Plan, the core consists of the high-income countries France, Italy, and Monaco. The middle-income countries of Cyprus, Greece, Israel, Malta, Spain, Turkey, and Yugoslavia fall into the semiperiphery. The periphery includes the low-income countries of Albania, Algeria, Egypt, Lebanon, Libya, Morocco, Syria, and Tunisia. The core has 43.3 percent of the region's population (1970) and 65.5 percent of the GNP (1978). The semiperiphery has 35.2 percent of the population and 26.4 percent of the GNP. The periphery has 28.2 percent of the population and only 8 percent of the GNP. Historical materialists believe that these structures of economic resources have historically biased most negotiated outcomes in favor of the core.

Moreover, by virtue of its former colonial relationship, France subtly shapes domestic decision making in many Maghrebine countries. In the realm of commercial ties and technical asssistance, France has played a predominant role in the Maghreb states since their independence. French technicians played a major role in planning economic development in the Maghreb states. Seconded French civil servants provided technical training and helped in the preparation of national budgets.[5]

The Maghreb states' ties with France have been much closer than with any other Mediterranean country. Table 7.1 contrasts French and Italian agreements with the Maghreb states.

The extent of foreign advisers' presence in the Maghrebine states, presented in table 7.2, demonstrates a similar reliance on France. Although still indicating a high degree of North African reliance on French technical assistance in 1966, French penetration of the policy formulation process in North Africa had declined dramatically from 1963, when there were over 27,000 French experts in the Maghreb.

This dominant French influence is most visibly demonstrated when contrasted with the Italian role in North Africa at the same time. In 1969 there were 481 Italian teachers in all three North African states, compared with 9,502 French teachers in Algeria alone (Van Buu 1974:84; some numbers are for 1966). Contrasted with the extensive French presence illustrated in table 7.2, there were twelve Italian

Table 7.1. Agreements Signed Between Maghreb States and France and Italy, 1956–1973

	France	Italy
Algeria	58[a]	5
Morocco	27	5
Tunisia	37	10

Source: Centre de Recherches et d'Etudes sur les Societés Mediterranéenes (1974), pp. 104–6, 139. Covers scientific and technical, cultural, financial and economic, and commercial agreements with Italy. French agreements are for the same categories, and also include social and administrative agreements.

[a] Between 1962 and 1973 only.

advisors in Algeria in 1971 training technicians, engineers, and architects, as well as teaching (Fuglestad-Aumeunier 1974:128–29). In 1971 there were only eighteen Italian advisors in Tunisia, establishing a hotel school, a television network, instructing architects, and training personnel in land use management. There was one Italian viniculturist in Morocco (Fuglestad-Aumeunier 1974:128–29).

Table 7.2. French Technical Assistance to North Africa, 1966 (in number of advisers)

	Algeria	Morocco	Tunisia
Public administration	158	198	35
Planning and statistics	172	134	96
Agronomy/veterinary	403	209	127
Public health/medicine	593	585	105
Professional training	54	22	44
Transport/communications/ energy/public works	1,491	373	155
Industry/mining	249	51	34
Teaching	–	49	20
Other/tourism	4	8	55
Total	3,124	1,629	671

Source: Van Buu (1974), p. 84.

THE GEOGRAPHICAL DISTRIBUTION OF
MED PLAN BENEFITS

UNEP's staff set out to avoid the unequal distribution of gains from participation through its principle of geographic distribution. By distributing benefits to all Med Plan participants, the Med Plan secretariat deflected France's efforts to appropriate the majority of such Med Plan benefits as Blue Plan activities, staffing positions, and commercial opportunities. The developing countries actually gained more from their participation than did the developed countries.

Med Pol lead laboratories were distributed equitably around the basin. Lead laboratories were assigned to Malta, Yugoslavia, Turkey, France, Algeria, Egypt, and Italy: two for the core, two for the periphery, and three for the semiperiphery. UNEP targeted other benefits from Med Pol away from France and the core, hoping to reinforce domestic self-reliance in scientific matters, as is seen in table 7.3. Given that 35 percent of the region's marine science institutions are in core countries and 53 percent are in the semiperiphery (UNEP 1977), the distribution of monitoring contracts reflects the secretariat's deliberate attempt to diversify the training benefits away from the core countries.

RACs are also equitably distributed. France got the Blue Plan,

Table 7.3. Distribution of Med Pol Benefits
(in percentage of total)

	Low Income	Middle Income	High Income
Total assistance received	33	60	7
Monitoring equipment worth over $5,000	33	67	0
Trainees sent to other laboratories	34	61	6
Number of participating institutions	13	50	37
Number of research contracts signed with national institutions	20	57	23

Source: Table 4.1.

Yugoslavia got the Priority Action Programme, Tunisia got the Specially Protected Areas office, Greece got the Med Plan headquarters unit, Malta received the Regional Oil Spill Combating Centre, and Spain was named the legal repository for regional agreements.

Professional-level positions in the administration of the Med Plan, which are nominated by UNEP and paid from the Med Plan's Trust Fund, went to more developed-country nationals than to developing-country nationals. Their distribution is shown in table 7.4. U.N. positions are graded as follows: general staff, professionals (P1 and P2), directors (D1 and D2), and executives (Assistant Secretary General, Under Secretary General, and Secretary General).

Frenchmen are well represented in the administration of the program,[6] although French nationals do not control the headquarters unit. Observers suspect that early French acquisition of the directorships of the Malta Regional Oil Spill Combating Centre (D1; see table 7.3) and the Blue Plan (P5; see table 7.3) worked against them in seeking to control the administrative positions in the headquarters unit. Although the French Foreign Ministry strongly supported a French candidate for the directorship of the Med Plan in 1980, Mostapha Tolba selected an Italian from within UNEP. Later UNEP tried for five years to hire a North African economist for the office.

Consultants hired for the first round of Blue Plan studies came from all of the Mediterranean states. Countries providing consultants were: France (three), Greece (three), Egypt (three), Tunisia (three), Italy (two), Algeria (two), Spain (two), Yugoslavia (two), Morocco (two), Syria (one), and Lebanon (one).[7] This breaks down to 21 percent from the core, 29 percent from the semiperiphery, and 50 percent from the periphery, contrary to patterns based on the core's regional prevalence.

In fact, as a whole the semiperiphery does much better from the Med Plan than does the core. Core countries support the Med Plan financially, and do not recoup their costs. The periphery received back $US70,000 more than it provided ($222,000, excluding Syria and Libya); and the semiperiphery got back $1.8 million, while the core ran a deficit of $5.1 million. Aggregated costs for the programs's support and monetary benefits from the various components are presented in table 7.5.

Although it is unreasonable to expect the same proportions to be distributed equally among different regional issues and indicators, the distribution of immediate benefits anaylzed above reveals proportional benefits that are dramatically lower for the core than the pat-

Table 7.4. Distribution of Med Plan Professional Staff,* 1981–1987

Nationality and Grade	1981–1984		1984–1987	
	Annual Salaries (in $US thousands)	% of All Salaries	Annual Salaries (in $US thousands)	% of All Salaries
France[a] D1 (1978–1984) P5, P2	180.0	39	100.0	24
Italy D2, P2/3	110.0	24	110.0	26
Spain P5 (1981–1984)	61.0	13	0	0
Malta P4	51.2	11	51.2	12
Turkey P2	32.9	7	32.9	8
Egypt D2 (1979–1984) 1/3rd time	24.0	5	0	0
Yugoslavia P5 (1984–)	0	0	65.9	16
Libya P4 (1984–)	0	0	56.5	14
TOTAL	459.1	100	416.5	100

	1981–1984	1984–
	% of All Salaries	% of All Salaries
Core	63	50
Semiperiphery	32	36
Periphery	5	14

Source: UNEP/IG 49/5, annex 7; UNEP/BUR/16, Annex 4; UNEP/IG 56/INF 3, pp. 32–33; UNEP/IG 56/5, annex 8.

*Includes headquarters unit, Blue Plan, and ROCC. Does not include PAP, which has a Yugoslav director and deputy director with unclear grades. Nine general services staffs work for the headquarters unit. Other nationalities working for other UN agencies at the headquarters unit are a P5 from Malta paid by WHO, a P5 from Cyprus paid by FAO, and a P3 from Yugoslavia paid by the IAEA. The UNEP Regional Seas Programme staff involved in the creation of the Med Plan and subsequent support activities came from Yugoslavia (1), Egypt (1), Morocco (1), and the United States (2).

[a] Does not include a 1/3d time D2 from 1977–1979.

Table 7.5. Costs Versus Benefits of Participation for Med Plan
Participants, 1974–1983 (in current $US)

	Paid[a]	*Received*[b]	*Net*
Malta	8,715	2,244,883	+2,236,168
Yugoslavia	498,990	2,063,616	+1,564,626
Tunisia	17,607	600,505	+582,898
Egypt	57,766	201,566	+143,800
Cyprus	7,854	77,925	+70,071
Algeria	79,032	129,905	+50,873
Lebanon	23,101	38,210	+15,109
Morocco	38,780	53,585	+14,805
Monaco	7,854	6,635	−1,499
Syria	17,458	0	−17,458
Israel	162,756	128,275	−34,481
Turkey	255,417	186,505	−68,912
Libya	136,704	0	−136,704
Spain	938,845	49,113	−889,732
Greece	1,139,970	80,621	−1,059,349
France	4,971,333	2,689,560	−2,281,773
Italy	2,863,964	80,700	−2,783,264
EEC	1,079,081		
UNEP	8,028,300		
Other UN agencies[c]	1,599,900		

[a] Includes payments to the Mediterranean Trust Fund, Greek annual contributions to the headquarters unit ($450,000/year from 1982), French support for the Blue Plan headquarters ($100,000/year from 1978, assuming an average annual exchange rate of 7 French francs to $US 1.00), Yugoslav support for the Priority Action Programme headquarters ($186,000/year from 1983). Amounts include actual disbursements through 1982 plus pledges for 1983.

[b] Includes total assistance received in Med Pol Phase I, plus budget line allocations for the Regional Oil Combating Center (to Malta), budget line allocations for the Blue Plan (to France), budget line allocations for the Priority Action Programme (to Yugoslavia), and budget line allocations for the Specially Protected Areas Programme (to Tunisia). Does not include $6,405,000 spent for meetings, coordination, and training, which was spent throughout the region.

[c] Other UN agencies include ECE, UNIDO, UNDP, FAO, UNESCO, IOC, WHO, WMO, IMCO, IAEA, IUCN, and others. Their contributions include cash, kind, and services.

Sources: UNEP/IG 14/4, annex 4, p. 17; UNEP/IG 43/3/add 2, annex 1, pp. 1–2; UNEP/IG 36/4/ Rev 2, annex 1; UNEP/IG 43/CRP 4/Add 1/Rev 2; UNEP/BUR/18, table 2 and annex 4, p. 18; UNEP/WG 46/3.

tern of regional distribution of resources would lead one to expect.
Despite obtaining a disproportionate number of positions and share
of Med Plan salaries, France and Italy received less than 20 percent of
the benefits from other Med Plan projects, and actually paid the most

for the program's maintenance. By pursuing a principle of geographic distribution and encouraging technical self-reliance, UNEP was able to channel Med Plan benefits throughout the region. UNEP itself was insulated from direct French pressure by its activist secretariat.

WHOSE EXTERNALITIES?

Some delegates from Egypt, Algeria, and Turkey suspected that the Med Plan was a "trick" perpetrated by developed countries to further dominate and exploit developing countries by making them pay for pollution problems caused by the developed countries. Some foreign ministry officials from Algeria and Morocco thought that the core countries were attempting to defray the future pollution control costs that they would have to sustain at home. With pollution of the shared Mediterranean being portrayed as a "public bad," mutual sacrifices by all littoral states would be required to clean the sea. These foreign ministry officials doubted the collective nature of many of the Mediterranean pollutants, seeing them solely as externalities of the industrial development in the northwest basin. They suspected that European leaders hoped to defray their own domestic costs with the partial financial assistance of the North African countries by casting the Med Plan's scope in concert with their own needs.

Samir Amin, among others, writes that pollution is a problem only of capitalist externalities, where social costs are not adequately absorbed by individual enterprises. At a conference convened in Dakar to develop a common African position for UNCHE, Amin urged the consideration of the true problems facing developing countries, not the "imported" ones from developed countries. He argued that developing countries and developed countries face fundamentally different environmental problems, and that developing countries should be sure not to be stuck with paying the cost of cleaning up pollution caused by developed countries (Barlion 1972:10–11). Pollution problems may be solved by more efficient national planning (Amin 1976:66–67).

Early on, all participants in the Med Plan were convinced of the collective nature of pollution from tankers and dumping. None of these substances were Amin's "imported" pollutants; all were substances that LDC leaders already recognized as legitimate problems facing LDCs as well as DCs.[8] Turkish and Algerian negotiators at Med Plan meetings were attuned to the possibility that the Med Plan would only treat French and Italian externalities. Despite French efforts to immediately control as many pollutants as possible, LDCs delayed accepting additional pollutants to control jointly until they were convinced that they were truly jointly produced and threatened all coastlines.

Through participating, the LDC negotiators learned that a more comprehensive approach was needed, and that more pollutants must be controlled. But the identification of such pollutants was not imposed by the North. The composition of a list of pollutants to be controlled was based on studies by LDC scientists, as well as on materials supplied by UNEP. The acceptance of such studies by LDC foreign ministries (and the commitment of these ministries to the collective management of the identified pollutants) awaited the domestic discovery—as much as seven years later—of their importance. Within the context of the UNEP-administered Med Plan negotiations, developing-country delegations could not be forced to accept joint solutions that they did not favor. The Med Plan's scope reflected autonomous northern and southern concerns.

POLLUTION CONTROL, FOREIGN TRADE, AND THE INTERNATIONAL DIVISION OF LABOR

Many LDC officials were also afraid that the Med Plan would freeze the international division of labor. Controlling marine pollution would inhibit domestic efforts to industrialize because of the additional costs of installing pollution abatement technologies. Delegates were not sure whether this was a deliberate goal of the French, intended to protect their regional comparative advantage, or whether it would be just an unpleasant side effect of the agreements they were considering.

Such outcomes did not come to pass. The motivations and effects of northern industries were actually quite ambiguous. Moreover, LDCs postponed their support for the Med Plan until they were assured that their industrialization goals would not be jeopardized. LDCs, sensitive to the possibility of the Med Plan impeding their industrial efforts by curtailing comparative advantage, were able to bide their time. In fact, they were eventually given an effective comparative advantage over the North, because they do not have to control the grey-listed substances as quickly as does the North, due to differences in the ambient quality of the coastal waters.

The motivations of the industrial countries and of regional industries are ambiguous, even when seen from the point of view of the South. It is not at all clear whether the LDCs would be better served by attracting foreign manufacturing industry or repelling it. Nor was it clear whether the DCs' motivations were to protect domestic jobs and impede industrial relocation, or promote public health by encouraging it.

Many LDC representatives, keeping in mind potential trade effects, encouraged the movement of heavily polluting industries to the Southern Hemisphere because of the economic benefits that would accrue to their economies, and because of the perception that the LDC physical environments were less degraded, and hence could sustain greater industrial pollution than could the physical environments of the North.

> Given Man's new understanding of environmental pressures, a more widespread siting of industrial regions, more use of areas with very little local risk of pollution—in a word, clearer recognition of the poor nations' pressing need for technological advance on all fronts—is not incompatible with a steady, mandatory increase in world environmental safeguards. The technologies of clean production, soil and forest-conserving husbandry, air and water purifying techniques and pollution-free settlements can be discovered and spread as the technological revolution brings its gains—and risks—to every continent.[9]

In a similar vein, Houari Boumedienne asserted: "I can assure (the developed countries) that many of us would be very happy to help you solve your pollution problems by processing (raw materials) in our own countries."[10]

In contrast, Samir Amin warns of the public health affects of such a transfer:

> But to acquiesce in the transfer of industrial pollution is also to accept the transfer of its eventual costs from capital to the peoples of the Third World. It means accepting a new unequal international division of labour, continued unequal relations between a dominant centre and dominated periphery, and a growing gap between their standards of living. (1977:141–42)

Looking at the North, other North African writers speculated that the industrialized countries intended to transfer their polluting industries to the South, effectively converting the LDCs into a toxic waste dump for the developed economies. They suspected that collaboration was being encouraged by the European countries "for the shifting towards underdeveloped countries of industries considered polluting or harmful to the environment of developed countries" (Keramane 1974:135).

Others thought that the North was acting to preserve jobs at home by ensuring that the North African countries did not obtain a comparative advantage either through lower production costs resulting from the introduction of unilateral pollution control legislation in France, or as a form of nontariff trade barriers to prevent pollution-intensive European manufacturing industries from relocating their production facilities to the South (Strong 1973:691–92; Juda 1979).

These conflicting interpretations of motivations for regional pollution control and its effects were never resolved. Elsewhere, though, industrial location decisions have only been affected at the margin by pollution controls.[11] A study of factors influencing multinational corporation (MNC) relocation concludes:

> Most MNCs have not yet found real benefits in a unified multinational approach to environmental management. The differences among nations in competitive situations and in the substance, intensity, and timing of national environmental policies are commonly viewed as being so great that little can be gained from standardizing MNC environmental objectives, policies, and programs. Environmental affairs in the MNC today are . . . most typically viewed as a strictly local problem. . . . Investment decisions are usually the result of a complex amalgam of factors, with costs in rival locations frequently playing only a minor role. (Gladwin and Welles 1976:196)

Even if policymakers' motivations about industrial relocation were clear, the Med Plan would have been unlikely to strongly influence such policies. Despite concern on the part of Third World delegates and analysts, international environmental protection policies do not seem to have had a significant effect on foreign trade. Fairly extensive research on the United States and on decision making in multinational firms reveals that environmental protection costs play a fairly minor role in foreign investment considerations. The uncertainty associated with variable environmental regulations may not justify short-term relocation to a developing country where the regulations may change later, and where political risks may be greater. MNC planners are generally poorly informed about national environmental regulations. A time horizon of five to ten years for investments transfers

MNC planners' attention to long-term market opportunities rather than immediate short-term gain. Other locational cost considerations, such as the availability of infrastructure, plant construction costs, and transport costs are all more important than the 5 percent difference in production costs resulting from environmental protection. In the long run, environmental controls would be more likely to balance out worldwide.

Even though the motivations of industrial firms and the full social effects of their relocation were unclear, LDCs did not wish to have their industrialization objectives hampered by pollution control agreements. A Turkish naval representative suspected that marine dumping agreements could serve as nontariff trade barriers against Turkish ships. Algerian representatives, at the earliest meetings in Barcelona, feared higher production costs for their petrochemical industry, and continued to participate only after they were reassured that Italian petrochemical firms would have to treat their wastes as well.

The LDCs' fear of the reproduction of dependency was dispelled through the advice provided by LDC scientists and by UNEP regarding the necessity of controlling industrial wastes. Awaiting the domestic provision of scientific advice, the LDCs acceded to the DCs' and UNEP's urgings for controlling a wider variety of pollutants, even given the economic costs for the controlling countries. Moreover, the grey list of the Land-Based Sources Protocol is to be made effective on the basis of ambient environmental quality, thereby giving the LDCs, with cleaner coastal waters which can absorb more pollution, a short-term comparative advantage; northern industries face more stringent controls than do southern plants. The LDCs avoided reinforcing the regional division of labor by awaiting domestic proof of the need for controlling pollutants and by bargaining for concessions for their industries in the Land-Based Sources Protocol.

DEEPENING COMMERCIAL TIES

The secretariat tried as hard as it could to furnish new trading partners for the LDCs. However, due to the historical fact that most marine pollution control equipment is manufactured in the West, there was very little that could actually be done to avert dependence on traditional trading partners, even though much of the equipment was bought with UNEP funds.

The recipient of technology is dependent upon the source for continued supply. Michel Flory writes that "the fundamental goal pursued in giving assistance is the maintenance of developing countries in the shifting world capitalist system and the preservation of general interests of the group of the imperialist countries" (Flory 1974:59). He "views (collaboration) as simply a reinforcement of dependency in a new guise—not the domination of an enclave export sector by the world market and foreign firms, but the technological and market subordination of dependent industrialization."[12] Galtung also explains North-South technical cooperation as a way for northern firms to extend their access to the southern economies:

> [Depletion and pollution] . . . are expensive and make the products even less accessible for the masses of the world, at the same time as they create new dependence on antidepletion and antipollution technologies. As such they are likely to reinforce the dominance structure, bringing in transnational corporations with world-encompassing economic cycles, specializing in undoing some of the evils perpetrated on humankind by the other corporations, but structurally identical with them. Like intergovernmental agencies, they tend to reproduce world structures, even to reinforce them. (1980:151)

Faced with the increased cost of oil imports in the mid-1970s, France and Italy would be looking for new sources of exports to balance their trade accounts.

UNEP officials deliberately strove to avoid using only French suppliers. Conducting the research and monitoring exercises laid out in Med Pol requires sophisticated gas chromatographs and atomic absorption spectrophotometers. Contracts for this equipment were signed between UNEP and the Swiss offices of the American-based VARIAN corporation for all of the necessary scientific equipment, because the UNEP officials did not want contracts to go to a Mediterranean state. Nitrogen gas, which is necessary for use of the equipment, is available only from the USA, the Federal Republic of Germany, Italy, and France; obtaining it requires expenditures of foreign exchange by the North African countries and necessitates the expansion of their reliance on the global economy in a slight way, but not with regard to a particular economy. WANG computers were purchased for the Med Plan's Athens headquarters unit, despite active French efforts to obtain computer contracts for French producers. Although they went outside the Mediterranean for equipment, the LDCs were still reliant upon the core for sophisticated technology.

The Malta Regional Oil Combating Centre (ROCC) comes nearest to serving the putative trade-enhancing role. Annual training courses for national officials responsible for supervising responses to oil spills were given by the center, where procedures and equipment were demonstrated. French firms had the greatest regional experience and training in combating oil spills, following the 1967 *Torrey Canyon* spill and 1976 *Argo Merchant* spill.

Philippe Le Lourd, a French engineer who was director of ROCC, was a member of the ecological epistemic community. He shared UNEP's vision of interrelated ecosystemic problems. Le Lourd attempted to introduce Mediterranean officials to non-French suppliers, although he was most familiar with the capabilities of French firms. Officials from Algeria, Cyprus, Egypt, Greece, Israel, Libya, Malta, Monaco, Morocco, Syria, Tunisia, Turkey, and Yugoslavia received instructions at regional seminars in handling oil spills; most of them were given fellowships to fund their attendance.[13] Table 7.6 shows the number of training courses given between 1978 and 1981, their location, and the number of trainees attending them. Of course, the equipment and procedures of the host country were the ones most widely demonstrated at each course. ROCC also held annual trade shows and training seminars (MEDIPOL) to educate regional official to prevent and respond to oil spills. Between 1978 and 1981, France attracted thirty-four Mediterranean officials to trade shows exhibiting its oil pollution control technology, and Italian firms hawked their wares to thirty-eight officials.

Table 7.6. Oil Spill Cleanup Seminars

Year	Location	Attendance
1978	Italy	20
1978	France	5
1979	Italy	18
1979	France	2
1980	France	4
1981	France	18
1981	France	5
1982	France	

Source: ROCC brochure on its activities (June 1982), p. 13.
No data provided on attendance at 1982 seminar.

Le Lourd was aware that his seminars were used to promote the goods of the host country. He attempted to diversify the Mediterranean officials' knowledge of equipment suppliers through a number of techniques. He attempted to hold the annual MEDIPOL conferences in as many different countries as possible, splitting the meetings between France and Italy, and intending to hold future meetings in Greece and Spain. He keeps officials aware of other suppliers of merchandise by reviewing different products in the bimonthly newsletter *ROCC News*, although the manufacturers of such products are generally limited to Western Europe and the United States. Trainees were sent to the United States and the United Kingdom in 1982 to expand their range of familiarity with different techniques. This was much more expensive than sending them to continental European countries, and was discontinued.

The core countries, through their existing control over the regional market for pollution control equipment, were able to dominate the marketing of their equipment within the Med Plan. However, the secretariat attempted to expose officials to alternative technologies from other sources. Actual monitoring equipment used within Med Pol was purchased from outside the area. Although certain structurally determined patterns persisted, they were modified slightly.

OVERCOMING DC ATTEMPTS TO SHAPE LDC INTERESTS AND IMPOSE WESTERN MODELS OF DEVELOPMENT

More subtly, the Med Plan was perceived by some historical materialists as a possible way of shaping LDC industrialization plans so that they weighed environmental protection and economic development equally, contrary to the interests that the LDCs had expressed earlier. Michel Nancy criticizes the "hegemony of models" of development that occurs when LDC leaders copy and apply models of development, or pollution control, from abroad. Such inappropriate planning results in "irrational economic choices" in the periphery, constituting the mere reproduction "pure and simple" at the cultural, educational, and economic levels (Nancy 1974:37). Such an analysis questions the fundamental choices of issues to be settled by collaboration, asserting that the very range of pollution topics is shaped by the coercive effect of the North on the formation of preferences in the South. Writers question the creation of an LDC development ideology that is in fact controlled by the ideology of the developed states, and see the policies espoused by LDC negotiators at North-South discussions as a reflection of the "context of distortions" (Duvall 1978:55–57) imposed by or resulting from northern penetration. Closely related to the trade effects discussed earlier, this pattern of shaping domestic policy choices was averted as LDCs learned autonomously of the need for more comprehensive notions of development and pollution control.

The substances controlled by the Med Plan strike at the essential sectors of the LDCs' plans to develop a modern materials-processing sector and require a massive investment in municipal sewerage. By extension, the entire Med Plan was suspect, since LDC leaders viewed all pollution control measures as potential methods to retard economic growth, control domestic industry, and guide national industrial development in a more expensive direction.

Delegates to the Med Plan meetings were aware that research on styles of development (such as the Blue Plan and PAP) and agreements for technical standards covering industrial emissions (such as the Land-Based Sources Protocol) could have significant consequences for economic development and the availability of economic resources to other groups in the countries. Writers and some LDC delegates viewed integrated management with great suspicion, seeing it as an instrument of control over LDC industrialization, or as a northern device to get LDCs to divulge sensitive socioeconomic data. A Greek member of the Blue Plan's Group of Coordination and Synthesis wrote:

> It is obvious that an unqualified recommendation for the adoption of environmentally sound development strategies can be easily considered a controversial proposition. The restrictions for the type of industry to be included, and most important, the financial burden of such a strategy, can be easily taken as an obstacle to industrialization imposed by developed countries upon the developing ones. (Lagos 1982:181)

LDC representatives were not gullible about the economic implications of controlling the pollutants preferred by the North. Many delegates were aware of the variety of pollution problems that faced them before the Med Plan negotiations began, by virtue of their preparations for UNCHE. These preparations had been made without the assistance of foreign consultants and created a rudimentary domestic infrastructure for evaluating the extent of domestic pollution problems and conveying its importance to policymakers. They had to be convinced of the need to deal with the full collection of pollutants before they firmly approved the rest of the Med Plan, which covered additional pollutants and sources of pollution. Thus, although the French and other DCs wished to control land-based sources of pollution and promoted integrated planning, the LDCs waited several years to approve their inclusion in the Med Plan. The extensive involvement of UNEP and LDC nationals in the development of the Blue Plan and PAP ensured that they both came to reflect LDC development interests as well as those of DCs.

For instance, Algeria drafted a report for UNCHE based on submissions from the National Economic and Social Council, the Ministry of Transport, the Ministry of Foreign Affairs, the Ministry of Agriculture, the Ministry of Industry and Energy, the National Organization for Scientific Research, the Ministry of Public Health, the Ministry of Information and Culture, the Ministry of Planning, and the Ministry of Hydrology. Environmental problems were cast entirely within the framework of the tension between the need for both economic development and environmental protection. From the outset leaders realized that Algeria suffered from a lack of roads; urbanization and overcrowding in cities; soil erosion; deforestation; and waterborne contaminants and sewage affecting public health. Algerian officials cited marine pollution problems as consisting of oily wastes on beaches from tanker traffic, and harbor pollution resulting from unprocessed municipal sewage.[14] It took ten years for them to acknowledge the need to control industrial wastes. Tunisia cited erosion, deforestation, and agricultural development as its key environmental problems at the time.[15] Syria was particularly concerned about coastal marine pollution by oil.[16] The specific projects identified in the Blue Plan and PAP echo these early LDC concerns.

Writers from other developing countries in the early 1970s confirm the North African countries' accurate identification of their problems and their ranking them below their industrialization objectives. They acknowledged that developing countries experience pollution problems, but they are often different problems from those experienced in developed countries. Writers differentiated between a "pollution of poverty" in the developing countries (essentially, pollution problems affecting public health that could be resolved through economic development and an improved quality of life) and the "pollution of affluence" in the developed countries. LDCs were concerned with "precarious housing conditions, poor health, and low sanitary standards, not to mention starvation" (de Araujo Castro 1972:245). In concrete terms, LDC problems consisted of poor sanitation and food and water contamination, and (in rural areas) the major pollutants are micro-organisms disseminated because of the lack of appropriate sewage and other disposal facilities. In urban areas the same problems exist together with quite a few others linked to excessive urban densities at very low income levels. . . . [and] problems of agricultural soil conservation and of different types of urban deterioration. (de Almeida 1972:52)

A Brazilian delegate to UNCHE identified (de Almeida 1972:46–48) a number of true marine pollutants facing developing countries as well as developed ones: phosphates, mercury, lead, oil, persistent organochlorines, and radionuclides. All of these are covered by the Med Plan protocols.

LDC delegates were consistently suspicious about the substances listed in the annexes to the Land-Based Sources Protocol; they lacked detailed information about the extent to which banning or controlling emissions of the substances included in the black and grey lists would affect their economies. However, very few objected to specific substances. Rather, their strategy was to drag their heels until they were convinced of the overall necessity of banning such substances. Only after being convinced by their own scientists and by materials provided by UNEP did they agree to the inclusion in the protocol of the full list of banned substances.

The LDCs took several years to accept the need to confront industrial pollutants at home as well. Moreover, many of them were suspicious of the political role of information provided by experts from developed countries that underscored the importance of dealing with this problem. LDC governments were very leery of information provided from the North, and would only accept the value of numbers when they were provided by domestic scientists. When uncertain they demanded advice from domestic scientists, and effectively delayed negotiations until they were firmly convinced of the need to control industrial pollution.

Thus, rather than being imposed on LDCs from the outside, the control of industrial pollutants domestically and through the Med Plan occurred with the domestic provision of information. Other components of the Med Plan also reflected the concerns of LDCs. Although LDCs did not draft these components, the Blue Plan, PAP, and Med Pol all reflect their concern with treating the concrete pollution problems associated with underdevelopment.

As argued in chapter 4, the Land-Based Sources Protocol was successfully negotiated by compromise. The LDCs' interest in technology transfer and the coverage of rivers-transmitted and airborne pollutants was satisfied, and they were given an effectively preferential schedule for controlling grey-listed substances. Such an outcome clearly modifies historical materialists' expectations of recurrent patterns of outcomes that impose DCs interests on LDCs. However, the DCs, although making concessions, were able to distance themselves from the concessions they found most repellent: discussions of the annex covering airborne pollutants were deferred to GESAMP; and France withheld information on emissions of radionuclides into the Rhone, and demoted to a resolution Morocco's proposal at Barcelona for an Interstate Guarantee Fund. Even these ploys were met by UNEP, which obtained data through other transgovernmental channels and needled GESAMP to speed up its activities.

Although the LDCs were able to avoid the subtle penetration of Western development models into the Med Plan, electing to support elements only after they were convinced that they truly reflected their own legitimate concerns, the DCs were still able to retreat from concessions extracted by the LDCs. The LDCs were able to ensure that elements that the DCs did not wish to face were not excluded from the agenda, but the DCs in turn were able to postpone discussion on those elements. The DCs' tactics are at best a delaying move, though, as UNEP's active role in the negotiations ensured that the issues would be dealt with by other UN bodies and picked up later in the Med Plan.

MARINE SCIENTISTS' ROLE IN ARTICULATING LDC INTERESTS

The nature of the epistemic community and the actions of marine scientists combined to avert the reproduction of a more insidious form of dependency. Because the form of ecology motivating the epistemic community is inherently integrative, DC notions of pollution did not prevail on the agenda; LDC notions made it to the agenda as well. Because the marine scientists allied with UNEP typically received their training at a variety of institutions, their own outlooks were not shaped by graduate experiences in the North. As is seen below, most did not receive training in the northern countries with the most clear cut Mediterrenean interests. Marine scientists in LDCs providing policy advice to their governments expressed the interests of their own countries when they were consulted to mitigate the uncertainty surrounding regional pollution.

Once they were assured access to their governments, which was the case by the late 1970s, the content of marine scientists' advice to their governments did not echo what historical materialists commonly observe about technical advice. Many patterns of structural influence on experts were absent from the Med Plan because of the training marine scientists had received and the nature of the ecological discipline that motivated UNEP to integrate the various marine sciences under one broad umbrella notion of pollution control.

Historical materialists commonly expect that, as a result of frequent exposure to cultural, commercial, and educational messages from the North marine scientists' policy advice embodies the interests of the North rather than of their own countries (Galtung 1980:ch. 4). The educational experiences of these individuals would be presumed to condition the advice they proffer to their governments.

But, unlike many areas of technical training, few Mediterranean marine scientists were educated in France or Western Europe and hence they did not bring external notions of pollution problems to the Med Plan talks. The graduate training for Mediterranean marine scientists, as available from a UNEP survey, is presented in table 7.7. None of the scientists in the most prominent LDCs, Algeria and Egypt, were trained in France or Western Europe, although some Algerians received one or two years of postgraduate training there. Only 20 percent of the Greek marine scientists have ties to France, and 50 percent of the Syrians are so dependent. The relatively short period of postgraduate training compared to university education and length of time working in the LDCs is too short to transfer the scientists' short-term interests to the core away from their own professional or national ambitions. The advice proffered by these marine scientists to their governments was relatively free of structured impurities.

CONCLUSION

UNEP and LDC negotiators were able to avoid the common patterns of North-South interactions observed and described by historical materialists. Many dimensions of dependency were not reproduced. The Med Plan does not reflect a French or core negotiating victory at the expense of the North African countries. Developing-country delegates were able to withstand French claims at meetings,

Table 7.7. Training of Marine Scientists

Country[a]	Number of Marine Science Institutions	Number of Scientists with a Ph.D or Doctorate 3eme Cycle	Number of Institutions Surveyed
Algeria	3	5+	1
Egypt	5	47+	1
Greece	17	76+	2
Israel	13	256+	2
Spain	8	23+	2
Syria	1	5	1
Turkey	6	22+	1

[a] Surveyed marine scientists account for 23 percent of the marine scientists with a Ph.D. or doctorate 3eme cycle for these seven countries. Without Israel, the surveyed scientists account for 56 percent of the marine scientists.

[b] Includes Italy (4), Federal Republic of Germany (4), Israel (2), Belgium (2), Canada (2), Switzerland (2), Austria (1), the German Democratic Republic (1), Japan (1), the Netherlands (1), Norway (1), and Poland (1).

Source: UNEP (1977),

and hold out for their own preferences. The LDCs learned of the need to control a wider range of pollutants, and elevated pollution control considerations to roughly the level of their prior focus on industrialization. The agenda-setting process was not shaped contrary to LDC interests. The Blue Plan and PAP reflect LDC preferences, and the Land-Based Sources Protocol is a compromise in which both sides' interests are represented. Nor does the Med Plan represent a conversion of LDC preferences through the process of negotiations: the LDC preferences were formed before the regional politicization of marine pollution took place and LDC interaction with the DC delegates occurred.

Still, certain historical patterns persisted. France consistently attempted to control the program. UNEP and the LDCs could not escape retaining trading ties to those sectors in which France and the core had been historically dominant, such as with sources of pollution control equipment. The Med Plan modifies outcomes within a system of unequal control over economic production. These novel outcomes occurred despite relatively invariant regional economic structures. Although the division of labor was altered, and the program did not mask the interests of the North, the actual location of production remained unaffected, and unquestioned.

Origin of Surveyed Scientists' Advanced Degrees					
France	*U.S.*	*Domestic*	*USSR*	*U.K.*	*Other*[b]
0	0	5	0	0	0
0	1	2	14	0	3
8	6	0	0	7	19
2	6	9	1	1	0
0	0	20	0	0	0
2	1	0	0	0	1
0	3	0	0	2	0

The Med Plan does demonstrate that actors have more flexibility within a given structure than historical materialists' analyses commonly indicate. UNEP and LDC delegates achieved joint outcomes that were relatively free from structural penetration. With time to develop their positions domestically, LDCs were able to learn to accept new and more comprehensive agreements than they initially deemed tolerable.

EIGHT

Effluents and Influence: The Emergent International Political Order for the Environment

The Mediterranean Action Plan exemplifies an incipient new order of international cooperation for environmental protection, based on more comprehensive patterns of national and international environmental policy making. This growth of international environmental cooperation was discussed in chapter 1. Subsequent chapters analyzed the process by which such an order emerged, and how such a change could be explained, by looking in detail at the Med Plan. Since the Med Plan constitutes a "hard case" for cooperation because it emerged under very difficult political circumstances due to the broad disparity of political interests and power in the region, an explanation of its development provides a strong basis for understanding the process by which order may emerge elsewhere in international politics. In the future, cooperation may develop in complex and uncertain international issue areas in which there are mobilized epistemic communities. This concluding chapter reiterates the new forms of behavior that make up this order; their causes, as illustrated by the Med Plan; how the behavior may be understood; and its implications for future international cooperation.

THE INTERNATIONAL POLITICAL ORDER
FOR THE ENVIRONMENT

An international environmental consciousness developed during the 1970s and 1980s, as governments developed new patterns of behavior for coping with transboundary pollution. Governments began to cooperate to control a variety of sources of environmental pollution, and these efforts became increasingly comprehensive to cope with the full range of ways in which pollutants are transmitted across national boundaries by biogeochemical cycles. Arrangements grew in their geographical scope, in the number of pollutants controlled, in the sources of pollution that were regulated, and in the range of control over the environmental channels through which they were transmitted. This new order consists of broad international and national efforts to control the spread of environmental pollution.

Although evidence is still scarce regarding true changes in environmental quality, the direction of collective movement is clear. By 1987, most sources and types of marine pollution were covered for most of the global oceans under UNEP's ten Regional Seas programs. Pollution of the high seas from oil spills and from dumping was covered by numerous pieces of IMO legislation. The atmosphere is protected as well. Treaties are in place to protect the global ozone layer from damage by chlorofluorocarbons, and to control the long-range transport of European air pollution. By now almost all countries are party to at least one multilateral treaty for pollution control.[1] Pollution of the open seas by pollution from tankers and dumping of chemicals and other wastes has been largely regulated through treaties drafted by the IMO, which has banned dumping of specific substances, developed design standards for new tankers, and established navigation and tank-cleansing practices for tankers. Marine dumping in the North Sea has been virtually eliminated. Land-based discharges have been regulated in the North Sea and the Mediterranean, although sewage remains one of the principal threats to coastal ecosystems elsewhere. Air quality and water quality in large Western cities has improved over the last decade, whereas air and water quality in rapidly growing third world cities continues to deteriorate (UNEP 1987; UNEP 1988:10–12).

Of course, much remains to be done. There is little surveillance of national compliance with these arrangements. Global rain forests and river basins lack protection. Nor are there any arrangements to control the emission of greenhouse gases into the atmosphere, which may contribute to an overall warming of the global climate by 1° to 3°C.

The form of this cooperation is new. International agreements were adopted that were more comprehensive and stronger than previous efforts. They came to control many more pollutants, including a number of chemicals, pesticides, herbicides, fungicides, and organic wastes, as well as pollution from a variety of sources: tankers, marine dumping, coastal industry, municipal sewerage, and emissions into the atmosphere. Many of the agreements included technical annexes establishing emission standards or environmental ambient quality standards and lists of substances to be regulated.

In the Med Plan, governments accepted a number of more comprehensive efforts to control Mediterranean pollution. The sources of pollution covered in the legal protocols grew from oil and marine dumping to land-based sources, including agricultural spraying, municipal wastes, and industrial wastes. The particular regulated pollutants grew in number and in the precision with which they were identified, through the, at least, interim adoption of emission and ambient standards for certain specified uses of coastal waters. Arrangements for environmental assessment of the Mediterranean grew increasingly more sophisticated and extensive.

Many domestic measures became more comprehensive and stringent as well. More pollutants were controlled, more sources of pollution were covered, and the supporting measures for such activities were stronger. Such national actions are converging around a common approach to controlling environmental deterioration which reflects a new sensitivity to cross-border flows of pollutants, supported by efforts to control emissions from a number of sources into all of the media by which such pollutants are transmitted.

HOW THE MED PLAN DEVELOPED

This new international political order for the environment was deftly masterminded and guided by an ecological epistemic community. Members of this community staffed UNEP and served in the administration of several Mediterranean countries. They shared common beliefs about the causes of pollution which informed their policy advice and action in the issue area. They also shared common political objectives in reorganizing and creating new governmental and intergovernmental institutions that would be responsible for more comprehensive forms of environmental protection. Through such institutions they ultimately hoped to lower the amount of pollution produced rather than develop ways to clean up existing wastes.

They all considered themselves ecologists. They all believed in the need to protect the human environment. They believed that the Mediterranean was endangered from a number of different sources of pollution, and that protecting the Mediterranean required the multilateral control of all pollutants. They identified common sources of pollution and proposed similar comprehensive pollution control policies when government officials solicited their advice. Later, when installed in environmental ministries or as consultants to national delegations to Med Plan meetings, they continued to provide concordant policy advice. In addition, they formed a transnational alliance with regional marine scientists who shared some concerns with controlling specific pollutants but lacked the full scope of vision held by the epistemic community.

After encountering widespread coastal oil pollution in the late 1960s, Mediterranean governments became concerned about the health of the sea. Uncertain of the full range of other sources and types of pollution, they solicited the advice of scientists whom they considered authorities in marine pollution. Allied with the ecological epistemic community and UNEP, they advised their governments to pursue congruent and more comprehensive pollution controls.

The epistemic community whipsawed governments. At the international level it promoted a comprehensive set of arrangements which exceeded the initial interest of any of the regional parties, and encouraged delegates to consider taking broader measures for pollution control. Nationally, through its members and its scientific allies, it successfully pressed for support of the Med Plan and for enforcement of its protocols.

As members of the secretariats of the FAO and UNEP, members of the epistemic community drafted the Barcelona convention and Land-Based Sources Protocol to include land-based sources of pollution as well as the marine-based ones with which most of the governments were preoccupied. The epistemic community pressed governments to consider regulating pollutants other than oil, as well as pollutants transmitted through the atmosphere and by rivers. By approving a broad range of research and monitoring projects at the 1974 IOC/ICSEM/UNEP meeting, scientists spread the net of possible sources and forms of pollution sufficiently widely to be able to include in protocols any pollutants about which they were concerned. Through Med Pol, UNEP supported research that demonstrated the need to create a more comprehensive set of pollution control arrangements. The definition of pollution promoted by UNEP was sufficiently broad to include all possible concerns, and cemented such a wide scope into the international bargaining process that as broad a range of pollutants as possible could be covered. Finally, UNEP commissioned the 1977 Med X Report, which identified land-based sources of pollution as a sufficiently strong threat to Mediterranean quality that delegates from foreign ministries could not avoid agreeing to control it, despite their interests in protecting their own coastal industries from control. At the 1980 Conference of Plenipotentiaries for the Land-Based Sources Protocol the UNEP secretariat suggested compromises that would protect the environment and satisfy the political qualms or national representatives as well. All of these examples were discussed in much greater detail in chapters 3 and 4.

The continued access of the epistemic community to international negotiations was facilitated by political rewards to parties for participating in the Med Plan. Countries received research contracts, regional activity centers, and new technology and training in its use. In order to receive such rewards they continued to attend negotiations, at which the epistemic community sought to influence them. The success of this political tactic was also supported by a number of fairly simple features of the Mediterranean negotiations: a neutral forum insulated the parties from each other; and a technically capable secretariat generated respect from national officials and belief in the data it submitted.

Domestically, the epistemic community penetrated policy-making as well. Its members and allies served on delegations to Med Plan meetings and staffed environmental ministries as they were established throughout the region. They consistently encouraged their governments to comply with the arrangements developed internationally. As they became involved in developing and enforcing national policies for pollution control, they pushed for stronger and more comprehensive measures. More forms of pollution were covered, and measures for their control became more stringent.

The strongest supporters of the Med Plan were the countries in which the epistemic community was most active. Such environmental consciousness was slow to develop in countries unconnected to the epistemic community. Algeria, Egypt, France, Greece, and Israel—the states where the epistemic community became most strongly entrenched—adopted more coherent forms of pollution control through the coverage of industrial wastes as well as other forms of pollution. These countries also established procedures for conducting environmental impact assessments of new development projects.

Elsewhere—where the epistemic community was weaker—states signed and ratified the Land-Based Sources Protocol, but have not taken steps to integrate such objectives into the rest of national policymaking. Domestic environmental policy in these countries became correspondingly broader and was more strongly enforced.

Due to its holistic approach, the epistemic community suggested policies that included all Mediterranean countries' concerns with how to control pollution. The integrative and synergistic nature of the ecology discipline's beliefs about cause-and-effect relationships in the physical environment prevented the penetration of key core concerns into the agenda-setting process. The ecological epistemic community's views did not reflect broader systemic influences, and hence helped to promote integrative outcomes that reflected different countries' concerns with environmental protection. The Med Plan did not merely establish the legitimacy of French interests or exclude or subordinate LDC interests. Critiques of the way in which ecology embodies core political values misrepresent the form of ecology motivating the epistemic community in the Med Plan.

Ecology as a discipline has been viewed as a possible inhibition to LDC industrialization because of its focus on constraints to economic development that must be introduced in order to preserve environmental quality. A former Brazilian ambassador to the United States argued that pollution control is merely a facade that allows industrialized countries to reinforce their systemic control over the developing countries' economies:

> Interest in the field of ecology, which is centered in the developed countries . . . [and] the methods envisaged to resolve on a world basis the so-called environmental crisis were inspired by the realities of a fraction of that very same world: the family of the developed countries. Furthermore, the bulk of the solutions in hand, mainly of a technical nature, seek primarily to make healthier the consequences of the Industrial Revolution without

necessarily providing a tool for a further distribution of its benefits among states. . . . The working hypothesis is that the implementation of any worldwide environmental policy based on the realities of the developed countries tends to perpetuate the existing gap in socioeconomic development between developed and developing countries and so promote the freezing of the present international order. (de Araujo Castro 1972:237)

Thus, the scientific disciplines that were introduced to manage Mediterranean pollution could have masked "a structure consisting of taken-for-granted assumptions, preferences for symbol systems and analytical devices within which an observer's inquiry proceeds" (Holzner and Marx 1979:99) and utilized concepts "to the extent to which they do or can satisfy vital material and symbolic interests."[2] With regard to environmental issues, ecological concerns have been criticized for fundamentally encouraging status quo values (which are of benefit to the core) because of their concern with equilibrium, and for contradicting or subsuming demands by LDCs for economic redistribution and systemic restructuring.[3] Policies based on the static notion of economic development exceeding carrying capacity would be inappropriate to LDCs, because they distract attention from "the global setting, replete with inequities, injustice, twisted historical heritage—all superimposed on unequal natural resource endowment, physical and climatic differences, and social, national and international barriers—even the most objectively inspired scientific statements acquire controversial and conflictual connotations" (Gosovic 1984:142). Excessive attention to ecological constraints on development omits such social processes as innovation, technological change, and technological transfer from consideration by planners, which could allow them to surmount the inhibitions to their development objectives.

Hence, the extent to which makers of foreign policy transfer the resolution of environmental problems to technical analysis and accept the various technical characterizations of the problem and the allocation of costs for its resolution, might mask the ideological power vested within the authoritative position of the scientific disciplines that are invoked. "Knowledge is ideologically determined insofar as it is created, accepted, or sustained by concealed, unacknowledged [or] illegitimate interests."[4] In short, with the acceptance of disciplines of knowledge presumably grounded on core concerns, all negotiators become "prisoner[s] of an intellectual context, characterized by the map of a geographic and temporally situated idea."[5]

However, UNEP's ecological viewpoint enabled it to build a program that transcended these patterns of exclusion from the international agenda. Such LDC interests as poverty-generated pollution, technology transfer, and the possible loss of comparative advantage to DCs were included on the agenda. The definition of pollution and the scope of problems covered at the original 1974 IOC/UNEP/ICSEM conference reflected those intrinsic LDC concerns. They remained cogent throughout subsequent negotiations.

In part, the intellectual history of ecology facilitates its ability to integrate diverse concerns. The earlier critique of ecology's static focus involves only a partial reading of the literature. A dynamic ecological concept exists as well and was held by the members of the epistemic community. By appropriating a variety of social concerns and adding them to a focus on ecological cycles in order to obtain a full understanding of the causes of environmental disruptions, this notion does not serve to perpetuate structural political and economic inequalities. Because the ecological principles at the heart of the epistemic community constituted more of a framework—an interdisciplinary synthetic approach to problem solving rather than an analytic deductive science—they were amenable to incorporating diverse concerns into the Med Plan. These LDC concerns emerge within both the technical scope of Med Pol, with its monitoring of municipal wastes, and the integrated management component, with its focus on the evolving dynamic between social trends and environmental quality.

Ecology is a "hybrid science" (McIntosh 1985:49), consisting of elements drawn from all scientific disciplines pertaining to the uses of the oceans. Because of its inherently synthetic nature it includes a host of other disciplines within its rubric (Worster 1977), each with its own source of institutional support by UN agencies; no particular group's interpretation of pollution has prevailed. Ecology is a broad link that has joined the diverse marine science disciplines and identified them as viable candidates for promoting collective pollution control policies; no one discipline was specified as preferable or more correct. Rather than stressing tradeoffs between approaches ecologists amicably indicate the need to pursue them all. Until there are budgetary crunches, which UNEP avoided having to cope with, there are thus few sources of conflict.

Thus, the application of various marine sciences by the secretariat resulted in a potentially integrative outcome, rather than an outcome that inherently favors certain interests. The broad rubric of the consensual definition of pollution and the variety of disciplines that were deemed appropriate at the earliest meetings led to the inclusion in negotiations of a broad variety of problems that incorporated all concerns. Because of the heterogeneous nature of the problem, technical policy proposals included all of the existing political preferences: oil pollution control, fisheries protection, public health, the control of industrial and municipal wastes, and even the transfer of technology. The range of alternatives was expanded through the application of all of the marine sciences, rather than being circumscribed. Of course, these scientific proposals were subject to political approval, which extended the length of time necessary to negotiate UNEP's slippery slope. In conjunction with the diversity of backgrounds of the marine scientists, the epistemic community, with its transnational alliance with regional marine scientists, was able to transcend the shaping forces of historical materialists' political and economic structures.

Over time governments learned to adopt new patterns of environmental policymaking. The epistemic community had stressed how the biogeochemical transmission of environmental contaminants requires more comprehensive and coordinated action. Governments realized that in order to maintain the quality of the Mediterranean, a greater range of pollutants must be controlled, more sources of pollution had to be managed, and countries had to better coordinate their policies. Such learning entails the attachment of new means to existing ends. As such, it is well within the realm of the outcomes that systemic theorists expect. Foreign affairs ministries did not learn to make more coherent policies to deal with complex interlinkages, but they did learn to solicit, and defer to, advice from marine scientists.

However, a number of governments, in fact those in which the epistemic community was strongest, developed new organizations and methods to understand and balance the interplay between different uses of the Mediterranean. Regulatory environmental ministries responsible for environmental impact assessments of new development projects focus on the tradeoffs between different uses of the environment. To the extent that these procedures are truly respected, these countries have adopted a new, more comprehensive form of reasoning that relates environmental protection to economic development objectives. Economic development is seen in conjuncture with other competing uses for the Mediterranean, thus requiring a comprehensive policymaking style rather than a style of pursuing discrete objectives in isolation from one another. These states now try to optimize the use of the Mediterranean, satisfying industrial, recreational, and fishery interests while protecting public health. It must be stressed that such learning occurred by virtue of the epistemic community appropriating the policy debate and usurping actual bureaucratic control over decision making and enforcement.

Few governments, however, fully accepted UNEP's integrative pattern of reasoning to relate environmental quality, economic development, and pollution control. For instance, the integrated management component of the Med Plan, which directly attempts to apply UNEP's interest in rational planning, has seen the least support of any of the Med Plan activities. The Blue Plan, the explicit articulation of such a desire, remains principally a French artifact, a result of the idiosyncratic French penchant for prospective planning. Conservation of species also remains at best a desultory interest of the Mediterranean governments.

The UNEP secretariat learned from the Med Plan, which it applied when it recreated the Med Plan model in nine other regional seas. In a review of its experience in promoting marine pollution controls, UNEP summarized what it had learned (UNEP 1982a, 1982b). It realized that action at the regional level is the most effective way to protect the marine environment, and that such efforts must contribute to economic development as well as environmental protection. A number of successful tactics were identified as well: regional governments must be responsible for defining their own problems and regional boundaries; UNEP should take care to promote its interdisciplinary approach by soliciting input from a variety of international organizations as well as national institutions; and UNEP should reinforce national technical capacities whenever possible. UNEP learned of the efficacy of its strategy of geographic distribution of all benefits, as well as the need to foster indigenous scientific and monitoring capabilities. UNEP also quickly realized the desirability of designing research and monitoring projects that would include all scientists' preferred variables and methods, even if it gave rise to unwieldy and expensive projects and ultimately to a list of substances demanding regulation that was more complicated than UNEP's initial goal of more simple targets.

UNEP also learned that its holistic "slippery slope" goal may have been too ambitious. Although all of its other regional seas programs are grounded on the common process of developing an action plan leading to subsequent protocols for enforcement, their scope is limited to controlling oil pollution and developing monitoring networks (UNEP 1982a, 1982b; Hulm 1983). None of the other Regional Seas

Action Plans have an integrated planning component, although they often have more specialized projects—similar to the Priority Action Programme—that have been established to demonstrate the utility of broader forms of economic planning. Whereas most governments learned to pursue new means and ends through more comprehensive and sophisticated policies, UNEP realized that instilling entirely new reasoning patterns was an unrealistic objective. The UNEP staff moved from its globalist rhetoric to a more pragmatic approach of dealing with specific problems as they emerge regionally. UNEP became more modest in its other Regional Seas programs (UNEP 1986a).

EXPLANATIONS OF THE MED PLAN AND OF AN EMERGENT ORDER

The Med Plan's evolution confirms a number of the propositions about epistemic communities that were introduced in chapter 2. An ecological epistemic community was consulted by governments in order to dispell uncertainty about the extent of environmental pollution. Such concern was precipitated by a crisis; the alarm that the Mediterranean was in danger of dying. This epistemic community significantly influenced the form and duration of environmental cooperation. The epistemic community made itself felt internationally and nationally.

Through international secretariats, especially that of UNEP, it successfully engaged in publicizing concern; agenda setting; identifying sources of pollution, pollutants, and channels of pollution for regulation; proposing specific standards; and setting the general universe of discourse by extending concern with discrete pollution problems to a more generalized discussion of coastal land use patterns and integrated planning. As a consequence, it influenced the range of pollutants that were controlled, the sources of pollution, and the channels by which they are transmitted. Through the provision of timely scientific evidence, it influenced the pace of negotiations as well as its content. Contrary to the expectations of historical materialists, it did not exclude LDC concerns from the agenda due to its broad beliefs in cause-and-effect relationships, which led it to easily accept other sources of pollution and pollutants.

At international discussions, members of the epistemic community pushed for a more comprehensive scope of pollution control through shaping the international agenda and at times persuading foreign ministry delegates of the need to control specific pollutants. Med Plan meetings at which the epistemic community was present were more amicable than meetings at which they were not. For instance, the 1979 scientific meetings went very smoothly, whereas delegates at concurrent legal ones were unable to reach agreement. In general, meetings where epistemic communities are widely represented can be contentious, but they are likely to yield consensus.

The epistemic community made its mark in the areas in which it was involved. In drafting documents and providing the secretariat with services for meetings, its members persistently pushed delegates to adopt measures that reflected their own concerns with broader and more comprehensive pollution control efforts.

The epistemic community extended its influence through alliances with like-minded domestic groups of scientists. True to expectations, countries in which members of the epistemic community or its allies held important administrative positions pursued congruent policies. They were the most constructive supporters of the Med Plan, and took the strongest measures at home. The countries taking the strongest measures for pollution control were those in which the epistemic community and its allies were most strongly entrenched in the bureaucracy, commonly in regulatory environmental agencies. These domestic measures were strongly informed by the policies adduced from the cause-and-effect beliefs of the epistemic community. By controlling domestic environmental bodies, they pushed for compliance with the Med Plan and the development and enforcement of more comprehensive domestic measures.

Other propositions about epistemic communities are confirmed as well. Once in place, the epistemic community's access was not seriously questioned. Even though Mediterranean pollution control was widely perceived as a collective good in the early 1970s, being a commons problem of the open seas, the problem of Mediterranean pollution is increasingly becoming only a bilateral or national coastal problem as oceanographers realize that many pollution problems are localized. Currents are insufficiently strong to transport them further. In the words of a UNEP official, the notion of the public nature of Mediterranean pollution is "utter nonsense." Yet such improved scientific understanding was not converted into changed governmental behavior. Already in place in their governments, subsequent scientific discoveries did not receive much attention by governments, as there was no constituency to publicize the new findings.

Most governments, except that of France, had other things on their hands, and were quite content to leave the marine scientists and ecologists in charge of issues that they did not fully understand and that were not characterized by recurrent crises. Although supervised at international meetings, scientists had much more latitude domestically in areas to which they had regulatory authority delegated to them and in which they were not closely supervised. In countries with smaller and more harassed bureaucracies, such as Egypt and Algeria, the marine scientists and the epistemic community were relatively independent, once their governments conferred decision-making responsibility upon them. After the early reports of extensive Mediterranean degradation in the early 1970s, no subsequent reports seriously challenged their authority. Nor did their common beliefs shift, so that governments had no information that could possibly undermine their faith in this group.

This confirms the proposition raised in chapter 2 about the "elasticity of demand for expert advice." Governments' willingness to question the authority and policy advice of the epistemic communities varied with respect to the size and capability of the administrative framework. Larger bureaucracies had more administrative resources, and were able to more frequently reassess the input from the epistemic community and environmental ministries. Smaller bureaucracies had less time for such activities, and hence ceded more autonomy to the environmental ministries. Thus, epistemic communities may have a more enduring role in LDCs than in DCs, where the elasticity of demand for their input is much higher. Also, as suggested in chapter 2, most Mediterranean policies have been remedial, as governments responded to tangible signs of failed policies.

The epistemic community also contributed to governmental learning. The countries in which the epistemic community was most strongly lodged came to adopt the most comprehensive styles of environmental policymaking, informed with the cause-and-effect beliefs of the epistemic community.

These new styles of environmental policymaking are tantamount to a recalculation of state interests. Governments realized that the existence of intricate ecological cycles required the balancing of discrete state objectives, which had formerly been pursued in isolation. The move to the use of environmental impact assessment and the adoption of the Land-Based Sources Protocol reflect the acceptance of a new equivalence between economic development in the coastal zone and the preservation of the quality of the Mediterranean. The objective of economic development was tempered by the need to preserve the Mediterranean for other possible uses, including fishing and recreation, as well as the need to protect public health. Instrumental interests may now be served by international cooperation, and by accepting new state responsibilities for environmental protection. Thus, although state security may well remain the fundamental objective for Mediterranean states, they realize that such security may only be obtained by linking issues in a previously unprecedented manner. Those governments in which the epistemic community was most active may now recognize the need to consider the possibility of incompatible tradeoffs between formerly discrete state objectives. Thus, even the pursuit of fundamental aims of autonomy and sovereignty may become muted.

However, it must be stressed that very little learning occurred by persuasion. Other government officials did not come to accept a more integrative and conceptual vision of environmental problems (an environmental consciousness) as a result of their accepting the correctness of the ecological epistemic community's consensual knowledge. Few of them fully understood the technical dimensions of the region's environmental problems, or were able to critically assess the advice offered by scientists. Rather, government learning came from the political power of the epistemic community, once it was entrenched in domestic administrations, which converted consensual knowledge to new domestic and foreign policy. The epistemic community usurped control over environmental policymaking, and shifted policy in accordance with their shared values and understandings. Regional scientists learned of new techniques and data from each other, through the networks sponsored by UNEP.

The learning that did occur is still well short of UNEP's grand aspirations to instill governments with entirely new environmental responsibilities, and to infuse them with a holistic style of environmental policymaking. Governments did not fully accept UNEP's view of nondecomposable holistic environmental problems, all of which require common planning to manage. The relative failure of regional integrated planning testifies to the limitations on governmental learning. Although the epistemic community did lead to an unusual new order, old systemic theories are still useful for understanding the constraints influencing the range of changes that the epistemic community could hope to accomplish.

In short, many propositions about epistemic communities explain the process and form of the Med Plan's evolution. Environmental cooperation may emerge from technical consensus among a politically influential set of specialists. As a consequence of their insinuating themselves into state bureaucracies, and through their coordinative role in international secretariats, members of the epistemic community led Mediterranean states to adopt new patterns of more comprehensive collective behavior and to recognize new state interests to which they would direct their resources. Yet such an analysis of state motivations and beliefs fails to take into account the range of inhibitions on that behavior.

The Med Plan is a case of systemic modification; it is not fully transformative.[6] Although systemic influences persist, their full influence was tempered by the epistemic community. Weak states were willing to cooperate, strong states continued to cooperate past hegemony, and outcomes did not fully reproduce deeper regional economic inequalities. Although the reflectiveness of governments and the development of comprehensive outcomes does indicate a remarkable systemic flexibility that systemic theorists are not fully capable of explaining, systemic features persist. As much as it stresses a greater degree of systemic flexibility than is commonly considered to be possible, the Med Plan also demonstrates the remarkable resilience of international systemic features.

The systemic principles from which systemic theorists derive their analysis remain unaffected by the new environmental order and by epistemic communities. Anarchy still exercises a significant influence on the degree of constraint on state policy that governments will tolerate. In the Mediterranean, scientific interest in holism encountered international anarchy, and holistic policy gave way to incrementalism. The reflective pattern of policy change that the epistemic community helped promote did not progress as far as its architects hoped it would.

States successfully defended their sovereignty. Governments only learned as much as, or were willing to pursue new goals that did not severely interfere with their traditional responsibilities. The organization of the international sphere by nation-states is not in doubt. In fact, the power of the state has been reinforced as governments are entrusted with a wider array of regulatory authority and surveillance over private sector operations within their territory and granted a new responsibility: pollution control. Although international scientific exchanges were stressed in the Med Plan, research monitoring was still conducted on a purely national basis by laboratories in the relevant coastal state. In effect, Mediterranean states extended their legitimate physical sovereignty to include their coastal waters.

Yet the range of action they may take is circumscribed. By articu-

lating common pollutants and standards for their control, the epistemic community helped craft a set of constraints on the range of
state behavior. Although not superceded, sovereignty may be in the
process of being redefined and circumscribed.

In fact, one may argue that governmental learning was itself circumscribed to some extent by these preexisting political systemic
features. Namely, the form of learning was that which was least
threatening, at least in the short run, to states' pursuit of autonomy
and security. States could have learned to make their environmental
policies more comprehensive in at least three ways. Policymaking
could have been accommodated to the functional, temporal, or spatial
interaction of pollutants. That is, they could have acted to manage
their impacts on future generations, through reduced discount rates;
they could have managed the spatial flow of these pollutants through
efforts to monitor and manage transboundary flows of pollution, and
they could have acted to manage the functional effects on other issues
that would be sensitive to environmental pollution—for instance,
fishery management or public health. In fact, most action occurred in
the latter category, which does not question the territorial integrity
of the sovereign nation-state. If anything, as noted above, it extends
its responsibility. Spatial obligations would impugn that territorial
definition. Accepting temporal obligations to future generations would
undermine the autonomy of elected governments. Thus, the type of
linkages about which governments learned were those that posed the
least threat to the persistence of an international political system
grounded on state sovereignty. Although such learning is still dramatic and significant, these limits on the range of cognitive lessons
learned by the governments suggests some limits on the flexibility of
behavior within international political structures.

The global logic of capitalism also remained unquestioned. Although attempts were made to redistribute trading partners, no efforts were made to relocate major sources of industrial production.
The Green strategies of massive decentralization, rejection of the industrial model of development, and transforming consumer preferences were never even considered. Even the integrated planning projections were extrapolated from existing patterns, rather than from
envisaging new development strategies. Individuals identified better
strategies within the social system as it existed. Any possible relationships between the variety of strategies available, or between the root
causes of environmental pollution and modes of production, as expressed by radical critics, were not raised.

Although fundamental systemic features remained unaltered, systemic theories proved incapable of fully explaining the Med Plan's scope and duration. This flexibility exceeds the explanatory capability of neorealism and historical materialism. They find it inconceivable, because of their theoretical presuppositions, that new forms of behavior are possible without the tranformation of their systemic principles, grounded on invariant and manifest economic and political structures. These traditions automatically presume that future behavior may only change from past patterns if the underlying systemic principles are altered. Otherwise, future actions will resemble those of the past. Both sets of structural traditions are caught in a Catch-22: international behavior is shaped (or determined) by international structures, yet there is no compelling explanation for why these structures exist in the first place. This means that there is no way to anticipate how new structures will emerge that would change behavior.

Algerian behavior poses the strongest anomaly for these interpretations. Such structural analyses focus on unchanging interests and the role of the distribution of power in explaining Mediterranean collaboration. Since Algerian leaders thought that French emissions were the principal causes of Mediterranean pollution, and France was already compelled to reduce its pollution by EEC obligations and arrangements for the North Atlantic region, the question remains of why Algeria introduced national pollution controls when it could easily have ridden freely. Why did Algeria continue to support pollution control measures when they knew that France was going to cooperate, and a defection would yield the higher gains for the Algerians?

Furthermore, Algerian leaders became concerned with more sources of pollution. They developed an interest in industrial wastes, one that was absent at the beginning of their Med Plan negotiations. This behavior, in excess of Algeria's narrowly proscribed systemically derived interests and beyond its initially expressed goals, indicates a change of national preferences. Algerian preferences changed from ranking economic development above environmental protection to ranking the two at least equally.

Neorealists were stymied by the willingness of small, weak states to cooperate in the absence of tangible rewards, and the willingness of a strong state to continue to cooperate past its hegemony. By assuming the invariant nature of international anarchy, they presume that new forms of behavior are unlikely to occur. Such orthodox structural accounts are, to some extent, ideal types. The formal assumptions that interests are invariant and that states constantly pursue forms of power may not always hold. Although Keohane, Krasner, and Gilpin acknowledge that actors may learn or utilize knowledge to recognize new causal patterns, and redefine their policies accordingly, they neglect them in their formal analysis.[7] Moreover, such adjustments are likely to be limited to instrumental rather than fundamental interests. States' behavior can only change if their systemic position changes, or if the nature of the international system changes. Analysts' rationality assumptions allow analysts to deduce behavior from a study of circumstances rather than of the actors. Thus, without looking at the actors' actual views of the world and manners of processing information about it, they predict new forms of behavior solely from systemic changes. Although such changes occur only infrequently, neorealists as well as historical materialists lack a compelling genesis story to explain how the set of structural conditions that so shape behavior came to bear in the first place.[8]

Because they accept the relatively enduring and undifferentiated presence of such structures, such theorists are blind to smaller accommodations within them, or to seeds of possible transformation. By rigorously clinging to their formal assumptions, analysts are hamstrung in their efforts to identify or explain new orders of behavior. They minimize or neglect the possible influence of nonstate actors such as scientists and international organizations who are armed with less conventional power resources, such as information and knowledge. Thus, in their view, without a redistribution of power or supercession of anarchy little new behavior is possible. If national interests, preference functions, and decision-making processes may change, then the distribution of benefits by the resulting institution will no longer directly represent the initial distribution of power within the region producing the institution. Moreover, states may act based on interests that are derived internally, rather than on those provided externally from their systemic positions. As states recalculated their interests following the recognition of greater ecosystemic interlinkages, governments were able to resist temptations to defect from the collective agreements that neorealists identify. Even in the absence of systemic transformation, states may recalculate their interests based upon the penetration of new actors with new images into decision making. As seen in this analysis, an ecological epistemic community was able to identify and successfully imposed new state interests which did not directly reflect systemic or structural principles.

For historical materialists, the relatively egalitarian nature of the Med Plan arrangements is surprising. They expect to see the continued domination of the South by the North, yet the Med Plan truly reflects the interests of both groups, as well as ceding a temporary comparative advantage to southern industries.

More generally, because of its deep structural orientation, such a tradition cannot explain the variation between behavior or outcomes in the Third World. Since all actions by weaker parties are necessarily shaped and conditioned and possibly determined by their exposure to stronger parties, there is no possibility of a systematic positive theory of international behavior. It is also blind to explanations of Third World wealth and behavior that are independent of the South's historical experiences or structured relationship with the North.[9]

Furthermore, this approach is excessively deterministic in its assumption of systemic penetration of lower level knowledge and perception. At the cognitive level, most of such analysis regards interpretations of past events as remaining static. Studies of intellectual history have found bodies of thought to be remarkably resistant to social pressures in the medium to long term. Such studies have also found that collective interpretations of events change, so that social influences often wash out in the longer run, as shared frameworks are constantly reevaluated in the face of subsequent events (or anomalies) and theoretical challenges.[10] The process of human inquiry may lead to a reformulation of collective concerns, the identification of new problems, and the development of entirely new responses.

Although some fields of study may reflect the inherited influence of powerful social groups, these fields lack the systemic penetration proposed by ardent structuralists. Epistemic communities organized around more reductionist disciplines may be more likely to lead to outcomes that are more penetrated by systemic principles, shaped by structural distributions of power, and explicitly influenced by interest groups. All bodies of knowledge from which events are defined, located, and interpreted need not be equally determined. Thus, the extent to which subsequent issues in which epistemic communities assume influence will significantly be influenced by deeper social, political, or economic structures depends upon the intellectual history of the specific epistemic community that becomes involved in dispelling uncertainty and articulating policy.

Ultimately, a compromise must be struck between midlevel and systemic analyses. By looking at epistemic communities one may understand the origins of state interests and the ends to which they will deploy their resources, as well as the role that some international organizations may play in insulating interstate conflicts of interest. If states do not accurately and promptly interpret the political and economic structures that condition their behavior, then the group that is responsible for identifying and interpreting such often ambiguous signals may prove influential in explaining how states actually behave, even within a context of anarchy or capitalism. Even without influencing more deeply held interests, instrumental state behavior changed, out of a new recognition of ecosystemic interconnections between social practices.

Actors are constantly buffeted in their efforts to recognize, comprehend, and respond to the conditioning factors in their milieu. To stress the conditioning factors imposed from outside tells only half of the story of international behavior; it is too narrow a view. It addresses the external factors influencing cooperative aspects of international political orders, but gives short shrift to beliefs. Such factors as standard operating procedures, perceptions, values, norms, prevailing modes of thought, consensual knowledge, the nature of diplomacy, and elements that are frequently organized under the "cognitive" heading may also influence behavior (Krasner 1983a, 1983b). Structures shape, but may not fully condition, the array of incentives and constraints facing actors. Robert Cox writes that

> [structures] are in one sense prior to individuals. They are already present in the world into which individuals are born. People learn to behave within the framework of social and political structure before they can learn to criticize or oppose or try to change them. . . . [but they are also subject to change since] they are transformable by collective human action. (1987:395)

Focusing on either voluntary action or structures, each at the expense of its counterpart, arbitrarily overpredicts responses and neglects key elements of international behavior. Steven Lukes insightfully notes the tension between structural constraints on actions, and the unit-level capability to extend the parameters of action:

> Social life can only properly be understood as a dialectic of power and structure, a web of possibilities for agents, whose nature is both active and structured, to make choices and pursue strategies within given limits, which in consequence expand and contract over time. Any standpoint or methodology which reduces the dialectic to a one-sided consideration of agents with-

233

out (internal and external) structural limits, or structures without agents, or which does not address the problem of their interrelations, will be unsatisfactory. (1977:29)

Studying the development of social welfare policies in Britain and Sweden, Heclo offers the complementary view that studying power without considering actors' considerations of how to deploy such power "would only replace one form of myopia with another. . . . Each without the other has been inconsequential for policy" (1974:311).

Taken alone, neither structures nor cognition can fully describe the world or explain changes in behavior. Weighting the importance of any of these factors in determining behavioral responses is an uncertain business. The link between outcomes and the distribution of power is often tenuous (Jervis 1980) but the link between outcomes and beliefs is equally unclear (Vasquez 1983).

The systemic approaches continue to provide a means of analyzing the constraints on such processes of learning; for states continue to act and interact in an international context shaped by power, and new objectives must be pursued in light of the recurring problems of reciprocity and weakness, which are so thoroughly analyzed by more orthodox approaches. Even if it is imbued with new policy objectives, a weak government is unlikely to be able to successfully accomplish them. Such systemic constraints still provide boundaries beyond which reflection cannot prevail, such as issues involving high-security considerations, and hostile confrontations in which power considerations are paramount.

OTHER CASES OF ENVIRONMENTAL COOPERATION

Other environmental cases further confirm the role of specialists in promoting more comprehensive forms of cooperative efforts to protect shared environmental resources from transboundary pollution. Crises and uncertainty recur as important themes. The causal links between the existence of an epistemic community and changes in government policy are less clear than they were in the Med Plan, due to the fact that this discussion is based on secondary sources. A stronger demonstration would require interviews with the involved scientists to determine their beliefs and values.

The Baltic Sea

The Baltic Sea is the world's largest brackish body of water. With a residency time of twenty to forty years for pollutants, a solution to pollution requires coordinated policy for a wide variety of pollutants. The Baltic is extensively polluted from municipal sewage, industrial wastes, fertilizer and pesticide runoff, airborne pollutants, and pollution from ships. Some 70 million people, producing about 15 percent of the world's industrial output, live along the coast (Rytovuori 1980:93; Carroz 1977:213; Hagerhall 1980). In the early 1970s the Baltic Sea was perceived to be in grave danger from pollution, and was popularly pronounced "dead or moribund" (Carroz 1977:213).

Arrangements have grown in scope from regional fishery management to controlling land-based sources of pollution. In September 1973 the seven Baltic states adopted the Convention on Fishing and Conservation of the Living Resources in the Baltic Sea and the Belts. The Convention on the Protection of the Marine Environment of the Baltic Sea Area (the Helsinki convention) was signed on March 22, 1974 by all seven littoral states: Denmark, Finland, the German Democratic Republic (GDR), the Federal Republic of Germany (FRG), Poland, Sweden, and the USSR. Preliminary discussions on the living resources convention had begun in 1969, at a subnational level, following an invitation by the Finnish government. Participants viewed the Baltic as a commons, but intergovernmental agreement was impossible before the formalization of relations between the Germanies in December 1972 (Rytovuori 1980).

The Helsinki convention entered into force on May 3, 1980, following ratification by all seven states. Each state had been complying with the terms of the convention before its entry into force, and had been attending meetings of an interim commission. The convention covers emissions of oil, noxious liquid substances, and chemicals; dumping from both land- and sea-based sources; and pollution transmitted through the atmosphere; it also controls all pollution resulting from seabed utilization and research.[11] Contracting parties agree to "counteract" emissions of DDT and PCBs and to "control" emissions of heavy metals and a number of other substances.

The Helsinki convention responds to all of the marine pollution problems faced by the region's advanced industrialized countries. Because the countries faced similar problems, interests were initially fairly harmonious, and the adoption of a broad treaty was not as contentious as in the Mediterranean. All officials were concerned about the problems of harmful substances, such as DDT and PCBs, and oil spills. The Soviet Union may have been more concerned than other countries about freedom of navigation, but it was relatively less interested in the overall topic of Baltic pollution, because the economic significance of the Baltic for the USSR is lower than for the other states (Rytovuori 1980:97).

The Helsinki convention also grew in strength. By 1984 the use of DDT had been banned in all seven countries; the use of PCBs was severely restricted in the Baltic countries; and a new group of hazardous substances—PCTs—had been added to the list of banned substances in the Helsinki convention. Discharges from ships had been strictly limited; port reception facilities to handle ships' wastes had been built; rules and guidelines for cooperation in combating oil spills had been drawn up; and various measures were in place for coordinating maritime traffic in the Baltic.[12] Governments now pursue new means and ends. Their learning did not extend to new reasoning processes, as the Baltic arrangements lack any integrated management components.

The Helsinki convention's implementation is guided by the Baltic Marine Environmental Protection Commission (the Helsinki commission), which is composed of a secretariat in Helsinki and two technical working groups. The Scientific-Technological Working Group (STWG) deals with dispersing water protection technology, the establishment of criteria and standards of water quality, and monitoring the marine environment. The Maritime Working Group (MWG) handles problems related to pollution from ships, particularly dumping, tracking oil residues, and international coordination in cases of accidental spillages (Caldwell 1984:127–28; Hagerhall 1980). Before the convention entered into force in 1980, the commission met informally, and the states unilaterally bore the costs of the program. Until 1977 Finland paid for the interim commission's costs, and Sweden paid for the MWG's expenses. After 1977 the costs were divided equally among the seven parties, with Finland paying for the extra expenses of the commission's Helsinki offices. After 1980, the interim commission became the Helsinki commission. Collaborative costs and benefits were distributed equitably among the parties. Finland was responsible for the chairmanship for the first two years of intergovernmental meetings, and officers were appointed to the commission for three-year terms. The executive secretaryship went to the Finland, the office of the secretary of the IWTG to Denmark, and the office of the secretary of the MWG to the USSR. The commission's budget went from $US

189,000 for 1980, to $295,450 for 1981, to $333,333 for 1982/1983.[13] The budget is small, but the commission does not have many responsibilities. Pollution control is funded nationally and monitored by several international nongovernmental and intergovernmental scientific organizations.

This evolution of collective concern was shaped by the Copenhagen-based International Council for the Exploration of the Sea (ICES), an intergovernmental organization dedicated to supporting and coordinating ongoing marine research in its eighteen member states. It established the Working Group on Pollution of the Baltic in 1968 to survey the pollution situation. In 1970 it produced a survey of loads and levels of various pollutants. In 1970 and 1971 ICES supported a baseline study of pollutants in the region, with the Scientific Committee on Oceanic Research (SCOR) of the International Council of Scientific Unions (ICSU). In 1977 it released its findings of high levels of mercury, cadmium, lead, and of organohalogen compounds in certain fish and invertebrate species. There were no clear "hot spots."[14] Subsequent provision of data moved states toward an agreement governing the environmental quality of the region. Monitoring of the Baltic is largely administered by ICES, with two regional professional scientific organizations, the Baltic Marine Biologists and the Baltic Oceanographers.

Along with the members of the countries' environmental ministries, the familiar alliance of an ecological epistemic community and various marine scientists was in place. Information was provided by a group with common concerns. The ICES secretariat, SCOR, and environmental ministries would constitute an ecological epistemic community. Research and monitoring contracts were drawn up with the region's marine scientists, who were concerned with more specific types of marine pollution. Throughout the region there was a high level of scientific competency before the program began (evident in the number of national ocean research institutions presented in table 8.1), so the marine scientists could easily advise their governments on the need for more comprehensive marine pollution controls. For comparison, figures from the same source, which differ from figures collected by UNEP (presented in chapter 3), are given for the Mediterranean states. The governments all had large environmental ministries, or similar large centralized bodies responsible for environmental protection. An environmental movement seems to have arisen in the USSR in the 1960s that had access to makers of foreign policy and promoted national environmental awareness.[15]

Table 8.1. Ocean Research Institutions, 1976

Baltic	Number	Mediterranean	Number
FRG	68	France	69
USSR	55	Italy	40
Sweden	34	Israel	21
Denmark	33	Yugoslavia	21
DRG	29	Spain	13
Poland	23	Turkey	12
		Greece	8
		Egypt	7
		Monaco	4
		Tunisia	4
		Morocco	3
		Malta	3
		Lebanon	2
		Algeria	2
		Cyprus	1
		Libya	1
		Syria	1

Source: Varley (1976). No data for Finland.

To some extent the scientific evidence reinforced existing political preferences by the major parties. The USSR is regionally dominant, as is clear from table 8.2. Although the range of economic and scientific disparities in the Baltic region is not as extreme as in the Mediterranean, the USSR's military presence cannot be overlooked. The USSR's hegemony is even greater if the USSR is viewed as leading and controlling the bloc of Eastern Baltic countries.

Environmental cooperation here is overdetermined. The value of an explanation based on epistemic communities rather than the distribution of power is unclear in this case, as the movement to control a wide variety of marine pollutants also correlates with the interests of the hegemonic USSR. The epistemic community may have generated initial interest in Baltic pollution and facilitated de facto policy coordination during the 1970s before the formal entry into force of the Helsinki convention. The additional explanatory value of the epistemic community in this progression would be clearer if the USSR chose to limit its foreign exposure in other international arenas, or decided to continue to respect its Baltic pollution control measures in the face of strong incentives to cease.

Table 8.2. Major Economic Indicators for Baltic Countries (in $US)

	GNP, 1978 (in billions)	GNP Per Capita, 1978	Average Real Growth of Per Capita GNP, 1970–1978
USSR	967.8	3,710	+4.3
FRG	631.6	10,310	+2.4
Poland	127.6	3,650	+5.9
GDR	107.6	5,670	+4.8
Sweden	87.3	10,540	+1.1
Denmark	54.0	10,580	+2.1
Finland	34.0	7,160	+2.2

Source: World Bank, *1980 World Bank Atlas*. Washington, D.C.

Acid Rain

The development of coordinated European controls over the long-range transport of air pollution ("acid rain") reveal a similar progression toward more comprehensive coordinated environmental policies following the involvement of an ecological epistemic community. European governments have moved from a framework convention without specific targets to controlling emissions of sulphur dioxides and nitrogen oxides, supported by monitoring efforts. Governments have learned that prior measures were insufficient to accomplish established goals, and so have pursued new means.

Acid rain consists of the deposition of highly acidic substances in rainwater that lead to the death of lakes, fish, and forests. Scientists have gradually determined that the principal sources of acidification are fossil fuel–fired power plants, whose emissions are converted into sulphur dioxides in the atmosphere, and automobile exhaust, which is converted to nitrogen oxides. Once emitted into the atmosphere, these pollutants are often transmitted hundreds of miles by wind and weather patterns. The real diffusion patterns of regional air pollution are not well understood, and are widely disputed. An OECD study established that sulphur traveled long distances and that the primary downwind producers of sulfur dioxides were the United Kingdom and Federal Republic of Germany. There two countries were the most vehement in denying the accuracy of models of atmospheric transfer of these pollutants, because their economies would stand to suffer the

239

most from installing stack scrubbers or other methods to limit the emissions of such substances. The Scandinavian countries and Canada are the principal receivers, or consumers, of acid rain, and have long urged its control (Wetstone 1987:165).

In November 1979 thirty-four states and the EEC signed the Convention on Long-Range Transboundary Air Pollution. Thirty-one of the signatories ratified the treaty, and it entered into force in March 1983 (UNECE 1987). Although it does not establish actual standards, the convention charges signatories "to limit, and, as far as possible, gradually reduce and prevent air pollution, including long-range transboundary air pollution." The convention established an executive body to review its implementation and develop targets and schedules for reducing specific pollutants. The United States has not ratified the 1979 protocol, insisting that it should be credited with reductions in emissions that were achieved before 1980, because air pollution control efforts began earlier in the United States than in Europe. In September 1984 twenty-one countries signed a protocol to the 1979 Convention on Long-term Financing of the Cooperative Programme for Monitoring and Evaluation of the Long-Range Transmission of Air Pollutants in Europe (EMEP), which established funding and arrangements for a network of monitoring stations, now totaling ninety-two stations in twenty-four countries with a 1987 budget of $US 970,000 (Sand 1987:16–17; Dovland 1987). Evaluating the data indicated that sulphur and nitrogen oxides are important sources of acidification, and that they are transported between countries by regional atmospheric patterns (Dovland 1987; United Nations Economic Commission for Europe 1987b:annex 1). In July 1985 twenty-one countries committed themselves to reduce their emission of sulphur dioxides by 30 percent by 1993 from their 1980 levels. These countries called themselves the Thirty Percent Club (see table 8.3). Nine of the countries plan to reduce their sulphur dioxide emissions by 50 percent or more (Rosencranz 1986:48). EMEP studies found that nitrogen oxides were also responsible for acid rain, leading the executive body to propose freezing their emissions as well.[16] In November 1988 the Sophia Protocol on Emissions of Nitrogen Oxides and Their Transboundary Fluxes was signed by the United States and twenty-four other states, and twelve Western European states adopted a declaration calling for 30 percent reductions in nitrogen oxide emissions by 1998. France, Italy, and the United Kingdom had resisted such a protocol on the grounds that it would require small cars, which they produced, to install catalytic converters, which would impede

Table 8.3. Signatories to the Convention on Long-Range
Transboundary Air Pollution and Details of Those Countries Who
Have Joined the Thirty Percent Club

Signatory	Ratification Date		Date of Accession to the Thirty Percent Club		Promised Reductions of SO_2, from 1980
Austria	Dec.	1982	June	1983	50% by 1995
Belgium	July	1982	June	1984	50% by 1995
Bulgaria	June	1981	June	1984	30% by 1993
Byelorussian SSR	June	1980	June	1984	30% by 1993
Canada	Dec.	1981	June	1983	50% by 1994
Czechoslovakia	Dec.	1983	Sept.	1984	30% by 1993
Denmark	June	1982	June	1983	50% by 1995
Finland	April	1981	June	1983	50% by 1995
France	Nov.	1981	March	1984	50% by 1990
Germany (Democratic Republic)	June	1982	June	1984	30% by 1993
Germany (Federal Republic)	July	1982	June	1983	60% by 1993
Greece	Aug.	1983			
Hungary	Sept.	1980	April	1985	30% by 1993
Iceland	May	1983			
Ireland	July	1982			
Italy	July	1982	Sept.	1984	30% by 1993
Liechtenstein	Nov.	1983	June	1984	30% by 1993
Luxembourg	July	1982	June	1984	30% by 1993
Netherlands	July	1982	March	1984	40% by 1995
Norway	Feb.	1981	June	1983	50% by 1994
Poland	March	1985			
Portugal	Sept.	1980			
Spain	June	1982			
Sweden	Feb.	1981	June	1983	65% by 1995
Switzerland	May	1983	June	1983	30% by 1995
Turkey	April	1983			
Ukrainian SSR	June	1980	June	1984	30% by 1993
USSR	May	1980	June	1984	30% by 1993
United Kingdom	July	1982			
USA	Nov.	1981			
European Community	July	1982			

Source: Derek Elson, *Atmospheric Pollution* (New York: Basil Blackwell, 1987), p. 261.

their fuel efficiency and power; they argued for the imposition, instead, of common speed limits. Germany, on the other hand, as a producer of higher-powered cars, supported such a move, as it would not require significant automobile redesign for its industry.

The arrangements for controlling European acid rain have grown significantly in scope from 1979 to 1987. Supporting national air pollution control measures have also grown in strength, as air pollution legislation, regulatory measures, and investment policies encouraging the shift to alternative fuel sources and the installation of control technologies have been widely introduced in Europe (United Nations Economic Commission for Europe 1987b:47).

Germany reversed its position in 1982, following extensive domestic evidence of forest damage from acidification. "By 1982 . . . West German officials had become convinced by their scientists and foresters that massive forest death *(Waldsterben)* was resulting in Germany and elsewhere in Central Europe from air pollutants, including the sulphur and nitrogen pollutants that are the principal components of acid rain" (Rosencranz 1988:174; see also Pallemaerts 1985). The FRG joined the Thirty Percent Club, and promised to reduce its emissions of sulphur dioxides by 60 percent by 1993 from 1980—twice as much as was targeted by the Thirty Percent Club (Rosencranz 1986). The foreign environmental policy reversals were followed by domestic energy conservation measures and the requirement that catalytic converters by used in new automobiles. After 1982 the government promptly introduced a series of new measures to phase out older inefficient power plants and to install expensive control technologies (Wetstone 1987:189). In light of the clear-cut benefits of not cooperating for upwind countries, the decision by the FRG to control emissions that contribute to acid rain are all the more striking. The United Kingdom has not acceded to the 30 percent target, although its awareness is "increasing very rapidly" and a coalition of six British environmental organizations has formed an acid rain coalition to lobby the government (Rosencranz 1986:48).

By examining the role of a transnational epistemic community we may also better understand how such cooperation emerged. To the extent that studies by EMEP and the OECD led to the adoption of new controls, governments have responded to the political clout of the scientists who are able to reduce the uncertainty surrounding the extent of damage caused by acid deposition, the pace at which damage is occurring, and the relationship among different emission sources, different pollutants, and different social and economic conditions. In downwind countries, where evidence of environmental degradation is more manifest, such groups have been able to seize public attention to the issue, and press governments to support stronger and more comprehensive international efforts. Domestically, they pushed for stronger measures. However, in up-wind countries such groups have encountered much more resistance, because the benefits from cooperation are much smaller (Wetstone 1987:192–93). In Germany environmentalist scientists also generated sufficient environmental consciousness to move the government to support new international and national measures for air pollution controls, although Germans' deep cultural bonds with nature and the Black Forest surely helped the environmentalists' cause.

Such cooperation still exceeds neorealist hegemonic stability explanations of behavior, because a large number of states with relatively equal power resources all cooperate. The three strongest parties are the United States, the United Kingdom, and the Federal Republic of Germany. They are the principal producers of acid rain, and they are upwind countries, so that the rain does not fall on them. Neorealist analysis would presume that they would be the least cooperative states—those standing to lose the most through participation and the most able to withstand pressure to participate. However, structural forces only prevailed for the United States and the United Kingdom, who have not ratified the 30 percent protocol. The FRG's reversal is an anomaly for such analysis.

This international environmental order has not extended to North America, where the United States has refused to join the Thirty Percent Club and to conclude a treaty with Canada that would limit American emissions, which the Canadians claim cause acid rain to fall in their country. This gap in the environmental order may be explained in light of the absence of circumstances that contribute to the empowerment of an epistemic community. In North America there has been very little uncertainty surrounding the transmission of acid rain between Canada and the United States. Public utilities in the Midwest emit sulphur dioxide into the atmosphere; this is deposited in eastern Canada and the northeastern United States, where forests are thinned and fish die. The payoff matrix is unmistakable; Canada is more affected by the phenomenon than is the United States, and the costs to midwestern states for its treatment would exceed the value of the benefits accruing to New England through averting the loss of fishing, tourism, and timber revenues. Thus, with little uncertainty, there was no reason for the makers of foreign policy in the

United States to consult atmospheric scientists who might be members of an ecological epistemic community, and such a group has had little access to bilateral negotiations.

THE FUTURE

This final section will discuss the future of the international environmental order, and the possibility that other international orders will arise by a similar process. Epistemic communities may play significant roles in the future as the conditions that encourage their entry into decision making become more widespread.

The future of the Med Plan is unclear, and necessarily conjectural. It will depend upon whether the ecological epistemic community can retain its influence over regional marine pollution control. Ultimately, this depends upon whether it retains control over environmental ministries and maintains its scientific consensus.

Without a major regional pollution catastrophe to dispel its domestic authority, the alliance between UNEP's epistemic community and national marine scientists is likely to continue to drive pollution control efforts in the region. A small oil spill, coastal epidemic, or shoreline industrial accident could reinforce the scientists' standing in their own countries, and enable them to press for stronger domestic pollution control measures. But too large a crisis would undercut their tenuous domestic standing by laying open to question their ability to effectively control pollution.

The falsification of a number of key ecological causal beliefs would lead to elimination of the epistemic community's intellectual basis and hence the loss of its common policy preferences. Although a logical possibility, such an event is unlikely in the short run. Since Galileo, few intellectual revolutions have rapidly overthrown existing bodies of thought. Even Einstein and Newton continue to equitably divide up the analysis of physics.

The Med Plan's focus is likely to remain on the control of land-based sources of pollution. In the absence of much pollution from offshore oil and gas drilling in the region or uncertainty surrounding its extent or effects, governments have little reason to conclude treaties covering these sources. Studies have not revealed any new sources of pollution that require collective attention. Activity is likely to continue at the national level, as the epistemic community continues to pressure governments toward more convergent pollution control practices. The most fruitful area of work for the Med Plan may well be the dissemination of information regarding methods of compliance with the Land-Based Sources Protocol, which may result in its greater enforcement, and may also reinforce UNEP's ties with domestic scientists.

Epistemic communities may prove influential in other international issue areas as well. As international vulnerabilities and complex interstate flows become more acute with the globalization of the world economy and mounting interdependence, groups able to attenuate the accompanying uncertainty for decision makers may become increasingly important in identifying problems, setting agendas, and proposing and enforcing domestic and foreign policies, particularly for issues with a large scientific and technical component, such as international finance, technology transfer and acquisition, telecommunications, and information flows. In such areas decision makers must handle a new constellation of complexly intermeshed issues, where the effects of decisions made in one issue area often flow to other issue areas that are analytically distinct.

There is often great uncertainty about the policy choices involved in such issue areas, due to the multiple interlinkages that decision makers must consider. These interdependencies span three dimensions: effects of actions are felt in the future; effects are felt in other, formerly functionally discrete issue areas; and their effects are felt elsewhere in space. Their features also elude effective management through the patterns of behavior developed to cope with issues that appear nationally. Although the effects cross borders, leaders are accustomed to dealing only with problems confronting them within their own sovereign territory. Moreover, due to their longer-term appearance, their effects are strongly discounted. Yet because they are felt in areas that are beyond the control of any country, such as in the oceans or the atmosphere, their control requires coordinated action.

As with the environment, uncertainty abounds:

The ecosystems which comprise the biosphere are incredibly complex interacting systems, and we have little present capacity to predict the effect of disturbances of these systems engendered by human activity. The fear is that we may do irreversible damage inadvertently through the fact that our capacity to alter nature to our purpose progresses much more rapidly than our understanding of nature's complexities and hence of the ultimate effects of our alternations. There is no agreement, for example, on how robust the system as a whole is with respect to the size of the perturbations we are capable of making in the natural biogeochemical cycles. Are we dealing with a highly resilient system, with many internal compensating mechanisms, or are we dealing with a system that is in very delicate balance, where a relatively small change might trigger a shift to an entirely new and less benign stable state? (Brooks 1982:293)

Facing such issues, decision makers as well as analysts are often uncertain about the likely effects of policies, and the significance of events which are publicized as being extremely high-risk.

Uncertainty takes two forms. Decision makers are often ignorant about the precise effects of actions because the scientific knowledge base is not sufficient to offer confident predictions. More importantly, they often lack enough information to determine the likelihood of an event, so they are unable to estimate the risks in order to calculate decision models of alternative outcomes or to rank the likelihood of different outcomes.[17]

As these types of issues with a high degree of uncertainty gain in salience for leaders—as is indeed the case—there is a greater range of influence for epistemic communities that possess authoritative claims to understanding the problems; analyzing them is also more useful. Activist scientists may be able to exercise some international influence through reaching out to groups with similar beliefs in other countries and exercising concerted pressure on their respective governments and international organizations. Epistemic communities with extremely comprehensive causal beliefs can influence governments to adopt policies that are more foreward looking, that acknowledge the broader geographic consequences of their actions, and that are more tightly linked to other functional activities.

The resulting political orders created for other issue areas will not all be the same. Their forms will vary by the nature of the epistemic community introduced to policymaking. The environmental order has been comprehensive because of the holistic world view of the ecological epistemic community. Other epistemic communities, with different visions, would influence other issue areas in different ways. Still, behavior is likely to remain reactive rather than anticipatory and require a crisis to instigate it.

A complicated vision of the future emerges. Patterns of interstate behavior may vary by issue and depend upon the scope of casual beliefs shared by the epistemic community that becomes involved. International cooperation and convergent state policies are increasingly possible for areas in which mobilized epistemic communities are able to influence policy. Current tendencies toward disarticulated national actions that ignore or resist global interlinkages may be offset by the involvement of epistemic communities with a global vision. In such cases, deft diplomacy by members of epistemic communities and international organizations can shape national and international behavior toward more internationally responsible policies.

Notes

Introduction

1. Some notable exceptions to this observation are Ruggie (1986) and Ruggie (1989); Pirages (1983); and Dahlberg (1979) and (1983).

2. Statement by Dr. Mostafa Kamal Tolba, UNEP executive director to the International Symposium on Toxic Chemicals and Aquatic Life, Seattle, Washington, September 17, 1986. UNEP Information 86/22 (October 1986), pp. 4–5.

3. Sand (1988); Hulm (1983); UNEP (1982a); UNEP (1982b); United Nations Environment Programme, "Cleaning up the Seas," UNEP Environment Brief No. 5. The other regions are the Gulf of Kuwait (or Persian Gulf) (1978), the Wider Caribbean (1981), West and Central Africa (1981), Eastern Africa (1985), the East Asian Seas (1981), the Red Sea and Gulf of Aden (1982), the South Pacific (1982), the Southeast Pacific (1981), and the South Asian Seas (in preparation).

3. Berger and Luckmann (1967); Hollis and Lukes (1982); Boulding (1956).

For a clear discussion of the epistemological views that are referred to here, see also Hesse (1982) and Knorr-Cetina and Mulkay (1983).

1. Effluents: The Development of International Concern About Environmental Pollution

1. United Nations (1980), p. 4. Earlier, Barry Commoner had argued that environmental issues are all intricately interlinked:

Everything is connected to everything else: the system is stabilized by its dynamic self-compensating properties; these same properties, if overstressed, can lead to a dramatic collapse; the complexity of the ecological network and its intrinsic rate of turnover determine how much it can be stressed, and for how long, without collapsing; the ecological network is an amplifier, so that a smaller perturbation in one place can have large, distant, long-delayed effects. (Commoner 1971:35)

2. United States National Academy of Sciences (1984), table I-1. Other sources are land based (48 percent), offshore platforms (1.5 percent), natural seepage (8 percent), and regular tanker operations (30 percent; discharge of contaminated ballast and water used for cleaning tanks).

3. Ward and Dubos (1972), p. 199. For a model of DDT transportation in the environment see Meadows and Randers (1972).

4. Wilson (1971), p. 6, quoted in M'Gonigle and Zacher (1979), p. 5. A popular bumper sticker and poster, still available from Environmental Action in the United States, presented the Earthrise photograph with the caption "love your mother." White 1987 describes the effect on astronauts of directly viewing the earth as a unitary entity.

5. Dolman (1981), p. 9. "Order" in international relations is of course a contentious term, varying from such usages as structures, processes, persistent behavior, and shared norms and values. At times it is a dependent variable, and times an independent one. See Hoffmann (1966) for a discussion of such different usages, and Cox (1981) for an effort to unify them within one multidimensional usage. As used here, order is a descriptive term, not an analytic one. It is an observable and hence verifiable pattern of behavior. It remains to be explained why certain orders appear and recur. This will be taken up in greater detail in chapter 2.

6. Lindblom (1973); Clark and Munn (1986), section 5; and Brooks (1986). For the general expression of such behavior see Lindblom (1959) and Simon (1985).

7. "Action To Save Our Environment," *UN Chronicle* (June 1988), p. 42.

8. *Ibid.*

9. For a sample of such exhortatory statements see Tolba (1987).

10. "Action To Save Our Environment," *UN Chronicle* (June 1988), p. 43.

11. For a lengthier discussion of these conferences see Biswas and Biswas (1985).

12. *The Environmental Digest* (November 1988), no. 18, p. 11.

13. Calculated from data provided by the Tanker Advisory Center, Inc., New York.

14. Data drawn from Kiss (1982) and OECD (1985b), pp. 275–77.

15. Haigh (1984) is the lone example. He studied the United Kingdom, and found that it did attempt to get its industries to comply with most of the directives.

16. Council of Europe *Naturopa Newsletter–Nature and Environment*, no. 88–4, p. 2.

17. *Report on the Environment* (April 1985), p. 1; United States Council on Environmental Quality (1984), pp. 505–6.

18. *International Environment Reporter* (July 8, 1987), vol. 10, no. 7, p. 313.

19. *Science* (May 15, 1987), p. 769; Aufderheide and Rich (1988).

20. *The Boston Globe*, August 6, 1987, p. 7.

21. UNEP/GC 14/4/Add 4, p. 6.

22. *UNEP North America News* (June 1988), 3(3):3.

23. Inglehart (1977); Milbrath (1984). A 1984 Eurobarometer survey found that Europeans' primary environmental concern was oil pollution of their beaches.

24. *Christian Science Monitor* January 13, 1987, p. 17.

25. Cited in Leonard and Morell (1981).

26. Enloe (1975); Lowe and Goyder (1983); Pilat (1980); Vogel (1986).

27. Compare, for instance, *The Global 2000 Report* (1980) and Simon and Kahn (1984).

28. See, for instance, Waterbury (1979) for the positive effects of the Aswan High Dam.

29. Strong (1973), p. 696. Meadows et al. (1971) and Woodwell (1985) sound similar alarms.

30. The Washington, D.C. representative of UNEP wrote:

The systems of nature confound and confuse national sovereignty; everyone is upwind or downstream from someone else. Animal and plant species often elude management by crossing national boundaries. This challenges governments attempting to reach international accords on such subjects as biological diversity, rangeland and watershed management.

The arbitrary imposition of national boundaries has often separated the watersheds, rivers, migratory routes, rangelands and forests, which has also defined tribal territories. . . . UNEP, in partnership with those sharing management of the Zambezi River . . . are now attempting to address this reality. (Martin-Brown 1987:11)

31. The reports are concisely summarized in Onuf (1983). The World Commission on Environment and Development (1987) is the most recent effort from this tradition, although not addressed to the Club of Rome.

32. Piddington (1989). He used the term "environmental intervener" in his presentation. Although not explicitly used in his paper, its meaning is expressed on p. 3.

33. Schultz and Hughes (1981); Porritt (1985); Devall and Sessions (1985). Many of these writers follow the ideas first expressed by E. F. Schumacher. All of these writings glorify a nature viewed as benign, and omit the continuous struggle for survival between species.

34. Boulding (1978); Dahlberg (1983); Pirages (1983); Jantsch and Waddington (1976); Clark and Munn (1986). This perspective has guided much of the work of the International Institute for Applied Systems Analysis (IIASA) and global modelers.

35. McHale (1969), p. 12. See also Markley and Harman (1982) for similar expressions.

36. Strong (1973), p. 697. For similar predictions see Independent Commission on International Development Issues (1980), pp. 13, 33. This was an uncommonly moderate view offered by a UNEP official, and Strong made many more dramatic statements as well.

37. For instance, Lee (1986); Bartelmus (1986); Riddell (1981); Holling (1978); Dasmann, Milton, and Freeman (1973).

38. Simon (1981); Simon and Kahn (1984). Kaysen (1972) critiqued the "limits to growth" model because it omitted the increasing price signals that would precede resource exhaustion.

39. Orr and Soroos (1979); Commission on the Organization of the Government for the Conduct of Foreign Policy (1975); Kay and Skolnikoff (1972); Sprout and Sprout (1974); Soroos (1986); Kay and Jacobson (1983); Rubin and Graham (1982).

40. Bahro (1984). He writes, "I believe that human evolution began to go wrong with the English industrial revolution. . . . I see exterminism as rooted in industrialism" (p. 212).

41. Ruggie (1986); Dahlberg (1983); Dahlberg (1979); Dunlap (1980); Sprout and Sprout (1965).

42. Kratochwill and Ruggie (1986); Ruggie (1983a); Ruggie (1989); and Cox (1981). Ashley (1984) argues that the extent to which writers neglect the change of context is an impediment to effective social responses. He may attribute an excessive degree of authority to scholarship.

43. Subsequent Syrian accessions to Med Plan protocols have specified that such agreements do not imply recognition of Israel.

44. "Toning Down the Mediterranean Blues," *The Economist*, June 11, 1983, pp. 97–100; Osterberg and Keckes (1977); Brisou (1976).

45. *L'Express*, July 24, 1987, p. 11.

46. Inter-Governmental Maritime Consultative Organization and United Nations Environment Program (April 1979).

47. *Spotlight* (fortnightly publication of the Institute for Political Studies, Athens), June 1, 1984, p. 3. See also Wenger (1975).

48. Commoner (1971), pp. 8–9; Roederer (1985). Commoner writes:

Understanding the ecosphere comes hard because, to the modern mind, it is a curiously foreign place. We have become accustomed to think of separate, singular events, each dependent upon a unique, singular cause. But in the ecosphere every effect is also a cause: an animal's waste becomes food for soil bacteria; what bacteria excrete nourishes plants; animals eat the plants. Such ecological cycles are hard to fit into human experience in the age of technology, where machine A always yields product B, and product B, once used, is cast away, having no further meaning for the machine, the product, or the user.

2. Influence: Explanations of International Environmental Cooperation

1. Aggarwal (1985) chooses to evaluate arrangements by their "strength, nature and scope" (pp. 21–22). Putnam and Bayne (1987) organize them by their intensity, scope, and duration (p. 2).

2. Morgenthau (1985), p. 5. In economic issues, "interest is defined as wealth."

3. For instance, see Pastor and Diaz-Briquets (1986), in which they argue that the Kissinger Commission Report on Central America neglected possibly destabilizing influences on governments and regional security coming from population movements, deforestation, and declining agricultural productivity.

4. Some exemplary works are Keohane (1984); Keohane (1983b); Waltz (1979); Gilpin (1975); Gilpin (1981); Krasner (1976). See Keohane (1983b) for a deeper analysis of the consistencies and differences among these approaches. Ashley (1981) regards such a move as a theoretical degeneration because it eliminates the art of diplomacy, which he found most accurate and attractive, from the classical realists.

5. See, for instance, Oye (1986), p. 1, n. 1.

6. Viner (1948); Gilpin (1986), pp. 308–13. These ends have been seen as reciprocal, as power facilitates access to more wealth, which in turn provides the wherewithall to furnish sufficient power to defend oneself.

7. Collective goods, or public goods, or commons, are characterized by two properties; if they are available to one country they are available to all countries (access cannot be restricted), and one country's use of the good does not reduce its availability to others. A clean Mediterranean Sea is an example of such a collective good. See Wijkman (1982) and Hardin (1968) for discussions of other environmental public goods.

8. Waltz (1979), pp. 196–99 and 209–10. See also Snidal (1985), p. 596; and Ruggie (1972), to which Waltz refers suggestively on p. 197, n.

9. Stremlau (1982). For a related argument about how economic development contributes to the *domestic* legitimacy and power of the state see Krasner (1985), chs. 1 and 3.

10. Keohane (1980); Krasner (1983b). Waltz (1979) also comments that cooperation is most likely when it is enforced by "agents with great capability" (p. 190).

11. Keohane (1980); Keohane (1983a); Kindleberger (1981). They point to such cases as international trade, where according to liberal theories of trade, all parties benefit from reduced barriers to trade. Once supported by the hegemon, all will truly benefit from the arrangements.

12. For Waltz, for instance, "only a structural transformation can abolish the international imperative—take care of yourself!—and replace it with the domestic one—specialize!" See Waltz (1986), p. 326.

13. Gilpin (1981), pp. 228, 230. He notes that leaders still have a space available to them for choice, and that learning seems to consist of making new choices. The rest of his book is devoted to analyzing the strong constraints acting on leaders from historical experience and structures, which presumably strongly inhibit any learning.

14. The term "historical materialism" is Cox's (1981). It incorporates Marxists, some non-Marxists, and dependency theorists. Some exemplary works are Amin (1974); Cardoso and Faletto (1979); Evans (1979); Wallerstein (1979); and Galtung (1980).

15. Johan Galtung argues that exchanges between the core and periphery are "cumulatively asymmetric." See Galtung (1980), p. 113.

16. *The Christian Science Monitor*, July 18, 1980, p. 12.

17. Balbus (1971), p. 153. See also Poulantzas (1973). For a study of the weaknesses of strong structural determinism see Lukes (1977), ch. 1.

18. Bourdieu (1977), p. 40; emphasis in the original. Foucault's works address the same concern. Schattschneider (1975) recognized that "the definition of the alternatives is the supreme instrument of power" (p. 66).

19. George (1979). Recent work with computer simulation indicates that expectations and belief systems may influence in an important way how specific events are interpreted, what motivations are ascribed to other actors, and their implied cause. See Carbonell (1981) and Winograd and Flores (1986).

20. Snyder and Diesing (1977); Jervis (1976); Boulding (1956). Stein (1982) notes that misperceptions need not lead to armed conflict.

21. Ascher (1983), p. 417. He goes on to note the various constraints on these groups in devising and promoting new policies. The Chernobyl nuclear accident also led the USSR to solicit advice from the nuclear engineers at the International Energy Agency (IAEA) and to abide by their technical proposals. Barkenbus (1987), p. 485. For other international studies see Rothstein (1984), and Putnam and Bayne (1987). Putnam and Bayne found that the economic summits that developed the most comprehensive, strong, and enduring concerted policies were those at which the major actors shared a significant understanding of the operation of the international economy. Richard Cooper suggests that effective macroeconomic cooperation is impeded by the inability of economists to agree on "means-ends relationships," or even on whether the key variables influencing economic performance are monetary or fiscal. See Cooper (1986), pp. 96–100, and Cooper (1985).

22. Ruggie (1975), pp. 569–70. The term comes from Holzner and Marx (1979), pp. 107–11. They use it in a broader sense than I do, considering, with Polanyi (1962), all scientists to constitute an epistemic community because they believe in the scientific method and logico-deductive reasoning. I use the term here with the assumption that such a faith in methods must be combined with a belief in specific causal relations and common political end values. Similar concepts are the "thought collective" (Fleck 1979), the "invisible college" (Crane 1972), the "episteme" (Foucault 1972), and the "scientific

community" (Kuhn 1970). Ruggie's usage is closer to Foucault's, referring to the broad unquestioned social beliefs that a culture or society holds, rather than their more immediate causal models shared by a scientific group. Haas (1989) applies a notion of epistemic community similar to mine, although according stronger weight to the community's common truth tests.

23. Most social scientists lack such shared rules.

24. See Sebenius (1984) for a description of how a report prepared at the Massachusetts Institute of Technology led to an early convergence of governmental positions at the Law of the Sea negotiations.

25. See the literature on the role of transnational and transgovernmental actors in international cooperation, such as Keohane and Nye (1971); Keohane and Nye (1974); Hopkins (1978); Evan (1981); Crane (1984).

26. Simon (1969), p. 118. Simon is calling national-level units *systems*, but the same process occurs as countries adapt to changes in the international system. Karl Deutsch has a very similar idea of learning as "the ability of any political decision system to invent and carry out fundamentally new policies to meet new conditions. . . . related to its ability to combine items of information into new patterns." See Deutsch (1966), p. 163.

27. At the level of individual moral development in women, Carol Gilligan has found that there is a progression in moral conception that closely follows this conceptualization of types of learning. She observes a "shift in perspective towards increasingly differentiated, comprehensive and reflective forms of thought." See Gilligan (1982), p. 73.

28. Heclo (1974) offers this as a contagion model.

29. Brewer and deLeon (1983), p. 36; Steinbruner (1974); Stein and Tanter (1980), part 1. Argyris and Schon (1978) call this single-loop learning.

30. Argyris and Schon (1978) call this double-loop learning.

31. Schank and Abelson (1977) speak of understanding the "intentional and contextual connections between events, especially as they occur in human purposive action sequences" (p. 4).

32. Prigogine and Stengers (1984), p. 13. See also Boulding (1978) for the argument that collective images of the world will evolve along with the complexity in the world.

33. See Gilligan (1982) for a discussion of such learning at the individual level.

3. The Origins of Awareness of Mediterranean Pollution and Early Negotiations for the Mediterranean Action Plan

1. Ritchie-Calder (1975), p. 43. This quote paraphrases Ritchie-Calder (1972).

2. Nineteenth-century researchers reported extensive organic pollution near Trieste and Marseilles; see Bellan and Peres (1972).

3. *Convention for the Protection of the Mediterranean Against Pollution*, article 4, paragraph 1.

4. *New York Times*, February 21, 1971, section 4, pp. 24–25.

5. *Algerian National Report to the United Nations Conference on the Human Environment*, mimeo, 1971. Available in UN library, Geneva.

6. WHO and UNEP (1979); Sittig (1975); *UN Yearbook of Industrial Statistics 1979*, vol. 1. New York: United Nations.

7. *El-Djeich* (Algiers) (April 1972), no. 107, p. 28.

8. Jon Marks, "Squeezed on the Margins," *South* (June 1987), p. 78.

9. Cited in McIntosh (1985), pp. 7–8. For a history of ecology see Kormondy and McCormick (1981); Worster (1977).

10. UNEP/IAMRS 1/6, Annex 2, pp. 4–5. Peter Thacher noted in an internal memo: "I continue to support FAO's tactic of stressing the effect on fisheries as a way to stimulate action on pollution in the Mediterranean, but suspect that the tourist angle is also one which should be played, particularly in relation to oil on beaches, but also in relation to sewerage." "Memo from PST to Dr. R. Frosch (March 19, 1974)." See also Tolba (1982) and Tolba (1987).

11. UNEP/IG 56/INF 8, p. 3.

12. "Thin Ice Over the Regional Seas." Interview with Stjepan Keckes in *AMBIO* (1983), 12(1):13.

13. ENI (1974), p. 243. Most trips in the Mediterranean are too short to allow the use of the load-on-top method, and few ports have the necessary deballasting facilities to accept residual oil clinging to the walls of holds, which otherwise gets flushed into the sea during routine cleaning operations; .01 percent of a tanker's load is usually emitted.

14. FAO FID:PPM/74/INF 6, p. 1.

15. United States Senate, Subcommittee on Ocean and Atmosphere of the Committee on Commerce (1972); Vadrot (1977), p. 37.

16. *The Economist*, March 31, 1973, p. 32.

17. M'Gonigle and Zacher (1979), p. 118, n. 134. This degree of hyperbole remained associated with the problem in the popular press; it is perhaps best characterized by an article titled "From Civilization's Cradle to Europe's Cesspool." See Linn (1974).

18. *New York Times*, May 23, 1971, section 4, p. 8.

19. *New York Times*, August 25, 1972, p. 12.

20. *Financial Times*, February 14, 1978.

21. Titanium dioxide wastes are dumped as "red muds" which discolor the water and which fishermen feared harmed fish. In 1974 the Scarlino plant installed new waste-processing equipment, and wastes are now disposed on land. A French court awarded the fishermen $US 13 million in compensation. In 1976 a Leghorn court overturned criminal charges against Montedison executives which had been imposed earlier. See Sand (1977), pp. 151–53; *Chemical Week*, December 8, 1976, pp. 65–67.

22. UNEP/WG 2/INF 6, pp. 4–5.

23. He observed that "harbors are evil smelling places, in some places with gas and oil bubbling to the surface." FAO FIRM/TRAM/672 (1972), p. 3.

24. Charbonier (1977), p. 375. See table on fish catches.

25. See tables on typhoid and paratyphoid.

26. See table on tourism.

27. A/CONF 48/IGWMP 1/5, Annex 7.

28. A/CONF 48/IGWMP 2/WP 8/Add 1.

29. UN, GESAMP, "Report of the Third Session, Joint Group of Experts on

the Scientific Aspects of Marine Pollution," GESAMP 3/19, Annex 6 (Paris: UNESCO, May 13, 1971), p. 5.

30. *Le Figaro*, June 8, 1973; *New York Times*, June 9, 1973; Boxer (1982), p. 331; *L'Apel* (Summer 1974), pp. 80–84.

31. Later reissued, with a slightly different name, as GFCM (1972).

32. GFCM Resolution 11/72/1.

33. FAO FID:PPM/74/Rep. 3, appendix E.

34. Cruises conducted by the IAEA subsequently confirmed his hunch. See Osterberg (1977), p. 30.

4. The Adoption of the Mediterranean Action Plan and the Development of More Comprehensive Measures to Control Pollution

1. UNEP/WG, 2/5 annex.

2. Individual studies of pollutants in the open waters of the Mediterranean were released as one report in 1986, although no efforts were taken to integrate the data for the entire open waters of the Sea. See UNEP and IOC, "Biogeochemical Studies of Selected Pollutants in the Open Waters of the Mediterranean (Med Pol 8," MAP Technical Reports Series No. 8 (Athens:UNEP, 1986).

3. UNEP/IG 11/INF 5.

4. FAO General Fisheries Council for the Mediterranean, "Joint FAO(GFCM)/ UNEP Coordinated Project on Pollution in the Mediterranean," Final Report (No. 7), Circular no. 8 (September 1981).

5. UNEP/IG 23/11, annex 4, p. 2.

6. UNEP/IG 11/3, p. 1.

7. UNEP/WG 91/5.

8. UNEP/WG 91/6, p. 17. The proportion of areas deemed satisfactory vary by whether one applies EEC standards or WHO standards. EEC standards allow a higher faecal coliform content in shellfish flesh and growing waters than do WHO criteria.

9. UNEP/WG 91/6, pp. 10, 13. Again, EEC and WHO criteria vary.

10. Cruzado (1984); UNEP/IG 49/5, p. 23.

11. UNEP/WG 62/4.

12. *The Siren* (October 1988), no. 38, p. 26. Institutions conducting monitoring and research came from Algeria, Cyprus, Egypt, France, Greece, Israel, Lebanon, Libya, Malta, Monaco, Morocco, Spain, Syria, and Yugoslavia.

13. UNEP/WG 28/3; UNEP/WG 118/8, p. 13.

14. GESAMP, "Atmospheric Transport of Contaminants Into the Mediterranean Region," UNEP Regional Seas Reports and Studies No. 68 (Geneva: UNEP, 1985).

15. 76/464/EEC, reprinted in *Official Journal of the European Communities*, no. L 129/23 (May 18, 1976). The EC has also had a long-standing controversy over ambient standards (supported by Britain) versus emission standards (supported by the countries on the Continent).

16. UNEP Press Release Press/82/37 (April 13, 1982).

17. UNEP/IG 5/7, pp. 7–8.

Reported Cases of Typhoid and Paratyphoid in the Mediterranean Area

	1966	1967	1968	1969	1970
Algeria					835
Cyprus	12	3	24	10	6
France	2,026	1,545	1,393	1,357	1,272
Greece	1,049	935	750		746
Israel	306	198	265	289	307
Italy	12,012	10,603	13,275	12,603	12,943
Lebanon	77	53	110		
Libya	151	90			
Spain	3,238	3,591	3,104	2,891	3,329
Tunisia					
Turkey	5,176	3,887	3,536	2,905	4,053
Yugoslavia	2,891	2,286	2,371	2,626	2,374
Malta	24	51	24	15	15

Source: WHO, *World Health Statistics Report* (various years).

[a] Figures do not cover entire country.

Total Fish Catches in the Mediterranean Sea and Black Sea, 1970–1979 (in thousand metric tons)

	1970	1971	1972	1973
Algeria	25.7	23.8	28.3	31.2
Cyprus	1.3	1.4	1.4	1.5
Egypt	12.0	14.0	13.1	9.6
France	45.6	49.9	59.9	49.6
Greece	59.1[a]	60.6[a]	55.2[a]	54.6[a]
Israel	3.2	3.8	4.0	4.2
Italy	320.3	321.1	348.7	334.2
Lebanon	2.2	1.9	1.8[a]	2.4
Libya	5.5	5.6	2.4	2.9
Malta	1.2	1.2	1.2	1.6
Morocco	10.3	13.7	17.4	19.6
Spain	124.2	124.2[a]	91.4	122.5
Syria	.1	1.4	1.1	.7
Tunisia	24.0	27.2	27.7	31.7
Turkey	165.3	146.8	172.6[a]	150.3[a]
Yugoslavia	26.7	30.9	30.6	30.5

Source: FAO, *1979 Yearbook of Fishery Statistics*, 48: 262, table C-37(b).

Note: In selected years Japan and Korea also fished in the area, but not in significant amounts.

1970–1973 show slower rates of growth, with a slight drop in total catch in 1973. Prior rates of growth resumed in 1974. This resumption was widely presumed to be a result of overfishing rather than pollution control. See M. Zei, "Perspectives for Mediterranean Fisheries and

1971	1972	1973	1974	1975	1976
1,141	1,346	1,320	2,125	3,081	4,746
3	9	2	15	3	4
1,260	1,040	1,150	1,037	1,045	994
466	594	522	510	470	603
156	193	154	122	125	166
11,975	10,483	11,413	7,125	12,403	10,289
137[a]	198	191	717		
91					103
2,533	2,235	2,183	2,415	2,185	2,092
	904		699	676	505
2,316	2,164	2,269	1,878	1,280	1,166
1,808	1,398	1,477	1,275	1,227	1,036
23	22	15	21	21	19

1974	1975	1976	1977	1978	1979
35.7	37.7	35.1	43.5	34.1	38.7
1.2	.9	1.0	1.2	1.2	1.3
8.4	5.4	6.2	6.7	11.8	20.0
44.6	46.8	50.1	44.0	40.5	44.8
56.8	62.7	71.8	69.8	73.0	88.0[a]
3.3	3.2	3.3	3.6	3.5	3.2
364.0	352.0	354.5	308.3	337.0	351.3
2.4[a]	2.4[a]	2.4[a]	2.4[a]	2.4[a]	2.4[a]
3.8	4.8	4.8[a]	4.8[a]	4.8[a]	4.8[a]
1.5	1.5	1.5	1.5	1.1	1.3
20.5	15.2	23.6	33.5	32.0	35.5
119.2	139.4	151.5	145.4	150.4	151.5
.7	.8	1.3	1.3	1.4	1.1
41.9	31.7	34.9	38.4	54.6	57.3
241.2[a]	182.7[a]	136.3[a]	136.3[a]	136.3[a]	136.3[a]
30.2	32.2	34.9	35.2	37.5	33.9

Aquaculture," paper presented to the Pacem in Maribus Conference, Malta, June 1972. Mediterranean fishery directors had been alerted to the problem of marine pollution by problems elsewhere (not in the Mediterranean).

[a] Estimate.

Incidence of Typhoid and Paratyphoid in the Mediterranean Area, 1970–1977 (Cases per 100,000)

	1970	1971	1972	1973	1974	1975	1976	1977
Algeria	5.8	7.7	8.8	8.5	13.0	18.4	27.4	
Cyprus	1.0	.5	1.5	.3	2.4		.6	.8
Egypt	1.4			41.4		32.6	27.6	
France	2.4	2.6	2.0	2.2	2.1	2.0	1.9	
Greece	8.5	5.3	6.7	5.8	5.7	7.5	8.4	6.8
Israel	12.4	6.1	5.1	4.0	3.7	4.2	3.4	
Italy	24.4	21.4	18.8	20.9	12.6	22.2		
Lebanon	1.4	5.4		7.1				
Libya	2.1	4.4	4.9	3.7	5.1	5.5	4.1	
Malta	4.2	7.0	6.9	4.4	6.6	3.6	5.6	2.7
Morocco	60.7	22.2	31.5	16.2	22.1	27.0	20.3	
Spain	9.8	7.4	6.5	6.3	6.9	6.1	5.8	
Syria	21.0	32.2	27.7	23.5	26.6	23.2	24.4	7.5
Tunisia	22.8	18.7	17.0	10.5	12.4		7.9	
Turkey	11.6	6.4	5.8	6.0	4.8	3.2		
Yugoslavia	12.7	8.2	6.9	7.2	5.9	4.6	4.8	4.0

Source: Planbleu, "Sante, population et mouvements de population," *Expertise* (1981), no. 5.

Tourism Receipts in the Mediterranean Area, 1967–1979 (in $US millions)

	1967	1969	1970	1971	1972
Algeria					
Cyprus	12.0	17.0	21.1	32.4	50.0
Egypt		65.6	71.3	86.5	101.2
France	1,040.5	1,058.4	1,189.2	1,451.3	1,760.5
Greece	126.8	149.5	193.5	305.3	392.7
Israel	52.3	85.8	103.5	178.3	211.9
Italy	1,423.7	1,632.4	1,638.6	1,882.3	2,174.0
Lebanon	80.0	102.8	131.5	179.6	203.6
Libya		13.5	11.2	6.6	10.8
Malta	15.3	28.3	29.4	25.6	22.8
Morocco	15.2	122.8	136.4	152.0	228.8
Spain	1,126.8	1,310.7	1,680.8	2,054.5	2,607.6
Syria		12.0		22.0	41.0
Tunisia		52.0	61.0	113.0	146.0
Turkey	18.5	46.1	51.6	62.9	103.7
Yugoslavia	150.3	241.0	274.2	381.6	490.5

Source: International Union of Official Travel Organizations, *International Travel Statistics* (various years); World Tourism Organization, *World Tourism Statistics* (various years).

18. UNEP/IG 11/INF 6.
19. UNEP/WG 29/3, annex 1.
20. UNEP/IG 5/7, annex 1.
21. UNEP/IG 56/INF 3, annex 2.
22. UNEP/IG 56/INF 3, annex 3.
23. *The Siren* (October 1988), no. 38, p. 26.
24. *The Siren* (September 1987), no. 34, p. 25.

5. Evolving National Measures for Pollution Control

1. The best estimates of Mediterranean pollution are in UNEP (1986b).
2. *New York Times*, October 21, 1986, p. C3.
3. *New York Times*, October 21, 1986, p. C3; Ress (1986), p. 267.
4. *El Pais*, November 8, 1984.
5. France, Secretariat Permanent par les Problemes de Pollution Industrielle de la Region de Fos-l'Etang de Berre, *Presse Environnement* (May 23, 1980), no. 379, p. 1.
6. *Le Monde*, June 18, 1980, p. 40.
7. France, Ministre de l'Environnement (1982), p. 179; *Le Monde*, April 4, 1985. For 1979 and 1980, the only years for which figures were disaggregated by region, the quality of Mediterranean beaches exceeded national averages.

1973	1974	1975	1977	1978	1979
20.0	23.0	51.0			
68.3	38.1	14.7	58.3	89.2	
96.6	145.6	278.6	658.0	594.0	
2,397.6	2,658.8	3,448.5			
514.9	447.6	643.6	980.6	1,326.3	1,662.8
230.3	194.9	233.3			
2,372.9	1,914.0	2,578.8	4,762.9	6,285.2	8,913.9
216.3	415.4				
11.5	26.0	18.0	7.5	5.7	
45.1	58.6	75.7	80.9	126.7	
317.8	349.3	434.0			
3,091.2	3,188.0	3,404.2			
56.8	83.1		58.3	89.2	
167.2	186.0	280.4			
171.5	193.7	200.9	204.9	230.4	280.7
630.0	768.4				

Quality deteriorated and then improved in the intervening years: 64.5 percent of beaches were of good and average quality in 1977, 56.2 percent in 1978, 61.3 percent in 1979, 60.2 percent in 1980, 71.0 percent in 1981, and 74.0 percent in 1983.

8. *The Siren* (September 1987), no. 34, p. 25.

9. USAID Interoffice Memorandum, "Survey of Environmental Attitudes and Needs in Africa" (Washington, D.C.: USAID, April 23, 1974); cited in Biswas and Biswas (1982), p. 482.

10. *International Environment Reporter*, September 9, 1987, p. 33.

11. "Un Jeune Ministère," *Les Cahiers Français* (November–December 1973), no. 163, p. 4.

12. *Environmental Science and Technology* (December 1974), 8(13):1060.

13. *L'Année Politique, Économique et Sociale en France 1979*, p. 28. Société des Editiohs ou Grand Siècle. Editiohs du Moniteur, Paris. May 1980.

14. *International Environment Reporter*, March 10, 1979, pp. 580–81.

15. OECD (1982), pp. 68–69. Subsidies and low-interest loans paid for 52 percent of industrial and municipal investment costs for the construction of treatment facilities. Fiesinger and Teniere-Buchot (1976).

16. Israel Ministry of the Interior (1979).

17. *Israel Environment Bulletin* (Autumn 1983), 8(3):9; *International Environmental Reporter*, September 10, 1986, p. 335.

18. Excerpts from *Journal Officiel de la Republique Algerienne Democratique et Populaire*, July 23, 1974, p. 647; reprinted in "Translations on Environmental Quality, No. 58" (October 10, 1974; distributed by NTIS), pp. 1–3.

19. *Journal Officiel de la Republique Algerienne Democratique et Populaire*, July 26, 1983, pp. 1325–27.

20. WHO and UNEP, *Protection of the Mediterranean Against Pollution from Land-Based Sources: A Survey of National Legislation* Geneva: WHO and UNEP (1976), p. Italy-1; Reich (1984), p. 386.

21. *The Environment in Europe* (November 1986), Bulletin of the Institute for European Environmental Policy No. 37, p. 3.

22. Spain, Commission Interministerial del Medio Ambiente (1984), pp. 269–74; Spain, Subsecretaria del Planificacion (1977), p. 128.

23. Baker, Bassett, and Ellington (1985), p. 129; ECE/ENV/R. 148, paragraph 58.

24. UNEP/WG 91/6, p. 21. France used total coliforms, faecal coliforms, and faecal streptococci. Greece only uses total coliforms; Israel uses only faecal coliforms; Libya and Yugoslavia use only total coliforms; and Italy, Malta, Spain, and Turkey used only *E. coli*.

25. *International Environment Reporter*, November 12, 1986, p. 417.

26. France, Secretariat d'Etat aupres du premier ministre, Commissariat General du Plan, Rapport du Groupe de Travail (January 1983), Annex 3.

27. France, Ministère de l'Environnement et du Cadre du Vie (1981), p. 33.

28. France, Ministère de l'Environnement et du Cadre du Vie (1982), p. 33.

29. *Medwaves* (1987), no. 9–II, p. 6.

30. INFOTERRA, response from the Ministry of the Environment, January 6, 1989.

31. *Journal Officiel de la Republique Algerienne Democratique et Populaire*, February 8, 1983.

32. *El-Moudjahid*, June 8, 1983, p. 7.

33. *The Siren* (January 1983), no. 19, p. 5; Kuwabara (1984), p. 87.

34. *UNEP News* (November-December 1987), supplement 8.

35. Domovik (1983), pp. 5–7, and UNEP/IG 43/INF 10, particularly Annex 2. A test of the network was conducted in June 1982. Each national focal point was contacted with a test message of an oil spill emergency. France, Israel, Malta, and Spain responded within three hours. Egypt, Greece, Monaco, and Morocco responded within twenty-four hours. Others took more than twenty-four hours to reply, or did not reply at all.

36. The International Tanker Owners' Pollution Federation, Ltd. (1980), pp. 129, 138.

37. *The Siren* (October 1982), no. 18.

38. *Actualité Environnement* (June 9, 1982), no. 18.

39. *International Environment Reporter*, November 2, 1981, p. 643; France, Ministère de l'Environnement et du Cadre du Vie (1982), p. 41.

40. *Medwaves* (1987), no. 11/5, p. 8.

41. France, Ministère de l'Environnement et du Cadre du Vie (1982), p. 15.

42. France, Secretariat d'Etat aupres du premier ministre, Commissariat General du Plan, Rapport du Groupe de Travail, January (1983), p. 30.

43. Calculated from Delorme and Andre (1983), annex 5.

44. Calculated from France, Ministère de l'Environnement et du Cadre du Vie (1982–1986), edition 1982, pp. 212, 352, 382, 382 bis.

45. Israel, Central Bureau of Statistics, "Public Expenditure on Environmental Protection 1982/83," *Monthly Bulletin of Statistics* (1985), no. 7, Supplement no. 7, p. 63.

46. Israel, Ministry of the Interior (1978), p. 29; *Newsweek*, September 3, 1979, pp. 21–22.

47. Greece, Center of Planning and Economic Research (1972).

48. Dr. Miltos Vassilopoulous, untitled mimeo (Athens: NCPPE, 1984).

49. Yusuf J. Ahmad, "Saving the Pearl," *The Siren* (November 1986), no. 32, pp. 11–14.

50. Minister of Cabinet Affairs, Minister of State for Administrative Development, and Egyptian Environmental Affairs Agency, "Environmental Plan of Egypt" (mimeo, no date, no location), pp. 1–8.

51. *International Environment Reporter*, February 11, 1987, p. 56.

52. Spain, Commission Interministerial del Medio Ambiente (1984), p. 179.

53. Ress (1986), p. 267; *Medwaves* (November-December 1985), no. 3, p. 3.

54. *International Environment Reporter*, July 9, 1986, p. 266.

55. Bakalem (1980); *Cahiers Geographiques de l'Ouest* (1980); Bakalem (1981); Bakalem and Romano (1982).

56. A UNDP consultant observed in 1972, following a trip to Tunisia and Algeria, that "harbors are evil smelling places, in some places with gas and oil bubbling to the surface." See FAO, "Fisheries Travel Report and Aide Memoire," no. 672 (May 1972), p. 4.

57. *Medwaves* (1987), 2(9):6.

58. Schiffman (1985), p. 184; Yishai (1979), p. 209 says that the EPS came from prodding by "elites."

59. *French Periodicals Index, 1973–1974, 1975* (Westwood, Mass.: F. W. Faxon, 1976).

60. *International Environment Reporter*, February 12, 1986, pp. 50–51.

61. In 1981 they thought that the environment was "very important" and "somewhat important." *Actualité Environnement* (December 17, 1981), no. 6 DOSSIER; Antoine and Navarin (1978); *L'Express*, May 16–22, 1977, p. 69.

62. Bridgford (1978); Journes (1979); *International Environment Reporter*, April 9, 1986, p. 109.

63. Panayote Dimitras, "Survey of Athenian Surveys" (Athens: EURODIM, 1982), mimeo.

64. Yishai (1979), p. 208. Only four small environmental groups existed in the country.

6. Assessing Neorealist Explanations of Cooperation

1. France remained the principal importer of Algerian wine and labor, but these two sectors waned in relative importance to Algeria, as exports of crude oil grew to account for 98 percent of Algerian exports by 1978.

2. *L'Année Politique 1964*, p. 326; cited in Kolodziej (1974), p. 464.

3. See M'Gonigle and Zacher (1979) for a discussion of the politics of the evolution of IMCO agreements.

4. *International Environment Reporter*, November 2, 1981, p. 643; *Presse Environnement* (May 23, 1980), no. 379, p. 1.

5. For discussions of nesting see Keohane (1984), pp. 90–91; Aggarwal (1983), p. 620.

7. Assessing Historical Materialist Explanations of Mediterranean Cooperation

1. See Indira Gandhi's address to UNCHE, reprinted in *Bulletin of the Atomic Scientists* (September 1972), pp. 35–36.

2. Isnard (1973); Seers et al. (1979). They note (p. 7) that the Maghreb states may be partially insulated from the penetration of Western values by Islam. A Tunisian minister of national economy also asserted that North Africa forms the Mediterranean periphery; see Ayari (1974), p. 112.

3. UNCTAD, *Handbook of International Trade and Development Statistics 1983* (New York: United Nations, 1983), pp. 148, 172.

4. *Ibid.*, p. 154.

5. Van Buu (1974), pp. 85–86. French experts' heaviest concentration was in foreign policy, defense, public administration, and the judiciary, however, and not foreign environmental policy.

6. In fact, men are well represented in all of the professional staff positions. Of the professionals listed in the previous table, only one P2 position was held by a French woman.

7. *The Blue Plan Letter*, no. 4.

8. De Almeida acknowledges them in the Founex Report (1972), pp. 46–50.

9. UNEP/GC 3/INF 4, "Draft Report of the UNEP/UNCTAD Symposium on Patterns of Resources Use, Environment and Development Strategies, Cocoyoc, Mexico October, 1974," p. 21; reprinted in *International Organization* (Summer 1975), 29(3):893–901.

10. *Times of London*, September 4, 1974.

11. Leonard and Duerksen (1980); Gladwin and Welles (1976); Rubin and Graham (1982); Koo et al. (1979); Leonard (1982); Pearson and Pryor (1978), ch. 3; Siebert (1974); Walter (1975); Duerksen (1983); Economist Intelligence Unit (1978); Gladwin (1977); Gladwin and Walter (1980), ch. 12; Pearson (1985); Pearson (1987).

12. Kahler (1982), p. 201. A number of pieces in Centre de Recherches et d'Etudes sur les Societés Mediterranéenes (1974) make similar arguments.

13. Le Lourd (1982), p. 16. The following countries received fellowships: Algeria (five), Tunisia (eleven), Morocco (four), Libya (three), Egypt (seven), Syria (three), Israel (ten), Turkey (seven), Cyprus (seven), Greece (four), Yugoslavia (eight), and Malta (one).

14. *Algerian National Report to the United Nations Conference on the Human Environment*, mimeo, 1971, UN Library, Geneva.

15. Tunisie, "Rapport National de la Commission sur l'Environnement" (1972).

16. Syria, Summary of the Syrian National Report in *The Human Environment*, vol. 2: *Summaries of National Reports, Environment Series 201* (Washington, D.C.: Woodrow Wilson International Center for Scholars, 1972).

8. Effluents and Influence: The Emergent International Political Order for the Environment

1. UNEP/GC/INF 11.

2. Bourdieu (1977), p. 38. Although specifically talking about anthropological theories, the point is generalizable to other scientific applications.

3. See Lowe and Worboys (1980); Enzenzburger (1979); Galtung (1973); Gorz (1980); and de Araujo Castro (1972).

4. Barnes (1977), pp. 32–33. Habermas offers a similar critique of modern science as obscuring the underlying natural interests of other social groups. At times, Mannheim takes a similar position.

5. Caire (1974), p. 8. A similar notion is that of the "captive mind," expressed in Alatas (1974), p. 691.

6. This is a much more modest conclusion than that reached by Lynton Caldwell. He argued that "the change marked by Stockholm is from the view of an earth unlimited in abundance and created for man's exclusive use to a concept of the earth as a domain of life or biosphere for which mankind is a temporary resident custodian. The older view saw this planet as a storehouse of resources to be freely developed for human use. The new view sees it as an ultimately unified system of living species and interactive, regenerative biogeochemical processes that may supply man's needs as long as he serves the system's rules." See Caldwell (1984), p. 19.

7. Krasner (1985), p. 9; Krasner (1983b), p. 368; Keohane (1984), pp. 131–32; Gilpin (1981), pp. 227–28.

8. See Ruggie (1983a) on Waltz's insensitivity to the shift from medieval to modern politics. See Zolberg (1981) and Skocpol (1977) on historical flaws in Wallerstein's origins of modern long-distance capitalism.

9. See, for example, Lewis (1978), who relates the lack of LDC prosperity to low rates of saving in tropical agriculture.

10. Laudan (1977); Toulmin (1972); Olafson (1979); Geertz (1985).

11. *World Environment Report,* May 19, 1980, p. 6; Boehmer-Christiansen (1984); Boczek (1978).

12. *The Siren* (May 1984), no. 24, p. 3. Boehmer-Christiansen maintains that compliance is more advanced in the Scandinavian countries than in the FRG. Poland's ability to comply with the convention's obligations was widely doubted as of 1980. See *Marine Pollution Bulletin* (1980), p. 90.

13. *Baltic Sea Environment Proceedings,* no. 1, p. 6; *Baltic Sea Environment Proceedings,* no. 2, p. 20; *Baltic Sea Environment Proceedings,* no. 3; *Baltic Sea Environment Proceedings,* no. 7, p. 7.

14. *Marine Pollution Bulletin* (June 1981), vol. 12, no. 6; UNEP (1982b), p. 7.

15. Kelley, Stunkel, and Wescott (1976), pp. 130–35; Goldman (1974); Gustafson (1979); Kamarov (1980).

16. Sand (1987), p. 18; United Nations Press Release ECE/ENV/8.

17. See Steinbruner (1974) and Simon (1979) for discussions of limited responses to such conditions.

Bibliography

BOOKS AND ARTICLES CITED

Abbas, Amar. 1981. "Les hydrocarbures surtout." *Algerie Actualité* (August), no. 825.

Accerboni, E. and L. Jeftic. 1980. "Yugoslav-Italian Multidisciplinary Program on the Investigation of Pollution in International Waters of the Adriatic Sea." In ICSEM and UNEP, *Workshop on Pollution of the Mediterranean*. Cagliari, Italy, October 9–13, 1980.

Adler, Emanuel. 1986. "Ideological 'Guerillas' and the Quest for Technology Autonomy: Brazil's Domestic Computer Industry." *International Organization*, vol. 40, no. 3.

Agarwal, Anil. 1985. *The State of India's Environment 1984–1985: The Second Citizens' Report*. New Delhi: Centre for Science and Environment.

Aggarwal, Vinod K. 1983. "The Unravelling of the Multi-Fiber Arrangement, 1981." *International Organization* (Autumn), vol. 37, no. 4.

Aggarwal, Vinod K. 1985. *Liberal Protectionism*. Berkeley: University of California Press.

Bibliography

Alatas, Syed Hussein. 1974. "The Captive Mind and Creative Development." *International Social Science Journal*, vol. 26, no. 4.

Allison, Graham T. 1971. *The Essence of Decision*. Boston: Little, Brown.

Alt, James E., Randall L. Calvert, and Brian D. Humes. 1988. "Reputation and Hegemonic Stability: A Game-Theoretic Analysis." *American Political Science Review*, vol. 82, no. 2.

Amin, Samir. 1974. *Accumulation on a World Scale*. New York: Monthly Review Press.

Amin, Samir. 1976. *Unequal Development*. Brighton: Harvester.

Amin, Samir. 1977. *Imperialism and Unequal Development*. New York: Monthly Review Press.

Andren, Leif. 1987. "Activities of the International Maritime Organization (IMO) of Relevance to Co-Operation for the Protection of the Marine Environment in the Mediterranean." *Etudes internationales* (April 1987), no. 25, special issue on Cooperation Marine en Mediterranée.

Anscombe, G. E. M. 1958. "On Brute Facts." *Analysis* (March), no. 184.

Antoine, Serge. 1985. "La Mediterranée 1985–2025: Un Travail de Developpement et Intégrée sur un Grand Region." *Revue Française d'Administration Publique* (July–September), no. 35.

Antoine, Serge and Jacques Navarin. 1978. "Les Français et la Qualité de la Vie." Futuribles (March–April), no. 14.

Argyris, Chris and Donald A. Schon. 1978. *Organizational Learning: A Theory of Action Perspective*. Reading, Mass.: Addison-Wesley.

Ascher, William. 1983. "World Bank and Development." *International Organization*, vol. 37, no. 3.

Ashley, Richard K. "Political Realism and Human Interests." *International Studies Quarterly* (June 1981), vol. 25, no. 2.

Ashley, Richard K. 1984. "The Poverty of Neorealism." *International Organization* (Spring), vol. 38, no. 2.

Asia-Pacific People's Environment Network (APPEN). *A People's Movement for Change*. No date.

Aufderheide, Pat and Bruce Rich. 1988. "Environmental Reform and the Multilateral Banks." *World Policy Journal*, vol. 5, no. 2.

Axelrod, Robert. 1984. *The Evolution of Cooperation*. New York: Basic Books.

Ayari, Chedly. 1974. "The Industrial Assets of the Mediterranean Basin." *Lo spettatore internazionale*, (April–June), vol. 9, no. 2.

Ayres, Robert L. 1983. *Banking on the Poor*. Cambridge, Mass.: MIT Press.

Bahro, Rudolf. 1984. *From Red to Green*. London: New Left Books.

Bakalem, Ali. 1980. "Pollution et sources de pollution marine d'origine industrielle sur la côte ouest algerienne: etude preliminaire." *VIes journées d'études sur les pollutions marines en Mediterranée*. Cagliari, Italy: C.I.E.S.M.

Bakalem, Ali. 1981. "Les sources de pollution sur la côte ouest algerienne: Note preliminaire." *Bulletin de la Societé d'Histoire Naturelle de l'Afrique du Nord*. (Alger) t 69, fascicule 3/4.

Bakalem, Ali, and J.-C. Romano. 1982. "Pollution et peuplements benthiques dans la region algeroise." *VIes Journées d'études sur les pollutions marines en Mediterranée*. Cannes: C.I.E.S.M.

Baker, Mark, Libby Bassett, and Athleen Ellington. 1985. *The World Environment Handbook.* New York: World Environment Center.

Balbus, Isaac D. 1971. "The Concept of Interest in Pluralist and Marxian Analysis." *Politics and Society* (February), vol. 1, no. 2.

Bandyopadhyay, Jayanta and Vandana Shiva. 1987. "Chipko: Rekindling India's Forest Culture." *The Ecologist*, vol. 17, no. 1.

Barkenbus, Jack N. 1987. "Nuclear Power Safety." *International Organization*, vol. 41, no. 3.

Barnes, Barry. 1977. *Interests and the Growth of Knowledge.* London: Routledge and Kegan Paul.

Barnes, Barry and David Edge. 1982. "General Introduction." In *Science in Context Readings in the Sociology of Science.* Cambridge, Mass.: MIT Press.

Bartelmus, Peter. 1986. *Environment and Development.* Boston: Allen and Unwin.

Bellan, G. and J. M. Pérès. 1972. "La pollution dans le Bassin Méditerranéen." In *Marine Pollution and Sea Life* West Byfleet, England: Fishing News (Books) Ltd.

Benedick, Richard E. 1986. "Global Environmental Change: The International Perspective." In EPA and UNEP, *Effects of Changes in Stratospheric Ozone and Global Climate*, vol. 1.

Benveniste, Guy. 1977. *The Politics of Expertise.* 2d ed. San Francisco, Calif.: Boyd and Fraser.

Berger, Peter and Thomas Luckmann. 1967. *The Social Construction of Reality.* New York: Doubleday.

Birnie, P. 1988. "International Law and Solving Conflicts." In John E. Carroll, ed., *International Environmental Diplomacy.* Cambridge, England: Cambridge University Press.

Biswas, Margaret R. and Asit K. Biswas. 1982. "Environment and Sustained Development in the Third World: A Review of the Past Decade." *Third World Quarterly* (July), vol. 4, no. 3.

Biswas, Margaret R. and Asit K. Biswas. 1985. "The Global Environment Past, Present and Future." *Resources Policy* (March).

Blau, Peter M. 1967. *Exchange and Power in Social Life.* New York: Wiley.

Bliss-Guest, Patricia A. 1981. "The Protocol Against Pollution from Land-Based Sources: A Turning Point in the Rising Tide of Pollution." *Stanford Journal of International Law* (Summer), vol. 17, no. 2.

Boczek, Boleslaw A. 1978. "International Protection of the Baltic Sea Environment Against Pollution: A Study in Marine Regionalism." *American Journal of International Law* (October), vol. 72, no. 4.

Boehmer-Christiansen, Sonia. 1984. "Marine Pollution Control in Europe Regional Approaches." *Marine Policy* (January), vol. 8, no. 1.

Borgese, Elisabeth Mann and Norton Ginsburg, eds. 1980. *Ocean Yearbook* Chicago, Ill.: University of Chicago Press.

Botkin, James W., Mahdi Elmandjra, and Mircea Malitza. 1979. *No Limits to Learning: Bridging the Human Gap; a Report to the Club of Rome.* New York: Pergamon Press.

Boulding, Kenneth. 1956. *The Image.* Ann Arbor: University of Michigan Press.

Boulding, Kenneth. 1978. *Ecodynamics.* Beverly Hills, Calif.: Sage Publications.

Bourdieu, Pierre. 1977. *Outline of a Theory of Practice.* Cambridge, England: Cambridge University Press.

Boxer, Baruch. 1982. "Mediterranean Pollution: Problem and Response." *Ocean Development and International Law* (April), vol. 10, nos. 3–4.

Braudel, Fernand. 1976. *The Mediterranean and the Mediterranean World in the Age of Philip II.* Vols. 1 and 2. New York: Harper and Row.

Braudel, Fernand. 1980. *On History.* Chicago, Ill.: University of Chicago Press.

Brewer, Gary D. and Peter deLeon. 1983. *The Foundations of Policy Analysis.* Homewood, Ill.: Dorsey Press.

Brewer, Marilynn B. and Barry F. Collins. 1981. "Introduction" in Marilynn B. Brewer and Barry F. Collins, eds. *Scientific Inquiry and the Social Sciences.* San Francisco: Jossey-Bass.

Bridgford, Jeff. 1978. "The Ecologist Movement and the French General Election, 1978." *Parliamentary Affairs* (Summer), vol. 31, no. 3.

Brisou, J. F. 1976. "An Environmental Sanitation Plan for the Mediterranean Seaboard." *Public Health Papers #62.* Geneva: World Health Organization.

Brooks, Harvey. 1982. "Can Technology Assure Unending Material Progress?" In Gabriel Almond, Marvin Chodorow, and Roy Harvey Pearce, eds., *Progress and Its Discontents.* Berkeley: University of California Press.

Brooks, Harvey. 1986. "The Typology of Surprises in Technology, Institutions, and Development." In Clark and Munn (1986).

Brown, Lester R. 1977. *Redefining National Security.* Worldwatch Paper 14. Washington, D.C.: Worldwatch Institute.

Bull, Hedley. 1977. *The Anarchical Society.* New York: Columbia University Press.

Burch, William. 1970. "Resources and Social Structure: Some Conditions of Stability and Change." *The Annals of the American Academy of Political and Social Science* (May), vol. 389.

Burlion, Jacques. 1972. "Les Africains et l'environement: Une prise de conscience," *France-Eurafrique* (April–May), no. 234.

Cahiers geographiques de l'ouest. Nos. 5–6. Special Seminaire, Developpement et Amenagement du Territorie en Algerie: Evaluation des Actions, June 8–10, 1980. Oran, Algeria: Université d'Oran.

Caire, Guy. 1974. "Ideologies du Developpement." *Tiers-Monde* (January–March), vol. 15, no. 57.

Caldwell, Lynton Keith. 1984. *International Environmental Policy.* Durham, N.C.: Duke University Press.

Caldwell, Lynton Keith. 1988. "Beyond Environmental Diplomacy." In John E. Carroll, ed., *International Environmental Diplomacy.* Cambridge, England: Cambridge University Press.

Caporaso, James. 1978. "Dependence and Dependency in the Global System." *International Organization* (Winter), vol. 32, no. 1.

Carbonell, Jaime. 1981. *Subjective Understanding: Computer Models of Belief Systems.* Ann Arbor: University of Michigan Research Press.

Cardoso, Fernando Henrique and Enzo Faletto. 1979. *Dependency and Development in Latin America.* Berkeley, Calif.: University of California Press.

Carroz, J. E. 1977. "The Management of Living Resources in the Baltic Sea and the Belts." *Ocean Development and International Law,* vol. 4, no. 3.

Castillo, Esther. 1982. "Los gastos estatales en proteccion del medio ambiente." *Boletin informativo del medio ambiente* (April–June).

Catton, W. R., Jr. and Riley Dunlap. 1978. "Environmental Sociology: A New Paradigm?" *The American Sociologist,* vol. 13.

Charbonnier, D. 1977. "Prospects for Fisheries in the Mediterranean." *AMBIO,* vol. 6, no. 6.

Christy, Francis T. 1975. "Property Rights in the World Ocean." *Natural Resources Journal* (October), vol. 15, no. 4.

Clark, William C. 1986. "Sustainable Development of the Biosphere: Themes for a Research Program." In Clark and Munn (1986).

Clark, William C. and R. E. Munn, eds. 1986. *Sustainable Development of the Biosphere.* Cambridge, England: Cambridge University Press.

Commission on the Organization of the Government for the Conduct of Foreign Policy. 1975. *Appendices,* vol. 4. Washington, D.C.: U.S. Government Printing Office.

Commoner, Barry. 1971. *The Closing Circle.* New York: Knopf.

Cooper, Richard N. 1968. *The Economics of Interdependence: Economic Policy in the Atlantic Community.* New York: McGraw-Hill.

Cooper, Richard N. 1985. "International Economic Cooperation: Is It Desirable? Is It Likely?" *Bulletin of the American Academy of Arts and Sciences* (November), vol. 39, no. 2.

Cooper, Richard N. 1986. "International Cooperation in Public Health as a Prologue to Macroeconomic Cooperation." Brookings Discussion Papers in International Economics No. 44 (March). Washington, D.C.: The Brookings Institution.

Cox, Robert W. 1977. "Labor and Hegemony." *International Organization* (Summer), vol. 31, no. 3.

Cox, Robert W. 1981. "Social Forces, States, and World Orders: Beyond International Relations Theory." *Millenium: Journal of International Studies* (Summer), vol. 10, no. 2.

Cox, Robert W. 1987. *Production, Power and World Order.* New York: Columbia University Press.

Crane, Barbara B. 1984. "Policy Coordination by Western Powers." *International Organization* (Summer), vol. 38, no. 3.

Crane, Diana. 1972. *Invisible Colleges.* Chicago, Ill.: University of Chicago Press.

Cruzado, Antonio. 1984. "Jellyfish Jitters." *The Siren* (September).

Dahlberg, Kenneth A. 1979. *Beyond the Green Revolution: The Ecology and Politics of Global Agricultural Development.* New York: Plenum.

Dahlberg, Kenneth A. 1983. "Contextual Analysis: Taking Space, Time, and Place Seriously." *International Studies Quarterly* (September), vol. 27, no. 3.

Dasmann, Raymond F., John P. Milton, and Peter H. Freeman. 1973. *Ecological Principles for Economic Development.* New York: Wiley.

de Almeida, Miguel A. Ozorio. 1972. "The Confrontation Between Problems of

Development and Environment." *International Conciliation* (January), no. 586.

de Araujo Castro, Joao Augusto. 1972. "Environment and Development: The Case of the Developing Countries." In Kay and Skolnikoff (1972).

De Greene, Kenyon B. 1982. *The Adaptive Organization.* New York: Wiley.

Delorme, Robert and Christine Andre. 1983. *L'Etat et l'economie: Un essai d'explication de l'evolution des depenses publiques en France (1870–1980).* Paris: Editions du Seuil.

Deutsch, Karl W. 1966. *The Nerves of Government.* New York: The Free Press.

Devall, Bill and George Sessions. 1985. *Deep Ecology.* Salt Lake City, Utah: Gibbs M. Smith, Inc.

De Yturriaga Barberan, Jose Antonio. 1976a. "Convenio de Barcelona de 1976 Para la Proteccion del Mar Mediterraneo Contra la Contamination." *Revista de Instituciones Europeas* (January–April), vol. 2, no. 1.

De Yturriaga Barberan, Jose Antonio. 1976b. "La Communidad Economica Europea y la proteccion del medio acuatico contra la contamination." *Revista de Instituciones Europeas* (September–December), vol. 3, no. 3.

Di Castri, Francesco. 1984. *L'ecologie: Les defis d'une science en temps de crise.* Rapport au Ministre de l'Industrie et de al Recherche. Paris: Le Documentation Française.

Dobbert, Jean-Marie. 1980. "Protocol to Control Pollution in the Mediterranean." *Environmental Policy and Law,* vol. 6.

Dolman, Antony J. 1981. *Resources, Regimes and World Order.* New York: Pergamon Press.

Domovik, Darko. 1983. "Means of Communications and Alerts in Cases of Oil Pollution." Paper presented at Session F on Means of Surveillance and Alert at MEDIPOL 83. Malta: Regional Oil Combating Centre.

Dovland, Harold. 1987. "Monitoring European Transboundary Air Pollution." *Environment* (December), vol. 29, no. 10.

Duerksen, Christopher J. 1983. *Environmental Regulation of Industrial Plant Siting: How To Make it Work Better.* Washington, D.C.: The Conservation Foundation.

Dunlap, Riley, ed. 1980. "Paradigmatic Change in Social Science." *American Behavioral Scientist,* special issue (September–October).

Duvall, Raymond D. 1978. "Dependence and Dependency Theory: Notes Toward Precision of Concept and Arguments." *International Organization* (Winter), vol. 32, no. 1.

Eckholm, Eric. 1982. *Down to Earth.* New York: Norton.

Eckstein, Harry. 1975. "Case Study and Theory in Political Science." In Fred L. Greenstein and Nelson W. Polsby, eds., *Strategies of Inquiry.* Vol. 7 of the *Handbook of Political Science.* Reading, Mass.: Addison-Wesley.

Economist Intelligence Unit. 1978. "Corporate Investment and Production Decisions: Does Environmental Legislation Play a Role?" *Economist Intelligence Report* (November).

Ehrlich, Paul R., Anne H. Ehrlich, and John P. Holdren. 1977. *Ecoscience: Population, Resources, Environment.* San Francisco, Calif.: W. H. Freeman.

Eisenbud, Merril. 1978. *Environment, Technology and Health: Human Ecology in Historical Perspective.* New York: New York University Press.

El-Kassas, Mohammed Abdel. 1981. "Egypt." In Edward J. Kormondy and J. Frank McCormick, eds., *Handbook of Contemporary Developments in World Ecology*. Westport, Conn.: Greenwood Press.

El-Sharkawi, Fahmy and M. N. E. R. Hassan. 1979. "The Relation Between the State of Pollution in Alexandria Swimming Beaches and the Occurence of Typhoid Among Bathers." *Bulletin of the High Institute of Public Health in Alexandria*, vol. 9.

El-Wakeel, Saad K. 1976. "Overview of Marine Pollution Research in Egypt." *Proceedings of the International Symposium on Marine Pollution Research* (held in Gulf Breeze, Florida, January).

El-Wakeel, Saad K. 1984. "The Development of Marine Science in Egypt." *Deep Sea Research: Part A, Oceanographic Research Papers*, vol. 31, nos. 6–8a.

Elster, Jon. 1983. *Explaining Technical Change*. Cambridge, England: Cambridge University Press.

Emery, Fred. 1977. *Futures We Are In*. Leiden, Netherlands: Martinus Nijhoff, Social Sciences Division.

Emery, Fred and Eric Trist. 1972. *Towards a Social Ecology*. London: Plenum Press.

ENI. 1974. "Oil Industry Development and the Prevention of Oil Pollution." In Norton Ginsburg et al., eds., *The Mediterranean Marine Environment and the Development of the Region*. Malta: Royal University of Malta Press.

Enloe, Cynthia. 1975. *The Politics of Pollution in a Comparative Perspective*. New York: David McKay.

Enzenzburger, Hans Magnus. 1979. "A Critique of Political Ecology." In Alexander Cockburn and James Ridgeway, eds., *Political Ecology*. New York: Times Books.

Ercman, S. 1977. *European Environmental Law*. Bern: Bubenberg-Verlag AG.

Etheredge, Lloyd S. 1979. *Government Learning: An Overview*. Cambridge, Mass.: Center for International Studies, Massachusetts Institute of Technology (September).

Evan, William, ed. 1981. *Knowledge and Power*. Beverly Hills, Calif.: Sage.

Evans, Peter. 1979. *Dependent Development: Multinational, State and Local Capital in Brazil*. Princeton, N.J.: Princeton University Press.

Falk, Richard. 1979. "Forward." In Orr and Soroos (1979).

FAO. 1977. *International Directory of Marine Scientists*. Rome: FAO.

Farvar, M. Taghi and John P. Milton, eds. 1972. *The Careless Technology*. Garden City, N.Y.: The Natural History Press.

Fiesinger, François & P. F. Teniere-Buchot. 1976. "Pollution Fees Are for Real in France." *Water Spectrum* (Spring-Summer).

Firor, John. 1984. " 'Endangered Species' of the Atmosphere." *Journal '84*. World Resources Institute.

Fleck, Ludwig. 1979. *Genesis and Development of a Scientific Fact*. Chicago, Ill.: University of Chicago Press.

Flory, M. 1974. "Cooperation et Dependance au Maghreb." In Centre de Recherche et d'Etudes sur les Societés Mediterranéenes, ed., *Independance et Interdependance au Maghreb*. Paris: Centre Nationale de la Recherche Scientifique.

Foucault, Michel. 1972. *The Archaeology of Knowledge.* New York: Pantheon.

Foucault, Michel. 1980. *Power/Knowledge.* New York: Pantheon.

"The Founex Report." 1972. *International Conciliation* (January), no. 586.

France. Ministère de l'Environnement et du Cadre du Vie. 1982–1986. Direction de la Prevention des Pollutions. *Données Economiques de l'Environnement.* Paris.

France. Ministère de l'Environnement et du Cadre du Vie. 1981. *L'Etat de l'environnement.* Edition 1981.

France. Ministère de l'Environnement et du Cadre du Vie. 1982. *L'Etat de l'environnement.* Edition 1982.

France. Secretariat d'Etat aupres du premier ministre. 1983. Commissariat General du Plan. Rapport du groupe de travail. *Environnement* (January).

France. Secretariat Permanent par les Problèmes de Pollution Industrielle de la Region de Fos-l'Etang de Berre. "Lutte Contre la Pollution des Eaux Etat des Rejects Industrielles." No date.

Fuglestad-Aumeunier, V. 1974. "La Cooperation Italo-Maghrebine." In Centre de Recherches et d'Etudes sur les Societés Mediterranéenes, *Independance et interdependances au Maghreb.* Paris: Centre National de la Recherche Scientifique.

Galtung, Johan. 1973. " 'The Limits to Growth' and Class Politics." *Journal of Peace Research,* Vol. 10.

Galtung, Johan. 1980. *The True Worlds.* New York: Free Press.

Geertz, Clifford. 1965. "Ideology as a Cultural System." In David E. Apter, ed., *Ideology and Discontent.* New York: The Free Press.

General Fisheries Council for the Mediterranean (GFCM). 1972. "The State of Marine Pollution in the Mediterranean and Legislative Controls." *Studies and Reviews,* no. 51.

George, Alexander L. 1979. "The Causal Nexus Between Cognitive Beliefs and Decision-Making Behavior: The "Operation Code" Belief System." In Lawrence S. Falkowski, ed., *Psychological Models in International Politics.* Boulder, Colo.: Westview Press.

Gerakis, Pantazis A. 1981. "Greece." In Edward J. Kormondy and J. Frank McCormick, eds., *Handbook of Contemporary Developments in World Ecology.* Westport, Conn.: Greenwood Press.

Gilligan, Carol. 1982. *In a Different Voice.* Cambridge, Mass.: Harvard University Press.

Gilpin, Robert G. 1975. *U.S. Power and the Multinational Corporation.* New York: Basic Books.

Gilpin, Robert G. 1981. *War and Change in the World Politics.* Cambridge, England: Cambridge University Press.

Gilpin, Robert G. 1986. "The Richness of the Tradition of Political Realism." In Keohane (1986b).

Gilpin, Robert G. 1987. *The Political Economy of International Relations.* Princeton, N.J.: Princeton University Press.

Glacken, Clarence J. 1967. *Traces on the Rhodian Shore.* Berkeley, Calif.: University of California Press.

Gladwin, Thomas. 1977. *Environment, Planning and the Multinational Corporation.* Greenwich, Conn.: JAI Press.

Gladwin, Thomas and Ingo Walter. 1980. *Multinationals Under Fire: Lessons in the Management of Conflict*. New York: Wiley.

Gladwin, Thomas and John Welles. 1976. "Environmental Policy and Multinational Corporate Strategy." In Ingo Walter, ed., *Studies in International Environmental Economics*. New York: Wiley-Interscience.

The Global 2000 Report to the President: Entering the Twenty-First Century. 1980. Vol. 1. Washington, D.C.: U.S. Government Printing Office.

Goldman, Marshall. 1974. *The Spoils of Progress*. Cambridge, Mass.: MIT Press.

Gorz, Andre. 1980. *Ecology as Politics*. Boston, Mass.: South End Press.

Gosovic, Branislav. 1984. "Population-Resources-Environment-Development Interrelationships in the United Nations: In Search of an Approach." *CEPAL Review* (August), no. 23.

Greece. Center of Planning and Economic Research. 1972. *Perspective Development Plan of Greece: Part 1, General Development Orientation*. Athens.

Greenberg, Daniel S. 1985. "Diplomat of Troubled Waters" *International Wildlife* (May–June 1985).

Greenwood, Ted. 1984. *Knowledge and Discretion in Government Regulation*. New York: Praeger.

Gustafson, Thane. 1979. "Environmental Conflict in the USSR." In Dorothy Nelkin, ed., *Controversy Politics of Technical Decisions*, Beverly Hills, Calif.: Sage.

Haas, Ernst B. 1980. "Why Collaborate? Issue-Linkage and International Regimes." *World Politics*, vol. 32, no. 3.

Haas, Ernst B. 1990. *When Knowledge is Power*. Berkeley: University of California Press.

Haas, Ernst B., Mary Pat Williams, and Don Babai. 1977. *Scientists and World Order: The Uses of Technical Knowledge in International Organizations*. Berkeley: University of California Press.

Habermas, Jürgen. 1970. "Technical Progress and the Social Life-World." In *Toward a Rational Society*. Boston: Beacon Press.

Habermans, Jürgen. 1971. *Knowledge and Human Interests*. Boston: Beacon Press.

Hager, Wolfgang. 1974. "The Mediterranean: A European *Mare Nostrum?*" *Orbis* (Spring), vol. 18, no. 1.

Hagerhall, Bertil. 1980. "International Cooperation to Protect the Baltic." *AMBIO*, vol. 9, nos. 3–4.

Haigh, Nigel. 1984. *EEC Environmental Policy and Britain*. London: Environmental Data Services.

Hardin, Garrett. 1968. "The Tragedy of the Commons." *Science* (December 13), vol. 162.

Hawley, Amos. 1950. *Human Ecology*. New York: The Ronald Press.

Heclo, Hugh. 1974. *Modern Social Politics in Britain and Sweden*. New Haven, Conn.: Yale University Press.

Heclo, Hugh. 1978. "Issue Networks and the Executive Establishment." In Anthony King, ed., *The New American Political System*. Washington, D.C.: American Enterprise Institute.

Helmer, Richard. 1977. "Pollutants from Land-Based Sources in the Mediterranean." *AMBIO*, vol. 6, no. 6.

Hesse, Mary. 1982. "Science and Objectivity." In John B. Thompson and David Held, eds., *Habermas Critical Debates*. Cambridge, Mass.: MIT Press.

Hirsch, Fred. 1976. *Social Limits to Growth*. Cambridge, Mass.: Harvard University Press.

Hirschman, Albert O. 1980. *National Power and the Structure of Foreign Trade*. Berkeley, Calif.: University of California Press.

Hoffmann, Stanley, ed. 1966. *Conditions of World Order*. New York: Simon and Schuster.

Holdgate, Martin W. 1982. "The Environmental Information Needs of the Decision-Maker." *Nature and Resources* (January–March), vol. 18, no. 1.

Holdgate, Martin W., Mohammed Kassas, and Gilbert White, eds. 1982. *The World Environment 1972–1982*. Dublin, Ireland: Tycooly International.

Holling, C. S., ed. 1978. *Adaptive Environmental Assessment and Management*. New York: Wiley.

Holling, C. S. 1984. "Ecological Interdependence." *IIASA Options* 1984, vol. 1.

Hollis, Martin and Steven Lukes, eds., 1982. *Rationality and Relativism*. Cambridge, Mass.: MIT Press.

Holzner, Burkart and John Marx. 1979. *Knowledge Application: The Knowledge System in Society*. Boston, Mass.: Allyn and Bacon.

Hopkins, Raymond F. 1978. "Global Management Networks: The Internationalization of Domestic Bureaucracies." *International Social Sciences Journal*, vol. 30, no. 1.

Hughes, Barry. 1985. *World Futures*. Baltimore, Md.: Johns Hopkins University Press.

Hughes, J. Donald. 1975. *Ecology in Ancient Civilizations*. Albuquerque: University of New Mexico Press.

Hulm, Peter. 1983. "The Regional Seas Programme: What Fate for UNEP's Crown Jewels?" *AMBIO*, vol. 12, no. 1.

Independent Commission on International Development Issues, 1980. *North-South: A Program for Survival*. Cambridge, Mass.: MIT Press.

Inglehart, Ronald. 1977. *The Silent Revolution*. Princeton, N.J.: Princeton University Press.

Institute for European Environmental Policy. 1986. "The Environment in Europe." Bulletin of the Institute for European Environmental Policy no. 37 (November).

IMCO (Intergovernmental Maritime Consultative Organization). 1979. "Executive Summary of the Report on Feasibility Study on Reception Facilities for Selected Ports in a Special Area Mediterranean."

IMCO and UNEP. 1979. "Executive Summary of the Report on Feasibility Study on Reception Facilities for Selected Ports in a Special Area Mediterranean" London: IMCO.

International Conference on Oil Pollution of the Sea. 1968. *Report of Proceedings*. October 7–9, Rome.

International Oceanographic Commission (IOC). 1975. *Report of the IOC/GFCM/ICSEM International Workshop on Marine Pollution in the Mediterranean*. Monte Carlo, September 9–14. Workshop Report No. 3.

International Registry of Potentially Toxic Chemicals. 1978. *Data Profiles for*

Chemicals for the Evaluation of Their Hazards to the Environment of the Mediterranean Sea, vols. 1 and 2. Geneva: UNEP.

International Tanker Owners' Pollution Federation, Ltd. 1980. *Measures to Combat Oil Pollution*. London: Graham and Trotman.

International Union for the Conservation of Nature (IUCN). 1980. *World Conservation Strategy*. Morges, Switzerland.

Isnard, Hildebert. 1973. "Le Monde Mediterranéen Peripherie de l'Europe." *Revue de l'Occident Musulman et de la Mediterranée*, nos. 15–16, 2eme semestre.

Israel. Ministry of the Interior. 1978. Environmental Protection Service (EPS). "Israel in the Mediterranean Ecosystem." EPS Publication No. 78-01. Jerusalem: EPS.

Israel. Ministry of the Interior. 1979. Environmental Protection Service (EPS). *The Environment in Israel*. EPS Publication No. 79-01. Jerusalem: EPS.

Jacque, Jean-Paul. 1986. "The 'Single European Act' and Environmental Policy." *Environmental Policy and Law*, vol. 16, nos. 3–4.

Jantsch, Erich and Conrad Waddington, eds. 1976. *Evolution and Consciousness*. Reading, Mass.: Addison-Wesley.

Jervis, Robert. 1976. *Perception and Misperception*. Princeton, N.J.: Princeton University Press.

Jervis, Robert. 1980. "Political Decision Making: Recent Contributions." *Political Psychology* (Summer), vol. 2, no. 2.

Jervis, Robert. 1983. "Security Regimes." In Krasner (1983c).

Jervis, Robert. 1986. "From Balance to Concert: A Study of International Security Cooperation." In Oye (1986).

Jervis, Robert. 1988. "Realism, Game Theory, and Cooperation." *World Politics* (April), vol. 40, no. 3.

Johnson, Brian. 1972. "The United Nations' Institutional Response to Stockholm: A Case Study in the International Politics of Institutional Change." In Kay and Skolnikoff (1972).

Journes, Claude. 1979. "Les idees politiques du Mouvement Ecologique." *Revue Française de Science Politique* (April), vol. 29, no. 2.

Juda, Lawrence. 1979. "Perspectives of and Implications for Developing States." In Orr and Soroos (1979).

Kaak, Moncef. 1987. "Contribution de la Direction de l'Environnement dans le domaine de la lutte contre la pollution marine par les rejets industriels." *Etudes internationales* (April), no. 25.

Kadushin, Charles. 1981. "Notes on Expectations of Reward in N-Person Networks." In Peter M. Blau and Robert K. Merton, *Continuities in Structural Inquiry*. Beverly Hills, Calif.: Sage.

Kahler, Miles. 1982. "Europe and Its 'Privileged Partners' in Africa and the Middle East." *Journal of Common Market Studies* (September–December), vol. 21, nos. 1–2.

Kamarov, Boris. 1980. *The Destruction of Nature in the Soviet Union*. New York: M. E. Sharpe.

Kay, David and Harold K. Jacobson, eds. 1983. *Environmental Protection: The International Dimension*. Totowa, N.J.: Allanheld, Osmun.

Kay, David and Eugene Skolnikoff, eds. 1972. *World Eco-Crisis.* Madison: University of Wisconsin Press.

Kaysen, Carl. 1972. "The Computer That Printed Out W*O*L*F." *Foreign Affairs* (July), vol. 50, no. 4.

Kelley, Donald R., Kenneth R. Stunkel, and Richard R. Wescott. 1976. *The Economic Superpowers and the Environment.* San Francisco, Calif.: W. H. Freeman.

Keohane, Robert O. 1980. "The Theory of Hegemonic Stability and Changes in International Economic Regimes, 1967–1977." In O. R. Holsti, R. M. Siverson, and A. L. George, eds., *Change in the International System.* Boulder, Colo.: Westview Press.

Keohane, Robert O. 1983a. "The Demand for International Regimes." In Krasner (ed.) 1983c.

Keohane, Robert O. 1983b. "Theory of World Politics: Structural Realism and Beyond." In Ada W. Finifter, ed., *Political Science: The State of the Discipline.* Washington, D.C.: American Political Science Association.

Keohane, Robert O. 1984. *After Hegemony: Cooperation and Discord in the World Political Economy.* Princeton, N.J.: Princeton University Press.

Keohane, Robert O. 1986a. "Realism, Neorealism and the Study of World Politics." In Keohane (ed.) 1986b.

Keohane, Robert O. (ed.). 1986b. *Neorealism and Its Critics.* New York: Columbia University Press.

Keohane, Robert O. and Robert Axelrod. 1986. "Achieving Cooperation Under Anarchy: Strategies and Institutions." In Oye (1986).

Keohane, Robert O. and Nye, Joseph S., eds. 1971. *Transnational Relations and World Politics.* Cambridge, Mass.: Harvard University Press.

Keohane, Robert O. and Nye, Joseph S. 1974. "Transgovernmental Relations and International Organizations." *World Politics* (October), vol. 27, no. 1.

Keohane, Robert O. and Joseph S. Nye. 1977. *Power and Interdependence.* Boston: Little, Brown.

Keramane, Abdelouaahab. 1974. "Algerian Imperatives for Fruitful Cooperation with Europe." *Lo Spettatore Internazionale* (April–June), vol. 9, no. 2.

Kindleberger, Charles P. 1981. "Dominance and Leadership in the International Economy: Exploitation, Public Goods, and Free Rides." *International Studies Quarterly* (June), vol. 25.

Kiss, Alexandre Charles. 1982. *Recueil de traites multilateraux relatifs a la protection de l'environnement.* UNEP Reference Series No. 3. Nairobi, Kenya: UNEP.

Knorr-Cetina, Karin D. and Michael Mulkay, eds. 1983. *Science Observed.* Beverly Hills, Calif.: Sage.

Kolodziej, Edward A. 1974. *French International Policy Under De Gaulle and Pompidou.* Ithaca, N.Y.: Cornell University Press.

Koo, Anthony Y. C., et al. 1979. *Environmental Repercussions on Trade and Investment.* Michigan State University International Business and Economic Studies, Graduate School of Business Administration, Michigan State University at East Lansing.

Kormondy, Edward J. and Frank McCormick, eds. 1981. *Handbook of Contemporary Developments in World Ecology.* Westport. Conn.: Greenwood Press.

Krasner, Stephen D. 1976. "State Power and the Structure of International Trade." *World Politics* (April), vol. 28, no. 3.

Krasner, Stephen D. 1983a. "Structural Causes and Regime Consequences: Regimes as Intervening Variables." In Krasner (ed.) 1983c.

Krasner, Stephen D. 1983b. "Regimes and the Limits of Realism: Regimes as Autonomous Variables." In Krasner (ed.) 1983c.

Krasner, Stephen D. (ed.). 1983c. *International Regimes*. Ithaca, N.Y.: Cornell University Press.

Krasner, Stephen D. 1985. *Structural Conflict*. Berkeley, Calif.: University of California Press.

Kratochwill, Friedrich and John Gerard Ruggie. 1986. "The State of the Art on the Art of the State." *International Organization*, vol. 40, no. 4 (Autumn).

Kuhn, Thomas S. 1970. *The Structure of Scientific Revolutions*. 2d ed., enlarged. Chicago, Ill.: University of Chicago Press.

Kuwabara, Sachiko. 1984. *The Legal Regime of the Protection of the Mediterranean Against Pollution from Land-Based Sources*. Dublin: Tycooly International Publishing.

Lagos, Panos. 1982. "The Blue Plan." *Ekistics* (March–April), vol. 49, no. 293.

Laudan, Larry. 1977. *Progress and Its Problems*. Berkeley. Calif.: University of California Press.

Lee, James A. 1986. *The Environment, Public Health and Human Ecology*. Washington, D.C.: The World Bank.

Le Lourd, Philippe. 1982. "ROCC: L'Idee . . . et la réalité." *The Siren* (October), no. 18.

Le Lourd, Philippe. 1983a. "Assistance to the Mediterranean Coastal States in the Preparation of Contingency Plans." Paper presented at Session A on Oil Pollution in the Mediterranean at MEDIPOL 83. Malta: Regional Oil Combating Centre.

Le Lourd, Philippe. 1983b. "Situation of Contingency Plans for Oil Pollution Combating in the Mediterranean." Paper presented to Session E on Contingency Plans and Regional Cooperation at MEDIPOL 83. Malta: Regional Oil Combating Centre.

Leonard, H. Jeffrey. 1982. "Environmental Regulations, Multinational Corporations and Industrial Development in the 1980s." *Habitat International*, vol. 6, no. 3.

Leonard, H. Jeffrey and Christopher J. Duerksen, 1980. "Environmental Regulations and the Location of Industry: An International Perspective." *Columbia Journal of World Business* (Summer), vol. 15, no. 2.

Leonard, H. Jeffrey and David Morell. 1981. "Emergence of Environmental Concern in Developing Countries: A Political Perspective." *Stanford Journal of International Law*, vol. 17, no. 2.

Lewis, W. Arthur. 1978. *The Evolution of the International Economic Order*. Princeton, N.J.: Princeton University Press.

Lieber, Robert J. 1980. "Energy, Economics and Security in Alliance Perspective." *International Security* (Spring), vol. 4, no. 4.

Lindblom, Charles E. 1959. "The Science of Muddling Through." *Public Administration Review*, vol. 19.

Lindblom, Charles E. 1973. "Incrementalism and Environmentalism." In U.S.

Environmental Protection Agency, *Managing the Environment*, EPA-600/5-73-010 (November).

Linn, Alan. 1974. "From Civilization's Cradle to Europe's Cesspool." *International Wildlife* (March–April).

Lipson, Charles. 1984. "International Cooperation in Economic and Security Affairs." *World Politics*, vol. 37, no. 1.

Lovelock, J. E. 1979. *Gaia: A New Look at Life on Earth*. Oxford, England: Oxford University Press.

Lowe, Philip D. and Jane Goyder. 1983. *Environmental Groups in Politics*. London: Allen and Unwin.

Lowe, Philip D. and Michael W. Worboys. 1980. "Ecology and Ideology." In Frederick H. Buttel and Howard Newby, eds., *The Rural Sociology of the Advanced Societies*. Montclair, N.J.: Allanheld, Osmun.

Lukes, Steven. 1977. *Politics and Society*. New York: Columbia University Press.

Lustick, Ian. 1980. "Explaining the Variable Utility of Disjointed Incrementalism: Four Propositions." *American Political Science Review*, vol. 74, no. 2.

Lyster, Simon. 1985. *International Wildlife Law*. Cambridge: Grotius Publications.

Majone, Giandomenico. 1982. "The Uncertain Logic of Standard Setting." In *Zeitschrift fur Umweltpolitik*, vol. 4. Deutscher Fachverlag GmbH.

Mann, Michael. 1986. *The Sources of Social Power: A History of Power from the Beginning to A.D. 1760*, vol. 1. Cambridge, England: Cambridge University Press.

Markley, O. W. and Willis W. Harman, eds. 1982. *Changing Images of Man*. Oxford, England: Pergamon Press.

Marsh, George P. 1864. *Man and Nature, or Physical Geography as Modified by Human Action*. New York: Scribner's.

Martin-Brown, J. 1987. "The Renaissance of Foreign Policy: The Role of Foreign Policy in Achieving Sustainable Development." Paper presented to New York University School of Law Symposium on Development and the Environment, December 3–4.

Mathews, Jessica Tuchman. 1988. "Redefining National Security: The Environmental Dimensions." Paper presented at the International Studies Association Meeting, March 31, 1988, St. Louis, Missouri.

McHale, John. 1969. *The Future of the Future*. New York: George Braziller.

McIntosh, Robert P. 1985. *The Background of Ecology*. Cambridge, England: Cambridge University Press.

McIntyre, Alastair. 1985. "So What Is Pollution" *The Siren* (September), no. 29.

Meadows, Dennis L. and Jorgen Randers. 1972. "Adding the Time Dimension to Environmental Policy." In Kay and Skolnikoff (1972).

Meadows, Donella, et al. 1971. *The Limits to Growth*. New York: Universe Books.

Meadows, Donella, John Richardson, and Gerhart Bruckman. 1982. *Groping in the Dark: The First Decade of Global Modelling*. Chichester: Wiley.

M'Gonigle, R. Michael and Mark W. Zacher. 1979. *Pollution, Politics and International Law: Tankers at Sea.* Berkeley, Calif.: University of California Press.

Michael, Donald. 1973. *On Learning To Plan and Planning To Learn.* San Francisco, Calif.: Jossey-Bass.

Milbrath, Lester W. 1984. *Environmentalists: Vanguard for a New Society.* Albany: State University of New York Press.

Mohan, V. C. 1987. "Environmental Action in Malaysia and Asia-Pacific: The Experience of SAM and APPEN in Environmental Protection and Resource Management." Paper presented at the 4th World Wilderness Conference, Colorado, September 13–18.

Moore, Gerald. 1976. "Existing and Proposed International Conventions for the Control of Marine Pollution and Their Relevance to the Mediterranean." Legal Office Background Paper No. 8. Rome: FAO.

Morgan, Joseph R. 1987. "Large Marine Ecosystems: An Emerging Concept of Regional Management." *Environment* (December 1987), vol. 29, no. 10.

Morgenthau, Hans. 1985. *Politics Among Nations.* New York: Knopf.

Mulkay, Michael. 1977. In Ina Spiegel-Rosing and Derek de Solla Price, eds., *Science, Technology and Society: A Cross-Disciplinary Approach.* Beverly Hills, Calif.: Sage.

Mulkay, Michael. 1979. *Science and the Sociology of Knowledge.* London: Allen and Unwin.

Mulkay, M. J. 1977. "Sociology of the Scientific Research Community." In Ina Spiegel-Rosing and Derek de Solla Price, eds., *Science, Technology, and Society.* Beverly Hills: Sage.

Nancy, M. 1974. "Analyse des relations entre les systemes hegemoniques et les specificités nationales; un case particulier: Urbanisation et developpement." In Centre de Recherche et d'Etudes sur les Societes Mediterranéenes, ed., *Independance et Interdependances au Maghreb.* Paris: Centre National de la Recherche Scientifique.

Nelkin, Dorothy. 1975. "The Political Impact of Technical Expertise." *Social Studies of Science* (February).

Nelkin, Dorothy, ed. 1979. *Controversy Politics of Technical Decisions.* Beverly Hills, Calif.: Sage.

Nelson, Richard R. and Sidney G. Winter. 1982. *An Evolutionary Theory of Economic Change.* Cambridge, Mass.: Harvard University Press.

NOVA. 1980. "A Mediterranean Prospect" Boston, MA: WGBH Transcripts.

Odell, John. 1982. *U.S. International Monetary Policy: Markets, Power, and Ideas as Sources of Change.* Princeton, N.J.: Princeton University Press.

Odell, Rice. 1977. "History Offers Some Warnings on Environment." *Conservation Foundation Letter* (October).

Odell, Rice. 1979. *Conservation Foundation Letter* (November).

Odum, Eugene P. 1975. *Ecology: The Link Between the Natural and Social Sciences.* New York: Holt, Rinehart and Winston.

Odum, Eugene P. 1977. "The Emergence of Ecology as a New Integrative Discipline." *Science* (March 25), vol. 195.

Olafson, Frederick A. 1979. *The Dialectic of Action.* Chicago, Ill.: University of Chicago Press.

Olson, Mancur. 1965. *The Logic of Collective Action: Public Goods and the Theory of Groups.* Cambridge, Mass.: Harvard University Press.

Onuf, Nicholas G. 1983. "Reports to the Club of Rome." *World Politics*, vol. 36, no. 1.

OECD (Organization for Economic Cooperation and Development). 1982. *Economic and Ecological Interdependence.* Paris: OECD.

OECD. 1983. *Environmental Policies in Greece.* Paris: OECD.

OECD. 1985a. *The State of the Environment 1985.* Paris: OECD.

OECD. 1985b. *Environmental Data Compendium 1985.* Paris: OECD.

OECD. 1985c. *Environmental Policy and Technological Change.* Paris: OECD.

OECD. 1986. *Environmental Policies in Yugoslavia.* Paris: OECD.

Orr, David and Marvin Soroos, eds. 1979. *The Global Predicament: Ecological Perspectives on World Order.* Chapel Hill: University of North Carolina Press.

Oslo and Paris Commissions. 1984. *International Cooperation in Protecting Our Marine Environment: The First Decade.* London: Chameleon Press.

Osterberg, Charles. 1977. "Taking the Pulse of the Mediterranean." *International Energy Agency Bulletin* (February), vol. 9, no. 1.

Osterberg, Charles and S. Keckes. 1977. "The State of Pollution of the Mediterranean Sea." *AMBIO*, vol. 6, no. 6.

Oye, Kenneth A., ed. 1986. *Cooperation Under Anarchy.* Princeton, N.J.: Princeton University Press.

Pallemaerts, Marc. 1985. "Judicial Recourse Against Foreign Air Pollution: A Case Study of Acid Rain in Europe." *Harvard Environmental Law Review*, vol. 9, no. 1.

Parkin, Sara. 1989. *Green Parties: An International Guide.* London: Heretic Books.

Pastor, Robert and Sergio Diaz-Briquets. 1986. "The Caribbean: More People and Fewer Resources." In Andrew Maguire and Janet Welsh Brown, eds. *Bordering on Trouble.* Bethesda, Md.: Adler and Adler.

Pearson, Charles S. 1975. "International Marine Environment Policy: The Economic Dimension." *Studies in International Affairs*, no. 25. Baltimore, Md.: Johns Hopkins University Press.

Pearson, Charles S. 1985. *Down to Business: Multinational Corporations, the Environment, and Development.* World Resources Institute Study No. 2.

Pearson, Charles S., ed. 1987. *Multinational Corporations, the Environment, and the Third World: Business Matters.* Durham, N.C.: Duke University Press.

Pearson, Charles S. and Anthony Pryor. 1978. *Environment: North and South.* New York: Wiley-Interscience.

Peccei, Aurelio. 1977. *The Human Quality.* Oxford: Pergamon Press.

Piaget, Jean. 1985. *The Equilibration of Cognitive Structures.* Chicago, Ill.: University of Chicago Press.

Piddington, Kenneth. 1989. "Sustainability in a Global Context." Address to the American Association for the Advancement of Science, San Francisco, Calif., January 15. Mimeo.

Pilat, J. F. 1980. *Ecological Politics: The Rise of the Green Movement.* Beverly Hill, Calif.: Sage.

Pirages, Dennis. 1983. "The Ecological Perspective and the Social Sciences." *International Studies Quarterly* (September), vol. 27, no. 3.

Polanyi, Michael. 1962. "The Republic of Science." *Minerva* (Autumn), vol. 1 no. 1.

Porritt, Jonathon. 1985. *Seeing Green: The Politics of Ecology Explained.* Oxford, England: Basil Blackwell.

Poulantzas, Nikos. 1973. *Political Power and Social Classes.* London: New Left Books.

Prigogine, Ilya and Isabelle Stengers. 1984. *Order Out of Chaos: Man's New Dialogue with Nature.* New York: Bantam.

Primack, Joel and Frank von Hippel. 1974. *Advice and Dissent: Scientists in the Political Arena.* New York: New American Library.

Putnam, Robert D. and Nicholas Bayne. 1987. *Hanging Together.* 2d ed. Cambridge, Mass.: Harvard University Press.

Redclift, Michael. 1987. "Mexico's Green Movement." *The Ecologist*, vol. 17, no. 1.

Rehbinder, Eckard and Richard Stewart. 1988. *Environmental Protection Policy.* Berlin: Walter de Gruyter.

Reich, Michael R. 1984. "Mobilizing for Environmental Policy in Italy and Japan." *Comparative Politics* (July), vol. 16, no. 4.

Repetto, Robert, ed. 1985. *The Global Possible.* New Haven, Conn.: Yale University Press.

Report on the Environment by the Technology, Growth and Employment Working Group. 1985. London: Her Majesty's Stationery Office (April).

Ress, Paul Evan. 1986. "Mediterranean Sea Becoming Cleaner." *Environmental Conservation* (Autumn), vol. 13, no. 3.

Riddell, R. 1981. *Ecodevelopment, Economics, Ecology and Development: An Alternative to Growth-Imperative Models.* New York: St. Martin's Press.

Ritchie-Calder, Peter. 1972. *The Pollution of the Mediterranean Sea.* Bern: Herbert Land.

Ritchie-Calder, Peter. 1975. "The Sick Sea." In Camera dei Deputati Secretariato Generale (Italy), *Proceedings of the Inter-Parliamentary Conference of Coastal States on the Control of Pollution in the Mediterranean Sea* (Rome, March 29–April 3, 1974).

Robert, Annette. 1980. "The EEC and the Maghreb and Mashreq Countries." In Dudley Seers and Constantine Vaitsos, eds., *Integration and Unequal Development: The Experience of the EEC.* New York: St. Martin's Press.

Roederer, Juan G. 1985. "Tearing Down Disciplinary Barriers" *Eos* (October), vol. 66, no. 40.

Rosenau, James. 1986. "Habit-Driven Actors in World Politics." *International Organization* (Autumn), vol. 40, no. 4.

Rosenberg, Nathan and L. E. Birdzell, Jr. 1986. *How the West Grew Rich.* New York: Basic Books.

Rosencranz, Armin. 1988. "The Acid Rain Controversy in Europe and North America: A Political Analysis." In John E. Carroll, ed., *International Environmental Diplomacy.* Cambridge, England: Cambridge University Press.

Rothstein, Robert L. 1984. "Consensual Knowledge and International Collaboration." *International Organization* (Autumn), vol. 38, no. 4.

Rowland, Wade. 1973. *The Plot To Save the World*. Toronto: Clarke, Irwin.

Rubin, Seymour J. and Thomas R. Graham, eds. 1982. *Environment and Trade*. Totowa, N.J.: Allanheld, Osmun.

Rudig, Wolfgang and Philip D. Lowe. 1986. "The Withered 'Greening' of British Politics: A Study of the Ecology Party." *Political Studies*, vol. 34.

Ruggie, John Gerard. 1972. "Collective Goods and Future International Collaboration." *American Political Science Review* (September), vol. 66.

Ruggie, John Gerard. 1975. "International Responses to Technology: Concepts and Trends." *International Organization*, vol. 29, no. 3.

Ruggie, John Gerard. 1983a. "Continuity and Transformation in the World Polity: Toward a Neorealist Synthesis." *World Politics*, vol. 35, no. 2.

Ruggie, John Gerard. 1983b. "International Regimes, Transactions, and Change: Embedded Liberalism in the Postwar Economic Order." In Krasner (ed.) 1983c.

Ruggie, John Gerard. 1986. "Social Time and International Policy: Conceptualizing Global Population and Resource Issues." In Margaret P. Karns, ed., *Persistent Patterns and Emergent Structures in a Waning Century*. New York: Praeger.

Ruggie, John Gerard. 1989. "International Structure and International Transformation: Space, Time and Method." In Ernst-Otto Czempiel and James N. Rosenau, eds., *Global Changes and Theoretical Challenges*. Lexington, Mass.: Lexington Books.

Rytovuori, Helena. 1980. "Structures of Detente and Ecological Interdependence: Cooperation in the Baltic Sea Area for the Protection of Marine Environment and Living Resources." *Cooperation and Conflict*, vol. 15.

Sabri-Abdalla, Ismail. 1978. "Heterogeneity and Differentiation: The End of the Third World." *Development Dialogue*, vol. 2.

Sachs, Ignacy. 1974. "Environnement et styles de developpement." *Annales: Economiques, Sociales, Civilisations* (May–June).

Saliba, Louis. 1978. "Protecting the Mediterranean." *Marine Policy* (July), vol. 2, no. 3.

Sand, Peter H. 1977. "The Role of Domestic Procedures in Transnational Environmental Disputes." In OECD, *Legal Aspects of Transfrontier Pollution* Paris: OECD.

Sand, Peter H. 1987. "Air Pollution in Europe: International Policy Responses." *Environment* (December), vol. 29, no. 10.

Sand, Peter H. 1988. *Marine Environmental Law in the United Nations Environment Programme*. London: Tycooly.

Sanson, H. 1974. "L'apres-cooperation." In Centre de Recherches et d'Etudes sur les Societes Mediterranéennes, ed., *Independance et Interdependances au Maghreb*. Paris: Centre national de la Recherche Scientifique.

Sapolsky, Harvey. 1971. "An Exchange Model of the Science Advisory Process." Paper prepared for delivery at the 1971 Annual Meeting of the American Political Science Association, Chicago, Ill., September 7–11.

Schank, Roger C. and Robert P. Abelson. 1977. *Scripts, Plans, Goals and Understanding: An Inquiry Into Human Knowledge Structures*. New York: Wiley.

Schattschneider, E. E. 1975. *The Semi-Sovereign People*. Hindsdale, Ill.: Dryden Press.

Schiffman, Irving. 1985. "The Environmental Impact Assessment Comes to Israel." *Environmental Impact Assessment Review* (June), vol. 5, no. 2.

Schlaim, Avi. 1976. "The Community and the Mediterranean Basin." In Kenneth J. Twitchett, ed., *Europe and the World: The External Relations of the Common Market*. London: Europa.

Schlaim, Avi and G. N. Yannopoulos, eds. 1976. *The EEC and the Mediterranean Countries*. Cambridge, England: Cambridge University Press.

Schneider, Jan. 1979. *World Public Order of the Environment*. Toronto: University of Toronto Press.

Schneider, Stephen H. and Starley L. Thompson. 1985. "Future Changes in the Atmosphere." In Repetto (ed.) 1985.

Schulman, Paul R. 1975. "Nonincremental Policy Making: Notes Toward an Alternative Paradigm." *American Political Science Review*, vol. 69, no. 4.

Schultz, Robert C. and J. Donald Hughes, eds. 1981. *Ecological Consciousness: Essays from the Earthday X Colloquium* (University of Denver, Colorado, April 21–24, 1980). Washington, D.C.: University Press of America.

Schumacher, E. F. 1973. *Small Is Beautiful*. New York: Harper and Row.

Sears, Paul B. 1954. "Human Ecology: A Problem in Synthesis." *Science* (December 10), vol. 120.

Sebenius, James. 1984. *Negotiating the Law of the Sea*. Cambridge, Mass.: Harvard University Press.

Seed, John, Joanna Macy, Pat Fleming, and Arne Naess. 1988. *Thinking Like a Mountain*. Philadelphia, Pa.: New Society Publications.

Seers, Dudley, Bernard Schaffer, and Marja-Liisa Kiljunen, eds. 1979. *Underdeveloped Europe: Studies in Core-Periphery Relations*. Hassocks, Sussex, England: Harvester Press.

Sideri, S. 1970. *Trade and Power*. Rotterdam: Rotterdam University Press.

Siebert, Horst. 1974. "Trade and Environment." In Herbert Giersch, ed., *The International Division of Labour: Problems and Perspectives*. Tübingen: International Symposium.

Simon, Herbert A. 1969. "The Architecture of Complexity." In *The Sciences of the Artificial*. Cambridge, Mass.: MIT Press.

Simon, Herbert A. 1979. "Rational Decision Making in Business Organizations." *The American Economic Review* (September), vol. 69, no. 4.

Simon, Herbert A. 1985. *Reason and Human Affairs*. Stanford, Calif.: Stanford University Press.

Simon, Julian L. 1981. *The Ultimate Resource*. Princeton, N.J.: Princeton University Press.

Simon, Julian L. and Herman Kahn, eds. 1984. *The Resourceful Earth: A Response to Global 2000*. Oxford, England: Basil Blackwell.

Sittig, Marshall. 1975. *Environmental Sources and Emissions Handbook*. Park Ridge, N.J.: Noyes Data Corporation.

Skocpol, Theda. 1977. "Wallerstein's World Capitalist System: A Theoretical and Historical Critique." *American Journal of Sociology*, vol. 82, no. 5.

Snidal, Duncan. 1985. "The Limits of Hegemonic Stability Theory." *International Organization* (Autumn), vol. 39, no. 4.

Snyder, Glenn H. and Paul Diesing. 1977. *Conflict Among Nations*. Princeton, N.J.: Princeton University Press.

Soroos, Marvin. 1986. *Beyond Sovereignty.* Columbia: University of South Carolina Press.

Spain. Commission Interministerial del Medio Ambiente. 1984. *Medio Ambiente en España.* Madrid.

Spain. Subsecretaria de Planificacion. 1977. *Medio Ambiente en España: Informe General.* Madrid.

Speth, James Gustave. 1988. *Environmental Pollution: A Long-Term Perspective* in National Geographic Society *Earth '88 Changing Geographic Perspectives.* Washington, D.C.: National Geographic Society.

Sprout, Harold and Margaret Sprout. 1974. *Multiple Vulnerabilities: The Context of Environmental Repair and Protection.* Princeton, N.J.: Princeton University Center for International Studies.

Stein, Arthur. 1982. "When Misperception Matters." *World Politics,* vol. 34, no. 4.

Stein, Eric and Brian Johnson. 1979. *Banking on the Biosphere.* Lexington, Mass.: Lexington Books.

Stein, Janice Gross and Raymond Tanter. 1980. *Rational Decision-Making: Israel's Security Choices, 1967.* Columbus: Ohio State University Press.

Steinbruner, John D. 1974. *The Cybernetic Theory of Decision.* Princeton, N.J.: Princeton University Press.

Streeten, Paul. 1986. "What Do We Owe the Future?" *Resources Policy* (March), vol. 12, no. 1.

Stremlau, John J. 1982. "The Foreign Politics of Developing Countries in the 1980s." In John J. Stremlau, *The Foreign Policy Priorities of Third World States.* Boulder, Colo.: Westview Press.

Strong, Maurice F. 1973. "One Year After Stockholm." *Foreign Affairs* (July), vol. 51, no. 4.

Strong, Maurice F. 1984. "Major Issues Facing the Conservation Movement in the Coming Decade and Beyond." *The Environmentalist* (Autumn), vol. 4, no. 3.

Sun, Marjorie. 1988. "Environmental Awakening in the Soviet Union." *Science* (August 26), vol. 241.

Sutcliffe, B. 1972. "Imperialism and Industrialization in the Third World." In R. Owen and B. Sutcliffe, eds., *Studies in the Theory of Imperialism.* London: Longman.

Talaat Abou Saada, M. 1987. "Environmental Protection in Egypt with Particular Emphasis on Wastewater Management." Cairo: Cairo Wastewater Organization. Mimeo.

Thacher, Peter S. 1977. "The Mediterranean Action Plan." *AMBIO,* vol. 6, no. 6.

Thacher, Peter S. 1983. "The Stockholm Process." *The Siren* (May), no. 20.

Thacher, Peter S. 1985. "Learning To Cope with Multi-Dimensional Problems." *Social Education* (March), vol. 49, no. 3.

Thacher, Peter S. and Nikki Meith. 1980. "Approaches to Regional Marine Problems: A Progress Report on UNEP's Regional Seas Programme." In Elisabeth Mann Borgese and Norton Ginsburg, eds., *Ocean Yearbook 2.* Chicago, Ill.: University of Chicago Press.

Thirgood, J. V. 1981. *Man and the Mediterranean Forest.* New York: Academic Press.

Thomas, William L., ed. 1956. *Man's Role in Changing the Face of the Earth.* Chicago, Ill.: University of Chicago Press.

Thompson, William Irwin, ed. 1987. *Gaia: A Way of Knowing.* Great Barrington, Mass.: Lindisfarne Press.

Tolba, Mostapha K. 1982. *Development Without Destruction: Evolving Environmental Perception.* Dublin: Tycooly International.

Tolba, Mostapha K. 1987. *Sustainable Development.* London: Butterworth.

Tolba, Mostafa Kamal, ed. 1988. *Evolving Environmental Perceptions from Stockholm to Nairobi.* London: Butterworths.

Tomassini, Luciano. 1980. "Environmental Factors: Crisis in the Centres and Change in International Relations of the Peripheral Countries." *CEPAL Review* (December), no. 12.

Tomczak, M., Jr. 1984. "Defining Marine Pollution: A Comparison of Definitions Used by International Conventions." *Marine Policy* (October), vol. 8, no. 4.

Toulmin, Stephen. 1972. *Human Understanding: The Collective Use and Evolution of Concepts.* Princeton, N.J.: Princeton University Press.

Ullman, Richard. 1983. "Redefining Security." *International Security*, vol. 8, no. 1.

United Nations. 1971. "The Sea: Prevention and Control of Marine Pollution. Report of the Secretary General." E/5003 (May 7).

United Nations. 1973. *Report of the United Nations Conference on the Human Environment.* Stockholm, June 5–16, 1972. New York: United Nations.

United Nations. 1980. *Interrelations: Resources, Environment, Population and Development.* New York: United Nations.

UNECE (United Nations Economic Commission for Europe). 1987a. *Environmental Statistics in Europe and North America.* New York: United Nations.

UNECE. 1987b. *National Strategies and Policies for Air Pollution Abatement.* ECE/EB. AIR/14. New York: United Nations.

UNEP (United Nations Environment Programme). 1977. *Directory of Mediterranean Marine Research Centres.* Geneva.

UNEP. 1982a. *Achievements and Planned Development of UNEP's Regional Seas Programme and Comparable Programmes Sponsored by Other Parties.* UNEP Regional Seas Reports and Studies No. 1.

UNEP. 1982b. *Guidelines and Principles for the Preparation and Implementation of Comprehensive Action Plans for the Protection and Development of Marine and Coastal Areas of Regional Seas.* UNEP Regional Seas Reports and Studies No. 15.

UNEP. 1984. *Pollutants from Land-Based Sources in the Mediterranean.* UNEP Regional Seas Reports and Studies No. 32.

UNEP. 1986a. *Assessment of UNEP's Achievement in "Oceans" Programme Element (1974–1985).* January 14.

UNEP. 1986b. "Review of the State of the Marine Environment: Mediterranean Regional Report." December 19. GESAMP WG 26. 26/C/1.

UNEP. 1986c. *1985 Annual Report of the Executive Director.* Nairobi, Kenya: UNEP.

UNEP. 1987. *1986 Annual Report of the Executive Director, Part 1.* Nairobi, Kenya: UNEP.

UNEP. 1988. "The State of the Marine Environment." *UNEP News,* April pp. 10-12.

USAID (United States Agency for International Development). 1981. Bureau of Science and Technology and United States Man and the Biosphere Secretariat of the Department of State. *Environmental Report on Tunisia* (revised draft). December.

United States Council on Environmental Quality. 1984. *Environmental Quality: 15th Annual Report of the Council on Environmental Quality.* Washington, D.C.:

United States National Academy of Sciences. 1984. *Petroleum in the Marine Environment.* Washington, D.C.

United States Senate. 1972. Subcommittee on Ocean and Atmosphere of the Committee on Commerce. *International Conference on Ocean Pollution* (92-49). 92d Congress. 2d Session.

Ural, Engin. 1987. "Environmental Protection and Foreign Private Investment in Turkey." In Pearson (1987).

Vadrot, Claude-Marie. 1977. *Mort de la Mediterranée.* Paris: Actuels Iseuil.

Van Buu, E. 1974. "Evolution de la Cooperation Franco-Maghrebine." In Centre de Recherches et d'Etudes sur les Societés Mediterranéenes, ed., *Independance et Interdependances au Maghreb.* Paris: Centre National de la Recherche Scientifique.

Varley, Allen, ed. 1976. *Ocean Research Index.* Guernsey: Francis Hodgson.

Vasquez, John A. 1983. *The Power of Power Politics: A Critique.* New Brunswick, N.J.: Rutgers University Press.

Viner, Jacob. 1948. "Power vs. Plenty as Objectives of Foreign Policy in the Seventeenth and Eighteenth Centuries." *World Politics,* vol. 1., no. 1.

Vogel, David. 1986. *National Styles of Regulation.* Ithaca, N.Y.: Cornell University Press.

Wallerstein, Immanuel. 1979. *The Capitalist World Economy.* Cambridge, England: Cambridge University Press.

Walter, Ingo. 1975. *International Economics of Pollution.* London: Macmillan.

Waltz, Kenneth N. 1979. *Theory of International Politics.* Reading, Mass.: Addison-Wesley.

Waltz, Kenneth N. 1986. "Reflections on *Theory of International Politics:* A Response to My Critics." In Keohane 1986b.

Ward, Barbara and Rene Dubos. 1972. *Only One Earth.* New York: Norton.

Wasserman, Ursula. 1984. "UNCTAD: International Tropical Timber Agreement." *Journal of World Trade Law,* vol. 18.

Waterbury, John. 1979. *Hydropolitics of the Nile.* Syracuse, N.Y.: Syracuse University Press.

Weir, Margaret and Theda Skocpol. 1985. "State Structures and the Possibilities for 'Keynesian' Responses to the Great Depression in Sweden, Britain and the United States." In Peter B. Evans, Dietrich Rueschemeyer, and

Theda Skocpol, eds., *Bringing the State Back In*. Cambridge, England: Cambridge University Press.

Wenger, Edith. 1975. "Survie ou mort de la Mediterranée: Un test pour la cooperation internationale." *Revue Française d'Etudes Politiques Mediterranéenes* (March), vol. 3.

Wetstone, Gregory S. 1987. "A History of the Acid Rain Issue." In Harvey Brooks and Chester L. Cooper, eds., *Science for Public Policy*. New York: Pergamon Press.

White, Frank. 1987. *The Overview Effect*. Boston: Houghton-Mifflin.

White, Gilbert F. 1986. *Geography, Resources and Environment*. Vol. 1. Chicago, Ill.: University of Chicago Press.

Whitehead, Cynthia. 1985. "EC Environmental Policy Is Model for Other Nations." *Europe* (September–October).

Wijkman, Per Magus. 1982. "Managing the Global Commons." *International Organization* (Summer), vol. 36, no. 3.

Wilensky, Harold. 1967. *Organizational Intelligence*. New York: Basic Books.

Wilson, Thomas W. 1971. *International Environmental Action: Global Survey*. Cambridge, England: Dunellen.

Winograd, Terry and Fernando Flores. 1986. *Understanding Computers and Cognition*. Reading, Mass.: Addison-Wesley.

Woodwell, George M. 1985. "On the Limits of Nature." In Repetto 1985.

World Commission on Environment and Development. 1987. *Our Common Future*. New York: Oxford University Press.

WHO. 1977. "Coastal Water Pollution Control." Report of a Workshop Jointly Convened by WHO and UNEP, Athens, June 27–July 1, 1977. Copenhagen: WHO.

WHO and UNEP (World Health Organization and United Nations Environment Program). 1979. *Principles and Guidelines for the Discharge of Wastes In the Marine Environment*. Copenhagen: World Health Organization.

World Resources Institute. 1986. *World Resources*. New York: Basic Books.

World Resources Institute. 1987. *World Resources 1987*. New York: Basic Books.

Worster, Donald. 1977. *Nature's Economy: A History of Ecological Ideas*. Cambridge, England: Cambridge University Press.

Wrong, Dennis. 1979. *Power: Its Forms, Bases and Uses*. New York: Harper and Row.

Yishai, Y. 1979. "Environment and Development: The Case of Israel." *International Journal of Environmental Studies*, vol. 14.

Zahlan, A. B. 1980. *Science and Science Policy in the Arab World*. New York: St. Martin's Press.

Zolberg, Aristide R. "Origins of the Modern World System: A Missing Link." *World Politics*, vol. 33, no. 2.

PERTINENT PERIODICALS

Actualité Environnement, published in France.

AMBIO.

Bibliography

Boletin informativo del mediio ambiente, published quarterly by CIMA (Commission Interministerial del Medio Ambiente) (Spain).
The Blue Plan Letter, published by the Blue Plan Regional Activity Centre, Sophia-Antipolis, France.
Development Forum.
Environmental Policy and Law.
Industry and Environment, published by UNEP's Industry Liaison Office, Paris, France.
International Environment Reporter, published by the Bureau of National Affairs, Washington, D.C.
Israel Environment Bulletin, published by the Environmental Protection Service, Jerusalem, Israel.
Marine Policy.
Marine Pollution Bulletin.
Mazingira.
Mediterrania, published in Barcelona, Spain.
MEDWAVES, published by the Med Plan Coordinating Unit in Athens.
Ocean Development and International Law.
Ocean Management.
Priority Actions Programme Bulletin, published by the Priority Action Programme Regional Activity Centre, Split, Yugoslavia.
ROCC News, published by the Regional Oil Combating Centre, Manoel Island, Malta.
The Siren, published by UNEP's Regional Seas Programme, Nairobi, Kenya.
UNEP News, published by UNEP, Nairobi, Kenya. Replaced *UNITERRA.*
UNITERRA, published by UNEP, Nairobi, Kenya.

INTERVIEWS

In 1982–1983, over ninety open-ended interviews were conducted with government officials, scientists, UN officials, and various observers of the Med Plan. Three more were conducted in 1986–1987. Although at times information has not been attributed due to the confidentiality of the sources, no information has been presented unless it was verified from a second source or from memos. In addition to those individuals listed below, several others were interviewed who requested anonymity. Affiliations listed are for the positions held by the person interviewed relevant to the Med Plan. Many of them no longer hold the same positions.

Countries

ALGERIA

Dr. Ali Bakalem, scientist, Centre de Recherches Oceanographiques et des Peches (CROP) (June 7, 1983).
Mohamed El Hadi Bennadji, sous-directeur de la sauvegarde des resources

biologiques naturelles, Secretariat d'Etat aux Forets et à la Mise en Valeur des Terres (June 7, 1983).

Dr. Chouikhi, directeur, Centre de Recherches Oceanographiques et des Peches (CROP) (June 6, 1983).

Captain Y. De Ridder, IMO consultant to Department of Maritime Navigation (June 1, 1983).

Moustapha Djebaili, directeur, Organisme National de la Recherche Scientifique (ONRS) (June 6, 1983).

Mohammed Kolai, Directeur Protection de la Nature, Secretariat d'Etat aux Forets et à la Mise en Valeur des Terres. Personal communication.

Mohammed Ladjouzi, secretary for foreign affairs, Ministère des Affaires Etrangeres (March 1, 1983).

Hamia Semichi, Ministère des Affairs Etrangères (June 7, 1983).

EGYPT

Aboul-Fotouh Abdel-Latif, vice president, Academy of Scientific Research and Technology (January 29, 1983).

Ithlas Abdul-Meguid, director, Executive Office for Environmental Information, Academy of Scientific Research and Technology (January 25, 1983).

Dr. Bayoumi, director, Institute of Oceanography and Fisheries, Academy of Scientific Research and Technology (January 25, 1983).

Dr. A. H. El-Sabae, University of Alexandria Research Center. Personal communication.

Dr. Gamel El-Samra, Department of Occupational Medicine, Faculty of Medicine, Cairo University; secretary general, National Committee on Environmental Affairs, Office of the Prime Minister (January 29, 1983).

Dr. F. M. El-Sharkawi, Department of Environmental Health, High Institute of Public Health, Alexandria University (January 20, 1983).

Dr. Saad El-Wakeel, oceanography department, faculty of science, Alexandria University; UNEP Regional Seas Porgramme (1976–1979) (January 20, 1983).

Dr. Mohammed Kassas, Faculty of Science, Cairo University (also head of IUCN); chairman, National Committee on the Environment, Academy of Scientific Research and Technology (January 25, 1983).

Dr. Sabet, Academy of Scientific Research and Technology (January 25, 1983).

Dr. Hamed Sultan, faculty of law, Cairo University (January 28, 1983).

Dr. Saad Wahby, marine chemistry department, Institute of Oceanography and Fisheries, Alexandria (January 21, 1983).

Ibrahim Youssri, deputy director, legal department, Ministry of Foreign Affairs (January 29, 1983).

FRANCE

Serge Antoine, chef, Mission des Etudes et de la Recherche, Ministère de l'Environnement (June 21, 1983).

Henri Crepin-Leblond, Ministère des Affaires Estrangères (June 17, 1983).

Bibliography

Helene Dubois, Division des Organisations Internationales, Ministère des Affaires Etrangères (June 21, 1983).
Mireille Jardin, Direction des Affaires Economiques et Internationales, Secretariat d'Etat a l'Environnement (June 20, 1983).
Ambassador Olivier Manet, Ministère des Affaires Etrangères (June 14, 1983).
Anne-Françoise Mathieu, Mission Etudes et Recherches, Ministère de l'Environnement et du Qualité de la Vie (June 20, 1983).
Patricia Maugain, Ministère de l'Environnement et du Cadre de Vie (March 2, 1983).
Philippe Piotet, sous-directeur des eaux marines, Ministère de l'Environnement et du Cadre de Vie (June 22, 1983).
Marcel Surbiguet, legal department, Ministère des Affaires Etrangères (June 17, 1983).
Mr. Stuyk-Taillander, Division of Scientific Cooperation, Ministère des Affairs Etrangères (June 13, 1983).

GREECE

Byron Antipas, secretary, Hellenic Society for the Protection of Nature (November 30, 1982).
Dr. Panayote Dimitras, president, EURODIM (November 30, 1982).
Panos Lagos, Secretariat of the National Council for Physical Planning and the Environment, Ministry of Coordination (November 25, 1982).
Mr. Oikonomou, Greek Federation of Industry (April 28, 1983).
Dr. Stelios Pikoulis, secretary general, ERYEA (December 1, 1982).
Jean Siotis, director of the Athens Bureau of the European Communities, served as head of delegation to the 1977 Split Med Plan meeting (December 1, 1982).
Mr. Trandas, environmental section, Union of Greek Shipowners (December 3, 1982).
Dr. Miltos Vassilopoulos, Secretariat of the National Council for Physical Planning and the Environment, Ministry of Coordination (November 23, 1982; November 29, 1982; October 14, 1984).
Ambassador Dimitrios Yannopoulos, deputy director, Department of International Organizations, Department of Foreign Affairs (November 26, 1982).
Marinos Yeroulanos, director general, Secretariat of the National Council for Physical Planning and the Environment, Ministry of Coordination (November 25, 1982).

ISRAEL

Harry Evan, Environmental Protection Service, Ministry of the Interior (February 4, 1983).
Uri Marinov, director, Environmental Protection Service, Ministry of the Interior (January 10, 1983), interview conducted by Edith Austin; and February 28, 1983).
Josef Tamir, chairman, Life and Environment (served ten years in the Knesset). Personal communication.

ITALY

Ambassador Carlo Calenda, Ministry of Foreign Affairs (December 7, 1982).
Ambassador Giovanni Falchi, Ministry of Foreign Affairs (December 6, 1982).
Arnaldo de Mohr, first councillor of economic affairs, Italian Mission to the
United Nations in Geneva; formerly head of the coordination unit in the
Office of International Cooperation in Environmental Matters, Ministry of
Foreign Affairs (through 1980) (November 3, 1983).

LEBANON

Dr. Naggear, chairman, National Scientific Research Council (February 28,
1983).

MALTA

Dr. Louis Saliba, Malta Human Environment Council, WHO senior scientist
at Coordinating Unit for the Mediterranean Action Plan (MAP), (November
30, 1982; December 2, 1982).

TUNISIA

Hedia Baccar, sous-Directeur chargée de l'environnement au Ministère de
l'Agriculture (March 2, 1983).

TURKEY

Aydan Bulca, director, Department of Environmental Affairs; Undersecretar-
iat of the environment, Office of the Prime Minister (March 5, 1983).
Lieutenant Kamil Yuceoral, Turkish Navy (March 3, 1983).

UNITED STATES OF AMERICA

Gus Curley, United States Environmental Protection Agency (USEPA) sec-
onded to USAID in Egypt (January 18, 1983).
Don King, Bureau of Oceans, Environment, Science and Technology, Depart-
ment of State (Septmeber 1, 1982).
Walt McAleer, USAID in Egypt (January 19, 1983).
Mr. Redman, USAID in Egypt (January 18, 1983).
Bill Salmon, Science and Technology Office of Security Assistance, Depart-
ment of State (September 21, 1982).

YUGOSLAVIA

Franjo Gasperovic, Committee for Building, Housing and the Environment of
the Socialist Republic of Croatia (March 1, 1983).
Ivo Slaus, director, Rudjer Boskovic Institute (July 13, 1989).

International Organizations

UNITED NATIONS ENVIRONMENT PROGRAMME

Patricia Bliss-Guest, legal officer, Regional Seas Programme (November 5, 1982; November 11, 1982; and February 25, 1983).
Dr. Robert Frosch, deputy executive director (February 17, 1987).
Dr. Stjepan Keckes, director, Regional Seas Programme (February 18, 1983; July 15, 1983).
Sachiko Kuwabara, New York Liaison Office (July 18, 1983).
Paul Ress, press officer, Regional Seas Programme, Geneva (November 12, 1982).
Mohammed Tangi, Regional Seas Programme (November 4, 1982).
Peter Thacher, deputy executive director (July 9, 1982; February 28, 1983).
Mostapha Tolba, executive director (July 15, 1983).

FOOD AND AGRICULTURE ORGANIZATION

Dominique Alheritiere, Legal Office (December 8, 1982).
J. E. Carroz, director, Fishery Policy and Planning Division, Fisheries Department (December 6, 1982; December 8, 1982).
Gerald Moore, chief, Forestry, Wildlife and Fisheries Legislation Section, Legislation Branch, Legal Office (December 7, 1982).
Dr. Heiner Naeve, fishery resources officer, Inland Water Resources and Aquaculture Service, Fishery Resources and Environment Division, Fisheries Department (December 7, 1982; December 8, 1982).
Mr. Nikolic, senior fishery resources officer, Fishery Resources and Environment Division, Fisheries Department (December 6, 1982).
Peter Sand (subsequently with IUCN and UNEP) (November 8, 1982).

INTERNATIONAL OCEANOGRAPHIC COMMISSION

Dr. Gunner Kullenberg (August 15, 1986).
Dr. Mario Ruivo (August 15, 1986).

WORLD HEALTH ORGANIZATION

Sev Fluss (November 15, 1982).
Dr. Richard Helmer (November 10, 1982). Interview plus subsequent personal communication.
Dr. George Ponghis (May 12, 1983).
Hans Schlenzka, formerly in FAO legal department through February 1975 (November 16, 1982).

UNITED NATIONS ECONOMIC COMMISSION FOR EUROPE

Dr. Amassa Bishop (February 8, 1983).
Dr. Claude Ducret (February 8, 1983).

MEDITERRANEAN ACTION PLAN—AFFILIATED GROUPS

The Blue Plan

Rene Bourone, first president of MEDEAS (June 16, 1983).
Michel Grenon, executive secretary, Group of Coordination and Synthesis (February 27, 1983).
Dr. Ismail Sabri Abdalla, coordinator (January 26, 1983).

Regional Oil Combating Centre

Philippe Le Lourd, director (March 1, 1983).

Coordinating Unit for the Mediterranean Action Plan

Antonio Cruzado, senior marine scientist (December 10, 1982).
Aldo Manos, director (November 24, 1982; December 2, 1982).

UNEP Industry and Environment Programme

Nay Htun (June 15, 1983).

Inter-Parliamentary Union

Frank Wilcox (February 8, 1983).

United Nations Educational, Social and Cultural Organization

Dr. Michel Batisse, assistant director general for sciences (Environment and Natural Resources) (June 16, 1983).

Other

D. T. Edwards, Intergovernmental Maritime Organization. Personal communication.
Mike Fowler, Disbursements Division, Loan Department, World Bank (June 21, 1985).
Dr. Edward Goldberg, Scripps Institution of Oceanography (December 28, 1982).
Elisabeth Mann Borgese, Department of Political Science, Dalhousie University, Halifax, Nova Scotia, Canada. Personal communication.
John Parry, *International Environment Reporter* correspondent, Geneva.
Sarah Rau, *International Environment Reporter* correspondent, Athens.
Prof. Michael Royston, International Management Institute, Geneva (November 18, 1982).
Dr. Ignacy Sachs, Le Centre International de Recherche sur l'Environnement et le Developpement, Ecole Pratique des Hautes Etudes (June 20, 1983).

Index

297